*Pearson and Canada's Role in Nuclear Disarmament
and Arms Control Negotiations, 1945–1957*

Pearson and Canada's Role in Nuclear Disarmament and Arms Control Negotiations, 1945–1957

JOSEPH LEVITT

McGill-Queen's University Press
Montreal & Kingston • London • Buffalo

© McGill-Queen's University Press 1993
ISBN 0-7735-0905-4

Legal deposit second quarter 1993
Bibliothèque nationale du Québec

Printed in Canada on acid-free paper

This book has been published with the help of
grants from the Social Science Federation of
Canada, using funds provided by the Social
Sciences and Humanities Research Council of
Canada, the University of Ottawa, and the
Cooperative Security Competition Program,
External Affairs and International Trade Canada.

Canadian Cataloguing in Publication Data

Levitt, Joseph.
  Pearson and Canada's role in nuclear
  disarmament and arms control negotiations,
  1945–1957
  Includes bibliographical references and index.
  ISBN 0-7735-0905-4
  1. Nuclear disarmament – Government policy –
  Canada. 2. Arms control – Government policy –
  Canada. 3. Canada – Military policy.
  4. Canada – Politics and government – 1948–1957.
  I. Title
  JX1974.7.L48 1993   327.1'74'0971   C93-090152-5

Contents

Acknowledgments / vii

Introduction / 3

1   The Strategic Setting / 11

2   Pearson on the Superpower Confrontation / 43

3   Canada and the Baruch Plan, 1945–46 / 75

4   The Propaganda Wars: Defending the Baruch Plan, 1947–49 / 107

5   The Erosion of the Majority Plan, 1950–53 / 137

6   Narrowing the Gap between East and West, 1954–55 / 166

7   Working to Maintain Franco-American Harmony, 1955–56 / 192

8   Final Negotiations 1956–57: The Nuclear Test Ban and Aerial Inspection / 225

9   Conclusion / 264

Appendix: Key Actors and Meetings / 287

Notes / 293

Bibliography / 317

Index / 327

Acknowledgments

I would like to thank the Social Science Federation of Canada, the Research and Publications Committee of the Faculty of Arts of the University of Ottawa, and the Cooperative Security Competition Program of External Affairs and International Trade Canada for their grants which made the publication of this book possible.

I would like to thank the folks at McGill-Queen's for their efforts in bringing this book out. I am grateful to Mr Dacre Cole of the Historical Section of the Academic Division of the Department of External Affairs for his kindness and patience in helping me with access to the necessary documents. I would like to thank David Russell for reading this text and making useful suggestions. I was extremely fortunate that Marion Magee, who is simply a superb editor, agreed to work on this manuscript; her standards are truly impressive; she has done much to improve the flow of the narrative as well as to strengthen its coherence. Finally, I would like to thank my wife, Marnie, not only for her steadfast support but also for her uncanny skill with a computer.

Lester Pearson at a meeting of the United Nations Security Council, 6 January 1949. George Ignatieff is on his right. United Nations Department of Public Information; National Archives of Canada PA117616

Lester Pearson addresses the eleventh session of the United Nations General Assembly, 19 November 1956. United Nations 51591; National Archives of Canada c189169

Prime Minister Attlee of the United Kingdom, President Truman of the United States, and Prime Minister King of Canada at the Washington conference on the control of atomic energy, November 1945. National Archives of Canada C23271

Lester Pearson and General A.G.L. McNaughton during the United Nations session of 1949. National Archives of Canada PA186305

Introduction

In the years from 1945 to 1957, Canada was a member of two United Nations commissions in which negotiations were conducted, largely between the United States and the Soviet Union, on the elimination or control of nuclear arms. The aim in these discussions was to reach agreement on general principles which reflected the strategic needs of each side in the Cold War rather than on the technical details necessary for an actual treaty. Two other major powers, Britain and France, were also at the bargaining table. Canada was the only small power to take part in these talks – a situation which arose from its wartime role in the West's development of atomic energy.

Little has been written on the Canadian role in these early negotiations. James Eayrs, in his volumes of *In Defence of Canada*, and John Holmes, in his two-volume work, *The Shaping of Peace*, devote only a few pages to this topic. The several authors of the *Canada in World Affairs* volumes for the period touch upon the subject only lightly. Nor do the biographies or autobiographies of various major figures involved in these events have much to say about them. The only full-length study of the subject is an unpublished doctoral dissertation written by Grant Davy in 1962. Although this work offers many valuable insights and much useful information, it was written at a time when the only papers available were the published records of the United Nations and the public speeches of the participants. Most recently, Albert Legault and Michel Fortmann have published *Une diplomatie de l'espoir*, a history of Canada's efforts in the disarmament field from 1945 to 1988. Only two of their thirteen chapters deal with the early period and their approach is a thematic one.

This book describes the step-by-step negotiations on disarmament and arms control that took place in the years following World War II, seen through the eyes of Canada's diplomats. In constructing the narrative, I have therefore depended, first and foremost, on the documents that are available in the Department of External Affairs and the National Archives on Canadian participation in the two United Nations commissions. This research has been augmented by the use of other published documentary sources as well as the secondary literature on the atomic policies of the great powers. The Soviet records remain closed.

By far the most popular characterization of Canada's role in the world in the decade covered by this volume has been that of "middle power" – a term used to refer to states which were not great powers but possessed some characteristics which meant that they were not minor powers either. "Canada," as John Holmes would write in 1962, "went through a remarkably swift transition from the status of wartime junior partner in 1945 to that of a sure-footed middle power with an acknowledged and applauded rôle in world affairs ten years later."[1] He saw Canada as a country that believed it should make efforts to shape the peace and help to construct a new and benign world order. This perception led to such activities as service on the tripartite commissions in Indochina, the efforts to defuse the crisis over Suez, and peacekeeping in the Middle East, in Kashmir, and in the Congo.

This view of Canada has been challenged by other commentators and some have described Canada's foreign policy role as that of a satellite and have argued that Canadian policy was so dominated by the United States as to be nothing more than a pale copy of its giant neighbour's.[2] Certainly in this book we shall see few instances of Canada disagreeing publicly with the United States over arms policy. Equally, however, the documents show that the Department of External Affairs believed that Canada was perfectly free to develop its own policies. That they were often similar to those of the United States merely reflected a common appreciation of the strategic situation.

Nevertheless, as John Holmes asserted, "the inclination to support the Americans, right or wrong, must contend constantly with Canada's independent assessment of the forces in the world and with its obligation to act in world diplomacy as an independent power."[3] Canada was not averse to distancing itself from American policies or even opposing the United States publicly. Hence, in the discussions about the North Atlantic Treaty, we find Canadian diplomats insisting, against stiff opposition from the Americans, on the inclusion of an article that called on the signatories to encourage economic collaboration among themselves. During the Korean War Canada attempted to moderate American policy to avoid a disastrous land war with China. In 1955 Lester Pearson announced that Canada would not support any American intervention in what he regarded as a civil war if the offshore islands of Quemoy and Matsu were attacked by the People's Republic of China. In these cases, Pearson, despite his steadfast friendship for the United States, disagreed fundamentally with a policy that went against the Canadian view of how global politics ought to be ordered.

But when we turn to issues of defence and security, the role of Canada as middle power is not so easy to support. On these crucial matters, there simply was no room for fundamental disagreement between Canada and its allies, particularly the United States. In the matter of continental defence Canada worked in the closest harmony with the United States to develop common strategies. There was no scope for a truly independent contribution. This was also true of the complex issues of disarmament and arms control which were directly tied to the security of all the Western allies. Here, as we shall see, Canada played a role much closer to the "junior partner" of the war years. Indeed, it is this phrase which best captures my assessment of the way Canada saw itself and acted in the nuclear negotiations. This role rested on a political and philosophical agreement with the goals set by the United States and a commitment to assist in their achievement. Despite minor differences over tactics – which were usually aired in private ("quiet diplomacy") – the main thrust of Canada's activities in the two United Nations commissions was to help the American-led Western alliance succeed in its strategy of compelling the Soviet Union to negotiate on disarmament and arms control on its terms or, failing that, to assist the West in winning the all-important propaganda war.

Lester Pearson is named in the title of my book because his was the final word in the making of Canadian disarmament and arms control policy for most of the period. As under-secretary of state for external affairs from 1946 to 1948, he had much to do with the development of Canadian policy in the Atomic Energy Commission based on the reports sent back to the department by General McNaughton, the Canadian representative on that body. It is true that after he became secretary of state for external affairs in 1948, Pearson left the details of working out and implementing policy to others. But he remained well informed by his under-secretaries about what was happening in the Disarmament Commission and its sub-committee. As Jules Léger, the under-secretary from 1954 to 1958, has noted, one of his tasks was to provide the necessary underpinnings out of which Pearson fashioned his policy.[4]

The Canadians involved in the disarmament talks both at home and abroad included some of the most prominent personalities of the postwar Department of External Affairs. Arnold Heeney, John Holmes, R.A. MacKay, and Jules Léger were sending instructions and receiving reports from Andrew McNaughton, David Johnson, and Norman Robertson. Those in the background included George Ignatieff, Charles Ritchie, and Hume Wrong. All of these men became fairly expert in atomic matters, but there is little in their individual stories, which have been told with flair elsewhere,[5] about their involvement in disarmament talks between 1945 and 1957. In addition to these professional diplomats, there was a politician who was a gifted amateur. Paul Martin, the minister of national health and welfare in the St Laurent government, had had a passionate interest in foreign affairs ever since he had attended the World Youth Congress in Geneva in 1936. He was the head of Canada's delegation to the United Nations General Assembly in 1946, in 1952, and, most notably, in 1955. During that meeting he was instrumental in promoting the important compromise resolution which both the Soviet Union and the United States accepted, thus permitting the arms negotiations to proceed. Unlike the others, Martin does describe this feat in his memoirs.[6]

There is little doubt that these men had strong personalities and well-defined views on many issues, and it is likely that their personal views did form part of the general mix out of which Pearson fashioned his policy. But if there were differences of opinion over Canada's policy on disarmament and arms control, they are not revealed in the documents on which this account is based. After all, as Ritchie remarked in a slightly different context, "the Ambassador's personal opinions are of no more importance to a foreign government than those of a taxi driver and often less interesting."[7] Pearson's senior officials understood very well his views on political relations between the West and the Soviet Union, on the central importance of Western unity on security issues, and on the direction he wanted the disarmament negotiations to take. Their task was to carry out the policy of their political masters. They therefore conducted their day-to-day work so as to further the goals which Pearson had set out.

Pearson believed that as a liberal and open society the United States would never launch an unprovoked attack on the USSR; he had little empathy for the security concerns of the Soviet Union. As he saw it, the sole cause of a major military superpower confrontation would be Soviet aggression. Only American military preparedness could deter the Soviet Union from reckless action. The various disarmament proposals put forward by the United States in the negotiations were designed to provide what it believed essential to its security and that of the West. The clash between the superpowers took place over these substantive questions. On these issues, Canada lacked the military capacity and political weight to make a useful contribution.

The Canadian premise was that only Soviet agreement to the American programme would guarantee peace. But if the West was to be successful in compelling the Soviet Union to accept the American plan, the Western allies must remain united behind that demand. It was here that Pearson saw a role for Canada. During the negotiations, Western unity was threatened by Soviet blandishments towards France and debates over European security. Canada worked in the sub-committee to keep France "on side." Later, the Soviet Union began to woo India whose influence in the Third World was very strong under the leadership of Jawaharlal Nehru. Pearson believed that the West needed to retain the support of India and, whenever and wherever possible, Canada sought to accommodate its increasing calls for a Third World voice on disarmament issues without disrupting the talks.

Apart from the substantive issues, the superpowers were engaged in a gigantic propaganda duel. Each wished to appear as the great force for peace. Canada worked to help package the Western programme in a way that would win the support of the lesser powers at the United Nations as well as world opinion in general.

I began this study with a naive question: was there anything that Canada could have done to halt the nuclear arms race? Examining what Canada actually did in the negotiations demonstrates the limits of its capacity to influence either of the superpowers on security issues. Canada as a small power had only a marginal affect. Nevertheless, the Canadian government had opinions on all the great arms issues of the day which were often as political as they were military. An analysis of these views reveals many of the assumptions, attitudes, and policies of Pearson and his colleagues about Western defence problems during the Cold War. It shows that ultimately Canada did not believe that disarmament was possible and that it continued to depend for its security on increasing Western power so as to keep the Soviet Union in check. Thus, it did not seek to constrain the American arms build-up in the late forties and early fifties. Some writers have left the impression that postwar Canadian diplomacy was marked by a profound concern for the amelioration of Cold War tensions. John English even suggests that Pearson attempted to "thaw the Cold War."[8] This was not true of Canada's activities in the two disarmament commissions. Its main interest was in helping the United States achieve its objective of using the negotiations to strengthen itself militarily at the expense of the Soviet Union.

Not surprisingly, this study tells us a good deal about the relations of Canada towards its two neighbours. For a decade Canada was part of the Western team negotiating with the Soviet Union on an issue of supreme importance. It is clear that Pearson shared the conventional attitude of his generation of Western politicians that the West was engaged in a desperate political conflict with the Soviet Union. This fact accounts for the profoundly hostile attitude towards the Soviet Union that characterized Canadian policies in the atomic negotiations. As for the United States, discussions between Ottawa and Washington regarding atomic policy went on for almost a decade. They show that Canada, sharing the strategic outlook of the Americans, approved their determination to build a military alliance with the West European powers through the North Atlantic Treaty Organization (NATO) as well as to continue to increase their nuclear strength. From time to time Pearson was unhappy about some aspects of American atomic military policy as well as some of the rhetoric the United States government and its representatives used. What he wished above all else was that the United States would consult its allies including Canada before making important policy changes. Pearson sought to influence Washington without breaking Western solidarity and thereby giving comfort to the Soviet Union. These atomic negotiations furnish a vivid case-study of this perennial problem of Canadian diplomacy.

This work also throws some light on the way the superpowers approached nuclear negotiations in the late forties and most of the fifties. The common thread running through most of the writing on the subject is that the negotiations were dominated by the United States and the Soviet Union, that the United Kingdom and France played only bit parts in the drama. But this interpretation underestimates, in my view, the influence on the negotiations exercised by West European countries. First Britain and then France decided to become nuclear powers and so developed disarmament and arms control proposals that often did not jibe with those of the Americans, let alone those of the Soviet Union. In addition, the United States wished to see a rearmed West Germany integrated into the NATO command while the Soviet Union strove to keep that country neutral. The West Europeans were not entirely happy with the American insistence on this development. In the propaganda battle, each side was always trying to win over European public opinion. In a word, the struggle between the two superpowers on disarmament issues was carried on against a background of disagreements over matters of political and military security in Europe. This is not always taken into account in discussions of arms control negotiations in this period.

The disarmament and arms control proposals designed to give each side military superiority over the other were decisively shaped by the steady improvement in nuclear technology and arms that took place during this period. Continuing changes in the defence policies of the two adversaries meant that the strategic relationship between the two was always in a state of flux. Previous studies do not take these military factors sufficiently into account. This study makes a modest attempt to show how they affected the various concrete proposals which were put on the negotiation table.

The negotiations in the two United Nations commissions examined in this book came close on the heels of a dreadful world war in which millions of men had been locked in ferocious combat using the most modern technology then available. That war had culminated in the use of a wholly new weapon – the atomic bomb. Hiroshima gave a vivid indication of what an atomic war would be like. While in theory each side might acknowledge that atomic arms were harmful, in practice neither could be sure that the other would not launch an atomic attack. The natural reaction of each side in the new "cold" war was to seek to improve its own security by developing more powerful weapons with which to threaten the other side. A small power could do very little, even when placed close to the negotiations as Canada was. If there was a peaceful way out of this frightening impasse, Pearson believed it would require the Soviet Union to accept the American proposals on nuclear disarmament and arms control. As the following narrative shows, the thrust of his policy would be to use whatever influence Canada possessed to obtain this objective.

CHAPTER ONE

The Strategic Setting

The disarmament and arms control programmes of the United States and the Soviet Union in the decade after the end of World War II were direct products of their postwar security needs. These, in turn, were defined by the strategic views of their respective military planners. The fundamental political fact on which these views rested was the unremitting hostility which had grown up between the superpowers towards the end of the war and immediately thereafter. While this enmity rested in part on ideology, it also arose from genuine fear of vulnerability to destructive attacks from the other side. To improve their security the Americans succeeded in integrating the Western-controlled sectors of Germany into the West's defence arrangements, thereby increasing the fears of the USSR. The latter responded by increasing the size of its army. Both developed their nuclear technology to the point where each seemed completely open to a devastating atomic strike from the other. This stalemate was the chief characteristic of the military confrontation in central Europe during the years between 1946 and 1957. And it was these strategic considerations that governed the content of the proposals for disarmament and arms control which each side brought to the negotiating table.

THE COLD WAR

Arthur Schlesinger Jr has rightly observed that "the more one broods about the Cold War, the more irrelevant the assessment of blame seems."[1] American historians have written extensively on the causes of the Cold War. Liberals like Schlesinger have claimed that the Soviet Union, originally only interested in "a free hand in Eastern Europe," increased its ambitions to the point where it sought world domination.[2] Revisionists have argued that the American government wished to make the world safe for American capitalism and never took into account the legitimate security fears of the Soviet Union, thus prompting the latter to maintain its domination of Eastern Europe. They have also pointed out that the fiercely anti-communist views of the American people, which were encouraged by their leaders, made any compromise politically out of the question.[3] A newer school blames Stalin himself, arguing that although his goals were not ideologically motivated, they were vague and ill defined. His methods of achieving limited objectives created distrust: even if the actions were purely defensive, they were perceived by the West as a threat to its security.[4]

The common thread in these interpretations is the idea that the Cold War could have been avoided. However, the blows inflicted on Germany at the end of the war by both the Soviet army and the forces of the Western allies had brought about the collapse of that state. This vacuum allowed the Soviet Union to extend its dominion into the heart of central Europe. In its own interests, the West was impelled to try to mitigate this shift in the balance of power. Consequently, as the war ended, conflicting strategic interests led to an outpouring of mutual recriminations. This hostile atmosphere naturally affected power and military relationships as well. It is true that the ideological dispositions of both sides to look at issues in moral terms made the resolution of concrete problems more difficult. But even had the superpowers shared the same ideology, a political struggle for influence would have developed.

The four individuals who dominated the early years of this global struggle were Presidents Harry Truman and Dwight Eisenhower of the United States and Premiers Joseph Stalin and Nikita Khrushchev of the USSR. Although differing greatly in experience, in personality, and in the problems they faced, these men shared the conviction that a struggle between a socialist Soviet Union and a capitalist United States was inevitable. They rightly believed that this conflict was the dominant feature of world politics, and they were also convinced that it would end only when one side had triumphed over the other. None accepted the possibility of a genuinely co-operative and peaceful coexistence. This was the crux of the Cold War.

John Gaddis has asserted that if it is necessary to select a date for the beginning of the Cold War, February 1946 would be as good as any. By then relations between the United States and the Soviet

Union had deteriorated alarmingly. In February, Stalin implied that so long as communism had not replaced capitalism as the most important form of economic organization, war between the two was inevitable. In March, in the approving presence of President Truman, Winston Churchill delivered his Fulton, Missouri, speech charging that an iron curtain had been rung down across the heart of Europe. Although negotiations continued over a final postwar settlement, the Americans made no further concessions to the Soviet Union. In fact the Americans were virtually abandoning diplomacy. By August relations had so deteriorated that Truman was prepared to use military force for the first time since the end of the war – in this case to prevent Soviet participation in the defence of the Turkish straits as the Soviet government demanded. In September 1946 a report on relations with the Soviet Union commissioned by President Truman advised that no concessions should be made to the Russians. It stated that "the language of military power is the only language which disciples of power politics understand" and maintained that, if necessary, the United States should be prepared "to wage atomic and biological warfare."[5] Perhaps the most complete expression of this policy was the Truman Doctrine, enunciated in March 1947, in which the United States announced military and economic aid to countries threatened by Soviet expansionism (in this instance, to Greece and Turkey) as part of a global crusade of good against the evil of communism.

Much of the American government's Cold War doctrine was set out in the celebrated March 1950 statement of the National Security Council (NSC–68), which was written by Paul Nitze, who was about to replace George Kennan as director of policy planning in the State Department. The document, which was approved by Truman in September 1950, began with the premise that the Soviet Union is "animated by a new fanatic faith, antithetical to our own, and seeks to impose its absolute authority over the rest of the world."[6] It already had overwhelming superiority in conventional arms in Europe and it was expected that by 1954 it would possess enough atomic bombs to make a devastating surprise attack on the United States. The memorandum argued that the United States should respond to this threat with an immediate and large-scale military build-up. In particular, it must increase the nuclear capability which was essential to American security. Meanwhile, the United States should avoid substantive negotiations with the USSR until it could approach them from a position of strength.

Here was a statement of the basic strategy of the United States: win the arms race and you will be in a position to dictate terms to the Soviet Union. Truman shared the view that it was no use talking to the Russians until the West had developed sufficient strength to force the Soviet Union to settle the outstanding issues between them. NSC–68 provided the intellectual framework for the doctrine of containment which justified the American administration's policy of pressing on politically with the Cold War to halt what it called Soviet expansionism. Top American officials accepted this posture completely. The memoirs of Dean Acheson, the secretary of state from 1949 to 1953, reveal an attitude of unremitting hostility towards the Soviet Union; every one of his global policies was shaped by the need to gain an advantage over the USSR. Seyom Brown believes that Acheson and his successor, John Foster Dulles, shared the attitude that "there were in fact no significant negotiable issues" between the Soviet Union and the United States and that if a settlement ever were possible, it would only come about when there was "a global imbalance of power clearly favoring the West."[7]

When elaborating on his hostile attitude towards the West in February 1946, Stalin had implied that there was no possibility of peaceful collaboration between the socialist and capitalist worlds. He warned his people that the consumer goods they so desperately wanted must wait on rearmament. A year later, his protégé, Andrei A. Zhdanov, proclaimed that the world was divided into two camps, each implacably hostile to the other. There is no evidence, however, that Stalin had any intention of launching his armies against Western Europe. The Soviet economy, which had been smashed by the war, could not have sustained this kind of military effort. But he was able to exert pressure on Western Europe through his influence on the powerful communist parties of Italy and France. Nor was Stalin averse to seeing local communist parties triumph as they did in Czechoslovakia. He did show particularly bad judgment in imposing a blockade on Berlin in 1948 and, if Khrushchev is to be believed, in not stopping the North Koreans from their reckless attack on the South in 1950. The Korean War was to prove a catastrophe for Soviet foreign policy in that it triggered a vast rearmament programme in the West.

The rapidly deteriorating relations between the two sides resulted in impotent diplomacy. The Council of Foreign Ministers (the United States, Britain, France, and the Soviet Union), which had been set up at Potsdam in July 1945, wrangled over the future of Germany without success, meeting for the last time in June 1949. At the nadir of the Cold War Acheson never talked formally with his Soviet counterpart, Andrei Vyshinsky. Although the Korean War was the most dangerous episode between the two nations in this decade, their foreign ministers did not meet until six months after its conclusion. It is true that each side made a feeble attempt at reconciliation. In the autumn of 1950, Truman made a gesture towards helping the disarmament negotiations and later, in 1952, Stalin said that a world war with the capitalists was no closer than it had been two or three years before.[8] But for all practical purposes, diplomacy between the two sides was frozen after mid-1949.

The situation improved somewhat during the administrations of Eisenhower and Khrushchev. This is not to say that their attitudes towards the adversary softened, however. In November 1956 Eisenhower told Churchill that "the Soviets are the real enemy of the Western world, implacably hostile and seeking our destruction."[9] As for Khrushchev, he made it clear that peaceful coexistence would lead to the triumph of world communism; it was merely that the struggle against the capitalist world would be carried on by political rather than military means. It was the advent of the hydrogen bomb which had changed the situation. With its development and production, both governments came to understand that its destructive power meant that there could no longer be a "limited" nuclear conflict; it was impossible to imagine any meaningful political settlement in a world emerging from the total wreckage of an H-bomb exchange.

Both nations were now anxious to avoid a war. Premier Georgi Malenkov declared in 1953 that there was no existing difference between the two countries that "cannot be decided by peaceful means,"[10] and three years later President Eisenhower would say that "the only way to win World War III is to prevent it."[11] Noting that the president's State of the Union message of 1954 had acknowledged that there had been a great strategic change in the world during the last year, Walter Lippmann went on to observe that "the change is marked by an open recognition in both great coalitions that their conflict – of which no settlement is in sight – cannot be waged or decided by overt military measures."[12] An active diplomacy had become necessary for survival, and in the next few years serious attempts to come to arrangements over various issues were apparent. In February 1954 the foreign ministers of the Soviet Union, the United States, Britain, and France met to prepare for a settlement in Indochina and Korea. There was an agreement on an Austrian peace treaty in May 1955, followed by a summit of the heads of the United States, France, Britain, and the Soviet Union at Geneva in the summer of 1955 and another meeting of their foreign ministers in November. There was a civil public exchange of letters in 1956 between Marshal Bulganin and President Eisenhower. Finally, in the spring of 1957, there was an intense period of negotiations over arms control, with both Eisenhower and Khrushchev actively engaged behind the scenes. Unfortunately, mutual fear and distrust and animosity made it very difficult to agree on any constructive measures.

INTEGRATING WEST GERMANY
INTO THE WESTERN ALLIANCE

Political confrontation meant quite naturally that military considerations were never far from the minds of the leadership on both sides. At the end of the war the Soviet Union and the United States emerged as the only potential threats to one another. What made the confrontation particularly dangerous was the enormous destructive power each side commanded. If the Soviet Union had a vast army, the United States possessed the atomic bomb. Each had sufficient strength to make it conceivable that each, under favourable circumstances, might be tempted to launch a pre-emptive attack on the other. The job of the military is to worry about security. It was therefore natural for them to speculate on what harm the other side could inflict if political relations soured. As early as the summer of 1944, the American Joint Chiefs of Staff warned that, with the defeat of Germany and Japan, "the United States and the Soviet Union will be the only military powers of the first magnitude."[13] Even without the onset of the Cold War, the military on both sides would have worried about their own country's safety. Postwar tensions naturally worked to make security concerns more immediate. By February 1946 the Joint Chiefs of Staff were warning that "from a military point of view, the consolidation and development of the power of Russia is the greatest threat to the United States in the foreseeable future."[14]

In May 1945 Walter Lippmann, in a prescient observation, had pointed out that any falling out among the wartime allies would result in the wooing of Germany. Germany always had the potential to be the economic powerhouse of central Europe – a power that could easily be translated into political and military capacity. Hitler's rule over Europe had demonstrated how powerful a military force a regime could produce if it had all of western Europe's resources at its disposal. It had taken the combined strength of the USSR, the United States, and the British Commonwealth to eliminate Nazi Germany. Even though it was only a section of the original Reich, the sectors of Germany controlled by the West had great potential; this region had possessed the most developed infrastructure in

Europe and contained substantial natural resources, and its population was highly educated. Fearing either a Germany under Soviet control or an independent but neutral Germany, the Truman administration decided to encourage Germany's integration into the Western side. The real danger, observed George Marshall, the secretary of state from 1947 to 1949, "would be a Germany controlled by the Soviet Union with German military potential utilized in alliance with the Soviet."[15] Stalin, of course, was equally concerned about Germany's potential. His foreign policy in central Europe and that of his ultimate successor, Khrushchev, was dominated by the fear that Germany would be drawn into the Western camp. Its power would thus be at the service of the United States which would thereby be much more capable of launching an assault on the Soviet Union proper. Khrushchev forcefully made this point to Lester Pearson when the latter visited Moscow in 1955: "we do fear the combination of American technology, industrial leadership, and German militarism."[16] Which side would co-opt Germany and its resources remained the fundamental political issue in Europe during the decade after the end of World War II.

By May 1946 General Lucius Clay, the American military governor in Germany, was already moving in the direction that Lippmann had predicted: cutting off reparations to the Soviet Union and wondering out loud about the possibility of a provisional government. A two-month conference of the Big Four foreign ministers, which began in March 1947, was unable to hammer out a common policy towards Germany. The West feared that economic chaos in Germany might provide a propitious atmosphere for the blossoming of communism. To avert this danger its officials hurried to create a German state in the Western zones of occupation. Early in 1948 the United States, Britain, and France agreed to merge their zones. A year later, in May 1949, the Western military governors approved a constitution for this new "state." In May and June of 1949 the Council of Foreign Ministers again failed to agree on what should be done about Germany. The West, attracted by Germany's economic and potential military strength, was more certain than ever that it was on the right track. In September 1949 the Federal Republic of Germany (FRG) was launched, with Konrad Adenauer as its first chancellor. However it was still ultimately controlled by the Allied High Commission made up of representatives of France, Britain, and the United States. One month later a Soviet-dominated republic was formed in the east, the German Democratic Republic. Thus Germany had been divided, with its two sections under the sway of opposing blocs.

Still, the Americans remained unhappy about the strategic situation in Europe. Although both the American and Soviet armies had been substantially reduced in strength between 1945 and 1949, Western experts calculated that the Soviet Union still had about 175 army divisions, of which some 30 were in Eastern Europe. Facing them in Germany were about two American, two and a half British, and a half-dozen poorly armed French divisions.[17] It seemed that the Soviet army could walk into Western Europe any time it wished. The United States could punish the USSR by inflicting Hiroshima-like damage on Soviet cities, but it lacked the quantity of atomic bombs and the delivery system to inflict widespread damage on the USSR in a single blow.

There was no real danger of war, however. Just as the United States had no means of invading the Soviet Union, the Soviet army would have been able to come west only with great difficulty because it had ripped up the main rail connections through Poland in the autumn of 1945. Stalin's only military action in this period was to impose a blockade of traffic into Berlin in March 1948, in an attempt to force the Western allies to abandon their sectors of that city which lay deep within the Soviet zone of occupation. That this was not intended as a serious attempt to take over Western Europe militarily seems clear, for Stalin had earlier given himself the luxury of reading Tito out of the world communist movement, thus increasing the potential opposition to him in the event of war. By the spring of 1949 it was clear that West Berlin could not be starved out, and Stalin gave up the attempt. Nevertheless, in moving from diplomacy to direct military pressure, he increased the anxiety of West Europeans about procuring American protection.

Meanwhile, the Western allies had been negotiating a collective security pact since the spring of 1948, and in April 1949 the North Atlantic Treaty Organization (NATO) came into being. Although its chief clause dealt with common defence, the alliance actually lacked the military capacity to defend Western Europe. The pact's main value was political. There was no feeling of urgency because hardly anyone, including the American Joint Chiefs of Staff,[18] believed that the Soviet Union intended to launch an attack. What Western leaders feared was a repetition of the events in Czechoslovakia, with hitherto Western-oriented countries being taken over by subversion. The North Atlantic Treaty, it was felt, would help to stiffen the European resolve to hold firm to the West. The main thing that needed to be done was to improve the economic state of Western Europe and so boost the confidence of the people in their ability to survive and to flourish.

The formation of NATO meant that the United States was firmly committed to the defence of Western Europe; yet until North Korea attacked the South in June 1950, the United States was unwilling to commit large forces to NATO. NATO's Council had approved a strategic concept whereby the United States would provide the atomic bombs and the European allies the necessary ground troops. Nor did the United States contemplate rearming Germany. In April 1950, the American high commissioner to Germany had affirmed that "our fixed policy has been to maintain effective controls against the revival of a German war machine."[19] Nevertheless, the Pentagon had begun to lay plans to rearm Germany and by April 1950 the Joint Chiefs of Staff had actually approved a scheme. There remained the difficult task of persuading President Truman of the validity of this radical new course. The precipitating event was the North Korean incursion into the South in June. Many feared that this attack was merely a feint, that the real danger was a probable Soviet blow at Western Europe. The willingness of the communists to use force convinced Truman of the need to increase United States military strength. The budget for defence and international affairs rose from US$17.7 billion in fiscal year 1950 to $53.4 billion in fiscal 1951.

At the meeting of North Atlantic Council in September 1950, the United States announced that it would send four to six divisions to Europe. Because of different number of men in an American division, this commitment was roughly equivalent to sixteen Soviet divisions. Looking back, President Eisenhower observed that when he was the supreme commander of the allied forces in Europe, he had believed that American troops were only in Europe on a "temporary or emergency" basis and that the United States could not and would not man "a Roman wall" in Germany.[20] However, this proved to be a fateful step. The United States would find that dispatching troops to Europe was much easier than bringing them back. For the Europeans, the presence of American troops became the insurance policy that the Americans were irrevocably committed to their defence. Then, too, American expectations that their European allies would shortly provide substantial numbers of troops were not fulfilled and American forces were actually needed to man the NATO ramparts against a potential Soviet attack. Finally, the United States continued to believe that it was necessary to do everything to bind West Germany to the alliance. The treaty of friendship between the Russians and the Germans, signed at Rapallo in 1922, and the Stalin-Hitler pact of 1939 had not been forgotten. It was thought that the presence of American troops in Germany would also do much to stem any sentiment in favour of neutrality. In this way, the United States became committed to stationing a considerable land army in central Europe. These forces would become one of the main sticking points in the arms control negotiations between the superpowers.

By September 1950 the American government had also decided to rearm West Germany. This announcement delighted Chancellor Adenauer. As he later recalled: "Rearmament might be the way of gaining full sovereignty for the Federal Republic. This made it the essential question of our political future."[21] Thus, at the September NATO meeting the United States also proposed a European command headed by an American and a national Germany army of approximately ten divisions that would be integrated into NATO. This proposal caused considerable difficulty for the French. Understandably, they were unalterably opposed to rearming German soldiers. Yet they not only wished to make sure that American troops remained in Europe but also sought some means of controlling if not constraining the potential military capacity of the Federal Republic. Consequently, in October, they countered with the Pleven Plan which proposed that West Germany have combat teams of a few hundred men operating within a European army instead of its own national army. Moreover, no European army would be formed until a complementary supranational political structure had been erected. The effect of the Pleven Plan would have been to delay German rearmament. The December NATO meeting accepted the French plan of a European army on condition that France accept the principle of German rearmament. The integrated army was to be under an American supreme commander. The planned subordination of all West German units to a central command would leave Bonn without any independent military command structure to direct its troops. In July 1951 it was agreed that a European Defence Community (EDC) would be set up. Its task was to create a European army that would include West German troops and would presumably become the military arm of NATO. Until the EDC arrangements were ratified by the governments concerned, the NATO military command continued in being.

Meanwhile, the Korean conflict was becoming more and more of a stalemate. The fear that it was a precursor of Soviet activity in Europe was fading and with it the fear of the Soviet Union. In January 1952 Acheson told Prime Minister Churchill that the danger of a Soviet attack in Europe appeared to be declining. This relaxation of tension led the Europeans to moderate their programmes of rearmament. Yet to halt a Soviet attack NATO would require

100 divisions, about the same number that Eisenhower had had deployed in Germany at the end of the war. To acquire such a number seemed impossible. In February 1952, at its Lisbon meeting, the NATO council set a target of approximately fifty divisions for that year, seventy-five in the next, and ninety-six by 1954. The European NATO governments did not, however, possess the resources to fulfil these goals. On the very day the Lisbon meeting opened, Churchill announced that the British could no longer afford to supply its quota of these ground forces and intended to rely on strategic bombing and nuclear arms. During the meeting the French government was overthrown because of its request for a tax increase to finance the new troops. In meeting the Lisbon force goals, therefore, German military formations would be more important than ever. Consequently the NATO Council endorsed the concept of an EDC army.

In March 1952 Stalin made one last effort to stop the continuing integration of West Germany into the West. He proposed a reunified Germany which could have its own military forces on condition that it adopt a policy of neutrality. Both the Western allies and Bonn rejected this offer, however, and in May West Germany, the United States, Britain, and French signed a number of treaties whose effect was to establish the European Defence Community. The humiliating Occupation Statute was to be repealed and the high commissions abolished. West Germany would now conduct relations with the three former occupying powers on the basis of equality. In return, West Germany would furnish a dozen divisions for the new European army.[22]

To be implemented the EDC treaty had to be ratified by the French assembly, which was not enthusiastic about the proposal – after all a good deal of France had been occupied by Nazi Germany only six years before. "The rearmament of Germany fills me with great anxiety,"[23] warned the speaker of the assembly, Édouard Herriot, and President Vincent Auriol, reflecting the strength of French sentiment against the restoration of German power, complained to Acheson that rearming West Germany was a dreadful mistake.[24] As long as the war in Indochina went on, most of France's armed forces would be tied up there; by default, the new European army would be dominated by the Germans. In consequence, there seemed no hope for ratification until the French troops returned from Indochina to redress that imbalance. The turnover in the American government, from the Democratic party to the Republicans under Eisenhower in the 1952 presidential elections, meant that the Americans were too preoccupied to exert a great deal of pressure on France. It was not until December 1953 that the new secretary of state, John Foster Dulles, warned the French about the possibility of an American reappraisal of the situation, if nothing were done. Then, in May 1954, the Indochina war came to an end with the French defeat at Dienbienphu. This defeat led to the fall of the administration led by Pierre Laniel and its replacement by one headed by Pierre Mendès-France. The latter was no great supporter of the EDC and allowed the treaty to go down to defeat in the assembly on a procedural issue in August 1954. But all was not lost; Britain intervened. Anthony Eden, its foreign minister, argued that it was essential to anchor Germany in the West rather than let it drift in central Europe, and after hurried negotiations among the Western powers in October, it was agreed that West Germany would become a member of NATO and would furnish twelve divisions to its combined forces. (Owing to domestic opposition the West Germans did not furnish their first division until the beginning of January 1958, and it was only in 1965 that they finally mobilized all twelve divisions.) On entering NATO the occupation laws ceased to apply, the Federal Republic achieved full sovereignty and participated as an equal in alliance deliberations. The Soviet Union recognized the irrevocability of this step when it agreed to establish diplomatic relations with West Germany in September 1955.

Curiously, the French quickly approved West Germany's entry into NATO. Mendès-France spoke strongly in favour of the decision, on the grounds that it was necessary to preserve the Western alliance. He argued that if the French turned down another plan, it was probable that the British and the United States would go ahead and rearm the Germans anyway. German rearmament was the price of the American guarantee of Europe's security. The French seemed to have drawn comfort from the supreme commander being an American who was thus (presumably) in a position to prevent the Germans taking any independent action. Nevertheless this difficult process had poisoned relations between France and the United States which were already strained because many in France blamed the Americans for not furnishing them with more help in Indochina. It is probable that this lingering animosity made the problems that arose between the French and the United States in the disarmament negotiations even more difficult to resolve.

A major goal of both Eisenhower and Adenauer – the integration of a fully sovereign West Germany into the Western side – had been achieved. The Federal Republic not only had great military potential but was staunchly anti-communist. On 9 May 1955 West Germany attended its first session of the NATO Council. A week later the Soviet Union responded by engineering the Warsaw Treaty Organization with members of the communist bloc – as a counterweight to NATO.

The alliance with West Germany was the keystone of American policy in Europe. As Samuel Huntington noted, the "participation of Germany in western defense efforts was a cardinal aim of American policy."[25] In this respect the motives of the Eisenhower regime were the same as those of its predecessor. Dulles was only repeating the view of Marshall when he wrote that "[Western Europe's] industrial plant represents so nearly the balance of industrial power in the world that an aggressor might feel it was a good gamble to seize it – even at the risk of considerable hurt to himself."[26] In return for their sovereignty, the West Germans would furnish United States strategic planners with a serious conventional deterrent against a possible Soviet attack.

Meanwhile Adenauer had won a pledge from the Western powers never to recognize the German Democratic Republic whose sovereignty had been acknowledged by the Soviet Union. The next phase of the East-West political struggle over Germany would revolve around the attempts of the Soviet Union to get the West to accept East Germany as a sovereign state. The German Social Democratic party accused Adenauer of sacrificing the unity of the country to secure the American alliance. Consequently, he was compelled to go on claiming Germany's right to unify itself by means of free elections and to associate with the West. Eisenhower, for his part, would declare, in one of his first presidential announcements, that an honourable European peace would require the emergence of a united German republic.[27] All through this period the United States continued to support the concept of a freely united Germany allied to the West, because the hard fact was that the most substantial land contribution to Western Europe's defence would have to come from the Germans. The United States believed that preserving the prestige and power of Adenauer was so important that they were prepared to sacrifice any possible gain in arms control rather than abandon their support for what they must have perceived to be an impossible goal.

THE IMPROVEMENT IN ATOMIC TECHNOLOGY

In July 1946 the atomic bomb, while formidable, was not yet a decisive weapon because there were only seven in existence. Even by the following year the United States was producing fewer than one every two months. Forty-eight hours were required for each bomb to be assembled laboriously by a team of physicists and engineers. By 1948 the United States had approximately 50 bombs, but they were so bulky that they could only be delivered by a specially designed bomber. Even if they had been used, they would have done no more damage to the vast Soviet Union than conventional bombing had done to a much smaller Germany.[28] Still, there was steady improvement in the technology. By 1949 a much more efficient method of using fissionable material for atomic bombs had been developed, and the bombs themselves could now be produced on an assembly line. The bombs were smaller, more efficient, and able to be used in a variety of forms including long-range artillery shells and land mines.

The nation's limited supply of fissionable material was preventing the production of the number of atomic bombs the military desired. In the autumn of 1949, however, despairing of achieving international control of atomic energy, Truman approved a substantial increase in production. The outbreak of the war in Korea led to further increases in October 1950 and again in 1951, and in 1952 Truman ordered another expansion of atomic facilities. By then the United States had sufficient supplies of uranium, and by January 1953 a construction programme was under way which would soon add eight plutonium production reactors and ten gaseous diffusion U-235 production plants to the five reactors and two gaseous diffusion plants already in operation.[29] So great was this expansion that it has never been necessary to build more capacity. There was now no limiting factor on the number of bombs the United States could produce. By 1950 it had perhaps 300 atomic weapons; in 1953, about 1,000. By 1957 it is probable that the total had reached about 10,000; and by the end of Eisenhower's second term the stockpile was over 30,000.[30]

The means of transporting the bombs was as critical as their production, and improvements in aircraft paralleled those in nuclear technology. In the late forties the United States had fewer than three dozen B-29 aircraft with a 4,000-mile range that were equipped to carry the bomb and they could only reach the USSR from overseas bases. The Berlin blockade prompted Truman to send two squadrons of B-29 bombers to Britain, and after the outbreak of the Korean War the Americans began a crash programme to establish bases on foreign soil from which to attack the USSR. They planned to use a medium-range bomber, the B-47, which had a range of some 3,200 miles. These overseas American bases would become an important issue in the disarmament negotiations. At home the United States deployed, first, the B-36 which had a range of some 8,000 miles and, later, an even more advanced long-range bomber, the B-52. By the end of the Eisenhower years the United States was gradually eliminating medium-range bombers (mostly B-47s) and moving towards a force of approximately 500 long-range bombers (mostly B-52s).

The Soviet Union developed its own atomic expertise more rapidly than expected. As early as June 1940 it had begun research. In 1942 the Russians realized that both the British and Americans were working on an atomic bomb. In response, Soviet scientists began to study the design of both the U-235 and plutonium bombs and by the spring of 1945 they were planning an industrial reactor for producing plutonium. At Potsdam in July 1945 Truman had told Stalin that the United States possessed a weapon of unusual force. Hiroshima confirmed this fact. The Soviet leader realized that the American possession of the bomb posed a dangerous threat to his country's security. As Stalin told his officials: "Hiroshima has shaken the whole world. The balance has been destroyed. Provide the bomb – it will remove a great danger from us."[31] He gave top priority to building a bomb and assigned the necessary resources. The occupation of Czechoslovakia provided access to a convenient source of uranium. Stalin made use of both German and Soviet scientists, many of the latter having been political prisoners. In September 1949, the Soviet Union exploded its first atomic device. The Americans had overestimated by six years the time the Soviet Union would need to become a nuclear power. Truman had been confident that the United States would enjoy a monopoly for at least ten years, but he did not reckon on Stalin's determination not to be left behind. By 1953 the Soviet Union probably had about 300 to 400 atomic bombs and had become a formidable nuclear power.

As early as 1948 the Russians unveiled their version of the B-29, the Tu-4. Although this aircraft could not reach North America, it was capable of return missions to Western Europe. By 1953 the Soviet Union had accumulated a force of about 1,000 Tu-4s. In the May Day parade of 1954 they created the impression of formidable air power by displaying a prototype of their long-range bomber – the M-4 Bison, but it and another long-range bomber, the Tu-95 Bear, do not seem to have come into service until 1956. These developments caused American strategists considerable concern. As early as 1951 Acheson had warned that in time the Soviet Union could strike the United States using a heavy bomber equipped with atomic bombs.[32] In the fifties the United States certainly reckoned seriously with the possibility of a direct Soviet blow on those elements of its Strategic Air Command (SAC) stationed at home. In fact, North America was not a feasible target because even the newer Soviet bombers were unsuitable for intercontinental missions. Later, Premier Khrushchev would concede that "the U.S. was out of the range for our bombers. We could blast into dust America's allies in Europe and Asia, but America itself ... was beyond our reach."[33] Fortunately for the Soviet Union the United States had little reliable intelligence about its military capacity until 1956 when Eisenhower authorized the taking of aerial photographs of the USSR using a new type of aircraft, the U-2. Khrushchev, by means of sheer exaggeration, had caused the United States military to believe that their country was much more vulnerable to a sudden Soviet strike than it was, and this drastically affected their whole strategic posture towards the USSR during the mid-fifties.

Another crucial stage in the arms race was the development of the hydrogen bomb. The Soviet atomic explosion in September 1949 caused enormous political pressure to be brought to bear on Truman for the United States to develop the super weapon. At this nadir of the Cold War, how could he resist steps to increase American strength? Lewis Strauss, a member of the United States Atomic Energy Commission who would go on to become its head under Eisenhower, expounded the perfect rationale for the arms race when he wrote to President Truman in November: "I believe the United States must be as completely armed as any possible enemy. From this, it follows that I believe it unwise to renounce, unilaterally, any weapons which an enemy can reasonably be expected to possess."[34] On 31 January 1950 Truman made the decision to go ahead with development of the hydrogen bomb. In November 1952 the United States exploded its first thermonuclear device and less than a year later the Soviet Union dropped its first thermonuclear bomb. In March 1954 the Americans tested a genuine thermonuclear bomb that could be delivered. In November 1955 the Soviet Union pulled even by demonstrating a hydrogen bomb with a yield four times greater than the one they had dropped two years before. Both sides were hard at work testing their H-bombs, a process which would lead to serious political consequences.

The hydrogen bomb itself differed a good deal from an atomic bomb. Given an atomic bomb to act as a trigger, a hydrogen bomb required no expensive fissionable material because it was fuelled by hydrogen, the most plentiful element in nature. Each H-bomb was at least a thousand times as powerful as an atomic bomb. The explosion of one gave off enormous amounts of lethal radioactivity. SAC planners now calculated that they could destroy three-quarters of the populations of 188 Soviet cities, with casualties approaching seventy-five million people. So great was the destructive power of the hydrogen bomb that Churchill was led to speculate that "mankind [would be] placed in a situation both measureless and laden with doom."[35] What its impact on the conduct of war would be was unclear. Unlike the atomic bomb, an H-bomb was so powerful that only a few might force another great state to surrender. Yet it was difficult to conceive of a situation where it would make sense to use them. There would have been no point in dropping them, even had they been available, in either Korea or Indochina because there were no suitable targets.

Nevertheless the existence of the hydrogen bomb had an immense effect on politics, helping to persuade the leaders of the superpowers that a nuclear war would simply end in mutual destruction. It is no accident that the H-bomb's successful development precipitated a period of détente. At the same time the possibility of complete disarmament was undermined because even a few hydrogen bombs in an enemy's hands could cause enormous destruction. The arrival of the hydrogen bomb greatly stimulated the peace movement. The memory of Hiroshima had faded in the late forties. In general people seemed not to have understood the significance of atomic weapons. The bomb, it came to be said, "was not so bad after all, and in any event it was here to stay."[36] The effect of radioactive fallout on Japanese fishermen as a result of the first American hydrogen bomb test was much easier to comprehend. There arose a world-wide movement which sought not so much to halt the arms race as to end the testing. In the United States, Lewis Strauss aroused considerable apprehension when he asserted that one H-bomb could destroy any American city. This possibility, along with the fear of radiation, ignited a movement in the United States that was strong enough to make the cessation of nuclear testing an issue in the presidential election of 1956.

The other important atomic technological improvement was the development of tactical nuclear weapons. These were miniaturized shells or bombs that used nuclear fuel to create a tremendous explosion. Tests in October 1951 had demonstrated their potential. Robert Oppenheimer had recommended them as a way of deterring the Soviet army from invading Western Europe, without the mass destruction that defence with hydrogen bombs would bring. This advice had impressed Eisenhower when he was commander of the allied forces in Europe,[37] and as president he enthusiastically supported their use. John Foster Dulles explained that tactical nuclear weapons would provide nations around the Sino-Soviet perimeter with an "effective defense against full-scale conventional attack and thus confront any aggressor with the choice between failing or himself initiating nuclear war against the defending country."[38] In October 1953 these weapons came into service in the United States forces and that month Eisenhower approved an NSC decision to employ them in response to any minor aggressions in Europe. Between the Lisbon meeting of February 1952 and that in Paris in December 1954 the Atlantic alliance moved from relying on conventional arms to agreeing in principle to adopt tactical nuclear weapons. They seemed ideal for bolstering NATO's defence against a possible Soviet conventional threat, especially when it became clear that the West's conventional forces were well below projected targets. At its December 1956 meeting NATO's dependence on tactical nuclear arms was made even more complete, with the decision to accept an American offer to put nuclear weapons and stockpiles at NATO's disposal in Europe.

The acquisition of nuclear weapons by the two superpowers made disarmament both more important and more difficult. But there was still another complication. Both Great Britain and France, without any American help, entered the nuclear club in the 1950s. That Britain did so was no great surprise. Its scientists had contributed greatly to the discovery of nuclear energy and its military applications. It had a scientific team of highly qualified nuclear experts in place and its military advisers understood that a nuclear defence was considerably cheaper than a conventional one. The British government was wary of becoming totally dependent on the United States for its security; it believed that an independent nuclear capability was necessary to guarantee Britain's security. But the more important reasons for becoming a nuclear power were prestige and self-image. Acquiring a bomb would be a signal to the world that despite its grievous economic and military position caused by the war Great Britain intended to remain one of the world's great powers.[39]

At first the British had believed that they could acquire an atomic bomb on the cheap by reason of their special relationship with the United States. But the McMahon Act of 1946 made it illegal for American authorities to hand over industrial atomic information to foreigners. The next year the British Defence Committee decided that Britain would build its own atomic bomb, and in 1948 the Labour government of Clement Attlee announced the decision to proceed. The project moved along swiftly and when Churchill came back as prime minister in November 1951 he found the work almost completed. The following February he announced the completion of the project, and in October 1952 the British exploded their first atomic bomb. But just as Britain was procuring its atomic bomb, the Americans and Russians were building hydrogen bombs. For both economic and political reasons Britain decided in 1954 to take this next step. In June 1956 Prime Minister Anthony Eden was able to announce considerable progress, and Britain tested its first H-bomb early in 1957.

Unlike Britain, France had decided that its nuclear research would be confined to non-military purposes, but even in 1946 this policy was conditional on the establishment of international control over the production of atomic energy. In 1951 the government announced a long-range plan to produce fissionable materials. Apart from the problems of international control, developments in Europe were to reinforce the move towards an independent atomic military capacity. France's original assumptions had been that the United States would provide protection against the communist menace and that Germany would play a subordinate role in Europe. By the end of 1954 these premises no longer appeared valid. The Soviet threat, now strengthened by a nuclear capability, seemed more formidable than ever. Meanwhile West Germany would soon acquire an army that would clearly be more powerful than that of France, which had been severely wounded by the war in Indochina and was increasingly occupied with retaining its position in Algeria. France's ability to maintain a great power role was being put more and more into question; it needed to acquire more military strength. Consequently, in December 1954, Premier Mendès-France decided to allow the launching of a secret programme of preparation for nuclear weapons.

The French were in a contradictory position. They were the most militant of the Western allies in demanding the abolition of nuclear weapons. But this disarmament campaign might not succeed. In that case they too must acquire nuclear arms if they were to remain a great power. This dichotomy explains the ambiguous statements of French politicians. In April 1955 France renounced the development of military applications of nuclear energy for at least three years but nevertheless continued its secret programme to allow France to join the nuclear club. In January 1956, Premier Guy Mollet claimed that France favoured a European atomic organization devoted to peaceful purposes, but by July he was saying that such an agency must not hinder France's right and ability to construct nuclear weapons. Doubtless the American failure to support the French in November during the Suez crisis reinforced the lesson they had already learned in Indochina: that no other great power was likely to help them militarily unless its own vital interests were involved. If the French wanted nuclear protection, they would have to provide it themselves. And in May 1957 the minister of defence announced that France would create its own nuclear force to allow it to remain a great power.

THE STRATEGIC VIEWS OF
THE SUPERPOWERS

In the early years of the Cold War each side assumed that the best way to guarantee its security was to strengthen itself militarily in relation to the other. It is easy to understand why both superpowers would have such a view, but the attempts of each side to strengthen its position only impelled the other to do the same. There was as yet no conception of nuclear danger as "a common problem,"[40] no realization that the only change in military arrangements that would be beneficial in the long run was one which made both sides feel equally secure. Because the defence policy of each side was based on a deep apprehension and distrust of the other side, there was an alarming increase in both the nuclear and the conventional weaponry at the disposal of each side during this period. The strategy of each was shaped by this ever accelerating arms race. There were also common assumptions underpinning the strategies of both sides. Stalin and Truman both expected that any future war would be a replay of World War II. Eisenhower and Khrushchev, however, prepared for a different kind of war – one that was short and devastating and might be decided by the side that launched the first blow.

The years from 1946 to 1953 were characterized by the overwhelming ground superiority of the Soviet army and the American possession of the atomic bomb. Soviet forces could occupy Western Europe but only at the cost of atomic retaliation from the United States. The United States could bombard Russian cities, but it had no way of preventing the Soviet Union sweeping west in Europe. As one writer commented: "The Soviet capability for occupying Western Europe, and the American capability for air attack, might seem to be of the same order of magnitude, and hence mutually deterrent."[41]

In these years the centrepiece of American strategy was the atomic bomb, on which they believed their monopoly would last for many years. There was no alternative because in 1947 Congress had rejected a peacetime universal draft and refused to pay for a strong conventional force. The Truman administration was compelled to rely on the bomb as the principal deterrent to Soviet aggression. At the peak of the Berlin crisis, in September 1948, the president explicitly authorized the use of atomic weapons in the event of war. Although Truman always regarded atomic bombs as horror weapons to be employed only in the last resort, it was important, if deterrence was to work, that he affirm publicly that, as in the case of Hiroshima, he would not hesitate to use them if necessary. Nevertheless, if a war were to break out in Europe, American strategists saw themselves doing what had been done in World War II. They could, to be sure, use atomic weapons to inflict heavy damage on the Soviet Union. But if the latter were determined, it could sweep into Western Europe; there might well be another Dunkirk where the remnants of Western Europe's forces would gather before being driven off the continent. Thus, a Western victory would again require some kind of Normandy-style landing and the liberation of Europe. As the Americans saw it, in this operation the United States would supply the air power and the finances and the West Europeans would furnish the land troops.

The Soviet atomic explosion in September 1949 made it less certain that the Americans would risk trying to slow down a Soviet invasion of Western Europe by an atomic strike against Moscow; they would now face Soviet nuclear retaliation. Dean Acheson pointed out that with the passage of time, Soviet nuclear forces would tend more and more to balance American atomic strength. He believed even then that in the event of war Soviet bombers might be able to drop as many as 200 atomic bombs on American cities. A state of mutual atomic deterrence was coming into being. "If Russia can maintain her relative superiority in ground strength while at the same time narrowing the gap in atomic striking power," he wrote, "the time comes when the Russian land army becomes the decisive weapon in the military balance."[42] Certainly the American possession of the atomic bomb would not deter the North Koreans from launching their attack. Consequently, Acheson worked to restore a conventional balance in Europe. Thus, the outbreak of the Korean War precipitated the American decision to send another six divisions to Europe and to persuade France to accept German rearmament.

But what was the purpose of these conventional forces? The first was to deter the Soviet Union from contemplating aggression. If that failed and the Russians did launch an all-out assault, NATO ground forces were to delay the Soviet army long enough to allow SAC bombers to strike the Russian heartland with sufficient force to prevent the Soviet Union from gaining control of the great war potential of Western Europe. When Acheson set out this scenario, he did not explain how bombing Moscow would prevent the Soviet army taking over in the West. Indeed, for Acheson's strategy to succeed, the West would have needed nearly a hundred divisions. But at the beginning of 1954 the French transferred four divisions from Europe for service in Algeria; in 1957 the British withdrew another two for financial reasons, reducing the number of NATO divisions to about seventeen. Meanwhile NATO continued to maintain that it confronted about 175 Soviet divisions. (A Soviet division was not nearly as large as a NATO one, but the difference in manpower available was still striking.)

Soviet military doctrine was based on Stalin's concept of permanently operating factors. This theory was rigidly adhered to not only because of Stalin's personal power but also because its virtues seemed to have been demonstrated by the victories gained in World War II. Stalin contended that to win, a government needed to be able to depend on a number of constants such as "stability of the home front, morale of the army, quantity and quality of divisions, equipment of the army, the organizing ability of the commanding personnel of the army."[43] Soviet propagandists also advanced a factor of historical determinism: the USSR had the advantage of representing a superior social and economic form of society. Stalin's strategy precluded seeking advantage through the element of surprise. In 1946 he declared that "atomic bombs are meant to frighten those with weak nerves, but they cannot decide the fate of wars since atomic bombs are quite insufficient for this."[44] No doubt this statement was designed to offset any pressure on the Soviet Union arising from American possession of the bomb. Since the USSR did not possess an atomic bomb in those early years, Soviet leaders could hardly admit that it was a winning weapon. Nevertheless, the great Soviet effort to build one shows that Stalin believed the atomic bomb to be a very significant weapon. Still, as late as 1952 theorists were quoting Stalin's dictum that deprecated the value of the atomic bomb.[45] There is some question about whether he ever believed his own assertion that an atomic bomb was not the ultimate weapon. It is probable, however, that Stalin failed to appreciate that nuclear and thermonuclear weapons had fundamentally altered the nature of war.[46]

Rhetoric aside, there was not that much difference between the strategic views of the superpowers in the early postwar years. Both continued to see the next war as a rerun of World War II; while each knew that the atomic bomb could inflict terrible destruction, neither thought it the decisive weapon. One writer has summed up the situation this way: "Until the appearance of the hydrogen or fusion bomb in 1952, the victors of the Second World War planned and trained their forces as if nothing had fundamentally changed, envisaging lengthy major campaigns on land, at sea, and in the air, conducted on the same lines as they had experienced between 1941–1945."[47]

When Eisenhower became president, he sought to continue the Democratic aim of containing potential Soviet aggression, but to do so with a smaller defence budget. The current level of defence spending was high because the policy of containment meant that the United States must be on guard along the whole border where the communist and non-communist worlds met, and this commitment required great numbers of men and vast amounts of equipment. But costs could be cut significantly if nuclear weapons were substituted for conventional ones. The basis of Eisenhower's policy was that nuclear defence against potential Soviet aggression was much cheaper than conventional means. (A ton of TNT cost US$1700 in 1952; fissionable material could produce the same explosion for $23.[48]) In October 1953 President Eisenhower approved NSC–162/2 which authorized the use of both strategic and tactical nuclear weapons wherever the military thought it desirable. For Truman, nuclear bombs had been weapons of last resort. Eisenhower proposed to treat them as ordinary weapons, no different from a bullet or a gun.

This was a major revolution in American strategic thinking. From now on, the new secretary of state, John Foster Dulles, announced, the United States intended to deter aggression by depending "primarily upon a great capacity to retaliate, instantly, by means and at places of our own choosing."[49] It appeared that for the first time the United States was ready to use massive nuclear strength to deal with crises and local wars outside Europe. It is true that Eisenhower told his chiefs of staff not to count on nuclear weapons in minor conflicts. Nevertheless, by 1955, he had shifted ground and announced that "the United States cannot afford to preclude itself from using nuclear weapons even in a local situation."[50] Both Eisenhower and Dulles soon conceded, however, that there were circumstances where something less than massive retaliation would be appropriate.[51] There was certainly no ambiguity in Eisenhower's declared policy of meeting any large-scale Soviet attack against Western Europe with a strategic nuclear blow at the USSR. He hoped that the mere threat of such massive nuclear retaliation would deter the Soviet Union. As he explained to his countrymen in 1954, he reasoned that in contemplating any war with the United States, Soviet leaders were bound to ask themselves what nuclear weapons would do to their homeland. (At the same time he rejected any idea of a preventive nuclear strike at Moscow.[52])

It has been suggested that Eisenhower departed sharply from NSC–68's insistence that a strong conventional force be maintained in central Europe. "Two more divisions or ten more divisions on our side," he insisted, "would not make very much difference against the Soviet ground force."[53] Yet this judgment is a little too strong. While Eisenhower wished to shift the emphasis in the American armed forces from the conventional to the nuclear, he continued to accept Acheson's argument on the need for strong allied forces in central Europe to delay any kind of Soviet aggression by land. He remained strongly committed to NATO and the rearming of West Germany. As we shall see, the Americans consistently refused to lower the numbers of their armed forces to the levels proposed by the USSR.

The decision to integrate nuclear weapons into the American arsenal was far from a panacea for American defence. It did not erase the possibility of a Soviet surprise attack on SAC installations in the United States which would eliminate the American capacity to retaliate. Such an unexpected strike was an old fear of Eisenhower's; he remembered the failure of intelligence at Pearl Harbor. It was the fear of such an attack that led him to propose to the Soviet Union a system of mutual aerial photography in the summer of 1955 and to authorize U-2 flights over the USSR in 1956.

Because the hydrogen bomb was so powerful, it ruled out a repetition of World War II with millions of men engaged in combat with conventional weapons. Eisenhower became convinced that there never would be another large-scale conventional war.[54] The United States was far ahead of its rival in stockpiling nuclear weapons, but the latter had sufficient quantities to inflict intolerable damage on North America. It appeared that any Soviet-American altercation would quickly result in nuclear destruction for all concerned. Thus the value of a doctrine of massive retaliation soon ran into a credibility problem. Was the defence of Western Europe so important to the United States that it would allow itself to suffer nuclear destruction rather than to go back on its pledge to defend it? And what about small incursions along the frontier? Would the United States use hydrogen bombs in a brushfire war if there was a chance of escalation into a major nuclear conflagration?

Some strategists sought to evade this difficulty by suggesting that the United States threaten to fight a limited nuclear war. If an all-out war meant mutual destruction, limited aggression could be fended off by the use of tactical weapons. Tactical weapons were thought to give the allies an advantage because those of the West were said to be superior to those of the USSR and because the damage they did would be limited. Both these propositions turned out to be false. The Soviet Union soon had efficient tactical weapons. Then, in June 1955, Carte Blanche, an exercise using tactical weapons, showed that in a real war there would be an enormous slaughter of civilians. A simulated attack using some 350 atomic bombs on military targets would have resulted in 1.7 million dead and 3.5 million wounded, without taking account of the effects of radioactive contamination. To make matters worse, the Soviet Union never accepted the possibility of the limited use of nuclear weapons; once a nuclear war began, they warned, there could be no limit to escalation. There was simply no way of guaranteeing that a comparatively minor tactical exchange would not develop into an all-out war.

There was, Robert Osgood suggests, a genuine difference between the United States and its European allies over the goals of the Atlantic alliance: "In American eyes the alliance ... was the essential instrument for redressing the military imbalance on the Continent; but in the eyes of most European members the major purpose [was] to commit the United States to come to their defense."[55] The United States wanted some means to slow down a Soviet conventional advance before it had to make the fearsome choice of using nuclear weapons. Yet in 1955 an independent *Time* survey found only ten effective divisions facing the Soviet army; of these, five were American and two were British. NATO's decision to acquire tactical nuclear arms had worked to lessen the pressure on its European members to supply ground troops. They wanted protection against a Soviet land attack without having to pay for a massive conventional force. They believed they had found it with tactical nuclear arms. The December 1954 NATO meeting that accepted these weapons refrained from even attempting to organize an increase in conventional forces. Instead, it adopted a new strategic concept of offsetting the numerical superiority of the Soviet army through nuclear arms. Because all such weapons were American, only the president of the United States could authorize their use. In effect the United States had assumed the main responsibility for fending off any Soviet attack on the alliance's front line.[56]

Both the French and the British had good economic reasons for relying on American nuclear weapons. As well, NATO acceptance of tactical nuclear weapons tended to undercut the urgency for the Germans to rearm: some West German politicians questioned the need to recruit conventional forces since NATO planned to use atomic bombs in any war that would destroy Germany. More and more European allies were "inclined to regard tactical, like strategic, nuclear weapons as a *deterrent* to aggression rather than as a *defense* against invasion if the deterrent should fail."NATO ground forces became "a kind of trip wire with scarcely a pretense of a defensive function."[57] But what guarantee was there that in case of a Soviet attack, the United States would not leave the Europeans in the lurch? The trip wire would only be credible if it included American soldiers. Thus the stationing of United States land forces in central Europe became the validation of the credibility of American nuclear deterrence. Tactical nuclear weapons made disarmament more difficult not only because of their number but also because they made it necessary for American troops to be stationed in West Germany.

In the Soviet Union the year 1953 not only brought the death of Stalin but also the development of the hydrogen bomb. These two events led to the first realistic assessment by Soviet leaders of the effect of that bomb on warfare. One of the first signs that Soviet leaders were rethinking Stalin's tendency to play down the effect of nuclear weapons was a statement in March 1954 by Premier Malenkov that "with the existence of modern means of destruction ... [war] would mean the destruction of world civilization."[58] Unfortunately the discussion on this issue in the Soviet Union rapidly became mixed up with the struggle to succeed Stalin. Evidently the group led by Khrushchev was able to make Malenkov back down, because in April 1954 he asserted that if the West, relying on nuclear weapons, began war against the Soviet Union, it would be crushed and the capitalist order itself would be destroyed. The implication was that Soviet society could survive a nuclear attack. In February 1955 the Khrushchev faction won the leadership struggle. That month *Pravda* was still expressing the old Stalinist viewpoint: "Only political adventurers can think that they will succeed with the help of atomic weapons in canceling the progressive development of mankind. Weapons have never altered or canceled the laws of social development." And both Vyacheslav Molotov and Anastas Mikoyan had continued to reiterate the idea that "only the imperialists will perish in an atomic war, but not civilization."[59] But this would have been cold comfort to Khrushchev. We can only speculate on whether he truly believed that the USSR could survive a war in which hydrogen bombs were used. It was clearly desirable to avoid one, however, and at the Twentieth Congress of the Soviet Communist Party he asserted that the destructive power of nuclear weapons made peaceful coexistence between East and West a necessity. Indeed, his main foreign policy departure from the accepted orthodoxy under Stalin was to assert that a war between the imperialist and socialist worlds was not inevitable.

At the same time the Soviet military were giving serious attention to the dangers of a surprise nuclear attack. In a celebrated article in February 1955, General Rotmistrov flatly asserted that "in the situation of the employment of atomic and hydrogen weapons, surprise is one of the decisive conditions for the attainment of success not only in battles and operations but also in the war as a whole."[60] The Soviet military came to believe that the first blow could be decisive. Logic led them to accept the concept of pre-emptive war. If they believed that the United States was preparing a nuclear attack against them, it followed that the Soviet Union must be able to strike first.[61] David Holloway, an expert on Soviet defence policy, has suggested that Soviet strategists never had a theory equivalent to massive nuclear deterrence. They never threatened to retaliate against a conventional attack with nuclear weapons. Like the Americans, however, they believed that their side must be militarily strong enough to deter an attack from the opposing powers. They sought to prevent war by means of a peace policy backed by military strength.[62] In the mid-fifties the Soviet Union certainly came to depend on nuclear weapons. At the same time, however, they abandoned their efforts to develop a strategic bombing force to match the one possessed by the Americans, opting instead for intercontinental ballistic missiles.[63]

PROSPECTS FOR DISARMAMENT AND ARMS CONTROL

At first sight, prospects for genuine negotiations on disarmament and arms control in the years from 1946 to 1957 were not very favourable. The great historian of the British atomic energy programme, Margaret Gowing, summed up the situation in the following elegant manner: "while waiting for mutual trust to be established and Utopia to arrive, each [world] power must look to its own interests and make itself as strong as possible with nuclear weapons, even if thereby mutual distrust was engendered and the chances of ultimate international control diminished."[64] It became easier and easier to produce as many nuclear weapons as the military thought it needed. They were much more efficient than conventional weapons and therefore the cheapest way to fend off an external threat. After 1953 they became an integral part of the war-making capacity of both superpowers. That the other side had nuclear weapons was always a powerful incentive to increase one's own nuclear arsenal. In the summer of 1949 President Truman had asserted that "since we can't obtain international control we must be strongest in atomic weapons,"[65] and in 1954 Marshal Bulganin stated that because the United States would not agree to renounce nuclear weapons, "the Soviet Union will need to have these weapons so that in the event of the unexpected happening, we shall not be disarmed."[66] Both the American policy of massive retaliation and the Soviet threat to deliver a pre-emptive blow if necessary were totally dependent on their increasing ability to strike the other side with hydrogen bombs.

As well, politics often worked against disarmament in this Cold War era. President Eisenhower gained votes at home by talking tough to the Soviet Union. He had to worry about the militant anti-communist wing of his own party as well as the Democrats accusing him of neglecting defence and being soft on communism. In the spring of 1957, at a time when disarmament negotiations were at a critical stage, Premier Khrushchev, locked in battle with his domestic opponents, similarly found it to his immediate political advantage to denounce the capitalist countries which want "a feverish arms race."[67] Such partisan considerations made it difficult for either side to make concessions. Nuclear weapons were also useful to make a point on the international stage. Eisenhower threatened to use atomic bombs to achieve American goals in Korea in 1953, and three years later the Soviet Union, desirous of increasing its prestige in the Middle East, intimated that it would use nuclear weapons against London and Paris if Britain and France did not halt their operations over Suez. The conventional military balance in Europe favoured the Soviet Union. To compensate, the United States worked hard to build a military alliance with West Germany. To maintain it, the Americans agreed to support Adenauer in his promise to reunify Germany and pledged that there would be no serious disarmament agreement until the Soviet Union allowed the East Germans to decide freely if they wished to join the West. The United States always subordinated disarmament to the kind of political settlements it wished to see in Europe.

Finally, the dynamics of the arms race made negotiations difficult. The atomic monopoly enjoyed by the United States in the early years gave it very little incentive to trade away a weapon it already had. President Truman was guided by the principle that "our country had to be ahead of any possible competitor."[68] A situation in which the United States had a monopoly offered little motivation for the Soviet Union to agree to a system of arms control which would prevent it developing an atomic bomb and thus achieving some sort of military parity. Moreover, building more arms while calling for their abolition was clearly a contradiction in intentions. Dean Acheson remarked that "we cannot ... carry conviction ... in advocating ... international control and abolition of atomic weapons if at the same time our military reliance on them is growing."[69] Official policy, as enunciated in NSC–68, was that the United States should avoid serious negotiations until it could bargain from a position of superior military strength. This was also the view of Dulles,[70] though perhaps not of Eisenhower. Because both sides were constantly engaged in military build-ups, each found it difficult to convince its opponent that it was sincere and serious when it put forward its disarmament proposals. Not the least harm which the arms race generated was an atmosphere of cynicism and distrust which made it very difficult to conduct fruitful negotiations on disarmament.

Nevertheless, there were almost continuous negotiations on nuclear issues between 1946 and 1957. The immediate impact of Hiroshima was strong in the West, especially in the United States. Among many politicians, opinion leaders, and journalists there was great revulsion at the atomic horror. John Foster Dulles signed a petition in 1945 against any further use of the bomb predicting: "If we a professedly Christian nation feel morally free to use atomic energy in that way, men elsewhere will accept that verdict. Atomic weapons will be looked upon as a normal arsenal of war and the stage will be set for the sudden and final destruction of mankind."[71] This widespread sentiment helped persuade Truman to initiate negotiations at the United Nations to establish international control over atomic energy. Once these began, neither superpower dared withdraw for fear of losing the propaganda war to prove which country was on the side of the angels. Truman himself always hoped that the atomic bomb would be outlawed: "I don't think we ought to use this thing," he maintained in 1948, "unless we absolutely have to. It is a terrible thing to order the use of something that is so terribly destructive beyond anything we have ever had ... It is used to wipe out women, children and unarmed people, and not for military use."[72] Not until 1949 did he give up hope of some sort of scheme for international control. Even then, he insisted, both for propaganda reasons and from personal conviction, that the negotiations be kept going. As late as October 1950 with the Korean War raging, he made a key proposal that allowed a resumption of negotiations.

Stalin's personal views on the ethics of using the atomic bomb are not known. But the support which left-wing and communist parties gave to the organized peace movement of the late 1940s, culminating in the 1950 Stockholm petition to ban the bomb, certainly assisted the Soviet Union's contention that it alone stood for peace. Cynics might argue that the demand to abolish the atomic bomb without any reduction in the Soviet army was meant to inhibit the United States politically from employing its main weapon if necessary. Even if this were the case, it would guarantee that the Soviet Union would keep disarmament and arms control on the political agenda. The yearnings of millions of people for peace and for a world free of atomic bombs made peace and disarmament a very important theatre in the political war between the United States and the Soviet Union. Neither side could allow the other to win that particular propaganda battle. The regular debates at the United Nations on these issues found both superpowers responding to public opinion; each had to be "for" peace and "against" the arms race.[73] The one positive result was to keep both powers at the bargaining table, proposing programmes of disarmament and arms control.

In 1953 the death of Stalin in March and the end of the war in Korea in July had served to ease tensions between the superpowers; an era of détente and active diplomacy was opening up. Michael Howard believes that there now began "a decade of relative mutual acceptance between 1955 and 1965; and it was no accident that this was the heyday of disarmament/arms-control negotiations."[74] In March 1954 the radioactive fallout from an American hydrogen bomb test dropped on a Japanese fishing boat. The fear of radiation spread to the United States and gave an enormous boost to the movement to halt the testing of nuclear weapons. The political leaders of both superpowers now spoke against the arms race. In the United States those who feared nuclear war found their most articulate and impressive spokesman in the person of Eisenhower himself. As a soldier with extraordinary experience, he enjoyed enormous credibility among the American people on military questions. The president was always sounding the alarm about the dangers of nuclear war. In September 1956, in a typical statement, he warned: "we witness today in the power of nuclear weapons a new and deadly dimension to the ancient horror of war. Humanity has now achieved, for the first time in its history, the power to end its history ... It makes world disarmament a necessity of world life."[75] In September 1954 the Soviet Union had detonated an atomic bomb in a military exercise. "After the atomic strike, there were not only no landmarks left on the terrain," reads the report, "but the area itself had become unrecognizable."[76] No doubt it was the growing knowledge and experience of the Soviet military with nuclear arms that caused Khrushchev to reiterate constantly what a catastrophe nuclear war would be for mankind. Thus the two leaders raised the consciousness of their peoples and, indeed, of Western Europe and thereby increased the pressure on themselves to come up with an agreement.

Lastly, something must be said about the personal views of both Eisenhower and Khrushchev on disarmament. That there were political pressures on them to negotiate there is no doubt. Both were coming to realize that a nuclear war would be completely destructive to both sides. An eminent biographer of Eisenhower claims that the president's most basic strategic insight was that "unlimited war in the nuclear age was unimaginable, and limited war unwinnable."[77] He had a genuine horror of nuclear war. He told the president of South Korea that "atomic war will destroy civilization ... There will be millions of people dead ... If the Kremlin and Washington ever lock up in a war, the results will be too horrible to contemplate."[78]

When Eisenhower came into office, he told the chairman of the United States Atomic Energy Commission: "My chief concern and your first assignment is to find some new approach to the *dis*arming of atomic energy."[79] The chairman's task was made a little easier because, as we shall see, the emphasis in negotiations shifted from the elimination of nuclear weapons to arms control. Nuclear disarmament became impossible to achieve, not only because no political leader took it seriously but also because it proved impossible to verify whether a country had indeed destroyed its atomic bombs. Arguments for nuclear disarmament were always judged pure propaganda. Arms control, however, was quite different. Both sides believed that measures to reduce the arms race might be of benefit and therefore a fit subject for serious negotiation. This possibility would engage the attention of both Eisenhower and Khrushchev. A recent study asserts that Eisenhower was the main force behind the Americans taking arms control seriously.[80] Arkady Shevchenko, a Soviet defector, who was working in the arms control section of the Soviet government in 1956, writes: "I believe that Khrushchev was making a genuine effort to reach an accord ... on at least some measures for limiting the arms race."[81] Charles Bohlen and Llewellyn Thompson, the American ambassadors to the Soviet Union at this period, were convinced that the Soviet leader's commitment to arms control was genuine.

President Eisenhower once maintained that "world tensions have got to be diminished or there is going to be no progress [in disarmament]. At the same time there has to be progress in some kind of disarmament or there is going to be no reduction in world tensions."[82] This implies that his approach to both political settlements in Europe and disarmament and arms control was evenhanded. But this was not so. John Gaddis believes that Eisenhower had a personal commitment to keep the arms control negotiations going but nevertheless gave it a lower priority than the "maintenance of a credible nuclear deterrent, the preservation of harmony among allies, and the determination to score 'points' at the expense of the Russians in the area of psychological warfare."[83] Paul Nitze considers him to have been a president whose "apparent sincerity ... derived from his uncanny ability to be able to believe in two mutually contradictory and inconsistent propositions at the same time." Nitze once attended a meeting where Eisenhower declared nuclear war "utterly unthinkable." Then, in the next sentence, "he gave the Joint Chiefs of Staff detailed instructions on how they should prepare to go about fighting one."[84] There is no evidence that these comments might not apply equally to Khrushchev. The truth was that each man was confronted with what John Newhouse has called "contesting priorities."[85] Each wished to halt the arms race but each considered it necessary to continue to work hard at strengthening his country's military capacity.

Still, disarmament was an important aspect of the strategic policy of both sides. When Dulles wrote a memo to Eisenhower in November 1954 suggesting that NATO adopt nuclear weapons, he included as one of the integral parts of overall American policy the proposition that "we will be prepared to explore reasonable bona fide disarmament proposals."[86] Disarmament and arms control measures were an important part of the programme by which each superpower attempted to limit the military capacity of the other – to its own advantage. The purpose of this book is to follow Dulles's advice and to explore these disarmament and arms control proposals and the Canadian response to them. But first let us look at the attitudes of Canada, and in particular Lester Pearson, towards the Soviet Union and the United States and the antagonistic relationship between its two giant neighbours.

CHAPTER TWO

Pearson on the
Superpower Confrontation

Lester Pearson had much to say about Canada's foreign policy when he became under-secretary of state for external affairs in September 1946 and still more once he became the minister two years later. Until the defeat of the Liberals in June 1957 his influence on Canadian diplomacy was enormous because he had such steady support from Prime Minister Louis St Laurent. He was ultimately responsible for fashioning Canada's policy on disarmament and arms control. His views on these matters were shaped by his profound hostility towards the Soviet Union, his affection and general support for the United States, and his apprehension about the danger of nuclear war.

THE SOVIET THREAT

Two beliefs shaped Pearson's attitude towards the Soviet Union in the postwar years. Communist Russia had set out to achieve world domination and therefore the West must arm itself to meet that threat. However, with the arrival of the atomic era any war between the two superpowers would destroy civilization; consequently, the West must negotiate with the USSR to prevent such a catastrophe. Coming to an agreement with the Soviet Union while simultaneously waging an all-out political war against it would prove to be a difficult diplomatic feat.

Pearson was not well equipped intellectually to deal with the Russians. His diplomatic skills shone in the North Atlantic arena, but he did not show the same sureness of touch in his dealing with the Soviet Union. The innumerable references to the Soviet Union in his speeches and articles demonstrate no great knowledge of its history and culture, and for an educated person he seems to have had a remarkable lack of interest in Marxism as an intellectual system. Describing the Soviet system as one "spawned by Marxist materialism out of Russian mysticism," he asserted in 1950 that there was much in it that would be difficult for any one brought up in the Western tradition to understand.[1] This is not particularly surprising. His education had prepared him for a diplomatic career in the North American triangle. As a professor of history at the University of Toronto, he had given courses in the development of the British Commonwealth and the events in European history which had led up to the First World War. There was little opportunity for him to gain much knowledge of the Soviet Union.

Nor were there greater opportunities to learn about the Soviet Union after he joined the Department of External Affairs in 1928. Canada had severed its diplomatic relations with the USSR the previous year. Pearson's first glimpse of a live Soviet diplomat seems to have come at the Disarmament Conference in Geneva in 1932. The Russian delegate, Maxim Litvinov, proposed complete disarmament, a proposition which Pearson no doubt thought completely impracticable. During the thirties he seems to have equated the Soviet Union with Nazi Germany. "God knows," he wrote in December 1938, "I would be delighted to see the sub-human Nazis and equally sub-human Bolsheviks batter themselves to pieces against each other, while the Anglo Saxons held the ring."[2] During the war Pearson's attitude – like that of many others – towards the USSR moderated. In 1943 he noted that all "agreed that the Russians were winning the war for us."[3] But again there was a turn as the war ended. In April 1945, he described the Soviet Union as "a force which we simply do not understand."[4] This ignorance was shared by his colleagues in the Department of External Affairs such as Hume Wrong and Norman Robertson. The only one with direct experience of the Soviet Union was Dana Wilgress, Canada's ambassador to Moscow (1944–6). Significantly, he maintained that far from being incomprehensible, the USSR resembled all other countries in its desire to protect its own security.[5]

Pearson's first extensive contact with Soviet diplomats came in allied committees. The Russians, when outvoted, would come back again and again to their original propositions. At the San Francisco conference to set up the United Nations in 1945, it appears they would have tried the patience of a saint. Canada's diplomats became impatient with and angry at the Soviet Union. Charles Ritchie wrote in his diary: "The Soviet delegates have got very little good-will out of this Conference. They use aggressive tactics about every question large or small. They remind people of Nazi diplomatic methods and create, sometimes needlessly, suspicions and resentment."[6] Pearson shared these sentiments. He became sceptical of Soviet intentions and convinced that the Russians were untrustworthy and devious. Nor were his feelings towards them made more cordial when he learned that they were ready to veto his appointment as the first secretary-general of the United Nations, a post he would have dearly liked.

Many of the clashes at San Francisco arose from the growing antagonism between the United States and the Soviet Union. But there were also profound differences over the proper functions of the new organization. The Soviet Union was rightly apprehensive that it would be consistently outvoted in all the United Nations bodies; consequently, it wished to give the General Assembly as little power as possible. It was also vociferous in its insistence on the primacy of the Security Council and the veto powers of the five permanent members. Acceptance of these principles weakened the possibility of Canada and other middle powers operating independently of the great powers. Pearson must have been irked by the Soviet insistence that middle powers like Canada be excluded in this way from having any real influence in the United Nations and on world affairs.

At San Francisco Pearson nonetheless worked hard to get the Americans to adopt a more reasonable approach towards the Soviet Union. Later, in March 1946, he would observe in a note to the under-secretary of state for external affairs, Norman Robertson, that there was "a lot of sense"[7] in a magazine article which asserted that the United States was partly to blame for the deterioration of the international atmosphere. Yet in his memoranda to External Affairs Pearson was advocating a tougher and tougher line towards the Soviet Union. That same month he wrote that it might well be that "Soviet policy is fundamentally defensive; an effort to exploit a fluid post-war situation for all it is worth." The only suitable response would be a Big Three conference where all the issues were confronted. If this failed, "the United States and the United Kingdom should convert the United Nations into a really effective agent to preserve the peace and prevent aggression." If the Russians veto such a revision, then "a new organization must be created which ... can function without the Russians and, as a last resort, against them."[8] By November his attitude towards the USSR seemed to have

hardened even more. In a memorandum advocating the strengthening of Canada's contribution to Anglo-American defence co-
operation, he warned that "without some fundamental change in
the Soviet state system and in the policies of its leaders, the U.S.S.R.
is ultimately bound to come into open conflict with western democracy."[9] Pearson seemed to be asserting that a war with the Soviet
Union was virtually inevitable. However, John English has suggested that Pearson may have worded the memorandum in this way
to play on Prime Minister Mackenzie King's fears of the Soviet
Union and thereby help assure his support for a policy of active
Canadian participation in international affairs – in this particular
case, to accede to American requests for defence co-operation in the
Arctic,[10] an agreement which was concluded in the spring of 1947.

Yet, in January 1947, speaking about a fellow Canadian who
wanted to stand up right there and then to the Russians, Pearson
commented: "I can certainly understand his pessimism at the
possibility of developing friendly relationships with the USSR.
Nevertheless, that is the only possible approach, ultimately, to
peace."[11] In August, the under-secretary of state for external affairs
offered the Soviet Union cultural exchanges and co-operation in
developing the Arctic. In principle, Canada stood ready to improve
relations with the Soviet Union. That same month Escott Reid,
assistant under-secretary of state for external affairs, composed his
celebrated memorandum on the implications for Canada's policy of
Soviet-American antagonism and the possibility of war, which Don
Page and Don Munton believe calls into question the assumption
that "Canadian policy-makers perceived the Soviet Union as an
inherently aggressive, expansionist power, driven by its communist
ideology." Because Pearson saw to it that Reid's memo was widely
circulated, they suggest that "it is a reasonable assumption that he
did not disagree fundamentally with [it]."[12] By late 1947, however,
the commitment of Canadian policy-makers to the American side in
the Cold War was becoming stronger. Soviet actions to consolidate
their hold on Eastern Europe stimulated indignant reaction in
Canada. There was a general conviction that Stalin's totalitarian
Russia, unless checked, would continue to expand and impose a way
of life which was offensive to Western values on unwilling populations in Western Europe.

Even had it wished to try and find a role for Canada as a neutral,
the government would have been confronted with a very formidable
task in view of Canada's close economic, cultural, and defence ties
with the United States. Any war between the superpowers would
undoubtedly involve Canada. Pearson himself had long believed

that there was no way of isolating Canada from American actions. Yet he sometimes wondered whether American diplomacy was altogether wise. Certainly he wished Canada to be in a position to influence the American administration as they confronted the Soviet Union in the crises that were bound to come. But such a capacity depended on Canadian credibility, the first requisite of which was full support for the anti-communist positions of the United States. To convince the Americans of Canada's "soundness," tough anti-Soviet rhetoric was essential. Equally, there was a need to convince the Canadian public that a strong stand against the Soviet Union was necessary.

In January 1948, Pearson first spoke out publicly in support of collective security in the face of potential Soviet aggression. Here he was following the example of his minister, Louis St Laurent, who had earlier raised the possibility of "an association of democratic and peace-loving states"[13] that might band together in a separate organization for greater security. After becoming secretary of state for external affairs in September, Pearson had many more opportunities to expound these views. From that time until he left the External Affairs portfolio in June 1957, he consistently maintained that the Soviet Union was the greatest enemy of the liberal democracies. One of Pearson's great abilities as a diplomat, notes one of his later colleagues, was that "he was deeply responsive to circumstances, able to take on the coloration of the place, the time, even the particular person with whom he was dealing at the moment."[14] In his speeches Pearson's task was to present the official government position, regardless of what he himself might have felt about it. And he performed this duty very well. Whether he had any private doubts about every phrase of anti-communist rhetoric that he uttered is not clear. What can be said is that there is nothing in his numerous memoranda or letters or in his actions which would belie his public statements during this decade.

In his January 1948 speech Pearson developed themes to which he would return again and again. The world was divided into two hostile camps, a division both "ideological and political." "A cold-blooded, calculating, victoriously powerful Slav empire that had harnessed the crusading and subversive power of communism" was locked in struggle with "free expanding progressive democracy" for world domination. He warned that it was impossible for Canada to return to its former isolationist policies. "There are no fire-proof houses in the atomic age," he insisted: "Our frontier ... is wherever free men are struggling against totalitarian tyranny ... It may run through the middle of our own cities, or it may be on the crest of the remotest mountain."[15] These words were uttered against a background of a sudden and enormous expansion of Soviet power. The Soviet army was in control of hundreds of thousands of square miles of non-Soviet territory in central and eastern Europe, most notably in Poland and eastern Germany. The USSR had threatened Iran and Turkey and appeared to have instigated civil war in Greece. In Asia the nationalist and revolutionary movement led by communists was rapidly gaining strength in China. These events led Pearson to refer constantly to the Soviet Union as an aggressive imperialist power. He never changed his mind about its nature: in January 1957 he would call the USSR the "greatest colonial power of all and the one which exercises that power in the most arbitrary and tyrannical fashion."[16]

Pearson's view of Soviet policies rested on his belief that the government was completely evil because it was a totalitarian one. It deprived people of their liberty, crushed individuality, and converted each person into a mere appendage of the state. No one had any rights beyond those permitted by the regime. "Every day and every hour," he charged, "every aspect of his life is under the control of the state."[17] Pearson never attacked the Soviet Union for the lack of a free market or the abolition of the capitalist system. What he objected to was the subordination of the individual to some grand plan on the grounds of the doctrine of historical determinism. In his view it was unacceptable to believe that people were "slaves of fate and playthings of destiny."[18] In consequence, Pearson demonstrated no animus towards the Soviet people whom he described as "warm-hearted [and] lovable." But he detested the unscrupulous way the Soviet leadership manipulated public opinion. Communist education created prejudice and hatred to suit the evil purposes of the ruling élite. Soviet students were fed with information about the worst features of American life and culture. Soviet leaders had brought down the Iron Curtain and systematically instilled in their people an unjustified fear of the United States. They prevented their satellites benefiting from the Marshall Plan. Obviously they feared the "gradual infiltration of Western ideas and news through to their own people."[19]

Pearson was convinced that the Soviet leadership believed that the Russian Revolution was merely the beginning of a vast historical change that would lead to the overthrow of the bourgeoisie everywhere; that it was inevitable that the capitalist powers would attempt to exterminate the world communist movement; that the USSR could only guarantee its security by building up its armed forces and seeking to control more and more of the territory from which it might be attacked; that it would only be safe when the global revolution had taken place and it was at last the dominant state in the world. Meanwhile Pearson saw the Soviet leaders probing for weaknesses in the capitalist world. "Today there is fighting in Korea," Pearson warned in August 1950, "yesterday there was pressure on Persia, Greece and Yugoslavia and a *coup d'état* in Czechoslovakia. Tomorrow there may be aggression against Indo-China or a civil war fomented in Germany."[20]

The communist coup in Czechoslovakia in February 1948 had certainly hardened Pearson's determination to support an anti-Soviet alliance. This coup had introduced the technique of "indirect aggression"[21] by which the Soviet Union could penetrate a neighbouring country. There had been no Soviet tanks in Prague when Czechoslovakia fell. Instead the capital had been taken over by the local communist party, which knew it could count on the help of the Soviet army stationed in the outskirts of the city. Pearson argued that this experience showed that indigenous communist parties were the willing agents of Moscow. Party members in Canada, for example, would follow "every twist and turn of soviet policy."[22] In a word, "international Communism" had become the "weapon of Soviet imperialism."[23]

Pearson believed that the potential for such subversion was a serious problem because it was linked to broader issues of good or evil. The doctrine of communism had arisen as a response to the abuses of the Industrial Revolution of the nineteenth century. Now it flourished in the soil of the "poverty and misery and injustice"[24] that existed in the free world. The great challenge of uprooting these evil social conditions had enlisted the energies of thousands of devoted men and women. In their anger and disgust, some became disciples of what was for them "a new religion,"[25] and some, though highly educated, cultured, and humane, would even disregard the suffering of millions of people to bring a new world into being.

Pearson decried the idea of attempting to defeat communism by force. "No idea," he argued, "however perilous or noxious, as communism is, can be killed by bayonets or even by an atomic bomb."[26] It was best resisted by the removal of abuses through imaginative economic and social programmes. And although he had described communism as a new religion, he maintained that, contrary to the Marxist contention that the human make-up was only physiological, man's nature contained a spiritual component at its core that made questions of good and evil basic to his entire existence. Pearson insisted that the "eternal spirit of man [can] never be permanently bound by slave institutions."[27] It was inevitable that tyrannical communist regimes must sooner or later evolve or explode. One reason for Pearson's strong support for article 2 in the North Atlantic Treaty was to encourage the kind of economic, social, and cultural collaboration which would help create a grand Atlantic community which would become, in its devotion to the material and spiritual needs of its peoples, a beacon of hope to the oppressed millions under communist rule.

Up to September 1949 Pearson's views of the Soviet Union were quite straightforward – the USSR was simply an evil expansionist power which the West must contain. The Soviet atomic explosion of that month which revealed the possibility of a nuclear strike at North America brought home to him the necessity of some sort of *"modus vivendi,* some agreement to live and let live." There needed to be a "process of genuine and mutual compromise and accommodation."[28] To accomplish this, it was more essential than ever that the Soviet Union stay in the United Nations. At a time when there were no substantive diplomatic negotiations (or even contact) between the superpowers, the United Nations was a crucial place for dialogue. One constant element in Pearson's attitude towards the Soviet Union was that nothing should be done that would give it an excuse to withdraw from that body. This was a difficult course to pursue because the Cold War coloured "every subject that appear[ed] on a United Nations agenda."[29] Even in the cut and thrust of debate over genuine issues, "the substantive and the propaganda aspects cannot be separated."[30] Nevertheless, as long as Western liberties were not "called in question, we must continue to examine every proposal that is made on its merits."[31]

Dealing with the communist states, however, was no easy matter. Their tactics of appealing to peoples over the heads of their governments tended to lower diplomacy to mere propaganda. Soviet words of "peace and goodwill [might] represent merely an orthodox and normal shift in party tactics, designed to disarm and deceive us."[32] Western statesmen who made concessions to the Soviet Union would be open to charges of deserting principle and going soft on communism. How could the West reach agreement with a regime that operated without "the limitation of scruples or sincerity or morality"?[33] As a spokesman for the West in the war to win world public opinion, Pearson condemned the Soviet government as an evil regime. But as a diplomat seeking to avoid nuclear war, he realized the need to talk to the Soviet Union about security matters in a practical way which eschewed considerations of moral righteousness. Time would tell whether these somewhat contradictory activities could still yield results.

Stalin's death in the spring of 1953 opened an era of improved East-West relationships. The post-Stalinist leadership publicly conceded that in a nuclear war both the socialist regimes and the capitalist states would suffer equally. But this was all they were prepared to concede. The two systems might coexist without open conflict, but the struggle for supremacy would continue as fiercely as ever. Pearson agreed that the "menacing shadow of a thermo-nuclear cloud" meant that no country could escape the challenge of coexistence. He also believed that what was being offered by the Kremlin was far from amicable co-operation. Indeed, he complained that the basic Soviet objectives in Europe remained the same: disso-lution of NATO, withdrawal of United States forces from Europe, and preservation of a communist East Germany. While Khrushchev and his colleagues believed that in the end the Soviet system would triumph, Pearson had faith that a "free society, despite all of its faults and weaknesses," would outlast a "rigid, monolithic Soviet Communism." He called on the West to make itself strong enough economically and morally to win the great contest, but to maintain its military strength as well, in case the Soviet Union decided against all reason to resort to war and the possible annihilation of the world.[34]

Relations between Canada and the Soviet Union had been so cool that neither country had had an ambassador in the other's capital since 1947. After 1953, however, the Soviet stance towards Canada became friendlier. No doubt the Soviet leaders hoped that it might be possible to loosen the Canadian-American alliance. Playing on rising nationalist sentiment in Canada in the fifties, Soviet publica-tions began to show sympathy for Canada because it was under such heavy pressure from Wall Street and the Pentagon. Soviet farm experts visited Canada in the summer of 1955. Most significant of all, in June of that year Pearson, to his astonishment, had received an invitation – the first issued to any foreign minister of a member-country of the North Atlantic Treaty Organization since 1947 – to visit Moscow for talks with Nikita Khrushchev and his colleagues.

Pearson spent a week in the Soviet Union in October of 1955. While there he told the foreign minister, Vyacheslav Molotov, that "the two super-powers had to realize that, far from resolving their differences, nuclear war would bring ... wholesale death and un-thinkable devastation."[35] According to a report he made to cabinet on his return, Pearson came away with three main impressions. The first was that Soviet tactics had altered because their leaders had come to understand from their own tests that their country could not survive a nuclear war. The second was that the Russians re-

mained eager to break up NATO and "get" the United States out of
Europe. They continued to reject any argument that a Germany in-
side NATO was less of a threat than one left outside; they regarded
a West Germany within NATO as simply an agent of the United
States. During this discussion, Khrushchev had presented the evidence which had convinced him that the United States was an aggressor nation. Lastly, the Soviet leaders were extremely proud of
the progress of their country and were confident that in the coming
duel with the West in the era of peaceful coexistence, they would
win because their people were ready to make more sacrifices.[36]

Pearson's contact with the Soviet leaders did not persuade him
that they could be trusted. Yet there were some interesting changes
in his public evaluation of their state of mind. In a speech the
following December he asserted that the rulers of the Soviet Union
"desire peace." Possessing the hydrogen bomb they understood the
terrible consequences of a third world war. Then, too, they were
now confident that under peaceful competition their social system
would prevail over that of the West. Pearson also noted that some
of the tough talk emanating from North America had caused Soviet
leaders to claim that they feared the United States, and he conceded
that "it is just possible therefore, though not probable, that [their]
fears might be genuine."[37] Characteristically, he blamed this fortress
mentality on their complete ignorance of what was happening outside their country. More importantly, he remained convinced of the
Soviet government's malevolent intentions towards the West and of
the need to continue to increase NATO's military strength.

In February 1956 Khrushchev gave his historic secret speech to
the Central Committee of the Communist party in which he condemned Stalin's crimes. The contents of this speech were gradually
leaked in the following months, and Pearson later acknowledged the
significance of this act and the measure of liberalism introduced in
the Soviet political system. He conceded that Khrushchev might be
prepared to break with the Leninist dogma that war were inevitable
as long as imperialism existed. Without giving up its ideology or its
ultimate political goals, the Soviet leaders appeared ready to eschew
violence in their conduct of foreign policy. But the conclusions
which Pearson drew were contradictory as ever. While the new
more flexible tactics of the Soviet Union might ease Western fears,
they could also undermine the cohesion of the Atlantic alliance.[38]

Whatever credence Pearson placed in Soviet reforms was dissi-
pated the following November when the USSR intervened in the
most brutal fashion to put down the Hungarian uprising. Pearson's
liberal sensibilities were outraged, and he later confessed in his

memoirs to the romantic impulse of hoping to see a committee of the General Assembly fly into Budapest to plant the United Nations flag. Instead, he pressed for a United Nations resolution demanding that the Hungarian people be allowed to establish a government of their own choice. As he observed later, the United Nations could do nothing effective because of the "big blunt fact of the Red Army."[39] Pearson's anger at the Soviet Union was exacerbated when it was learned during the Suez crisis that the Egyptian embassy in Moscow had contemplated asking for Soviet "volunteers" to help Nasser, not to speak of the Soviet hint that they might use nuclear weapons against London and Paris unless the Anglo-French operation in Egypt was called off. At this moment, it is probable that Pearson saw little to differentiate Khrushchev from Stalin.

Pearson's belief that the Soviet Union was an expansionist imperial power with an insatiable appetite for world conquest led naturally to his support for the view that the Soviet Union must be contained by a militarily powerful and united West. The main power and leader of the Western alliance was the United States. Pearson was confident that Canada could play an important role in this alliance, and he devoted a good deal of thought to shaping a satisfactory working relationship with the United States.

CANADIAN-AMERICAN RELATIONS

Pearson always believed that Canada was very lucky that its neighbour to the south was the United States. Both as a liberal and a Christian, Pearson had a good deal of admiration for the nature of American society. This is not to say that he wished Canada to join the United States. He believed a separate Canadian state was necessary to preserve certain "political legal and social values" which were "distinctive" to Canada,[40] such as the parliamentary system and the institutional arrangements which allowed the French minority to live in peace with the English majority. Moreover, John English asserts that he had "many doubts about the nature of American society and politics ... [although he] came to admire the openness of American life and politics."[41] This being said, he believed that there was a natural kinship between the two countries which both belonged to a "Western Christian civilization ... based on human freedom, co-operation and tolerance."[42]

Pearson could not help being impressed by the unique and commanding position that the United States occupied in the postwar era. Economically and politically, it towered over the rest of the world. American manufacturing output and per capita production shot up to astonishing levels. The average personal income far exceeded that in other countries. Through its virtual control of the International Monetary Fund, the World Bank, and the General Agreement on Tariffs and Trade, the United States dominated the global economy. It was rich enough to give Marshall Plan aid to a Western Europe devastated by war. All important international political decisions in the non-communist world were made under its guidance. Many non-communist countries found themselves constantly lobbying Washington. The United States took on the onerous task of establishing a Pax Americana in a turbulent world; its military power was to be seen on all the oceans and in all non-communist countries.

Best of all, from Pearson's point of view, the United States had taken up the responsibility of guarding the free world against the evil expansionist forces of communism. Pearson and his colleagues were forever haunted by a fear that the United States might retreat into the isolationism of the prewar period. No doubt Pearson was particularly sensitive on this score because of his own isolationist views in the 1930s. His original strong support for the League of Nations had faded with the failure of the London Naval Conference of 1930 and the World Disarmament Conference of 1932. He had come away from them disillusioned and cynical. (Later, in his memoirs, he would invoke the flavour of his reaction by describing how easily a number of younger diplomats had solved an issue that had perplexed their seniors: "We agreed at once ... that there *was* a valid distinction between an offensive and a defensive weapon: if you were in front of it, it was offensive; if you were behind it, it was defensive."[43] During the thirties he had had strong reservations about the ability of the League to play an effective role and had been particularly disillusioned in 1935 when Britain and France virtually abandoned Ethiopia to Italy. For the next four years he had abandoned all faith in collective security and had "flirted with the notion of Canadian isolation, primarily because the thought of another war repelled him so much."[44] Once a war with Nazi Germany seemed inevitable, however, his emotional ties with the mother country came to the fore. Like Prime Minister King, he came to believe that if Britain went to war against Nazi Germany, Canada ought to be at its side. Perhaps it was his mistaken judgment about how to deal with the threat of aggression in the thirties that made Pearson such a zealous advocate of collective security in the postwar period.[45]

In January 1942, in a lecture at Victoria College in Toronto, Pearson, then minister-counsellor at the Washington embassy, set

out some of his views on world politics. He reviewed the failure of
the disarmament movement in the thirties. He then defined the
disarmament problem "in all its naked simplicity: No disarmament
without security." And he added: "the problem, indeed, from the
beginning had been a political and not a technical one."[46] This was
a conviction he retained ever after. Others might argue that huge
armaments in themselves created tensions between powers, but
Pearson never accepted this view. Later, his strong belief that the
Soviet Union threatened the security of the West inhibited him
from throwing himself emotionally and enthusiastically into
fostering the disarmament process between the superpowers.

In his 1942 lecture Pearson went on to eschew any grand
economic or sociological explanation for the actions of great powers.
The cause of the present war, he argued, was the desire of Nazi
fanatics, playing on Germany's economic misery and sense of
humiliation because of its defeat in 1918, to climb to power "if
necessary over the corpse of Europe." The world in general, and
the United States in particular, had ignored the perceptive warning
of the Soviet commissar for foreign affairs, Maxim Litvinov, that
peace was indivisible. There had been no effective collective security
system in place to prevent Nazi aggression. Pearson did not blame
small powers like Holland and Belgium for this failure. Nevertheless, the war had shown that they could not rely on their own
strength for protection. To be safe, "they [would] have to subordinate their policies and their military plans to those of larger
powers."[47] Two years later, in March 1944, he insisted that the
"collective system which was spurned in peace has proven to be our
salvation in war ... There is no other way to win the peace."[48] Here
he was rejecting the more isolationist policies of his prime minister
and setting out a conviction from which he would not waver: the
paramount necessity for *unity* among all free peoples if they were to
defend themselves against aggression. Later, in 1945, he must have
been delighted by chapter VII of the United Nations Charter which
specified the commitment of the great powers to prevent the
recurrence of Nazi-like aggression.

During the war Pearson had worried that the Americans might
give up on collective security. "The fact of the matter is," he noted
in 1943, "that most Americans are natural isolationists."[49] As late as
February 1950, Canada's ambassador in Washington, Hume Wrong,
expressed the fear, in a letter to Pearson, that the frustrations of
fighting the Cold War brought the risk of the "slow withdrawal of
the US from the centre of the international stage." He wondered
whether many Americans accepted the necessity of the defence of

Western Europe as a matter of faith rather than conviction. He believed that "it is after all remarkable that there has been no retreat from internationalism in this country since the end of the war, in spite of the failure of the UN to achieve its central purpose."[50] Pearson also thought it possible that inadequate cooperation from other members of the Western alliance might discourage the Americans to the point that "Washington may decide to 'go it alone.' "[51] He therefore sought to use whatever influence Canada had in Washington to stiffen the internationalist forces against the isolationists whom he regarded as hopelessly reactionary.

Thus Pearson was most grateful that the United States took up its global responsibilities. Looking back on the unchecked rise of Nazi aggression, he believed that the willingness of the United States to use its military and economic strength to unite Western Europe against aggression was the most fortunate of circumstances. By September 1946 the Americans had taken their place at the head of those countries which feared possible Soviet expansion. "For Canadians such as ... Pearson," as John English observes, "this American commitment had been long and earnestly sought and was richly treasured. Although there was a price in terms of the unpredictability of American leadership, the unity of the democracies was a precious good that [Pearson's] experience led [him] to cherish."[52] These phrases underline three critical elements of Pearson's world view. The first was that if the West was to deter the Soviet Union, the United States, because of its power and wealth, must undertake its leadership. The second was that American judgment was not nearly as impressive as its power. Other countries like Britain and Canada would need to urge a certain calmness and restraint on the Americans to produce the best diplomatic initiatives. Lastly, the Americans lacked the manpower to stand up to Soviet land forces; they would need the help of other Western democracies. Thus diplomatic and military unity in the West was absolutely essential to deter Soviet aggression.

Creating and leading the anti-communist coalition was not always easy and sometimes meant dealing with shortsighted and obstinate allies which might make the most patient of diplomats yearn for the simpler isolationist policies. Yet the United States persisted, and Pearson was properly appreciative of this effort. He believed that the responsibility had only been accepted reluctantly: "There is certainly no aggressive imperialism here."[53] He always fervently denied that the United States would ever use its power for the purpose of "aggressive war."[54] And he often insisted that "there had never been a nation less grasping or ambitious for power; or one which has discharged its global responsibilities more unselfishly and less aggressively."[55]

Pearson's own experience had convinced him that Canada, though a small country, could conduct relations with the United States on the basis of "friendly understanding,"[56] without fear of being bullied. He believed that in this special relationship there was such good will that "we, almost alone of all in the world, on any occasion and in respect of any subject, even the most political and diplomatic, can tell them exactly what we think and in their own language."[57] The extensive correspondence between the two countries over disarmament supports this assessment. While always maintaining their own position, American diplomats were invariably friendly, polite, and apparently always ready to listen. While in Washington as Canada's ambassador in 1945 and 1946, Pearson had become close friends with such diplomats as John Hickerson and Dean Acheson. These personal connections gave him an entrée into the State Department which was very useful and perhaps even flattering. But how did American diplomats regard Pearson? One American diplomat reported from Ottawa that the Canadians were very jealous of their image of independence; they had a tendency "to play down" the effects of Canada's bilateral ties with the United States and there was almost a "compulsion" for External Affairs to believe that it must give leadership in international organizations.[58] And, looking back, Dean Acheson remarked that Ottawa had a tendency to raise matters "to the plane of high principle upon which the Department of External Affairs [preferred] to rest Canada's more mundane interests."[59] These two comments suggest a certain amused tolerance of Canada's tendency to take itself too seriously. Still, Washington trusted and relied on Pearson. No doubt they appreciated the Canadian contention that American diplomacy was directed at the advancement not only of national interests but also of those of the free world.

Pearson once defined the Canadian-American relationship in the following words: "In this coalition, we are a junior partner and you are the great leader."[60] What Pearson meant by the word "partner" was best elaborated in a directive produced when he was under-secretary of state for external affairs. Written for the guidance of the man who would be Canada's first representative on the Security Council in January 1948, the document began by observing that if there were any armed conflict between the superpowers, Canada would find it impossible to remain neutral. The Americans would demand Canadian support and the majority of Canadians would take such participation for granted. Canada should therefore do everything possible to "halt the deterioration in relations between the Great Powers, or failing that, to ensure that any conflict will be waged collectively and with an overwhelming superiority of power on the side of western democracies." This was a good summary of Pearson's approach to the Cold War. But it did overlook the difficulty that ensuring military superiority for the West might itself cause the Soviet Union to become even more hostile to the West.

In the Security Council deliberations, the directive advised the Canadian delegate to remain independent. This was important for the long-run interests not only of Canada but of the United States. For in the Security Council "our support or our opposition will mean little if we accept the position of a complaisant satellite." The Americans believed that they could always count on Canada, but the United States should not always expect such support. Sometimes American policy was uncertain; sometimes their delegates were too anxious to get representatives to stand up and be counted when the time was not yet ripe; sometimes they were more aggressive than the policy position they would eventually adopt. Canada should be on guard against "intemperate action" proposed by the United States. In particular, it should not support the Americans on procedural questions "when the United States is in the wrong and the Soviet Union is in the right."

Issues were nevertheless to be judged not only on their merits but also on "the way the present distribution of power in the world will be affected by a decision one way or another." On questions that might affect war or peace, Canada must clearly be on the side of the United States. Therefore Canada should endeavour not to find itself in the position of having to oppose the Americans on less important matters "in which we believe them to be wrong." It was thus essential to reconcile any divergence in views with the United States before the issues were debated in the Security Council. In this advice, the document reflected one of the guiding convictions of External Affairs: "It is often in these conversations that Canada may influence the trend of events for good."[61] The guidelines set out in this document were essentially those under which the Canadian delegates to the various disarmament commissions would always act. Their basic alignment was always on the side of the United States. At the same time they would always guard their independence so as to enable them both to moderate what they considered to be extreme American tactics and to work to win support for the Western position as a whole.

This directive was written at a time of comparative political calm. During the political crisis brought on by the Korean War, managing these relationships would become a much more complex task, as Pearson explained to Arthur Lower, the eminent Canadian historian, in a letter dated 12 October 1950. No doubt he had been reflecting on the fact that General Douglas MacArthur, the commander of the United Nations forces in Korea, had recently announced his intention to pursue the North Koreans beyond the 38th parallel, an initiative about which Pearson had profound misgivings.[62] He wrote that it was fortunate that the United States had assumed leadership in the Western world. There were "deep flowing springs of good will, idealism and political intelligence" in the United States. Unfortunately there were also "currents of immaturity, indecision, roughness and lack of comprehension of the problems of other people" which were perplexing and frightening. Canadian diplomats were always trying to influence American policy in a way that would both protect Canadian interests and be "good for the world." But these opinions had to be expressed privately so as not to involve Canada "in public quarrels with a great and friendly neighbour."[63]

There was always the danger of upsetting a giant neighbour with which Canada had the closest ties of friendship and common interest. During these years there began to be a good deal of collaboration in the common defence of the North American continent. Common goals in Europe also brought economic benefits; Marshall Plan funds spent in Canada amounted to more than one billion dollars. In the postwar period strong continental movements drew Canada closer to the United States. The Liberal government encouraged the importation of American manufactures and capital and sought to pay for them by the export of raw materials. The result was increased American control of the Canadian economy. Foreign investment in Canada grew from $7 billion in 1945 to $17.4 billion in 1957. More than $10 billion was direct rather than portfolio investment, and four-fifths of it came from the United States. Americans controlled 70 per cent of the Canadian petroleum and natural gas industry, 52 per cent of mining and smelting enterprises, and 43 per cent of the manufacturing sector. The same years saw a vast expansion of American cultural products into Canada: newspapers, books, magazines, and above all television. Politically, economically, and culturally, Canadians were beset by the American presence. It is true that there was a growing nationalist movement which would contribute to the Diefenbaker victory of 1957. Canadians did not wish their country to be a satellite of the United States, but neither did they seek unnecessary quarrels with the Americans. Pearson himself observed that when a country became too heavily dependent on a much larger one there was always the risk of political pressure.[64] It would take determination to stand up to the Americans on foreign policy issues which most Canadians might not understand or, worse still, when substantial numbers of them agreed with the United States.

In a speech to the Empire and Canadian Clubs in Toronto in 1951 Pearson spoke about the difficulties Canadian diplomats experienced in trying to influence American policy. The former Canadian preoccupation about whether the United States would assume leadership of the West had been replaced with questions about how it would do so and whether "the rest of us will be involved." The days of an easygoing relationship with the United States were coming to a close. What the United States, the leader of NATO, decided would now determine peace or war. Because its very existence was at stake in American decisions, Canada must retain its right to criticize American policy. But open criticism always ran the danger of splitting NATO and giving comfort to the Soviet Union. Thus the benefit which might be gained from criticism must always be weighed against the harm done by any appearance of disarray in Western ranks. Reconciling the Canadian right to differ with the necessity for alliance unity was a "tough problem."[65] Pearson proposed to deal with this difficulty by an elaborate system of consultation based on a continuous exchange of views.

One reason for Pearson's commitment to NATO was that, apart from private conversations, it was the best means at hand for contributing to Western political and military strategy. In his maiden speech to the House of Commons in April 1949, Pearson had enunciated a principle which he believed must guide Canada in NATO deliberations: "if Canada is to be asked to share the obligations of the group, it must also share in the responsibility for determining how those obligations shall be met."[66] Unlike the unhappy situation in World War II when allied strategy had been run by the Big Three, he hoped that the North Atlantic Council would make it possible for all the members of NATO to have a say in policy.

In this wish he was to be profoundly disappointed. Canada was given a foretaste of what might happen in NATO by the unilateral actions of the United States in Korea. The United States decided to send its forces across the 38th parallel without talking to fellow members of the United Nations command.[67] A much more serious instance of lack of consultation was revealed in December 1950 when President Truman admitted at a press conference that there had always been active American consideration of the use of the atomic bomb. Prime Minister Attlee of Britain flew to Washington to demand that the United Kingdom have a say in any such use. The Canadian ambassador handed in a note which stated that before such a decision was taken, there should be consultation among the principal governments involved. The American government replied that it was ready to offer Canada the same arrangement it had made with the United Kingdom. But what had the British won? Prime Minister Attlee believed that he had gained his point because President Truman had apparently given his verbal assurance that the allies would be consulted. But this was never written down, and the official American interpretation soon raised apprehension among the Canadians. As Pearson saw it, "the United States is satisfied that there is no commitment in regard to prior consent from any other government before atomic bombs are used."[68] Nor did consultation improve after this contretemps. The United Nations was not asked its opinion about the truce negotiations in Panmunjon[69] or on the calling of the Geneva Conference of April 1954 to attempt to settle the Korean issue. However, Arnold Smith has said that President Eisenhower did ask for a Canadian opinion about a possible atomic strike in Indochina during the siege of Dienbienphu. Both St Laurent and Pearson strongly objected to this suggestion.[70]

Only in the North American defence sector was it possible for Canada to exert some influence. Thus, in January 1951 when the United States proposed an agreement which amounted to advance consent for the Strategic Air Command to use Canadian bases for launching atomic strikes at the USSR, Pearson accepted the American argument that there would not be time for consultation in a case where immediate retaliation for an atomic assault was necessary. In other cases, however, Canada was to be asked for consent, although it was difficult to conceive of a situation in which the United States would wish to drop atomic bombs when there was no urgency. Still, Pearson was making a symbolic point. And he was able to insist on this condition because this was a rare instance when Canada had something the United States wanted – legal control of the bases that the SAC needed.

Because Canada had no bargaining power in the NATO theatre it had no means of forcing the United States to consult. In September 1952, Pearson complained about the lack of information on Pentagon strategy with regard to atomic warfare and European defence.[71] Then in January 1954 the Americans announced their new massive retaliation strategy without talking to their allies.[72] In December 1954 the agreement by NATO to adopt tactical nuclear weapons brought the whole question of consultation to a head. Did this mean that military commanders had the power to precipitate a nuclear war? Under pressure from both Pearson and the British foreign minister, the United States agreed that the final decision would be made by civilians, but it was not very clear whether they would be the fourteen NATO Council members or the three major powers in the Military Committee's standing group. Even then Secretary of State Dulles insisted that if an attack were made on NATO forces, "the decision to shoot back would be made by the commanders on the spot."[73]

Pearson had given up the idea of some sort of formal consultation arrangements quite early. The Americans made it clear that adopting a procedure of consulting each of the allies before any military action would be tantamount to giving each NATO member a veto over American action. Pearson came around to agreeing with Dulles that consultation would be more useful if it were informal.[74] Pearson nevertheless continued to press for the NATO Council to be given more authority and to insist that "no member [should] think of taking action which affected the others in any substantial way ... without prior discussion with those members in NATO."[75] In May 1956 NATO established a Committee of Three (which included Pearson) to make proposals on this matter of consultation. The failure of the British and the French to consult their allies before bombing the Suez Canal in October underlined the importance of the committee's work. In its report in December, the committee could only emphasize again the importance of "making consultation in NATO an integral part of the making of national policy."[76] But it offered no concrete suggestions about how this goal might be pursued.

In the European theatre, the United States needed the co-operation of the major European powers such as Great Britain, France, and West Germany on such issues as German reunification. To them the United States was at least willing to explain its policies so as to promote a "more sympathetic attitude towards USA policy."[77] In fact, real bargaining in the Western alliance went on behind the scenes and final decisions were taken in meetings between the political leaders, never in the NATO Council. Thus Pearson was left to complain endlessly over this matter. In the last interview that he gave before leaving office, he was still saying that the United States ought to give more consideration to the views of the West European countries and Canada before determining its policy.[78] But none other than Henry Kissinger had some wise words about consultation that explain Pearson's real difficulty: "In the long run, consultation works only when those being consulted have a capacity for independent action. Then each side takes the other seriously: then each side knows the other's consent has to be won. Otherwise consultation becomes briefing."[79] Pearson believed the NATO countries should move to concerted action only after extensive discussion and compromise. But a superpower like the United States would never allow smaller powers to prevent it from taking decisions that it thought vital for its national security. Canada was a marginal power and the United States saw no great reason to consult with it. Still, as we shall see, the need for consultation became one of the main Canadian themes in dealing with its allies on issues of disarmament and arms control. Canada would forever ask the United States to consult with its allies before meeting with the Soviet Union. But the United States continued to pursue its own agenda and operate on its own schedule, leaving Canadian diplomats perpetually frustrated and exasperated.

How independent did Pearson feel in speaking up against American policies with which he disagreed? Certainly the danger to Western unity was an inhibiting factor. It is impossible to overestimate the importance he placed on that unity. In one typical sentence, he asserted that "we must be sure we do nothing avoidable by our words and by our deeds to further that wrong end of disunity and division."[80] He was convinced that only a united Atlantic community could win the political battle against the Soviet Union, and he was ready to make almost any concessions to achieve it. One striking example of the lengths to which he would go occurred in January 1951 when he was working with India to bring about a ceasefire in Korea. The Americans insisted that Canada support a resolution in the United Nations condemning China for aggression. Although Pearson explained to the General Assembly that the resolution was unwise, Canada voted for it. John Holmes has suggested that the message Pearson was trying to send was that although he disagreed with these particular American tactics, in the end he considered the preservation of Western solidarity was more important.[81]

My thesis in this book is that in matters of disarmament and arms control Canada acted as a junior partner. But I do not suggest that Pearson adopted such a stance in all foreign policy matters. Holmes rightly maintained that Canada often acted as a middle power. This implied some public questioning by Pearson of certain American positions. If he felt strongly enough about an issue, he believed that it was his responsibility to speak up. If there were a serious split between the two countries, "any Canadian Foreign Minister would be negligent in his duty if he did not indicate to the people of his own country that everything was not going well; or prepare them for the troubles ahead," – as he wrote to Wrong in 1951.[82]

In a 1949 interview Pearson summed up Canada's relationship with the United States. He conceded that Canada was influenced by the Americans and justified this by remarking that "no country can have complete independence today in its foreign policy, because no country can guarantee its own security by its own actions." At the same time he denied Canada was a satellite. Of course he believed it would be folly not to work closely with the United States, but insisted: "that doesn't mean we have to be subservient to every aspect of United States policy."[83]

That he meant what he said is well illustrated by the way he handled a major disagreement with his Washington counterparts over how to deal with the People's Republic of China. Pearson was convinced that the Americans would never accept its communist regime, that underpinning their attitudes and policies towards China was the "acceptance of inevitable wars not so much against an aggressor as against communism itself."[84] But Pearson did not share this unremittingly hostile attitude. Instead, he saw the Chinese revolution as a product of a great tide of nationalism sweeping Asia. It drew its greatest strength from the "passionate desire of its people to escape from poverty and starvation, exploitation and hopelessness."[85] It would have erupted even if there had never been a communist revolution in Moscow.[86]

Because he disagreed with the American assessment, Pearson took some independent diplomatic initiatives in the Far East. In December 1950, despite American disapproval, he worked closely with the Indian delegates at the United Nations to arrange a ceasefire between the warring Chinese and American forces in Korea. In April 1951, he warned the American ambassador to Canada that if General MacArthur carried the war to China's mainland, Canada would reconsider its commitment of troops. Then in 1955 the Chinese communists began to bombard the Nationalist strongholds on the offshore islands of Matsu and Quemoy. So seriously did the Eisenhower administration take this threat that it considered dropping atomic bombs on the mainland. But Pearson believed that an attack on the islands by the mainland Chinese would be no more than a continuation of the civil war. And while he continued to maintain that Canada could not stand aloof from a major war that threatened the American people, he also made it clear that he did not consider that the clash between the two Chinese factions was such a conflict.[87] He publicly differentiated

Canada's position from that of the United States, declaring that "we will not intervene in Matsu or Quemoy if they are attacked by the forces of communist China."[88]

During the same years, Canada was a member of the International Control Commission in Vietnam and came to support fully the American decision to prop up South Vietnam. Yet Pearson was not being inconsistent. What worried him in the confrontation with China was the possibility of the United Nations getting bogged down in a "hopeless land war."[89] China with its inexhaustible manpower would drain away so many Western resources that it would leave Western Europe vulnerable to a Soviet assault. There was not the same danger in Vietnam where no American troops were actively involved. Thus, a political struggle could be waged against communist forces without any significant penalty.

On European matters, the issue of whether to differ publicly from the United States did not arise. Pearson shared the same goal of rearming Germany. When the French National Assembly failed to accept the proposal for the European Defence Community, he publicly proposed that West Germany be accepted into NATO. He sincerely believed that it would be best if West Germany were bound to the Atlantic community. In a security system which contained both the United States and the United Kingdom there would be no danger that West Germany would be the dominating power; instead, its economic and military power would be used only for the constructive purpose of defending itself and the rest of Western Europe and would never threaten either the Soviet Union or France.[90] Once West Germany joined NATO, the reunification of Germany became the main foreign policy objective of the Adenauer government. Pearson and his NATO colleagues continued to demand free elections in the whole of Germany with the ensuing government allowed to choose its own alliances. This was clearly a propaganda ploy. Western leaders including Pearson knew that such a step was unacceptable to the Soviet Union because the resulting shift in the balance of power would put it at a serious disadvantage. Given his outlook, he cannot be criticized for pushing for the rearmament of West Germany. But a public plea for German reunification as a propaganda ploy was another matter. NATO leaders including Pearson understood that the Soviet Union would never agree to this. Yet they gave this goal a much higher priority than serious measures for arms control.

This short sketch of Canadian diplomatic policy towards China and Germany shows that, if necessary, Pearson felt free to disagree with the Americans. In its China policy, Canada played something of the role of a middle power, standing some distance away from the Americans – indeed, attempting to mediate between China and the United States. In Germany, American troops directly confronted those of the Soviet Union. There is no evidence that Pearson disagreed with the American assessment of the strategic situation in Western Europe. Consequently, Pearson saw Canada's role as that of a junior partner offering full support. And so it was with disarmament and arms control: Pearson agreed with the American approach, differing only occasionally over tactics. Consequently, Canada acted as a loyal though subordinate ally in helping the United States pursue its goals during the negotiations.

Political agreement was not, however, the only reason for such a concurrence of strategic views. During these years Canada was in a firm military alliance with the United States. One of the most important areas of this co-operation was in the Arctic. As the military build-up of both superpowers proceeded, North American strategists feared that Soviet bombers would catch the American bombers by surprise, destroy them, and leave the United States without any means to retaliate. As early as October 1945 the American Joint Chiefs of Staff had expressed their unhappiness with northern defence and after a period of prolonged negotiations in which Pearson (as Canada's ambassador to the United States) played a prominent role,[91] the two countries agreed in February 1947 that while each would retain control of military activity on its own territory, they would exchange military personnel and co-operate in exercises. Even though the agreement was a limited one, Canada had taken the first steps towards a continental military alliance with the United States.[92]

These joint arrangements for defence were a logical outcome of the North American strategic situation. As Pearson observed in 1955, "this continent must be defended as a whole or lost as a whole."[93] Canada lacked the resources to defend its own territory; it needed American help. The danger in such co-operative arrangements was that Canadian sovereignty might be weakened. Both the Canadian government and the American government were sensitive to this difficulty, and, as Joseph Jockel has shown, American defence facilities were not imposed on an unwilling Canada.[94] Instead, there existed a genuine defence partnership pushed by the military but agreed to by the politicians of both countries.

It has been suggested that the integration of Canadian and American air defences made it more difficult for "Canada to speak, in the disarmament negotiations, with a particularly Canadian voice."[95] This might suggest that there was a distinct Canadian defence interest not shared by the United States. But this was not the case. Shared geography meant that what was good for the defence of Canada was good for the defence of the United States. In this respect Canada was different from its main West European partners. Great Britain, France, and West Germany all had defence problems which were far different from those of North America. Had Canada had a unique defence interest, it might well have brought a particular Canadian perspective to the negotiating table. But because its location quite naturally gave it a viewpoint much like that of the United States, Canada was often perceived to have no views of its own about defence but to be merely a satellite of the United States. This weakened the effectiveness of its presentations to its Western allies not to speak of the Soviet Union.

NUCLEAR ARMS

From the beginning Pearson had been frightened by the potential dangers of nuclear weapons. In November 1945, he predicted that without international control of atomic energy the development of technology would one day make every country in the world vulnerable to incoming nuclear rockets.[96] No doubt he referred to himself when he observed in 1948 that mankind was trying to catch up with the "shattering implications of the scientific revolution that has taken place."[97] Even the apparent American monopoly of atomic bombs provided little comfort. His apprehension greatly increased when the Soviet Union exploded its first atomic device and rose even more in the early fifties as each side developed hydrogen bombs. Nuclear war, he warned in the House of Commons, now threatened "the very existence ... of the whole human race."[98]

In opposing the American use of the atomic bomb in Korea in December 1950, Pearson had praised the political instinct of the great mass of the world's people for sensing that this bomb was different from other weapons in its power to destroy all life on the planet. It was the ultimate weapon. "Whether or not to use a weapon of that kind," he added, "should surely not be decided by the application of the same criteria applicable to other weapons."[99] Six months later, in a private letter to Hume Wrong, he regretted that the earlier horror of atomic warfare was weakening and that there was a tendency to "accept the atomic bomb as merely another weapon."[100] Yet, in public, Pearson rejected the demand of the Canadian Peace Congress that the atomic bomb be outlawed, asserting that "a victim is just as dead whether he is killed by a bayonet or an atom bomb."[101] A few years later he claimed that the "differences" between using several ordinary bombs and one atomic bomb are "technical, or psychological or even political. They are not moral."[102] It was because he believed that nuclear weapons were necessary for the defence of the West that Pearson gradually came to overlook their capacity for mass destruction and to accept their moral legitimacy.

Pearson believed that the USSR would resist the temptation of aggression only if it was certain that it could not win a war it chose to start. Because of the overwhelming superiority of Soviet conventional strength, it was therefore doubly important that NATO constantly improve its nuclear capability: "we must ... not lag behind in the development of knowledge and skill in the field of atomic energy," Pearson maintained,[103] for "atomic retaliation from the air"[104] was vital to deterrence. Pearson was clearly operating on a Western theory that deterrence depended on an imbalance of terror in favour of the West.[105] Only the preponderance of American nuclear forces and up-to-date technology would keep expansionist Soviet forces in check. The Western states, which had only peaceful intentions, did not need to be deterred. The new destructive weaponry was safe in their hands because they would never use it "for any aggressive warlike purpose."[106] Western powers were actively pushing for disarmament while strengthening NATO's nuclear capacity. But Pearson argued that both policies were necessary to keep the peace: "There is no inconsistency here for the two policies are complementary."[107]

Believing that the West lacked the manpower to deal with Soviet-inspired attacks along the vast length of its perimeter, John Foster Dulles had announced in January 1954 that the United States would instantly meet such assaults with means and in places of its own choosing; instead of sending land armies to deal with Soviet incursions, it would feel free to respond with a massive nuclear assault, presumably against Soviet cities. Pearson was clearly uneasy about this new policy. In a private memorandum to Prime Minister St Laurent, he asserted that "local aggressions cannot be answered by atomic bombs on Moscow ... If it becomes a question of the atomic bomb and all-out war, or nothing, it may be, too often, nothing." He feared that the new strategy would use fewer United States troops and so create the impression that what the Americans had in mind is that "Europeans ... will fight in the old-fashioned, bloody, man-to-man way, while victory will come from the skies by atomic retaliation."[108] Such an approach could only weaken NATO unity. Publicly, however, Pearson refrained from criticizing the new policy, which he conceded might "turn out to be the best deterrent against aggression."[109] His main concern was to make sure that all the NATO allies were consulted before such a devastating strike was ordered, and he wondered how this need for consultation could be reconciled with the word "instantly" which Dulles had used.

Pearson had pointed out that the great flaw in the strategy of massive retaliation was that it might put the United States in the invidious position of beginning what might be a nuclear holocaust over a minor frontier incident or of losing credibility for failing to act. Because NATO's conventional forces remained inferior, the Soviet Union was free to probe any point along the boundary with Western Europe. The development of tactical nuclear weapons seemed to offer a solution. With these arms NATO soldiers could be confident about fending off incursions by numerically superior Soviet troops. In December 1954 Pearson therefore voted with the rest of the NATO Council to allow their troops to accept such weapons. Nevertheless he worried that a response to a Soviet threat against a "big battleship or a small island" that entailed an attack on the Soviet Union with hydrogen bombs would put the whole world at risk. Except "in the event of a reciprocal spasm of mutual annihilation," he wished the free world's forces to be used only for "limited political objectives."[110] What he was advocating was a doctrine of measured retaliation – restrict the amount of force used in retaliation to what was necessary to achieve the limited objective of halting a particular aggression. But he pointed to the weakness in his own theory "the use by one side of tactical A-bombs may ... lead to strategic H-bombs against a metropolis."[111] He might well have added that there was no guarantee that tactical atomic weapons might not favour the Soviet Union. As it happened, a month after he made that speech, a NATO exercise demonstrated that even the use of tactical weapons in central Europe would mean millions of German casualties.

Pearson consistently supported the increase in Western nuclear might because he believed that a strong West could help to keep the peace; at the same time he agreed with Churchill that peace now rested on a balance of terror. The two views were at variance because the second proposition implied the possibility of a preemptive United States attack that was only restrained by the threat of Russian retaliation. Although he acknowledged that such a balance might be mankind's best safeguard, he drew only limited comfort from the situation. Both sides were searching for an intercontinental missile that might minimize mutual deterrence by providing a capacity to annihilate the other side without warning. The balance of terror was unstable because of the likelihood that it could be upset by some new discovery. "Thermo-nuclear devices are too dangerous," Pearson warned: "The threat that they pose to the very existence of this planet is too great for sane men anywhere to view with equanimity their existence in a divided and frightened world."[112] Pearson's pessimism also reflects that, like many politicians of his generation, he had never decided just why he wanted nuclear weapons. If their sole purpose was to prevent nuclear attack, then the West needed far fewer weapons than it was building. If they were needed to achieve certain NATO objectives such as the reunification of Germany then they were ill suited to this purpose. As George Kennan was to point out in 1958, "the weapon of mass destruction is a sterile and hopeless weapon ... which cannot in any way serve the purposes of a constructive and hopeful foreign policy."[113] Caught in the strategic net, Pearson "went along" with a nuclear policy for the West that made no sense. Clearly he was uneasy with the policy, but he had nothing better to propose.

PEARSON'S POLITICAL STRENGTH

In the years that Pearson was secretary of state for external affairs he was never compelled to withdraw or even modify any of the public stands he took on foreign policy matters. He was able to speak with such confidence because, politically speaking, he was in an impregnable position. The federal Liberal party, easily trouncing its opponents in the elections of 1949 and 1953, was at the height of its postwar power. Pearson's political chief, Louis St Laurent, took the same stand on the Cold War as he did.

When St Laurent was secretary of state for external affairs he had set forth his views on Canadian policy in international relations in a lecture at the University of Toronto in 1947. He had spoken of the importance of political liberty and the values of a Christian civilization. He had underlined his belief that Canada must accept responsibility in world affairs – a sharp reversal of the isolationist stands of Mackenzie King. When the Cold War began in earnest, St Laurent led the crusade to sell NATO to the Canadian public. Once he became prime minister in 1949, he supported active Canadian participation in Korea and the integration of West Germany into NATO. Like Pearson, he had a great admiration for the United States which he once described in the following glowing terms: "In the establishment of security and peace ... in the expansion of world trade ... and in the industrialization and diversification of the economies of other continents, there is only one nation with the wealth and the energy and the knowledge and the skill to give real leadership, and that nation is the United States."[114]

A few months after St Laurent became secretary of state for external affairs in 1946 Pearson was named under-secretary. St Laurent soon came to appreciate the skills of his new deputy. It was Pearson who drafted the speech that St Laurent gave in September 1947 at the United Nations when he opened the campaign for a North Atlantic alliance. When St Laurent became prime minister, he named Pearson to External Affairs. St Laurent must have thought very highly of him because in promoting some one who was still only a civil servant he passed over a powerful Liberal politician, Brooke Claxton, who was also interested in the job. St Laurent and Pearson established a very harmonious relationship. The prime minister came to rely on Pearson more and more. As he got on in years, St Laurent became less comfortable negotiating with other countries, and he was glad to leave the details to Pearson as he did, for example, at the Commonwealth conference of June 1956.[115] He readily took suggestions from Pearson; in his memoirs, the latter relates an incident when he found it necessary to dissuade St Laurent from sending an angry and unhelpful telegram to Eden during the Suez crisis.[116] Pearson, for his part, ensured that his superior was kept informed and was careful to discuss initiatives with him; in short, he never took the prime minister for granted.

This excellent relationship with St Laurent meant that Pearson had plenty of scope to implement his own ideas. He himself claimed that in the debate over Suez at the United Nations, he had virtually a free hand. "Don't worry," St Laurent told him. "Do what is best. Do the right thing, and I'll back you."[117] George Ignatieff believed that Pearson had such great "political clout" because he had the complete confidence of the prime minister.[118] Pearson was extremely lucky to have St Laurent as his prime minister; had King still been the prime minister, Pearson would have found himself on a very short leash.

Pearson was also fortunate in his parliamentary opposition. There were two parties to the right of the government. The most extreme of these was the Social Credit. It supported the government on NATO and German rearmament and on the non-recognition of communist China. The main concern of the Socreds seems to have been that NATO might be used to form a world federal government – a fear that had little credibility. The Liberals had little fear of any serious attack from that quarter. The Progressive Conservatives were the largest opposition party. Their strategy on foreign affairs was to portray the Liberals as soft on communism.

But this meant they were reduced to saying "me too" on major government hardline initiatives: they supported NATO, Canada's participation in Korea, and the rearmament of Germany. In Asia they accepted Pearson's contention that Canada should not involve itself in the conflict over Quemoy and Matsu. They publicly speculated that the Liberals might weaken and agree that the China seat at the United Nations should go to the People's Republic. They gained some ground with the Canadian public when they attacked the government for not taking the British side in the dispute over the Suez Canal, but in doing so they appealed to a growing anti-American sentiment in Canada. They did not challenge Pearson's fundamental policy of rearming the West as a deterrent to possible Soviet aggression.

Pearson was also quite safe from attack on his left flank. The Co-operative Commonwealth Federation (CCF) was a small party which was able to elect only eighteen members or so to parliament during this period. For the most part, it accepted Pearson's analysis of the issues in the Cold War. It supported NATO and the dispatch of Canadian troops to Korea. It is true that as time went on the CCF began to grow more impatient with American policies, especially those on Asia, and pressed for the admission of the People's Republic of China to the United Nations. In 1952, after the NATO meeting in Lisbon, M.J. Coldwell, the CCF leader, asserted that the decisions taken had been deeply influenced by American domestic and political considerations in an election year. NATO, he argued, was attempting to implement an excessive military programme. If this were done at the expense of lowering the level of financial aid, it would lead to the economic collapse of Western Europe, a development which "the Kremlin wants and what the Kremlin is banking on."[119] However Coldwell had been led to make his statement because of a misleading communiqué from Lisbon which had projected the totally unrealistic figure of fifty divisions for NATO by the end of the year. In fact, the NATO Council had decided to scale down the amount of conventional rearmament it was aiming for and this soon undermined any political impact which the CCF stand might have had. In 1955, much to their embarrassment, CCF parliamentarians found themselves split over German rearmament. Coldwell and four of his colleagues voted to accept rearmament, but twelve members of the party opposed it. Obviously, they were not in any position to mount much of a campaign against this government policy. On Suez, the CCF totally agreed with Pearson. In sum, except on the matter of Suez, Pearson faced no serious opposition in parliament. Their own party programmes meant that the

Conservatives and the CCF were compelled to support most of his policies.

Pearson was also fortunate in that the Canadian public was largely apathetic about foreign affairs during this decade. The one substantial debate in the House of Commons on the significance of the atomic bomb had taken place in December 1945. The five volumes in the *Canada in World Affairs* series that survey this decade cite no evidence of public concern over the nuclear danger. Because a godless communist state was perceived as the enemy, there was little opposition to the government's stands on foreign issues in Quebec. Pearson had little reason to be concerned about the effect of his policies on national unity. There was very little interest in these issues and the political opposition soon learned that there was not much to gain by harping on foreign policy. One poll showed that only one per cent of the population considered peace the main problem facing Canada. This apathy was no fault of Pearson; he made energetic attempts to explain the issues as he saw them to the public and to involve them in the general debate. But, as James Eayrs has noted: "Thinking about the unthinkable is hard enough at the worst of times; the years 1949 to 1955 were, for most Canadians, the best of times."[120] Engrossed in taking advantage of postwar prosperity, most Canadians, enjoying the protection of the American Strategic Air Command, thought nuclear questions academic, if they thought of them at all.

Despite the growing atomic peril, the peace movement in Canada was remarkably feeble in the decade under study. The main demand of its principal organization, the Canadian Peace Congress, was for the abolition of the atomic bomb. Pearson was able to discredit the programme of the Congress on the grounds that the organization followed Moscow's lead.[121] His task was made a little easier in December 1952 when the chairman of the Congress, Dr James Endicott, accepted the Stalin peace prize. Nevertheless, its existence seems to have caused Pearson some concern. In 1951 he told the Americans that the Soviet peace campaign had made "a good deal of progress" in Canada and that his government was under "some domestic attack" for seeming to place greater reliance on atomic armament than on international control.[122] And in 1956 John Holmes warned in a departmental memo that the pressure to ban nuclear tests was growing.[123]

With the full support of prime minister and cabinet, with his party in the majority in the house, and with no serious challenge to his views from the opposition and an uncaring public, it is no wonder Pearson dominated Canadian foreign policy in this decade.

A successful attack on his policies would have needed a determined and united opposition backed by a broad public consensus. But the parliamentary opposition sensed that Pearson spoke for a large section of the public on foreign policy. Consequently, they put little effort into foreign policy. This was especially true of disarmament and arms control issues. A reading of the foreign policy debates in parliament reveals minimal interest in these matters, even though Pearson often commented on disarmament negotiations in his speeches to the house, and in his appearances before the Standing Committee on External Affairs he proved willing to answer all questions. But the opposition, whether Conservative or CCF, showed very little interest in probing these issues, let alone challenging Pearson to score political points. While under-secretary of state for external affairs from 1946 to 1948, Pearson was a major influence on Canada's disarmament policy; once he became minister in September 1948 he was totally responsible for the creation and implementation of Canada's arms control policy and was never challenged by the opposition: he had an absolutely free hand. As John Holmes has observed, Canadian delegations could pursue "what looked like constructive internationalist policies without too cautious regard for political repercussions at home."[124]

CHAPTER THREE

Canada and the
Baruch Plan, 1945–46

The successful completion of the Manhattan project and the dropping of the atomic bomb on Hiroshima brought the world into the nuclear age. The first attempt by the world community to agree on nuclear disarmament and the destruction of all existing atomic bombs came in the summer of 1946 when a commission of the United Nations discussed the rival plans presented by the United States and the Soviet Union. Each had based its scheme on strategic principles from which neither would budge for most of the next decade.

Because of its possession of uranium Canada had become involved in the development of the new technology and emerged an atomic power at the end of the war. In 1945 the Chalk River experimental pilot atomic reactor, the first to function outside the United States, came into operation. Margaret Gowing, a historian of the British nuclear programme, has noted that this project gave "Canada a flying start into the nuclear age ... It also brought Canada a seat at the top diplomatic tables."[1] Canada's expertise would bring it into the very centre of negotiations over the control of this new technology.

Canada had made a fine beginning towards becoming a producer of atomic energy for peaceful purposes. But would it build a bomb? In December 1945, C.D. Howe, then minister of reconstruction, announced that Canada had no intention of manufacturing atomic bombs.[2] In 1949, now minister of trade and commerce, he would repeat the message: Canada was able to make an atomic bomb but had no intention of doing so.[3] This was an accurate statement. By 1951 the National Research Experimental Reactor at Chalk River north of Ottawa was capable of producing the plutonium necessary for the manufacture of atomic bombs,[4] and in this early period Canada's technical knowledge was also highly advanced. However, there was no real reason for Canada to become an atomic military power.

Unlike Britain and France, Canada had no aspirations to be a great power; it had no need for nuclear weapons as symbols of this status. As a small power, Canada's leaders knew that they must rely on effective diplomacy rather than military force. Moreover, building such a nuclear capability would have certainly evoked the disapproval of their American ally. The United States would have considered such a programme a needless proliferation of nuclear weapons and an extra drain on the available supply of uranium oxide. Nor would possession of a nuclear arsenal have been psychologically acceptable to Canadians who were proud of their unmilitary and peaceful image. On the more practical level, the government's military advisers could not have made a case that Canada needed atomic bombs for its own protection, even if they had wished to. After all, any Soviet attack on Canada would have constituted a threat to the United States and precipitated an American retaliatory attack. Moreover, to become an atomic military power would have required an enormously expensive bomber delivery system.[5] It would also have consumed a considerable amount of the money that was devoted to Canada's conventional contributions to the North Atlantic Treaty Organization and Arctic defence. To persuade the Canadian taxpayer that this was a necessary expenditure in peacetime would have been an impossible political task.

In the end not to build atomic bombs was the sensible decision for Canada. Yet the lack of a military nuclear capacity would weaken its effectiveness in arms negotiations. Its declining expertise in this area would limit the scope and influence of its proposals. Had Canada been neutral, it might have been able to act in negotiations as a minor power speaking for all non-nuclear governments which desperately wished to be rid of the nuclear terror. But Canada supported all efforts to increase Western nuclear might. Thus, in the talks it had no particular moral position and no very impressive military credentials. In consequence, its ability to influence others around the negotiating table was limited right from the beginning.

1945

WASHINGTON CONFERENCE

Canada was informed on 4 July 1945 that the Americans intended to drop the atomic bomb on Japan. Canada had not been a signatory of the Quebec agreement of August 1943, under which the United States and Britain had agreed never to employ the atomic bomb against a third party without the other's permission. Legally, therefore, it had no veto. Even if it had had the right of refusal, it is very doubtful that the Canadian government would have intervened. The Pacific war was the exclusive responsibility of the American command; the lives of their soldiers and sailors would be saved by its use. The necessities of war had hardened the hearts of Canadian politicians as they had those of other war leaders. The bombing of Dresden and Tokyo had made mass destruction from the air seem commonplace. On the surface what was being proposed was nothing more than an ordinary air strike delivered by an extraordinary technical device. At the dawn of the atomic age, there was no danger that the Japanese would retaliate with a bomb of their own. Canada had no moral or strategic reasons to raise objections.

Mackenzie King nonetheless confessed to "mixed feelings in my mind and heart."[6] He had always prided himself on being concerned with the morality of political acts. Before the bombing took place, the prime minister worried that "we are approaching a moment of terror to mankind," that men had "created the Frankenstein which conceivably could destroy the human race."[7] He was saddened by the prospect of the deaths of so many innocent people. Still, there was no doubt in his mind that the Americans were doing the right thing. After Hiroshima he shivered at the thought of what might have happened to the British, had the Germans won the race to manufacture the atomic bomb.[8] Here, at the very beginning of the nuclear era, we find the attitude which Canadian politicians would adopt towards atomic weapons: they would readily concede their horrors but nevertheless insist that if necessary they should be used.

On 9 August, three days after the bombing of Hiroshima, President Truman declared in a radio broadcast that Great Britain, Canada, and the United States would not reveal the secret of manufacturing atomic bombs until it was possible to control atomic energy and to protect their countries and the rest of the world from possible destruction. This ban against sharing atomic information included the USSR. Yet it should have been clear by then that any successful effort by the international community to guarantee that atomic energy was used only for peaceful purposes would require the co-operation of the Soviet Union.

Direct negotiations with the Soviet Union on this matter raised the spectre of sharing the secret of manufacturing atomic bombs. Because of their sense of unease about Soviet goals which had developed by the autumn of 1945, however, neither the American public nor Truman was prepared to do this. Yet, politically, Truman needed to respond to American liberal opinion which was pressing for international control of atomic energy. On 3 October, in a message to Congress, the president attempted a compromise. Because the theory of making atomic bombs was well known, it was only a matter of time until some other nations produced them. To prevent such a dangerous development, it was essential to persuade potential atomic powers to renounce the military use of atomic power. He therefore proposed to initiate discussions with Britain and Canada and later with other nations to find a means of preventing an atomic arms race. Yet, in the next month or so Truman emphasized that he would not share weapons technology, not even with the United Kingdom, let alone the Soviet Union, and indeed suggested that the world would be better off if the United States kept a monopoly of the atomic bomb.

Canada and the United Kingdom, as Washington's putative partners in the search to control atomic weapons, were soon trying to influence what was supposed to be a common atomic policy. Late in September, Prime Minister Clement Attlee of Great Britain had written to Truman urging the necessity of international controls. At the time Mackenzie King happened to be in London, and it was there that he learned that both he and Attlee had been invited by Truman to a conference on this matter in Washington. But apparently no date was set. Attlee continued to press for action. In October he warned Truman that a clear joint statement on atomic policy was necessary for the forthcoming meeting of the United Nations General Assembly. The upshot was that tripartite talks were scheduled for sometime in November 1945.

In Washington the relationship of the United Kingdom to American atomic policy was seen to be different from that of Canada. Britain was virtually a partner because of the Quebec agreement. Canada was in a different position. It had no legal claim to be consulted; yet in world atomic politics Canada was important. It possessed large sources of uranium and knew the secrets of atomic production. If Truman had decided on direct talks with the Soviet Union, then Canada's attendance at the conference might have been of marginal importance. But to justify the contrary course of action, Washington needed to offer a responsible alternative. The presence of even a minor atomic power like Canada would confer legitimacy on Washington's claim that the conference would speak not only to American atomic concerns but to those of other democratic countries as well.

Since the end of September Canada had needed an atomic policy of its own. On 2 October, Lester Pearson, Canada's ambassador in Washington, had a long conversation with the under secretary of state, Dean Acheson.[9] It is not known whether Pearson actually saw the memorandum on atomic policy which Acheson had drawn up for the president,[10] but we may surmise that Acheson very likely told Pearson about its contents. In any event, the eloquent and lucid memo which Pearson wrote to prepare King for the Washington Conference contains two key Acheson arguments. The first was that the marriage of atomic bombs to the rocket technology of the German V-2 would mean that there was no defence against atomic warfare. The second was that the method of manufacturing atomic bombs could not be kept secret. Thus mankind was confronted with the "most bitter and disastrous armament race ever run." The only constructive solution must be an "international" one. But Pearson did not conclude, as Acheson had done, that the United States and the United Kingdom should approach the Soviet Union directly. Instead, he proposed that the three atomic powers exploit their temporary monopoly to bring atomic energy under international control; they ought to trade knowledge of atomic technology for the renunciation of atomic weapons by all nations. To guarantee no violations of such a pledge, there would need to be a system of inspection by "an international commission of scientists of world reputation" which would report to the General Assembly.[11]

James Eayrs believes that the Pearson memorandum "deserves a place among the great diplomatic state papers."[12] But whatever its fine qualities, Pearson's recommendations were constrained by his knowledge that none of Truman's statements demonstrated any intention of dealing directly with the Soviet Union on this matter. Pearson understood that his political master, Mackenzie King, was not likely to press the Americans on a proposal they thought unacceptable. Consequently, Pearson invoked the possibility of using a temporary advantage to persuade the USSR to renounce its military atomic programme. But if, as he conceded in the memorandum, the USSR would probably discover the secret within five years, why would it allow itself to be coerced into giving up its efforts to achieve atomic parity with the United States? Pearson's argument, infused with the necessity of sacrificing national control on this matter, would have been stronger if he had suggested that the United States be pressed to open immediate negotiations with the Russians and to be ready, if such a concession became necessary, to divulge the technology of manufacturing an atomic bomb. But such a proposal was obviously a non-starter, and being a competent and intelligent civil servant, Pearson suggested only what was politically possible. In any case it is not very probable that the Soviet Union would have given up its atomic programme and submitted to international inspection in exchange for the kind of technical information they were well on the way to discovering for themselves.

Truman, Attlee, and King met for more than three days. During the meeting the president asked everyone around the table for his views. Thus Pearson was able to suggest to Truman directly that the United States should be prepared to give up its atomic weapons and seek the co-operation of the USSR to draft an agreement for their international control. This effort, he maintained, should be pursued through the United Nations. McGeorge Bundy comments that "Canadians, on balance, were a force in support of working through the UN, not directly with Moscow."[13] It is easy to see why Pearson, a diplomat for a minor state, would be apprehensive about direct big-power negotiations. Canada would have little or no input. Because of his desire to enhance Canadian prestige, his commitment to functionalism, and his conviction that smaller powers had something important to contribute to a peaceful world order, it was natural for Pearson to think the United Nations was suitable for nuclear talks. But, as a wartime memorandum to Truman had suggested, the Soviet Union was not likely to take seriously the opinions of "many small nations who have not demonstrated their potential power or responsibility in this war."[14] And if what was wanted was disarmament, was it not naive to think that atomic issues could be settled in a United Nations commission open to press scrutiny and therefore bound to give rise to public posturing by the countries involved? "It seems unlikely," Bundy was later to remark, "that any one understood at the time how readily the idea of 'going to the UN' could become a substitute for action."[15]

Nevertheless, the three leaders decided to send the problem of the control of atomic energy to the United Nations. Pearson was the Canadian on the drafting committee which produced the statement signed by the three leaders on 16 November 1945. It stated that their aim was to use atomic energy for peaceful purposes. They wished to encourage the widest dissemination of basic scientific information about atomic energy but were anxious to prevent practical industrial techniques from being exploited for military goals. Consequently, such technology would not be revealed until "effective, reciprocal, and enforceable safeguards acceptable to all nations"[16] were in place. They proposed that a United Nations commission make recommendations for the exchange of basic scientific information, for means to control atomic energy to ensure its peaceful use, for methods to eliminate atomic weapons, and, finally, for the institution of effective safeguards to protect complying states against the hazards of violations and evasions. The work of the commission was to proceed by stages, the successful completion of one phase furnishing the necessary confidence to go on to the next. It was suggested that the work might begin by considering a wide exchange of information and then, as a second step, a compilation of information on the sources of relevant raw materials.

The Washington declaration has been criticized because it failed to make any approach to the Soviet Union.[17] Although such a gesture might have produced a slightly better atmosphere, in the end the Soviet Union did agree to a United Nations commission and the guidelines under which it would operate. But there were other weaknesses in the declaration such as the notion that there should be full disclosure of the sources of raw materials. Why would the USSR agree to reveal its stocks of uranium ore and therefore its potential as an atomic power without getting anything substantial in return? Worse still, the declaration showed that Truman and his colleagues had failed to consider the effect of the elimination of atomic bombs on the strategic relationship between the United States and the USSR; in time, they would come to see that this could be done only as part of a package that included the scaling down of Soviet conventional arms, if Western security was not to be undermined. Lastly, the declaration assumed that the Soviet Union would be content with a control process under which the Americans would retain exclusive possession of the atomic bomb. Nevertheless, it set forth two important principles which the USSR would eventually accept: that safeguards were necessary and that arms control and disarmament must proceed by stages.

For Canadian diplomats the Washington Conference was an unqualified success. In 1943 King's role had been limited to that of a helpful host who watched Roosevelt and Churchill initial the Quebec agreement. Now he, along with Truman and Attlee, signed the Washington declaration signifying the latter's acceptance of Canada as an equal. The Canadian functionalist dream that its possession of uranium and atomic expertise should allow it a voice in this extremely important area of policy conflict between the

United States and the USSR had seemingly been fulfilled. It is true that at the conference itself King had taken a back seat; he had only made a few minor suggestions.[18] Still, Canada had emerged as an important player in world atomic politics.

In December King reported on the Washington Conference to parliament. He explained why he had opted for international control and also justified keeping the manufacturing process for the bomb secret. His most perceptive remark was that "the solution of the problems presented by atomic energy must be sought in the realm of world politics."[19] In theory, a United Nations committee was to assume that all nations wished for disarmament and arms control and that its task was a technical one of finding a fair formula that would satisfy everyone. The reality was that the Cold War would cause each side to bargain so as to end up militarily stronger than its rival.

King's speech was well received by all members except Fred Rose, the Labour Progressive (Communist) member for Cartier. Rose brought a touch of realism to a debate distinguished by idealistic rhetoric by reminding his listeners that the Washington declaration left the Americans with the power to use the atom bomb "at their discretion"[20] and the door thus remained open for an arms race. He was right. Joseph Stalin would never rest content while the United States enjoyed an atomic monopoly. The arrest of Rose the following March – for transmitting secret information to the USSR and conspiring to violate the Official Secrets Act – meant that there was no longer any voice in parliament warning that an arms race was getting under way. The government could truthfully claim that the opposition parties supported its policy. It was virtually given a blank cheque to make policy on the military aspects of atomic energy for the next decade.

SETTING UP
THE ATOMIC ENERGY COMMISSION

None of the diplomats at the founding conference of the United Nations in the spring of 1945 had been even remotely aware of the development of the atomic bomb; consequently there were no provisions in the Charter for ways to go about controlling atomic energy. How, then, should the proposal for a commission be presented to the United Nations? Canadian diplomats thought it was a bad idea to ask the Soviet Union to join the atomic three in sponsoring a resolution. They argued that it was unlikely that Moscow would associate itself with a statement on which it had not been consulted and might complicate matters by insisting that the whole subject be considered by the Security Council instead of the General Assembly. They proposed that the United States, the United Kingdom, and Canada reach agreement among themselves and then simply inform the USSR without asking for its comments. On 30 November Pearson sent an aide-mémoire[21] containing this message to the American secretary of state, James Byrnes, but the latter, under some pressure from the press for having ignored the USSR at the Washington Conference had decided to approach Moscow directly on atomic policy.[22] The American government understood that the proposed commission could succeed only if its composition and terms of reference were acceptable to the Soviet Union.

Byrnes must have been a little uneasy about his reception when he left for Moscow on 12 December. The Soviet leaders had made no secret of their disapproval of the Washington Conference. Soviet propaganda claimed that the United States was planning to use the atomic bomb to bully the Russians. But in Moscow Byrnes was pleasantly surprised to find that his hosts were receptive towards his proposals. For one thing, and this was very important to Canada, they accepted the proposition that Canada must always be represented in the new commission. It was agreed to invite Canada along with the other three permanent members of the Security Council, Britain, China, and France, to sponsor the resolution in the United Nations. The USSR also accepted the proposed terms of reference. It also agreed that the work of the commission should proceed by stages.

Nevertheless Byrnes made one important concession. He agreed that the future commission should take direction from the Security Council and not the General Assembly. The Soviet leaders knew that American influence in the Assembly would be far greater than theirs; in the Security Council, however, they could use their veto to protect themselves against any harmful measures. This part of the 27 December communiqué did not sit well with Canadian diplomats. They had hoped that the commission would report directly to the Assembly. Now it appeared that its reports would reach the Assembly only if the permanent members of the Security Council, each of whom had a veto, gave permission. Canadian officials found this change especially disappointing because their main field of diplomatic action would be the Assembly where they might claim to speak for a large body of like-minded small countries. However, the Canadian government naturally accepted the Moscow agreement. After all, alone among the smaller countries, it would be a co-sponsor of the resolution setting up a commission on which it would have a unique position. Pearson thought that the Soviet agreement to the establishment of this commission was a "very considerable achievement, even though it does not commit the U.S.S.R. to anything except the establishment of the Commission with agreed terms of reference." He went on to observe that the battle for international control of atomic energy remained to be fought. This was absolutely true. The principal powers had nothing to lose by agreeing to *talk* about atomic issues. Still, as Pearson concluded, "a good beginning [had] been made."[23]

1946

On 24 January 1946, on the motion of the five permanent members of the Security Council and Canada, the Assembly unanimously voted to establish the Atomic Energy Commission (AEC). It was to be composed of the representatives of the eleven members of the Security Council and Canada. The AEC, working under the guidance of the Security Council, was to be a technical commission. It would attempt to find a compromise among conflicting national interests so as to reach a consensus on how to: (a) extend the exchange of basic scientific information on atomic energy for peaceful ends; (b) control atomic energy to ensure its use solely for peaceful purposes; (c) eliminate atomic weapons; and (d) institute effective safeguards against violations and evasions. It was to submit its reports and recommendations to the Security Council and these were to be made public unless the Council ruled otherwise. The AEC could not by itself institute a system of international control of atomic energy. Only the Security Council had the power to act on AEC recommendations.

In March 1946 the Canadian cabinet named General Andrew G.L. McNaughton as the Canadian representative to the AEC. He was a fine choice. McGeorge Bundy observes that "an American reviewing that debate [on the international control of atomic energy] can hardly avoid the conclusion that the basic case for international control would have been more widely persuasive – though not in Moscow – if it had been made not by Bernard Baruch but by the Canadian member, General A.G.L. McNaughton."[24] Both a military man and an engineer, McNaughton had a good scientific background and understood nuclear weapons. He had been named one of the military advisers to the Canadian delegation at the Geneva Disarmament Conference in 1932 but had soon departed claiming that he could serve no useful purpose there. (Later he reflected that that conference "began in a perfectly good atmosphere but, by reason of the very fact that statesmen started measuring their potential and actual forces one against the other, qualitatively and quantitatively, their minds were insensibly turned from the possibilities of agreement in the spheres where agreement might have been achieved to thoughts of armed aggression."[25]) As the Canadian representative to the AEC, McNaughton would display impressive diplomatic skills.

The cabinet had also set up an Advisory Panel on Atomic Energy which included representatives from the Department of Reconstruction and Supply, the National Research Council, the Department of National Defence, and the Department of External Affairs. McNaughton was of course a member of this panel which discussed all atomic issues including Canada's work in the AEC. Although the panel would remain active for a couple of years, from the beginning the work of the AEC was seen as a responsibility of the diplomatic mission at the United Nations. McNaughton received his day-to-day directions from the Office of the Under-Secretary of State for External Affairs, and the cabinet also sent to New York George Ignatieff as diplomatic adviser and Dr George Lawrence of the National Research Council as scientific adviser.

John Holmes has remarked that Canadian diplomats were "sceptical"[26] about the political possibilities of international control. Yet for Canada the establishment of the AEC was a vindication of its functionalist views: because of its resources and atomic expertise, Canada would now take part in negotiations with the Soviet Union on a vital issue that affected the Cold War. Membership in the AEC fitted in perfectly with the ideal diplomatic role which Canadian diplomats perceived for their country. Because of the wide publicity that would be given the commission, Canada would be able to demonstrate its diplomatic skills and show that smaller powers had something of value to give to the world debate. This gratifying role would go on as long as the AEC continued.

THE ACHESON-LILIENTHAL REPORT

To keep the AEC functioning would become one of the prime goals of Canadian foreign policy in the next few years. The other was to win support for the American plan that would be proposed in July by Bernard Baruch, the American representative to the AEC. The Baruch Plan was based on an American government study, the Acheson-Lilienthal Report published in March 1946. The previous January, Secretary of State Byrnes had instructed his under secretary, Dean Acheson, to head a committee to draft a plan for the international control of atomic energy. Acheson and his committee had named a board of consultants headed by David Lilienthal, the future chairman of the United States Atomic Energy Commission, and including the most eminent of American atomic scientists, Robert Oppenheimer, to formulate a set of proposals. It was the latter's ideas which dominated the report. Its conclusions provided the foundation of the Baruch Plan.

The report began with the premise that uranium was indispensable to the production of the fissionable material necessary for both the peaceful and the military uses of atomic energy. Atomic activities could be divided into "safe" and "dangerous" ones, but the same nuclear fuel could be used either for "dangerous" atomic bombs or for "safe" electric power. A small reactor in a laboratory was harmless. Even a high-power reactor that used uranium in which the U-235 was below the concentration required for explosive purposes was relatively safe. Oppenheimer believed that fissionable materials could be "denatured" by adding a less fissionable isotope of uranium to highly fissionable uranium-235 and plutonium; thus the latter elements could be rendered useless for bomb production.[27] But this idea proved "unrealistic."[28] Thus there was a possibility of using atomic energy for fruitful purposes. Unfortunately, nuclear fuel was also the key element in atomic bombs. Once it had sufficient fissionable material, any state could easily manufacture the casing and detonating mechanism required for an atomic weapon. Controlling atomic energy thus boiled down to regulating the way nuclear fuel was used.

One method was to leave the development of atomic energy in the hands of individual nations, which would undertake only to use it for peaceful purposes, and to institute a system of international inspection to ensure that there was no cheating. The weaknesses of this approach lay in the difficulty of detecting uranium mining (so that it was impossible to monitor the amount of raw material each nation would possess) and the possibility of new ways of refining the raw material into nuclear fuel. Oppenheimer feared that national rivalries would cause each nation to operate as close to actual evasion as possible. There was no way of knowing the purpose for which a nation undertook atomic development. "It's very hard to tell," he wrote, "whether a man is mining uranium because he is interested in cancer or interested in war." The way to escape this difficulty was to have a situation where "all those critical activities ... essential for going from the mine to the weapon, are not to be conducted by nations."[29]

The Acheson-Lilienthal Report therefore proposed to eliminate the national right to produce nuclear fuel. Instead, an international agency would own or control the supplies of uranium, construct and operate all atomic reactors and separation plants, and conduct unlimited research activity. This did not mean that the agency alone would produce atomic energy. There was certainly room as well for either governments or private companies to conduct "safe" atomic activities that would be licensed and inspected by the international agency to ensure that their purposes were peaceful.

The report offered a way to accommodate domestic political considerations. It would meet the widespread liberal sentiment that, in principle, atomic bombs should be done away with. At the same time, to satisfy those suspicious of the Soviet Union, the United States government would hang on to its bomb until it decided it was safe to do without it. "That decision," wrote the historians of the United States Atomic Energy Commission, would "have to be made by the United States ... in the light of the world situation."[30] The bomb would only be given up if there was an end to the Cold War and an elimination of mistrust between the superpowers or a build-up of conventional arms by the United States sufficient to match the armed might of the Soviet Union. Acheson believed that the report combined a "broad internationalist position with safeguards against the abuse of that position by any other country which might have unfriendly ... or at least negative intentions." He arranged to have it published to cut the ground "from under the feet of the more reactionary, nationalistic elements" who rejected giving up the atomic bomb under any circumstances. In the context of American opinion, he was quite right to regard it as an "intelligent and liberal" analysis.[31]

Canadian diplomats were very excited by the report. Because of the Chalk River plant, they knew something of the practical difficulties of operating a system of control.[32] George Ignatieff reported that Norman Robertson, Lester Pearson, Charles Ritchie, and Hume Wrong had all shown "an unqualified enthusiasm"[33] for the report. The cabinet's provisional instructions of 7 June guiding McNaughton's approach to the first meeting of the AEC stated that the Acheson-Lilienthal Report was the "most constructive and imaginative approach yet made towards a long-term policy on the international control of atomic energy"[34] and ordered him to support it. McNaughton himself agreed with this judgment.[35] One reason that he would be so dedicated and zealous in supporting the American proposals for international control was that he sincerely believed that they offered the best chance for dealing with the problem.

The Acheson-Lilienthal Report promised a civilized and rational solution to preventing atomic energy from being used for military purposes. To Pearson, who had seen the nationalist movements of the thirties run amok, it seemed a portent of a new era in world development in which selfish and narrow national interests would give way to international co-operation for the common good. In addition, Canada as a nation would gain more prestige in the international community. Presumably any international authority would be under the direction of a United Nations body on which Canada would have a seat. Because of the fortuitous circumstance of its uranium resources and atomic expertise, Canada might expect to enjoy a substantial influence in an agency of enormous international importance.

McNaughton's instructions also advised him on the conduct of relations with the United States and the United Kingdom in the AEC. Because of its industrial strength and power, the United States would "call the tune" in the commission – in the end, its policy would be decisive. This was not to say that Canada should "slavishly" follow American policies, but "we shall not wish to go further or faster" than the United States and the United Kingdom were prepared to go in advocating international control. McNaughton should avoid the Australian tactic of trying to mediate between the Russians on the one hand and the British and Americans on the other. "Such an initiative," warned the instructions, "would be resented by the British and the Americans as an irresponsible piece of meddling. It will be made use of by the Russians for their own purposes." Obviously, in so far as Canada had "constructive suggestions" to make, these would be designed to make the Western case more effective and not specifically to bring the two sides together.[36]

THE BARUCH PLAN

On 18 March President Truman had appointed Bernard Baruch, a 75-year-old businessman who enjoyed great esteem with the Senate, to be the American representative to the AEC. With Truman's approval, he made a few but significant changes to the Acheson-Lilienthal design. The most critical was his proposal to punish violators of the plan and to deprive the five permanent powers in the Security Council of the right to use the veto to escape such reprisal.

On 14 June Baruch revealed the American plan to the first meeting of the AEC. It proposed the creation of an International Atomic Development Authority to control the development and use of atomic energy. The authority would either manage or own all atomic energy activities which were potentially dangerous to world security. It would have the power to control, inspect, and licence all other atomic activities. It would also be responsible for being in the forefront of research to develop atomic energy for peaceful purposes. Only after the means to control atomic energy had been agreed upon and put into effect, along with a system for "condign punishment" for violations of the rules of control, would the manufacture of atomic bombs stop and existing ones be destroyed. At that point the authority would be in complete charge of all existing nuclear technology. Central to the plan was the proposition that none of the five permanent powers in the Security Council should be able to use the veto to protect itself from punishment for breaking its word not to develop or use atomic energy for destructive purposes.[37]

In the end the Baruch Plan would be totally rejected by the Soviet Union. The Russians apparently believed that the board of member-nations running the authority would be dominated by the United States. Thus, an American-controlled agency would dictate the pace of Soviet atomic development, gain enormous knowledge about natural resources in the USSR, and open up the entire country to a malign Western influence. Foreign inspectors might reveal facts about Soviet military capabilities which would undermine its security. As a Soviet official would put it in October 1946, when explaining his government's opposition to the Baruch Plan, the Soviet Union wished the "freedom to pursue its own policies in complete freedom and without any interference or control from outside."[38]

The Soviet Union would also be concerned by the proposal that the plan be instituted by stages. Only after the United States was satisfied that the system of control and punishment was in place, would it stop building atomic bombs. Even if the United States kept its word, it would still have its plants for producing nuclear fuel as well as the necessary expertise to build bombs, in contrast to the USSR which long before would have been deprived of any capacity to produce an atomic bomb. The USSR's atomic military inferiority would be perpetuated. If a crisis erupted between the two superpowers, the Americans could simply begin to manufacture the atomic bombs they needed. Thus the Americans would continue to wield a potential atomic threat to the security of the Soviet Union. In addition, it was far from certain that the United States would destroy its atomic bombs. The Baruch Plan did not propose a timetable that would be agreed to by all contracting parties. The Americans were to make this decision on their own. The Russians were being asked to run the risk of having their atomic development controlled from outside and to abandon their efforts to catch up in atomic might to the United States in return for an American promise to disarm which they had no guarantee would be kept.

Finally, the Soviet Union believed that giving up its veto in one area would set a dangerous precedent. It counted on its veto for protection within the United Nations from the proposals of the American-led majority. Surrendering it would be tantamount to weakening the power of the Security Council to determine what should be done with a country that transgressed the proposed regulations. The system of condign punishment for violations might have sinister consequences. According to Baruch, a violation might be as major as the actual possession of an atomic bomb or as minor as doing atomic research without a licence. The Russians believed that the Baruch Plan would make it easy for hostile capitalist countries to claim that the Soviet Union had violated the agreement and provide a handy legal pretext to launch a war against it. Baruch's statement did not specify what kind of sanctions he had in mind as punishment, but since the American army in March 1946 was down to some 400,000 men, the Soviet Union might be pardoned for thinking that it would be a pre-emptive atomic strike. Walter Lippmann could see why the Soviet Union objected to the veto clause. "No great power," he wrote, "will sign an agreement saying that the other nations may make war on it." Evidently he believed that the overall Baruch proposal was foolish, for he observed: "The UN charter is silent on what must be done if great powers violate agreements for the reason that the only thing that can be done is war."[39]

Canada's diplomats liked the Baruch idea of an international atomic authority but had grave doubts about the proposals on punishment and the veto. Their views on Baruch himself only reinforced this scepticism. Pearson believed that Baruch was inflexible and impervious to advice from the professionals at the State Department.[40] The Canadians knew that Acheson had little confidence in Baruch; indeed, he was to tell the Canadian minister in Washington that he would accept no responsibility for policies put forward by Baruch,[41] an extraordinary comment for a civil servant to make about one of his country's official policies. The talk of enforcement was "really paper talk";[42] the only "effective" punishment of a great power meant war.[43] Acheson believed the veto proposals "added nothing to the treaty and were almost certain to wreck any possibility of Russian acceptance of one."[44]

The statement which McNaughton had intended to make at the AEC merely supported the principle of the international control of atomic energy. But Baruch's proposals for sanctions against violators and the removal of the veto evoked considerable discussion and criticism. Both McNaughton and Pearson believed that the emphasis on the veto was "unwise" and that "it was causing concern to the State Department."[45] External Affairs believed that the Baruch statement opened up very difficult questions which might affect the entire structure of the United Nations. The abandonment of the veto for atomic questions but its retention for others would create a double standard, difficult to maintain. Then, too, how could the proposed authority take action against illegal activity by a nation bent on aggression unless it received atomic bombs from the United States in addition to manufacturing its own?[46] It might also have asked where the authority would get the air force to deliver them. Clearly External Affairs thought the whole sanctions proposal ill conceived.

Pearson set out to find some way of counteracting Baruch's "over emphasis"[47] on the veto issue. He suggested an additional paragraph in the Canadian statement that would urge the AEC to concentrate on creating the international authority itself and the principles and practices which should "govern its work" before discussing the questions of sanctions and vetoes which were "not ... primarily the problems of the Commission."[48] The McNaughton statement to the AEC on 19 June followed this line. It endorsed the principles underpinning the Baruch Plan but suggested that the commission "should not concern [itself] unduly over the procedure whereby the decisions of the proposed International Atomic Development Authority should be taken." Instead the AEC should concentrate on the proposals necessary to bring the authority into being. Baruch had failed to indicate where or how the AEC should begin its work and McNaughton suggested that it might start with the first point in the mandate given it by the United Nations the previous January: the development of proposals for the exchange of basic scientific information for peaceful purposes.[49] At the meeting of the AEC on 25 June Canada formally endorsed the principles of the Baruch Plan; nevertheless its diplomats retained considerable doubts about the wisdom of the sanction/veto proposals and would continue to make serious efforts to alter these aspects of the Baruch Plan.

THE SOVIET PLAN

Meanwhile, on 19 June, Andrei Gromyko, on behalf of the Soviet Union, offered his resolutions. Although he ignored the Baruch

Plan, he made it clear that the Soviet Union would resist any tampering with the veto. His main proposal was an agreement that the manufacture and use of atomic weapons be prohibited. All nuclear stocks were to be destroyed within three months after the agreement was signed. Any violation of this agreement was to be considered a crime against humanity. Within six months after the agreement was in force national legislation would be passed to provide severe punishment for violators. Although the Soviet Union agreed to the principle of supervision and control, it provided no details on what form these would take. Furthermore, the agreement to prohibit atomic bombs was to precede discussion of these issues. Gromyko also proposed the establishment of two committees: one to work out the means of exchanging scientific information and the other to develop control measures, including sanctions, to ensure the outlawing of atomic bombs. The effect of the Soviet plan would have been to improve its military position at the expense of the United States. The main means of United States defence, the atomic bomb, would have been destroyed. Moreover, the Soviet Union was asking that this be done without offering the Americans any guarantees that it would not begin manufacturing atomic bombs.

Pearson was concerned about the evident impasse between the two superpowers. In a telegram from Washington, he wondered whether the West ought not accept the Soviet proposition to outlaw atomic bombs. Such a convention would meet the Russian demands up to a certain point and perhaps persuade them that it was worthwhile discussing the Baruch Plan. The United States would, of course, retain its atomic bombs – otherwise the Russians would maintain their overwhelming military advantage in Europe. Still, a purely declaratory banishment of the atomic bomb while not giving them up would be somewhat analogous to nations retaining their poison gas although agreeing to prohibit gas warfare. Because the Russians omitted international sanctions from their plan and relied on good faith and national punishment, "they could not logically argue that the above proposal for prohibition without immediate destruction of bombs was valueless." But this rather ingenious proposal received short shrift from his superiors at External Affairs. Wrong, the associate under-secretary, thought that it "would deprive the United States of most of the influence of the possession of the atomic bomb as a deterrent." Robertson, the under-secretary, maintained that renouncing atomic war would leave the United States open to the demand that it not only destroy its bombs but also "disclose the processes for the production of plutonium on a substantial scale."[50] Yet, as the editors of the *Bulletin of the Atomic*

Scientists, pointed out: "The actual 'making of bombs' is such a minor part of the procedure leading from raw materials to finished bombs, that [the] United States could agree to Gromyko's request to stop assembling bombs and still retain practically all the advantages she has as far as atomic armaments are concerned – advantages which stem first from the possession of large plants producing fissionable materials and second, from the know-how of this production and of the bomb assembly."[51] But American public opinion would prevent United States negotiators from making any concessions that differed from the Baruch Plan.

Pearson's keen interest in finding a way to induce the Soviet Union to consider seriously American proposals for controlling atomic energy was in line with the two main objectives of Canadian atomic diplomacy in the late forties: keep the Soviet Union at the negotiating table and encourage it to accept the Baruch Plan. Compromise between the superpowers was difficult because of deepening mutual distrust. If the Russians believed that the United States desired a monopoly in atomic bombs, George Kennan, the director of Policy Planning Staff for the State Department, was equally convinced that the USSR wished to "turn the tables on us and to produce a situation in which the Soviet Union, rather than the United States, would be the sole power able to use atomic energy in war."[52] Then, too, each gained military strength from the deadlock. The failure of the USSR to agree to the Baruch Plan left the Americans free to increase their atomic military arsenal, a development their strategic planners considered vital, given the weak state of their conventional forces. Stalin may have doubted that the atomic bomb was the ultimate weapon, but he would not have wished for any constraints on the Soviet ability to catch up with the United States in the atomic race. The proposals that each nation advanced were also of great advantage politically. The Soviet insistence that atomic bombs had to be destroyed before control and inspection could be considered allowed the Russians to claim that because of imperialist greed the Americans would not give up these horrible weapons that threatened global destruction. The United States, in maintaining the need for an international authority to have access to Soviet territory before it would consider destroying its atomic bombs, was able to play on the theme of the wickedness of a closed communist totalitarian state. Each believed that its proposals not only strengthened its security but also enhanced its relative political strength. With such benefits it was no wonder that each would cling to its basic propositions for the next eight years. Neither Truman nor Stalin appears to have believed that eliminating atomic bombs was either possible or even desirable. At any rate the issue mattered so little to them that their respective positions were presented by minor spokesmen. This lack of commitment meant that there was no real bargaining, as had taken place during the war between the Soviet Union and the United States at Teheran, Yalta, or Potsdam. Each side merely continued to present its position for the public record. The consequence of this fierce national rivalry was that mankind missed its only opportunity to eliminate nuclear weapons – a possibility which existed then because they had not yet been integrated into national military strategies. The next set of serious negotiations would begin with the premise that nuclear weapons were here to stay – the only option left was how to control them.

MCNAUGHTON AT WORK
IN THE COMMITTEES

The mandate of the AEC was to offer the Security Council advice on how to reconcile these conflicts. At its meeting on 25 June the commission constituted itself a working committee that would meet in closed session to prepare a first draft of a general plan for the international authority. A few days later it appointed a sub-committee – made up of France, Mexico, the United States, the Soviet Union, and the United Kingdom under the chairmanship of the Australian representative, Herbert Evatt – to work out a skeleton outline of a system for control and development of atomic energy. Between 1 and 11 July this sub-committee held five informal meetings. The highlights of these were Gromyko's insistence that the AEC ought to agree to outlaw the atomic bomb and a fuller elaboration by the United States delegate of the American plan. In other words, the two sides rehearsed their arguments again. As Canada was not a member of the sub-committee, McNaughton contributed nothing to the discussion. On 12 July Evatt informed the working committee that while the majority of the sub-committee agreed with the United States proposals, they had not been able to win over Gromyko. Evatt proposed that work should proceed by setting up two committees (with all AEC members represented on each): one was to deal with the political problems involved with the control of atomic weapons and the other would examine its scientific aspects.[53]

The latter committee would be called the Scientific and Technical Committee. The level of conflict between the two sides is well illustrated by the inability of the AEC to agree even on a name that would define the task of the other committee. In desperation, Evatt decided to call it Committee 2. After their first organizational meeting on 17 July, each delegation was to catalogue the subjects that Committee 2 should consider. The outline which Canada proposed was designed to place the emphasis on "possible areas of agreement rather than fixed attitudes of disagreement" which had been so painfully evident in the earlier meetings of the sub-committee. After McNaughton and his colleagues drew up their list, they discussed it for five hours with their American counterparts who "welcomed the idea of further co-operative efforts of this kind on an informal basis."[54] Here was the beginning of a pattern; throughout the coming years in the AEC and later in the Disarmament Commission we shall find Canadian diplomats eager to talk things over with their allies, especially with the United States, to ensure that the West would present a united front to the Soviet Union.

The second meeting of Committee 2 on 24 July discussed the establishment of an international development authority. This furnished Gromyko with the perfect opportunity to attack the Baruch Plan. He asserted that the powers of the proposed authority could not be reconciled with national sovereignty. He complained that the United States wished the authority to be independent of the Security Council. He reiterated his objection to the elimination of the veto. He announced that the Soviet Union could not accept the American proposals "either as a whole or in their separate parts."[55] McNaughton nonetheless remained optimistic. He reported to External Affairs that although Gromyko had rejected an autonomous international authority or any limitations on the powers of the Security Council, "he had not closed the door on negotiations." The United States had put forward its views on the relationship between the authority and the United Nations prematurely; consequently, Gromyko was obliged by his instructions to reject the proposal. At an informal meeting with representatives from France, Australia, and the United States, McNaughton had therefore proposed that "we should now try to seek out an area of agreement by discussion in committees of the detailed aspects of the plan and not to continue emphasizing differences in prepared statements which separate the United States and Soviet positions."[56]

Two days later Gromyko returned to the attack. Again he proposed to outlaw the production and use of atomic weapons. Existing stocks should be destroyed. If all countries agreed that atomic weapons should not be used, why not prohibit them? Individual violators should be dealt with by national legislation and countries who broke the agreement by the Security Council. The Americans were now in a quandary. They were worried about how this dead-lock would affect the forthcoming Paris Conference to consider the peace treaties for Italy, Hungary, Bulgaria, Romania, and Finland. Since they had announced the Baruch Plan with great fanfare, they could not allow the work of the commission to end in failure. Yet they could not accept Gromyko's argument that inspections and vio-lations were matters for each country to decide. McNaughton ad-vised them to give Gromyko an opportunity to explain his proposals and to "lead him gradually to recognize that they were not in accord with the full terms of reference of the Commission as de-fined in the Assembly resolution unless they were accompanied by safeguards."[57]

At the next meeting of Committee 2 on 31 July, McNaughton asked Gromyko whether an agreement without safeguards would ease the natural anxiety of countries faced with the possibility of a crippling attack. He thought the Soviet proposal implied the estab-lishment of safeguards, and he wondered what specific measures they had in mind. But Gromyko maintained that the ultimate guar-antee lay in the desire of member-states to co-operate if they wished to maintain international peace and security. He went on to assert that the importance of the idea of inspection was greatly "exag-gerated." Complaints about violations could be taken not only to the national government but to the Security Council itself. He went on to define the American position as one of telling the world to accept their plans or they would not conclude a convention outlawing atomic bombs. Their attitude, he insisted, was neither right nor lawful: "Public opinion and the peoples of the world will not understand the reasons for refusing to conclude a convention as proposed by the Soviet government."[58]

In McNaughton's view, the Soviet Union seemed to be sending mixed signals. He was gratified that they agreed that international action might be necessary to constrain some nation from secretly preparing to use the atomic bomb. In case of violation Gromyko maintained that the Security Council should have the power to put an "aggressor in his place and punish him." Although he was not prepared to give details of exactly how this process would work, he did concede that the Council ought to act according to a system of specific recommendations prepared in advance. McNaughton be-lieved that this acceptance of Security Council action against a possible aggressor left room for more bargaining. He was not overly concerned about the possibility that the Russians were accepting international action by the Council on the understanding that they would retain their veto. What worried him was the apparently fixed

Soviet belief that inspection as a measure of control was "not in conformity with the principle of national sovereignty of States."[59] Canada's diplomats had come to believe that inspection was critical to guarantee an agreement to disarm. For the next half-dozen years Canada's criticism of Soviet atomic policies would focus on this issue. And Canadian hopes for an agreement would never die because from time to time the Soviet Union would drop tantalizing hints that it was prepared to be a little more open on this matter.

By early August the practical question of the value of carrying on discussion in Committee 2 arose. The superpowers were clearly at loggerheads. Publicly, they were both on the record as wishing to abolish atomic weapons but they disagreed on the necessary safeguards. Because of the need to court world public opinion, neither could afford to shatter its image as a peace-loving nation by breaking off the talks. McNaughton reported on 5 August that the Americans were especially anxious not to allow the Soviet Union to make any claim that its proposals had not been given "the most thorough consideration."[60] Fortunately, there was a means of continuing the negotiations without engaging in sterile controversy. On 30 July Committee 2 had agreed to ask the Scientific and Technical Committee to report on whether effective controls on atomic energy were possible and if so by what methods they could be achieved. After one more futile meeting on 6 August, Committee 2 unanimously agreed to wait until there was a report from their scientific advisers before meeting again.

The work of the Scientific and Technical Committee proved to be one of the few successes of the AEC. The scientists had the happy thought of ignoring politics and confining themselves to answering the question of whether control of atomic energy was technically feasible. They agreed with the central premise of the Acheson-Lilienthal Report that nuclear fuel could be used for both peaceful and military purposes. The difficulty was to prevent the manufacture of bombs if plutonium or separated U-235 was available. However they concluded that they did not find "any basis in the available scientific facts for supposing that effective control is not technologically feasible."[61] By 3 September the committee's report was ready. McNaughton liked everything about it. It justified the views on control expressed by the Baruch Plan but had the political advantage of being an AEC report. But the Soviet scientist, who personally had no objection to the report, possessed no authority to give formal approval. This caused McNaughton considerable anxiety for the next three weeks because he believed that further progress in the broader negotiations depended on whether the Soviet Union accepted this report. "The importance of the Soviet agreement," he explained, "lies primarily in the psychological consideration that we would have, as a starting point of discussion, an agreement as to a statement of the basic scientific facts."[62] Soviet assent finally came on 26 September. The next day McNaughton reported to External Affairs with obvious satisfaction that "there was general enthusiasm at the unexpected Soviet acceptance of the Report."[63] At the very least the Soviet leaders were sending a message that they wished the negotiations in the AEC to continue.

In the middle of August McNaughton had assumed the chairmanship of the AEC for a month. He had won the support of the Advisory Panel on Atomic Energy for the view that Canada's main aim must remain the reconciliation of the opposing views of the USSR and the United States, but that if a deadlock between the two became inevitable, it would be better if this occurred at the Paris Peace Conference or the coming General Assembly than in the commission. Keeping the AEC going and Canada's role within it was important. The panel failed to discuss the genuine security problems that the Baruch Plan presented to the Soviet Union; no doubt it could not even conceive of an American atomic attack on the USSR. Instead, it maintained that the problem within the commission "resolved itself into a question of whether the Russians would accept the U.S. proposals for control." Having agreed that the AEC negotiations must be kept alive, the panel reasoned that this might be accomplished by placing the problem "on a functional rather than political basis."[64] The trick would be to confine the discussion to a technical analysis of control (as the Scientific Committee was then doing) and eschew political debate.

The experience of the Scientific Committee had shown that agreement was possible if political considerations were excluded. After consulting with the United States, McNaughton therefore proposed to other delegates to the AEC that Committee 2 set up an informal procedure to determine what specific safeguards were necessary at each stage of the production and use of atomic energy to prevent the illegal manufacture of weapons. He hoped that this would build up a "climate of opinion among the twelve nations favorable to a solution along the lines of the U.S. proposals."[65] In any case, these findings would help educate the rest of the world on the steps necessary to achieve foolproof controls. All the members of Committee 2 accepted his proposal on 8 October and a week later the work was under way.

The committee met informally nineteen times before convening in formal session on 18 and 19 December. It completed its report on 26 December. McNaughton was obviously happy with its work: it was now possible to describe "with some precision and in detail" what safeguards were necessary to prevent the misuse of nuclear materials.[66] McNaughton had good reason to be pleased. The main findings, in addition to specifying in detail the nature of the controls that were needed, also lent support to the American plan: it found that a single international agency must be responsible for operating this system of safeguards although it did not suggest how it would come into being, what powers it would have, and how these would be enforced. McNaughton was also happy that the Soviet Union had continued to work in the committee. The Soviet diplomats must have been in a quandary. In October Stalin had conceded that it was necessary to have strict international control of atomic energy. Yet to offer support for an agency to monitor that control might raise awkward questions about its powers to inspect atomic facilities in national territories. As the deadline for completion approached and the thrust of the report became clearer, the Soviet delegation opted to solve this dilemma by ceasing to be active collaborators and instead adopting a posture of non-participation. They did not take part in the final approval of the draft report of the committee on 26 December – but neither did they walk out.

THE GENERAL ASSEMBLY MEETING

Gromyko's unexpected agreement to allow Committee 2 to continue its work seems to have been only one of several encouraging signs from the Soviet Union. That autumn Stalin was emphasizing co-operation with the West.[67] Molotov was helpful at the Council of Foreign Ministers meeting in New York, and as a consequence there was agreement on peace treaties for Italy, Bulgaria, Finland, Romania, and Hungary. And McNaughton reported that Gromyko had even observed that it was a pity that the United States and the Soviet Union had not met for direct talks before the AEC began work.[68] At the end of October Stalin had conceded that "a strong international control is needed."[69] Up to this point the Soviet view on this issue had been in doubt. Gromyko had hinted that control might be assigned to each national government. But the task of the AEC was to find a way by which competing nations could co-operate to control atomic energy. At the very least this implied some sort of international control. Had Stalin not accepted this principle, it would have been very difficult for the AEC to fulfil its mandate.

Nevertheless, on 29 October Molotov attacked the Baruch Plan ferociously while introducing a Soviet disarmament resolution in the

United Nations General Assembly. But in late November he presented a resolution to the First (Political) Committee that called for the prohibition of the atomic bomb and provision for establishing, within the framework of the Security Council, two special organs of inspection to control the reduction of arms and the military use of atomic energy. He later dropped this resolution in favour of an American one that called for the early establishment of the international control of atomic energy with effective safeguards by way of inspection and other means "to protect complying States against the hazards of violations and evasions."[70]

After more bargaining, there finally emerged on 14 December a disarmament resolution that received unanimous support in the General Assembly. The United States had agreed that the international system of control should operate through the Security Council and that the objective of eliminating atomic bombs was urgent. For its part the Soviet Union agreed to work through the AEC and to talk about safeguards and inspection and had conceded that the proposed control agency would derive its authority from a treaty ratified by member-states and not from the Security Council. At bottom, this was a compromise on the major issue of how much restraint the Soviet Union should exercise over the work of the proposed international control agency by means of its veto in the Security Council. What had not been decided was whether the new agency would begin its work by prohibiting atomic bombs or by setting up an efficient system of control by inspection and other safeguards. But this would be a future concern; for the present, United Nations members could take pride in a notable achievement.

Canada's attitude towards these resolutions reflected its commitments to an effective international agency as well as to keeping the Soviet Union at the negotiating table. It both criticized and lent support to the Soviet position. Canadian diplomats proclaimed their unhappiness about the Soviet proposal to prohibit the production and use of atomic energy for military purposes on grounds that it might be taken to mean that no attention should be paid to atomic energy produced ostensibly for peaceful purposes. Canada wished the USSR to agree that control over the whole process was necessary to ensure that atomic energy was only being used for peaceful purposes. It urged that the AEC (which the Soviet Union had ignored in its resolution) should be allowed to complete its task of investigating how this could be done efficiently. Molotov had proposed to give the powers of inspection to the commissions that were to supervise conventional disarmament and the prohibition of atomic weapons, but they were to work "within the framework of the

Security Council." Did that mean that the Soviet Union could veto inspection of its own territory? To counter this, Canada proposed a commission of control possessing the "freedom of access to inspect anywhere in any state."[71] Molotov would not accept the Canadian desire for freedom of access to the Soviet Union. This would be a difficult and contentious issue for the future. But he did take a small step by agreeing that the veto would not apply to the day-to-day workings of the control agency.

At the same time External Affairs did give full support to the Soviet determination to retain its veto against sanctions. In the Assembly debate, the secretary of state for external affairs maintained that eliminating the veto would not be realistic. He reiterated the generally held view that if the situation were such that sanctions needed to be applied to a great power, it would mean total war whether or not the opposition to the aggressor initially took the form of a veto. Sanctions could only be applied through the use of force, and the "use of force against a great power means war."[72] This public declaration was a calculated and open attack by Canada on one of the main principles underpinning the Baruch Plan supported by the United States.

The United States resolution also presented a problem for Canada. Its second paragraph contained a recommendation that the "Security Council give first consideration to the report which the Atomic Energy Commission will make to the Security Council before December 31st, 1946." McNaughton feared that this would encourage the American delegation to the AEC to press for the endorsement of the Baruch Plan including the establishment of an international authority although the commission had not yet even discussed this concept except in the vaguest terms.[73] Other Canadian diplomats at the United Nations agreed with this objection, but they had another practical reason for wanting this wording changed. In view of its opposition to the veto proposal, the Soviet Union would hardly endorse a resolution that could be taken to mean unqualified support for the Baruch Plan. However, the United States agreed to replace the offending clause by the words "expedite consideration of the reports which the Atomic Energy Commission will make to the Security Council."[74] The use of the plural "reports" meant that the American plan might be only one among others.

On 4 December the Political Committee of the United Nations appointed a sub-committee of twenty states including Canada to draft a resolution that would find unanimous acceptance. The main amendment which Canada persuaded others to accept was a reference to the necessity of a treaty providing not only for the prohibition of atomic weapons but also for sufficient control over the production of atomic energy to ensure that it was used for peaceful purposes. Throughout the session Canada had worked hard to ensure that the superpowers respected the integrity of the AEC. It had adopted a sensible and flexible attitude towards the veto. If Canada was an effective participant, it was because the session itself was comparatively harmonious; both superpowers still wished to explore the possibilities of constructive action. When the session had opened on 23 October, Canada had not expected the Assembly to achieve unanimous agreement on this important first step towards disarmament. It therefore welcomed the Russian desire for some sort of accommodation. "I was particularly impressed and heartened," wrote McNaughton to External Affairs, "by the remarks of Vishinsky reminding the committee of the pronouncements made by Stalin, Molotov and himself in respect to international inspection and ending with his emphatic statement, 'We don't go back on our word.' "[75] The Canadians emerged from this session of the General Assembly in a positive mood.

THE AEC'S FIRST REPORT

Despite all these positive developments the possibility that the AEC would unanimously endorse the Baruch proposals remained a worry to the end. The Soviet Union was hostile to the plan. The Canadian tactic, as we have seen, was to postpone the decision as long as possible, hoping that a better political climate would induce the USSR to change its mind. But Baruch became impatient. On 17 September he wrote to Truman, reviewing the differences between the Soviet Union and the United States, and proposed that the plan should be brought to a vote within the AEC in a reasonable time. This should be done rather quickly because three supporters of the American position – Egypt, Mexico, and the Netherlands – would be leaving the Security Council and therefore the commission on 1 January. Baruch did not expect the negotiations with the Soviet Union to be successful. On 5 November Truman gave the American delegation permission to press the AEC to approve the original Baruch Plan. And so Baruch had his way. On 30 December the AEC decided to send what was essentially the Baruch Plan on to the Security Council. Ten members, including Canada, voted for this motion; only the Soviet Union and Poland abstained.[76]

This episode has been of considerable interest to Canadian historians because Canada had publicly disagreed in the General Assembly debate with one clause in the Baruch Plan, namely, its insistence that each permanent member of the Security Council agree to give up its veto against sanctions being applied in the event it violated the atomic treaty.[77] Canadian diplomats believed this proposal would have only harmful effects. If a situation developed in which sanctions were required against a great power, they would be useless since the crisis could only be resolved by war. Yet retaining the veto clause gave the USSR an excuse to disown the whole Baruch Plan while avoiding the onus of not supporting international control of atomic energy. As the 1 January deadline approached, Canadian diplomats had gone to extraordinary lengths to dissuade the United States from what they considered to be a foolish step. Rumours of the dispute had even found their way into the press. In the end Prime Minister King had intervened and instructed McNaughton not to press his views on the veto any further. Consequently, in the final vote Canada had fully endorsed the American plan. King's policy of placing allied unity first had prevailed. If the others had had their way, Canada would have continued to oppose Baruch.

All along, McNaughton had feared the negative effects on the AEC and even on the United Nations itself if the USSR were offended. He had hoped that elimination of the reference to the veto might encourage the Soviet Union to vote for the rest of the Baruch Plan. The USSR would never have endorsed a scheme calling for the elimination of the veto, but it was unrealistic to think that this was the only obstacle to winning Soviet support. The USSR had fundamental objections to an international authority in the first place and even more to giving it unimpeded access to Soviet territory. Even had there been no reference to the veto, it is highly unlikely that the USSR would have supported an international authority equipped with inspection rights. Perhaps the Americans insisted on retaining the veto proposal as the only means of persuading the United States Senate to agree to a potential treaty prohibiting atomic weapons. In any event, their intransigence provided the USSR with a handy means of justifying its suspicions about American intentions in the all-important propaganda war. Still, all was not lost. Gromyko had not voted against the AEC report. He had only abstained; the door remained open for negotiations. Yet McNaughton sensed that since the heady days of autumn prospects for agreement had receded. He noted, for example, that Gromyko's attempt in December to return to his June proposal of prohibiting atomic bombs was "rather disappointing in the light of the apparent progress in Soviet thought during the discussion on disarmament in the General Assembly."[78]

In his book on McNaughton, John Swettenham claimed that the
general told him that the veto question and the punishment clause
made the Baruch Plan "insincerity from beginning to end," that the
plan was only a sop to public opinion and a means to ensure that
the American monopoly would continue.[79] Others have assessed
McNaughton's activities as an intense effort to "mediate"[80] between
East and West. John Holmes speaks of "a dogged effort to meet the
needs of the Russians" and maintained: "The record of Canadian
policy in the United Nations Atomic Energy Commission indicates
the exhausting effort to avoid closing doors. McNaughton got himself into difficulties with the Americans by his efforts to avoid
putting the Russians on the spot. He told the Advisory Panel in
Ottawa on 23 September 1946 that his delegation's efforts had been
directed for the most part to seeking a rapprochement between the
United States and the USSR delegations and in getting the Americans to agree to a moderate and patient approach."[81] These activities of McNaughton might leave the impression that he was sceptical about the Baruch Plan itself and trying to find a compromise
between the fundamentally opposite approaches of the superpowers. This was not so. McNaughton strongly favoured the main
thrust of the Baruch Plan, differing only, as he said, over "some of
the details of his proposals."[82]

This is not to say that McNaughton was optimistic that the
Russians could be persuaded to accept it. He believed that the
Baruch Plan implied that the Soviet Union must surrender "a
sufficient degree of freedom of action in this field [of atomic energy]
in the interests of security."[83] Verification was essential but he
doubted that the USSR would accept outside inspection. The Soviet
Union, he explained, can maintain their "mood of exultation"
derived from defeating the Nazis only "through never permitting
through outside contact the Russian people to realize the standard
of living of the democratic world. Therefore there can be no
permitted penetration of the Eurasian continent by the democratic
countries. For this reason alone, Russia will never permit disarmament by inspection, since that inspection would mean foreign setups
within the limits of the Soviet border."[84]

McNaughton might not believe that the Russians would co-
operate; nevertheless, he was convinced that the essence of the
Baruch Plan – the control of the production and use of atomic
energy by an international agency of the United Nations was the
only guarantee against an uncontrolled atomic arms race. Thus in
opposing Baruch, McNaughton was not seeking a compromise between the principles guiding the atomic policies of the two powers.

He knew which side he was on. His interest was tactical; he advocated removal of the veto clause simply to make it easier for the Russians to accept the American plan.

Whether McNaughton would have continued to hold out against American pressure, had he been left on his own, is an academic question. The fact was that his political master, the prime minister, intervened. After the Washington Conference King had asserted quite rightly that international control of atomic energy could only be obtained through the agreement of the superpowers.[85] Evidently this judicious opinion had been altered the following year by his growing belief that "we are headed into an inevitable conflict which will mean either civil war or revolution ... or open conflict between East and West with Communism versus Capitalism or Atheism versus Christianity. The war will be in the nature of a religious war as well as class struggle and may result in a sort of Armageddon."[86] His perception of such an intense Cold War atmosphere with the two sides absolutely polarized worked to make him disregard the fine nuances of the Pearson-McNaughton diplomacy in favour of declaring himself openly to be on the side of the United States. On 30 December, the day of the final vote, he wrote in his diary: "Before waking I had an interesting dream. A very clear one. It was President Roosevelt – standing at full length but needing someone to support him. He beckoned to me to give him my arm and we walked together first of all across some carpeted floor and then down a number of steps and along a level and up some other steps. He was very pleasant and friendly and seemed anxious that others should see that we were very close together. When I wakened I thought of that vision. It seemed to me to be related to the stand that Mr St Laurent and I agreed upon on Saturday should be taken at the meeting of the atomic commission today, namely that no doubt should be left as to any power of veto making impossible the punishment of Russia ... should she be guilty of criminal acts against any other nation."[87]

King never seems to have understood that, veto or no veto, the Soviet Union would use military force to protect itself from being punished by the West for breaking an atomic treaty. This points to a factor which Canadian diplomats needed to take into account. Politicians might not be interested enough in atomic issues to make sophisticated judgments, but they set the limits within which their civil servants could act. In this case all atomic negotiations were to be subordinated to the need to preserve the alliance with the United States. This being his goal, King was happy about his intervention, especially when Pearson, who had become under-secretary of state of external affairs in September, told him that "the Americans had been greatly pleased with our decision to support the [Baruch] resolution; that they owed more to Canada than to any of the other countries for having brought everything into line ... We had been helpful too with Russia. Gromyko had abstained from voting and the Polish representative with him."[88] King also set a precedent. In the next decade Canada would never again challenge United States atomic policy publicly.

CHAPTER FOUR

The Propaganda Wars: Defending the Baruch Plan, 1947–49

Relations between East and West deteriorated steadily in the years following 1946, culminating in the outbreak of armed conflict in Korea. It is difficult to believe that either the United States or the Soviet Union had any hope of – or was really interested in – an agreement on nuclear disarmament at the conclusion of the AEC meetings of December 1946. In consequence, Bernard Baruch resigned on 4 January 1947 and the United States representative at the United Nations, Senator Warren Austin, became his country's representative on the commission. His deputy, responsible for the day-to-day work, was General Frederick Osborn. For the moment, at least, "one great state had a temporary monopoly that it would not surrender except on conditions that a second great state was wholly determined not to accept."[1] There had been no serious negotiations, no real bargaining, between the two sides in 1946. Andrei Gromyko and Bernard Baruch had not even met privately to exchange views. This pattern would continue for the next three years. Neither side would make any effort to "narrow the difference by negotiation."[2] Even had it wished to, there was little Canada could have done to bring the sides together. But Pearson and his colleagues showed little interest in such a role. Most of the energy of External Affairs in these years went to helping the United States build and justify its case for acceptance of the Baruch Plan. The blame for the impasse in negotiations was laid at the door of the Soviet Union. At the same time, however, Canada's diplomats attempted to moderate American criticism, lest the Soviet Union abandon the talks altogether and perhaps use their failure as an excuse to leave the United Nations itself.

1947

THE AEC'S SECOND REPORT

In February the Security Council turned to consider the first report of the AEC. Canada was not at this time a member of the Security Council, but General McNaughton was able to attend as an observer, and it was he who suggested that the next step should be a study of the functions and powers of the proposed International Control Agency (ICA). (This was the new name for the International Atomic Development Authority in the Baruch Plan.) He also said that he hoped the Soviet Union would speak frankly about its objections to the first report. Gromyko needed no encouragement. In two devastating speeches, he completely rejected its main thrust. He demanded the unconditional prohibition of atomic weapons. He complained that the powers of the ICA would limit the sovereignty of individual states. He insisted that the American proposal to constrain the right of a Security Council member to veto the imposition of sanctions contradicted the principles on which the United Nations was founded. Nevertheless, he offered to consider the report item by item and put forward twelve amendments.

Commenting on Gromyko's stand, George Ignatieff, McNaughton's adviser, pointed to three matters on which there were fundamental differences between the two sides – the use of the veto in relation to enforcement by the Security Council; the timing of the prohibition of atomic weapons; and the powers of the ICA and its relationship to the Security Council.[3] The secretary of state for external affairs would not be nearly so open in his report to Parliament in March on the arms control talks.[4] It is true that St Laurent quoted an American statement that accepted the objections to the American position on the veto that Canada had voiced in the General Assembly in December. But he failed to mention the reasons for Soviet unhappiness with the timing of the prohibition of atomic weapons or with the powers to be assigned to the ICA. These omissions could only reinforce the impression that the USSR was entirely unreasonable in its objections to the first report.

On 10 March the Security Council directed the AEC to continue its work and report back to the Council as quickly as possible. There were now two matters before the AEC: the proposed Soviet amendments to the first report and the elaboration of the functions and powers of the proposed ICA. It was agreed unanimously that the Working Committee should deal with the Soviet amendments and that Committee 2 should consider the structure of the ICA.

The work of these two committees may be briefly summarized. In the Working Committee, the Soviet amendments expressed that country's objections to the first report. They wished to preserve the veto. They wanted atomic bombs prohibited before any system of inspection was instituted. On these measures, the Soviet Union was outvoted by the Western members of the AEC. It had no better luck in Committee 2. The first report of the AEC had concluded that there must be an international agency responsible for a system of safeguards and controls, but it had made no specific recommendations on its powers. In its discussions in 1947, the committee concluded that the agency must own the nuclear fuel, the raw materials out of which it was produced, and the industrial plant that produced it. Despite Soviet objections, all these proposals would be adopted by the AEC on 11 September as its second report.[5] Canadian delegates were active in both committees, emphasizing that international inspection was absolutely necessary to any *meaningful* agreement on atomic energy as well as seeking to fulfil what the government believed was its responsibility to support the United States.

McNaughton had recognized in August 1946 that the issue of inspection might prove a major sticking point in negotiations. The Soviet amendments revived this worry. In the early discussions in the Working Committee, Gromyko asserted that individual nations should carry out the necessary control and inspection measures. McNaughton feared that this implied that states signing the treaty would not be subject to inspection by the proposed ICA. McNaughton told the committee that he failed to see how such a system of self-inspection would reassure other nations that "atomic war was not being prepared."[6] Other Western delegates also pressed Gromyko to be more specific, but while he continued to reiterate the need for strict international control and inspection he did not explain what he meant. McNaughton even went so far as to submit a written question as to whether the Soviet Union accepted the proposition that ICA inspectors would have "access to all countries"[7] to ensure that they were complying with the treaty, but Gromyko responded that the query was out of order because it was unrelated to the supervision of plants which was the item under discussion. The next week McNaughton again demanded that Gromyko explain what he meant by inspection. "I urged," he wrote his Ottawa superiors, "that we should concentrate on getting a precise understanding of the terms control and inspection."[8] Discussion of the third Soviet amendment, which was taken up by the Working Committee early in June, confirmed McNaughton's worst fears. It called for a treaty that outlawed atomic weapons with a system of international inspection to ensure compliance. But Gromyko ruled out any additional control mechanisms such as supervision and ownership by the proposed ICA. Once again McNaughton asked the Soviet spokesman to explain what he meant by inspection but once again Gromyko evaded the issue, saying this was a matter for discussion at a later date.[9]

Reporting to the Standing Commons Committee on External Affairs on 5 and 6 June, McNaughton explained why Canada believed inspection to be so crucial to the control of atomic energy. The Russians proposed to prohibit atomic bombs without effective inspection. The United States was being asked to give up its atomic bombs without any assurance that the Soviet Union would not soon be manufacturing their own. Soviet scientists knew how to build bombs, and there was no reason to believe that the USSR did not possess the uranium from which nuclear fuel could be produced. What upset McNaughton was Gromyko's stubborn refusal to explain what he meant by international inspection. Without this information the West was unable to judge whether the Soviet proposals made any sense. Gromyko was saying that there ought to be an international law that would compel the United States to disarm unilaterally and that if this was done, the USSR would be willing to talk about what it meant by international control and inspection.[10] Clearly, Gromyko's persistent failure to be more specific had increased McNaughton's distrust of Soviet motives. The general also wished to see atomic bombs abolished, but he understood that the United States would not give up its bombs without a system of inspection in place because to do so might put its own security – indeed the security of the West – at risk.

By early June, however, the Soviet authorities had come to accept that it was necessary to be much more explicit about their views on the international control of atomic energy. At a special meeting of the AEC on 11 June, Gromyko offered what would prove to be the Soviet Union's most complete statement on this matter.[11] It proposed the international control of facilities engaged in the mining and production of atomic materials. It called for an international control commission that would work within the framework of the Security Council and would carry out inspections of these facilities "periodically." If there were violations of the treaty, the control commission would make recommendations to the Security Council about the treatment of the transgressors.

Gromyko may have believed that the Soviet Union was making an important concession by accepting periodic inspections, but this proposal failed to satisfy the Western side. Ignatieff was surely speaking for more than Canada when he criticized the Soviet plan at an AEC meeting early in August. The proposed inspection procedure left nations able to do as they wished, subject only to periodic visits from the international commission; it ignored other vital safeguards such as giving the "operational and developmental functions" to an international agency. Periodic inspections could easily be manipulated and thus offered no protection against clandestine activities; they would merely amount to a routine accounting of what nuclear materials were in production or in use. The powers of the commission to redress any dangerous situation would be limited to advising the Security Council; there would be no assurance that their recommendations would be acted upon. All in all, this was a bad plan. There was nothing in it, concluded Ignatieff, that would prevent "a nation from accumulating and having at its ready disposal unlimited quantities of nuclear fuel, convertible at any time to atomic bombs."[12]

This criticism was justified. It is true that the USSR had now accepted the principle of international control by an international commission. It had even conceded that there ought to be "periodic" inspections. But the Soviet Union still feared yielding powers to a commission over which it would have no ultimate control. Under its own plan, each nation would continue to run its own nuclear facilities and govern the access which outside inspectors would enjoy to its mines and plants. Moreover, the Soviet Union continued to insist that there must be an agreement to outlaw atomic weapons before a treaty providing for a control system could even be considered. This procedure quite naturally failed to satisfy Western security needs. Canada's opinion was expressed in a resolution which it offered on 15 August – and which was accepted by ten members of the Working Committee. It stated that the Soviet proposals failed to provide for an effective system for the international control of atomic energy.

The discussions in the Working Committee had shown that Canada objected to the Soviet amendments, but some differences with the United States were revealed as well. The eighth Soviet amendment proposed to substitute the word "destruction" for the original term "disposal" with regard to the fate of existing atomic weapons. But Canada and some other countries preferred "disposal," arguing that nuclear fuel was too valuable to be destroyed. To meet these objections, Gromyko asked whether the other members of the committee would agree to the statement "that all atomic weapons should be destroyed, and the nuclear fuel used only for peaceful purposes." The United Kingdom immediately said "yes" followed by China, Australia, Canada, and Brazil. But the American representative complained that such a decision would prevent the control agency from having a supply of atomic bombs to deter an aggressor. Gromyko replied that the majority were agreed that atomic bombs should be destroyed, and his suggestion that a sub-committee be named to draft a resolution to this effect was accepted.[13]

This exchange created an awkward situation for Canada. Apparently the Americans were by no means committed to the destruction of atomic weapons, despite the 14 December resolution which had unanimously bound the United Nations to this principle. Yet McNaughton had recently reiterated to the Commons Committee the Canadian government's view that once the atomic energy treaty came into effect, stock of atomic bombs would be eliminated. He therefore asked for guidance from External Affairs on this matter. His superiors agreed with his interpretation of the United Nations resolution. They could also understand the American "reluctance to accept the principle of complete prohibition of atomic weapons," but "the difference between acceptance of the principle and signature on an Agreement is surely great enough, however, to make it worth while for the United States, at least for tactical reasons, to admit the principle."[14] For propaganda reasons, it would be better for the United States to stay true to the principle of prohibition; at the same time, it should be possible, with a little ingenuity, to avoid actually giving up their weapons. This indeed proved to be the case.

The Americans made considerable efforts to eliminate the differences between themselves and their allies.[15] They reiterated their readiness to dispose of atomic weapons. The Soviet Union wished this to be done soon after the treaty was signed; the others, including McNaughton, now argued, however, that the timing of the destruction of atomic bombs could not be decided in isolation from an agreement to ensure the peaceful use of nuclear fuel.[16] The sub-committee assigned to draft a resolution on the destruction of atomic weapons limited itself to reporting the deadlock between the Soviet Union and its other members who refused to approve the destruction of atomic weapons immediately subsequent to a treaty on atomic energy. Canada, like the others, was retreating from its previous position. American pressure had forced McNaughton to qualify his views on the destruction of atomic bombs.

In 1947 Committee 2's task was to determine the specific powers the new international agency ought to have. Its report proposed to clothe the agency with enormous ownership powers with respect to mining and nuclear fuel. Because of its substantial uranium deposits, Canada was apprehensive about these proposed ICA powers over mining. The promise of the peaceful use of atomic energy meant that the Canadian uranium mine, Eldorado, was a potential source of enormous wealth. The Baruch Plan proposed the agency exercise "dominion" over the world's supplies of uranium. This implied that it would decide the rate at which Canada would use up this valuable national resource – a situation about which the Advisory Panel on Atomic Energy had had considerable misgivings from the beginning.[17] It is probable that McNaughton, too, had doubted the practicability of such controls. Because it would be compelled to buy all the land which anyone claimed contained traces of uranium if it was to own all uranium mines, the ICA, as McNaughton noted, would "become the biggest owners of derelict real estate of any organization in the world."[18] In many of the mines it would administer, the uranium might be mixed with other metals such as gold and tungsten and this would greatly complicate the agency's work. To do a proper job would mean employing a large number of people and spending a great deal of money. The Americans were nevertheless giving serious consideration to the international ownership of mines; in his proposals of 5 December 1946, Baruch had left open this possibility. But there was considerable opposition from other countries; consequently, in its first report, the AEC concluded that the international ownership of mines was not mandatory.

By the end of the Committee 2 discussions the Americans agreed that the international ownership of the mines was not necessary, but they insisted that the agency take over ownership of the raw ore as soon as it was extracted from the ground. McNaughton had suggested that the ICA have the authority to set a maximum rate of production but not be able to force a nation to produce more than was economically sound. But he was not able to gain this concession. The United States was determined that the ICA should be able to set the rate of production to prevent nations from conserving this indispensable military resource and thus gaining a strategic advantage once the supplies of other countries were exhausted. The quota of raw material that each nation would be compelled to extract would be proportionate to its usable reserves. On the one hand, Canada would retain ownership of its mines, and the price it would receive for its uranium would be subject to market forces and bargaining. On the other hand, it would have given up control over the rate of production. St Laurent remained doubtful about such onerous controls. The secretary of state for external affairs drew a parallel between initiating the peaceful use of atomic energy and the discovery of electricity. In view of the enormous potential in the production of uranium, he was reluctant to accept any controls.[19] Yet in the end he agreed to support the plan. The advisory panel shared the same misgivings, but, as its chairman observed, "all members of the Panel, I think, have accepted the necessity of our going along with the U.S."[20]

Canada was an enthusiastic supporter of the main thrust of the second report of the AEC which was adopted on 11 September 1947 – namely, that mined raw materials, atomic facilities, and nuclear fuel should be owned by the international agency. In a world in which national rivalries might threaten the peace, it was dangerous to allow individual nations to own nuclear fuel. McNaughton believed that even the most comprehensive system of inspection could not guarantee that a nation might not manufacture atomic bombs. The only solution was to give the agency vast ownership powers over all phases of production. At the same time, the ICA, operating under the principles written into the treaty by participating nations, would not be free to act capriciously.

But this would not, of course, satisfy the USSR. The second report had practically ignored the whole matter of the prohibition of atomic weapons. Just as important, the powers of ownership given to the agency were incompatible with the Soviet view of national sovereignty. Indeed, Gromyko had asserted that the United States was building up under its control an international trust to dictate its will to the rest of the world on atomic matters. The Soviet Union was depending heavily on atomic energy to rebuild its war-shattered economy and catch up with the United States. Its requirements in this respect were tremendous. It feared that the Baruch Plan would interfere with its capacity to utilize atomic energy to the maximum extent and thus shackle the economy.

Gromyko had even warned small countries like Canada to beware of those who claimed that in the atomic age the concepts of national sovereignty and independence must be modified. But on this point Canada's representatives held different views. It was a key belief of Lester Pearson that there ought to be "a voluntary surrender of some measure of sovereignty to a world authority in the interest of peace and security."[21] McNaughton was equally clear that individual nations must give up some of their powers, although he was sensitive to the sacrifice each country was being asked to make. He declared that the power to be turned over to the agency controlling atomic energy must be the minimum required to assure security, that there must be "no undue interference"[22] with the economic and political life of any country. McNaughton's differences with Gromyko about the ownership of nuclear fuel were thus fundamental. He believed individual nations must give up some of their powers. He was convinced, as he told the Commons committee, "that the Soviets must be prepared with all other nations ... to relinquish some of their sovereignty and place that sovereignty ... in the hands of an international organization."[23] But the fact was that if Canada gave up some of its sovereignty, it would still be safe under the American atomic umbrella. If the USSR gave up some of its rights in the atomic field, it would lag behind in the manufacture of atomic weapons and thus place its security at risk.

After adopting its second report on 11 September, the AEC took a recess. The Security Council received the report but did not discuss it. During the meeting of the General Assembly which opened a few days later, the Soviet spokesman, Andrei Vyshinsky, attacked the United States with a four-point resolution condemning war-mongering. The fourth point proposed that the December 1946 resolution to do away with atomic arms be implemented. The Soviet resolution was voted down in the Political Committee. Instead, the Committee unanimously adopted a resolution co-sponsored by Canada, Australia, and France which condemned all propaganda that might disrupt the peace but made no reference to the control of atomic energy. There had been no debate on nuclear disarmament scheduled for the General Assembly. Nor were the Western allies anxious to begin one. They believed that there were so many issues confronting the Political Committee that the delegations would not have time to study the difficult questions raised by the AEC's second report, much less to understand them. Fortunately the Soviet Union seems to have felt the same way. There must have been a collective sign of relief when the Political Committee agreed to a Norwegian resolution to shelve the debate on atomic controls and simply to "note" the AEC report to the Security Council.

Although a confrontation in the General Assembly had been avoided, Canadian diplomats were apprehensive about whether the United States would continue to participate in the AEC negotiations. In his speech to the Assembly in September, the American secretary of state, George Marshall, had warned that if the Soviet Union persisted in its mistaken course the atomic talks would be doomed. To make matters worse, Hume Wrong, Canada's ambassador in Washington, reported that the State Department was considering announcing publicly a tripartite (the United States, Great Britain, and Canada) conference on atomic energy co-operation scheduled for December.[24] They were also thinking about broadening the talks to include other nations. Among the objectives of the talks would be not only the peaceful development of atomic energy but defence against nuclear war. Arnold Heeney, secretary to the Privy Council Office, believed that such a statement would be taken "as a decision on the part of the three nations concerned to jettison the United Nations Atomic Energy Commission." He even suspected that the American diplomats were coming to the "conclusion that the time has come for a clean break with the Soviet Union in all that pertains to the United Nations." But this was contrary to the declared view of the Canadian cabinet "that the time has not yet been reached when any of the issues dividing members of the United Nations should be pressed to a conclusion which would destroy the organization as it is at present constituted."[25]

Fortunately the Americans decided not to pursue this announcement. But they certainly expected very little result from continuing the discussions in the AEC. Their attitude was well illustrated by the announcement of the defense secretary in December that while his government would not terminate its participation in the talks, there was no real possibility of an agreement. No doubt the United States was going on with the talks merely to protect its public image as a peace-loving nation. This was also essentially the Canadian position, as summarized by Pearson, in a memorandum in November of 1947. The Soviet Union was standing in the way of the achievement of a system of effective controls for atomic energy, but nothing should be done to give the USSR an excuse for leaving the United Nations. AEC negotiations should be continued because one day the Soviet Union might wish to co-operate; in that case, it would be useful to be ready with a treaty on managing atomic energy. And if the AEC talks were to collapse, it was important that the responsibility for that failure not fall on the West.[26]

THE AEC'S THIRD REPORT

If the AEC negotiations were to continue, how should Canada approach them? McNaughton's view, as reported by Osborn, was determined by his evaluation of the atomic prospects of the two superpowers. The Soviet Union was apparently making very slow progress with developing an atomic bomb. He thought that they might have enough material for a single bomb in the next five or ten years but not enough to support an atomic war. He therefore expected the United States to have a rising measure of atomic ascendancy until at least 1957. He supported the continued build-up of American atomic might to prevent the Soviet army from over-running

Western Europe. Weakness was the one thing that might lead to war, observed McNaughton, repeating the catchword that Western politicians would use to justify the arms race for the next ten years. For this reason, he advocated standing firm by the second report of the AEC and giving the Soviet Union no opportunity to change it.[27] But cooler heads in other Western delegations prevailed, and it was decided that the West should propose that the Soviet proposals of 11 June be re-examined, this time in the Working Committee. And Committee 2 would deal with what further powers were needed to make the ICA operate efficiently – in the areas of staffing and organization, for example. On 18 December 1947 the AEC met and adopted this programme of work.

1948

The next year, 1948, which brought the end of democracy in Czechoslovakia and the Berlin blockade, was not particularly propitious for meaningful diplomacy. Since neither East nor West had any reason to change its mind, there was to be no movement in the discussions under AEC auspices in 1948. Committee 2 met only five times. Its task was to deal with the composition of the agency's board of directors. Naturally, the Soviet Union opted for national representatives, reflecting its view that the control of atomic energy ought to rest with individual nations. The West, wishing the ICA itself to control the production and use of atomic energy, proposed that the personnel of the board be regarded as international civil servants. Because this divergence on organization reflected a profound disagreement on the functions of the ICA, Committee 2 could do nothing useful; it met for the last time in March 1948.

The proceedings of the Working Committee, examining the Soviet proposals, proved equally sterile. The two main issues re-emerged. The Soviet Union insisted that a treaty prohibiting atomic weapons be concluded before proceeding to negotiate a convention on controls; and even at that Gromyko said, quite accurately, that since these would be new negotiations, he could not guarantee that they would be concluded successfully. Yet if the negotiations broke down, the United States would have undertaken to destroy its atomic bombs without being sure that the Soviet Union was not building its own. Nor was Gromyko more co-operative on a matter of intense concern to the West – inspection. He specified that when the Soviet Union said "periodic inspection," that meant there would be no continuous inspection. Anything that was continuous would be management or supervision. But to the West this added up to no effective system of controls and inspection. Consequently on 29 March the majority concluded that there was no point in continuing to study the Soviet plan. A week later, by a vote of 9 to 2, the committee adopted a lucid report of four powers – Canada, China, France, and Great Britain – that was extremely critical of the Soviet control plan: its inspection provisions could not guarantee that there would be no diversion of dangerous materials to secret atomic activities; the Soviet version of the ICA would have no powers to enforce its decisions; and even so limited an agreement could not be brought into being until after the destruction of American atomic weapons.

It is easy to see why McNaughton and his Western colleagues could never accept the Soviet plan which took no account of Western security, and it is doubtful that the USSR ever believed its proposals would be acceptable to the West. The Soviet Union claimed that it was rejecting the Baruch Plan because it interfered with its sovereignty, and Canadian diplomats agreed that this was the principal issue.[28] Clearly, Stalin wished to keep control of his country's atomic programme. To appease world public opinion, he was ready to make some gestures towards the international control of atomic energy, but these were essentially meaningless. He refused to leave Soviet security in the hands of an international body which he suspected might be controlled by the United States. McNaughton understood this to be the case: "Soviet objections [to the Baruch Plan] arise from the fact that in the present international political situation they do not feel that they can give up to an international body in which nations they consider unfriendly to them are bound to be in the majority, the degree of authority of which the other nations are convinced is essential for security."[29] Impelled by the same motive which would later drive Great Britain and France to follow his example, Stalin seems to have believed that if the Soviet Union was to remain a great power it must have its own atomic bombs. So anxious was he to acquire nuclear weapons that he would not guarantee that even if the United States were to stop building atomic weapons, he would not go on with his own programme. Stalin also feared that giving up such extraordinary powers over such a potential source of energy would enable an American-dominated world body to interfere with Soviet internal economic life. (It was on such grounds that he had also rejected the Marshall Plan.)

It had been apparent from the beginning that the negotiations in the committees would likely fail and that there might be no point in continuing the work of the commission. The Americans wanted a public showdown in the forthcoming General Assembly where they could pin the blame for the impasse on the Soviet Union. The third report of the AEC should therefore be written so as to frame the debate in a way that would give the West the tactical advantage. They proposed that the report ask the Security Council to support the majority and condemn the USSR for obstructing the only way to atomic peace. Such a demand would provoke a great public row at the Security Council and prepare the ground for a major propaganda battle in the General Assembly. The AEC should also recommend, the United States contended, that the third report along with the first and second ones be transmitted to member-states as a matter of special concern, because countries not on the commission which wished to be ready for the discussion in September would need time to study this material.

McNaughton was greatly troubled by this aggressive approach. He wanted the third AEC report to be confined to describing the situation which existed without making any judgments. He had always feared that the American determination to seek confrontation would only jeopardize the "prospects of continued cooperation with the Soviet Union within the United Nations."[30] He did not think that the situation called for "mutual recriminations."[31] External Affairs agreed with McNaughton that the commission should merely report that progress was not possible. It also warned that if it provoked a debate at the Assembly, the United States might not have everything its own way; the Russians might offer a plausible case for destroying atomic bombs immediately. Pearson had many reservations on this matter. He thought it unwise for the West at this stage to commit itself to a showdown with the Soviet Union over how to control atomic energy; he would rather wait to see how things developed and then decide in September. There was always a chance that after Canada and other countries committed themselves, unexpected circumstances would later cause the United States to change its mind about the advisability of such a debate. He nonetheless advised McNaughton that if the United Kingdom and France concurred with the United States, Canada should no longer resist the recommendation.[32]

In May, opposed only by the Soviet Union and Ukraine, the Western bloc in the AEC, including Canada, endorsed the third report which blamed the Soviet Union for stubbornly clinging to its views on national sovereignty and recommended both that the commission suspend its activities for the present and that the three AEC reports be transmitted to the General Assembly for discussion. In a memorandum for the cabinet, Pearson summed up the feelings of the Canadian delegation. There was no point in continuing the discussion until the Soviet Union agreed to the "essential technical requirements of control" – namely, that no safeguards were possible without international ownership of atomic materials and facilities. The main points in contention were: the Soviet insistence on the outlawing and destruction of atomic bombs before a system of control could be established; its wish to be able to veto any punishment proposed by the agency; its resistance to an adequate system of inspection. McNaughton was authorized to vote in the Security Council (on which Canada was now serving) for the approval of the three reports and their transmission to the General Assembly.[33]

In June the American delegate proposed a motion in the Security Council that endorsed the majority position on atomic energy and condemned the Soviet Union. After an acrimonious debate, Gromyko vetoed the resolution. The American and British delegates had foreseen this possibility and had asked McNaughton to be ready with an alternate resolution.[34] On the basis of a simple procedural motion put forward by Canada, the Security Council agreed to transmit the three reports to the General Assembly without commenting on them. The Soviet Union did not try to veto this motion, evidently believing that to suppress debate on such a vital issue would have aroused the wrath of the assembled members of the United Nations.

After this meeting of the Security Council, McNaughton had reason to feel satisfied. While there had been a fierce clash at the Council, Gromyko had not tried to stop the transmission of the AEC reports to the General Assembly. McNaughton now hoped to get United Nations members to approve the three reports. The debate would provide a splendid opportunity to educate the other members of the General Assembly and to win their support for what was essentially the Baruch Plan. The door would also be kept open to the possibility, slight as it was, of the Russians coming on side. McNaughton believed that in this new and terrible era of warfare, the failure to control atomic energy might bring about "an end to civilization."[35] Every effort must be made to win over the Soviet Union to the only plan that would prevent atomic rivalry between the great powers. Even if the USSR did not accept right away, at least a seed would have been planted that might bring a change in Soviet thinking in the coming years. There was always the possibility of a change in the Soviet regime: Stalin might die; a coalition of anti-communist forces might arise and need Western help. Before agreeing, the United States and its allies would be able to lay down the condition that these new leaders must accept "effective international control of atomic energy."[36] For the present, if the Assembly could be persuaded to endorse the three AEC reports, the

USSR would be compelled to negotiate on their principles or else defy the will of the General Assembly.

But this neat scheme was in danger of being upset by a British proposal that questions of atomic energy, disarmament, and security be treated as parts of a single problem – the refusal of the Soviet Union to abandon, in the common interest, any of its legal rights under the United Nations Charter. McNaughton believed that the presentation of such an omnibus resolution to the General Assembly could only lead to a fierce propaganda clash in which many United Nations members might well remain neutral. "If the reports of the Atomic Energy Commission were to be used only as an additional stick with which to beat the Soviet Union, the value of an objective endorsement of the proposals by the General Assembly would ... be virtually lost."[37] There would be no real consideration of the intrinsic merits of the AEC reports. More importantly, such a resolution would shut the door on any possibility of an eventual agreement with the Soviet Union. McNaughton was a sincere believer in the Western plan for the control of atomic energy. He was convinced that in the end reason must prevail and that the USSR must come around.[38] The West must never make this hard decision for the Russians even more difficult by making their acceptance of the majority AEC proposals an admission of responsibility for the Cold War. He sought to make the atomic question an issue of technical feasibility rather than of world politics.

McNaughton thus desired the discussion of the AEC reports to be a separate item on the United Nations agenda. He wished to explain them to United Nations members rather than win a propaganda victory over the USSR. Fortunately, the Americans agreed with him. While they were ready to take on the Russians, they believed they would be more successful if, instead of a general propaganda brawl, they were able to hold the Soviet Union to discussing the specific proposals of the AEC.[39] Their hope was that a factual debate would mobilize world opinion on their side of the issue. They asked McNaughton to open the debate for the West and present a resolution asking the General Assembly to endorse the concrete proposals of the AEC majority.[40]

On 30 September McNaughton presented his resolution to the Political Committee on which each of the fifty-eight members of the United Nations had a seat. In his speech, he warned his listeners about the horrors of atomic war, praised the views of the AEC majority, and condemned the Soviet proposal to outlaw atomic bombs before even pledging to take any steps towards control of atomic energy. His resolution endorsed measures enunciated in the first and second AEC reports to guarantee that atomic energy would be used for peaceful purposes as well as the third report which blamed the impasse on the Soviet Union and called for the suspension of the activities of the AEC.

Meanwhile, it appears that the Soviet Union had come to realize that its stance of prohibiting atomic weapons first and then perhaps instituting controls was becoming more and more difficult to defend. On 2 October, therefore, Andrei Vyshinsky tabled a draft resolution in the Political Committee asking the AEC to draft two conventions: one to ban atomic weapons and the other to institute international control of atomic energy, both of which were "to be signed and brought into operation simultaneously."[41] In Pearson's view this offer opened intriguing possibilities. If the Soviet Union meant that the banning would take place once the control system was announced, then this proposal would be a non-starter: the American bombs would have been destroyed long before the control system was in place. There would then be a period during which the West would have no guarantee that the Soviet Union was not manufacturing atomic bombs. If the Russians meant that the bombs would be outlawed only after the controls were prepared and ready to go, however, then serious negotiations were possible about what controls the Soviet Union would accept. But what Vyshinsky had really offered remained in doubt. Up till May 1955 the Soviet Union refused to say whether the prohibition of nuclear weapons would take place when the treaty for international control was signed or when the control authority had come into existence. For the next seven years Pearson would follow this elusive possibility and urge that the Soviet Union be pressed to reveal its real intentions.

Both the Americans and the British believed that the Russian move was only a cynical manœuvre. Still, to be seen taking the high ground in the struggle for peace was a brilliant propaganda coup. The USSR seemed to have altered course and drawn closer to the Western position. Where the Soviet proposal fell down was in its refusal to accept the safeguards proposed by the West. The Russians evaded McNaughton's query as to whether the proposed conventions would be based on the principles underpinning the three AEC reports. Consequently the Soviet resolution was consistently rejected by the great majority in the Political Committee. Nevertheless, many countries wished to see the West respond positively to what seemed to be a Soviet concession, however limited.

Perhaps the most important voice for conciliation was that of India, a leader among the underdeveloped nations and consequently a country of enormous political significance in Pearson's view of the world. In 1948 it was already seeking diplomatic paths that would allow it to remain aloof from both the great power blocs. In atomic negotiations its views would always be a source of anxiety to Pearson who suspected that India would be "soft" on the Soviet Union. In response to the new Soviet proposals, Indian diplomats began to ask whether the situation that had led to the suspension of the AEC had been overcome: ought the commission to resume its work of trying to draft a treaty? McNaughton continued to insist that the AEC could not do any useful work until there was common agreement on the principles embodied in the three reports, but this argument was more and more difficult to sell. In a sub-committee of eleven, an Indian motion was defeated by 4 to 1; significantly there were six abstentions. Still, the same sub-committee passed the Canadian resolution by a count of 9–2, with only the Soviet Union and Ukraine opposed.

Canadian diplomats sensed the unhappiness of important countries like Brazil, Ecuador, Sweden, and India. One of them reported that "many delegations are unwilling to see the activities of the AEC suspended even though they are prepared to support majority reports." If the recommendation for suspension remained in the Canadian resolution, he feared that, at the final vote in the Political Committee, Australia, China, India, and a good many Latin American countries might join the Soviet bloc in opposing it.[42] In the end Canada and the United States agreed that the Canadian resolution should be amended to provide for the reconvening of the AEC. There was another concession as well: all reference to the third report which had blamed the Soviet Union for the impasse was dropped. Finally, the resolution requested Canada and the five permanent members of the Security Council to consult again to see whether a basis for agreement did not exist and to report back to the Assembly. The Canadian resolution was passed on 4 November in the General Assembly, with only the Soviet bloc opposed. Countries not involved in the AEC had forced the change. They liked the safeguards proposed in the first and second reports but, fearful of the possible dire consequences of a continued deadlock, insisted that all options for negotiations be kept open. Without doubt the Soviet concession of simultaneous implementation of the two conventions had stiffened their resolve on this point.

In reviewing the work of the Canadian delegation in this momentous debate, McNaughton had good reason to judge the results to be "gratifying."[43] Canada had played a major role on an issue of global importance – atomic energy. Its resolution to endorse the principles underpinning the Baruch Plan had been supported by the majority of the United Nations. (From now on the West would refer to it, quite rightly, as the Majority Plan.) World opinion was now on the Western side and would eventually have an effect, Mc-Naughton believed, in Moscow. It was true that, against his advice, the AEC had been revived, but this would simply be an annoyance that he could live with; he certainly had no hope that it would accomplish anything constructive. Lastly, the Americans had wished to see a public condemnation of the Soviet Union by the United Nations as the agent responsible for frustrating the universal desire for the peaceful use of atomic energy. As the dropping of the reference to the third report indicated, this had not happened. This, too, fitted well with McNaughton's desire to use the forum provided by the United Nations General Assembly to educate world opinion and not to win a propaganda battle over the USSR.

1949

THE SIX-POWER TALKS

McNaughton turned out to be right in his suspicion that the coming AEC meetings would prove sterile. The only useful purpose he could see for the commission was to have it clarify some parts of the Majority Plan and to write it up in simple language so as to provide an educational tool with which to influence public opinion. On 18 February 1949, the AEC adopted a resolution that called on the United Nations secretariat to prepare a document setting out the recommendations of the United Nations Assembly on atomic energy as well as an index of the contents of the three AEC reports. In March, it was agreed that this task would be turned over to the Working Committee which completed its work by June. But the Soviet representative had no such luck with his proposal. On 25 February he had moved that the AEC endorse the same resolution for simultaneous treaties that had been rejected by the Political Committee the previous autumn. Because of the importance of carrying public opinion with it, the AEC majority always needed to appear reasonable and open; instead of rejecting the Soviet proposition outright, therefore, the AEC agreed that the Working Committee would discuss it again. But in late June both the Working Committee and, later, a majority of the AEC rejected the Soviet proposal. The debate between the two sides was totally acrimonious and uncompromising: each was only speaking for the record. Finally on 29 July, at what proved to be the AEC's last meeting, a majority adopted an American resolution which again blamed the Soviet Union, maintained that the differences were irreconcilable, and suggested that no useful purpose could be served by continuing the work of the commission until the original sponsors of the AEC could report that there was a basis for negotiation. Again External Affairs expressed reservations about the value of a resolution that censured the Soviet Union, believing that it was sure to bring about a strong debate in the coming Assembly; but in the end the department accepted McNaughton's judgment that "we have no alternative but to indicate to the U.S. ... we shall give it our general support."[44] In September the Security Council, by a vote of 9–2, rejected a Russian motion to continue the AEC, on the grounds that further work in the present circumstances was pointless.

McNaughton and his colleagues had given up hope of an immediate agreement in the AEC discussions. Their focus had shifted to winning world support for the Majority Plan. As External Affairs noted, "we should be thinking at least as much about the propaganda effect of our proposals as of the technical aspects." It feared that the Soviet Union would use the AEC as a forum to air the charges that the United States wished to perpetuate its monopoly of atomic energy and that the Majority Plan undercut national sovereignty. But there was no reason for the West, it believed, to be on the defensive. After all, to use atomic energy for peaceful purposes, it must be controlled according to "an agreed plan which only the Soviet Union and her satellites refuse to accept. We must be able to fence with olive branches as well as they."[45]

Nevertheless External Affairs believed that the Americans were vulnerable to Soviet criticism in the propaganda battle because they were not explicit about when they would accept full international control. The third report had only noted that the transition to full international control would be conditional on future technological development and conditions of world security. In time, these stages would be fixed by the AEC. The introduction of the concept of stages implied that there would be no establishment of simultaneous control over all stages of production. The first stage might be limited to control over atomic raw materials; meanwhile the plants producing nuclear fuel would not be under international jurisdiction. The American delegate to the United Nations had evaded the issue by asserting that there was no point in defining the stages of this process when agreement on other issues seemed remote. But this did not satisfy the Russians. The previous year McNaughton had reported a Soviet complaint that while other nations would suffer controls, the United States would retain for a considerable time at least "the possession of the bomb and the 'know-how' and that control over existing plants producing nuclear fuel would be delayed."[46] The Russians had again made a fuss over this question at the General Assembly and in the spring of 1949 they were about to return to the matter. External Affairs understood the political force of Soviet resentment: "To the uninitiated ... one of the most serious Soviet charges is that the majority proposals in their present form could mean that the United States would give up nothing during the first stage while demanding control and inspection rights within the Soviet Union and that this stage could be prolonged indefinitely."[47]

This was a rather large chink in the West's armour. External Affairs directed McNaughton to advise the Americans that in the spring AEC talks they ought to be more precise about what they meant by stages. The French shared the Canadian concern and made the same suggestion.[48] However, at the height of the Cold War, President Truman would have been in great difficulty with an extremely anti-communist Congress if he had announced a time-table for giving up the atomic bomb. As the American representative to the AEC had noted the previous year: "the United States position on stages, if written under the present circumstances of Soviet pre-paration for war would necessarily be very stiff."[49] McNaughton himself was sympathetic to the American position. He held that until the Soviet Union agreed to accept the fundamental features of the Majority Plan there could be no progress on this difficult issue.[50] Nevertheless he had transmitted External Affairs' message and had been told that the American diplomats "wish to ensure that the AEC does not embark upon a discussion of stages of the transition which ... would be embarrassing to the U.S."[51] External Affairs remained unhappy about the situation but made no vigorous attempt to press this point.

Both the Americans and the Canadians had expected the re-newed AEC talks to fail. The United States negotiators were soon pondering how to deal with the six-power talks that were to take place after the AEC suspended its work. They held that the goal of the West should be to prove, "conclusively," to the majority in the General Assembly that "it would not be to the advantage of the U.N. to continue the work of the AEC at this time."[52] But External Affairs was sceptical about the validity of this approach in view of the "widespread hope in the world that they will not fail." It also be-lieved that the Americans were attempting to force the Soviet Union into a "purely negative position." What was needed was a reason-able expression in the clearest language of the minimum requirements for the international control of atomic energy. The chances of the USSR finding them acceptable were admittedly pretty slim – but the possibility must be left open. The West had nothing to lose. After all, "the more reasonable a document they have to refuse, the greater our propaganda victory."[53] External Affairs was always consistent in advocating that Western proposals should be free of Cold War rhetoric so as to make it easier for the USSR to accept them. The offer must be genuine. If, unfortunately, the Soviet Union rejected it, then the propaganda effect would be all the greater if the original proposal was based on the merits of the case rather than on an appeal to ideological loyalty.

Fortunately, the statement which the Western five (Canada, the United States, China, France, and the United Kingdom) presented to their Soviet counterpart was reasonable. It listed the fundamental points on which the Majority Plan depended. It was agreed that there would be no verbatim reports of these six-power talks. (This was a procedure which Canada would favour more and more, because it permitted a much more frank exchange of opinion between the two sides.) Beginning in August there were ten meetings of the six powers, the last one taking place in the middle of October. The same two questions which had bedevilled previous exchanges remained unresolved. Which should come first – the prohibition of atomic weapons or the control of facilities in order to prevent clandestine manufacture of atomic bombs? What measures were needed to exercise such control? The Soviet Union insisted that control could be achieved while nations continued to operate their own atomic programmes and that periodic inspection was sufficient. These two propositions the West denied. In a public statement of 25 October they blamed the Soviet Union for putting its sovereignty ahead of the needs of world security. The six powers agreed to pass on the summary records of their discussions to the General Assembly which was then in session. In November they suspended their talks until the Political Committee of the General Assembly concluded its own discussion of atomic energy issues.

Canada had made a special contribution to the six-power discussions. McNaughton had long been annoyed by the Soviet representatives calling the majority proposals "the so-called Baruch Plan." He believed that the principles of the former differed fundamentally from those of the latter, and he was anxious to go on record to this effect. He got his opportunity at the meeting on 6 October. His point was that the agency suggested by Baruch had been clothed with great and arbitrary powers; under the current Majority Plan these would be derived from the terms of a treaty signed by all participating nations. There would also be full recourse through international and national courts against capricious action by the agency. Because of the methods of inspection and control which had been evolved in the commission, there would be timely warning of any preparations for atomic war. As a result, the emphasis had shifted "from the unattainable objective of prevention and condign punishment of a violator at the instance of an autocratic all-powerful central international atomic authority to a more reasonable and, we believe, realizable purpose of setting up an effective system by which adequate warning would be given with certainty."[54] The principal duty of the agency would be to warn other nations rather than to punish the violators. The implication was that the clause in the first report that the veto could no longer be applied by a permanent power to avoid punishment would no longer be operative.

But McNaughton's explanation failed to impress Jacob Malik, the Soviet representative. He maintained that the differences between the two plans were minor. Both postponed the prohibition of atomic weapons to an indefinite future. He suspected that in both plans provisions for control would cover only raw materials but not the fuel-producing plants of the United States.[55] He might have added that under both plans atomic facilities and fuel would be owned by an international agency directed by a board on which the Soviet Union would always be in a minority. It did not believe that under these circumstances it would be treated fairly and honestly.

During the six-power talks, McNaughton may have believed that his side was having the best of the argument and was generally speaking in control of events. But the Soviet atomic explosion, reported in September 1949, was to undermine all chance of the Majority Plan being accepted. It is true that at first Western politicians seemed to take this new development in their stride. Lester Pearson believed that it was no cause for surprise. Scientific knowledge could not remain one nation's monopoly. There should be no change in policies; there was merely a greater than ever need to bring atomic energy under international control. This was also the position of President Truman.[56] Like well-rehearsed actors, politicians continued to speak the lines they had learned, even though they no longer applied to the events at hand. Perhaps they were too close to the event to appreciate its long-term significance.

With this development the strategic balance between the two superpowers had been altered forever and the eventual outcome of the Soviet possession of atomic arms would be a nuclear stalemate. Hence the superpower rivals might find themselves in a confrontation where the issue might be decided not by nuclear but by conventional arms; the latter would have to be brought into the disarmament equation. The Soviet advance also stimulated an increase in the quantity and quality of nuclear weapons on each side, to the point where even the most rigorous inspection could no longer guarantee that some might not escape detection. Both sides came to understand that the issue between them had changed from disarmament to arms control. In 1955 the United States would mark this new era by formally abandoning its support for the international control of atomic energy.

The whole American strategy for gaining Soviet acceptance of its plan for the control of atomic energy had been based on the leverage to be derived from its monopoly of atomic weapons. Up to this point the USSR had failed to be intimidated. Now that it had an atomic capacity of its own, this strategy was even less likely to succeed. At the United Nations General Assembly in the autumn of 1949, Vyshinsky would be even more intransigent than before and more disdainful of the Majority Plan. Before the Soviet atomic explosion became known, the tactic of McNaughton and his colleagues had been to prevent a revival of the AEC. At the same time they had wanted to avoid a bitter dispute on atomic arms in the Assembly which might provide the USSR with another opportunity to win over any countries that were tending to be neutral. But the Soviet explosion underlined the necessity of some kind of control over atomic energy and a lively debate in the Assembly became inevitable. Pearson, who had become Canada's secretary of state for external affairs in September 1948, began to worry that smaller nations "may be inclined to rush into some ill-considered proposal for prohibition pending agreement on control."[57] He believed that without some kind of a prohibition resolution, the West would not continue to receive the necessary support from the United Nations for the Majority Plan.

But coming up with a satisfactory resolution proved difficult. One idea which the Canadians explored was to outlaw the use of atomic bombs except in cases where the Security Council operating without a veto decided that aggression had been committed. This decision would be taken by seven out of the eleven members including three out of the five great powers. But the problem was that there might be a disagreement about what constituted aggression. France would likely have to be persuaded that it had actually taken place. Then, too, there was no assurance that some of the nonpermanent members of the Council would not adopt a neutral stance any time there was a critical vote. The dilemma, as Pearson explained in a radio interview, was that without control "you have a prohibition in a set of political circumstances in which you haven't confidence between all the states who will accept the prohibition."[58] In any case, it was hardly likely that the United States would give up the right to use the atomic bomb to defend its security.

In the end, however, Canada was satisfied with the result of the debate in the United Nations. In November, the West managed to defeat a Soviet resolution recommending simultaneous conventions for prohibition and control as well as win overwhelming support for a Canadian-French resolution calling on every nation to limit its sovereignty sufficiently to permit the international control of atomic energy. Significantly, the latter resolution did not ask for explicit support for the Majority Plan; apparently its sponsors feared that such a clause would cause it to receive fewer votes than the previous year. As well as the USSR, India, Egypt, Haiti, and Argentina had all proposed resolutions that in one way or another called for the prohibition of atomic weapons even without agreement on inspection and control as defined by the Majority Plan. Canada and France got around these awkward demands by inserting in their original draft resolution a clause that called on the six powers to continue their discussions and to accept all concrete suggestions from other nations. This meant that countries like India and Argentina believed that what they wished would be seriously considered in these talks. According to the Canadian report from the United Nations to External Affairs, this move "played an important part in securing the large vote which this resolution eventually commanded, and forestalling or facilitating the defeat of a number of hasty and confused proposals."[59]

The debate on the Canadian-French resolution gave Pearson, who was leading the Canadian delegation to the General Assembly, his first opportunity to state his views on atomic energy to the United Nations. He differed somewhat from McNaughton in placing more emphasis on inspection and less on international ownership. The Soviet Union was vulnerable in the propaganda arena because it was only prepared to accept "periodic" international inspection. As well, persuading the Soviet Union to accept an efficient system of inspection was the key to breaking the deadlock. To the United Nations Pearson asserted that if "it can be shown that national operation with complete 100 per cent inspection would not be a menace to security, then we would be glad to re-examine the position."[60] Here was a hint that it might be possible to relax the ownership provision of the proposed atomic treaty in exchange for continuous and rigid inspection.

Unfortunately, there was no opportunity to probe the Soviet reaction on this possible compromise. The Communists had come to power in China in September 1949, and the Soviet Union claimed that the new regime had a right to the China seat in the United Nations. At the first working meeting of the six powers in January 1950, the Soviet delegate demanded the seating of the People's Republic. When this request was refused, he walked out. Without the Soviet representative, there was no point in continuing to discuss atomic matters. Thus ended the work of the AEC which had been begun with such high hopes four years previously. It says much about the lack of seriousness in these negotiations in later years that the commission's demise was caused by an issue not related to atomic concerns.

COMMISSION FOR
CONVENTIONAL ARMAMENTS

So far we have been discussing the control of atomic weapons, but in the remote background there had also been continual negotiations on conventional arms. Both sides put a low priority on these talks at this time. But after the Soviet Union exploded its first atomic device in September 1949, it became apparent that only an integrated discussion of atomic and conventional weapons would open the way to genuine negotiations.

The General Assembly disarmament resolution of 14 December 1946 had emphasized that the regulation of conventional arms was also important to international peace and security. In the January 1947 meeting of the Security Council, the Soviet Union proposed that the discussion of these weapons be combined with those on atomic energy within one commission. But Western representatives resisted the merging of the two sets of talks. Instead, in February 1947, the Security Council – with the USSR abstaining – voted to set up a new commission, the Commission for Conventional Armaments (CCA) to consider the regulation of conventional weapons. Composed of all members of the Security Council, the CCA was to operate in a rather casual fashion for the next three years.

Given that the USSR was far ahead in conventional arms, the stance of the United States on combined negotiations is not easy to understand; it would have gained by having some legal means of controlling the size of the Soviet Army. The Americans may have thought that if it was agreed to count conventional arms, it would be difficult not to have the same thing done for atomic ones. It has been suggested that Eisenhower warned that it would be dangerous to proceed with conventional disarmament until the Russians agreed to a workable plan of inspection, lest they apply their unacceptable standards to atomic control.[61] For whatever reason, the two sides clashed over whether the terms of reference of the CCA ought to encroach on the AEC and include control of atomic energy. In the end the United States had its way. In setting up the CCA, the Security Council explicitly excluded atomic energy from its jurisdiction.

From the Soviet point of view this defeat was bad enough, but the Western delegates were to go even further. In August 1948 the CCA passed a resolution which stated that the reduction of conventional arms could only take place under conditions of confidence and security and these included the successful conclusion of a treaty establishing an effective system of controlling atomic energy. Success in reducing conventional arms was thus contingent on agreement in the atomic field. The unhappy state of atomic negotiations would guarantee that the American military establishment would continue to be able to rebuild their conventional military strength both in the United States and Western Europe to meet what they regarded as the dangerous Soviet threat.

Although Canada was not a member of the Security Council in 1947 (and therefore not on the CCA), McNaughton attended meetings as an observer and followed the proceedings closely. In June, before the Standing Committee of External Affairs, he had justified the separation of the negotiations on atomic and conventional arms on grounds of efficiency. Merged talks would lead to a lot of "confused thinking ... which may obscure the issues." And if keeping the talks separate would lead to the resolution of the atomic question, it would then be easy to deal with limiting ordinary weapons.[62] Once McNaughton took his seat as Canada's representative on the Security Council (and the CCA) in January 1948 he was able to tell Gromyko directly that Canada believed that effective control of atomic energy was essential to establishing complete international confidence – a condition necessary for the reduction of conventional arms.[63]

McNaughton's attitude towards the CCA differed from that towards the AEC in one important respect. In May 1948 he had readily agreed that the latter should suspend its activity. But he had no such opinion about the CCA. The work had not yet gone far enough; there was not yet sufficient evidence to make a case against the Soviet Union. There had only been a dozen meetings of the CCA. Until "we had been through the drill" in the CCA, the West could not say that the talks should not continue, nor would the

General Assembly support such an adjournment resolution.[64] It was not that he thought that an agreement with the Soviet Union was possible under the prevailing circumstances but that it was necessary to handle the situation so as to best extract propaganda benefits.

In September 1948 Vyshinsky proposed to the General Assembly that there be a one-third cut in the Big Five's armaments coupled with a prohibition on atomic weapons. This would have perpetuated the crushing superiority of the Soviet Union in conventional arms as well as removing the main weapon with which the United States sought to protect its security. Such a self-serving recommendation was rejected by the General Assembly. Instead, it voted to ask the CCA to establish an international organ of control that would check and publish full information about the conventional armaments of member-states. This meant the USSR would be asked to furnish data about its conventional establishment while being kept in the dark about the American atomic arsenal.

Almost a year later the CCA adopted a French plan for a census and verification of the conventional armed forces and armaments of United Nations members. This proposal was taken up at a Security Council meeting in October 1949 along with a Soviet proposition that all states submit information on both conventional and atomic weapons. At this meeting, Pearson presented the Canadian view. He criticized the Soviet resolution because it made no suggestion on how the information it sought could be verified. He dismissed as baseless the Soviet charge that the French plan was merely a scheme aimed at making the United Nations a branch of the "Anglo-American intelligence service." He reiterated his conviction that the reason the USSR was rejecting such a census was because of an "outmoded and old-fashioned concept of unrestricted national sovereignty."[65]

The French resolution was vetoed in the Security Council by the Soviet Union. But in December, with only the Soviet bloc opposed, the General Assembly approved a resolution asking for full information on conventional arms. A Soviet resolution calling for information on atomic as well as conventional arms was defeated. Canada took no part in these debates. In sharp contrast to its role in the AEC, Canada was passive in the CCA, displaying little interest and taking no initiatives. As an atomic power Canada had a real stake in the outcome of the AEC talks. As a small military power it had no distinctive policy on conventional arms. When the CCA met again in April 1950, the Soviet delegate again walked out because of the refusal to seat Communist China. Because Canada's term in the Security Council was up, it was no longer a member of the CCA.

Without the USSR there was not much that the commission could accomplish and in the following August it suspended its activity.

CONCLUSION

"It is a melancholy fact that for the time being the Assembly debates on atomic energy have been essentially battles in the propaganda war between East and West," reported McNaughton to External Affairs after the Canadian-French resolution was adopted in November 1949.[66] But this had been true of the General Assembly discussions ever since the autumn of 1947. In 1948, the *Bulletin of the Atomic Scientists* had observed, quite accurately, that the attempt by the AEC to establish international control of energy collapsed owing to the "present climate of enmity and suspicion between the United States and the Soviet Union."[67] In 1948 and 1949 the Cold War deepened, and there were tremendous political clashes between the United States and the USSR over the Marshall Plan, the creation of NATO, and the establishment of a West German state. Neither Stalin nor Truman was greatly interested in disarmament; neither became personally involved; the talks were always conducted on a bureaucratic level. So little did Stalin believe in any real possibility of success that he eventually torpedoed both the AEC and the CCA to win favour with his new ally, the People's Republic of China.

With so little political support the negotiations on disarmament were bound to founder. It is true that as late as May 1948 Truman still hoped that nuclear weapons might come under international control,[68] but to the American diplomats at the bargaining table this must have seemed a very forlorn hope. The sides could not agree because each made proposals that strengthened its own security at the expense of the other's. There is no evidence to support the contention of John Holmes that the tactic of the West was to offer an international regime which "would make due allowance for the security of the Soviet Union."[69] Looking back a decade later, McNaughton explained that the United States would "concede nothing which might compromise the technological advantage thought to be held by the U.S.A. and which was considered to be important to balance the Soviet preponderance in numbers of men and in the amounts of conventional armaments they had available." The Soviet Union, for its part, proposed the outlawing of atomic weapons but this was to be "unaccompanied by any agreement to throw their territories open to inspection. This position the West could not interpret as other than that the Soviets intended to remain free to develop nuclear weapons in secret."[70]

Once it became clear that no agreement was possible, the real purpose of the negotiations was to score propaganda points in the United Nations so as to influence world opinion. One Canadian diplomat observed that "both the Soviet Union and Western powers were shadow boxing on the question of disarmament, each side wishing to appear to champion the idea but both reluctant to take any measures which would make it possible to put effective disarmament into practice."[71] In April 1949 communist leaders organized the First World Congress of the Partisans of Peace. In the resolution he presented to the General Assembly of September 1949, which condemned American and British preparations for a new war and demanded the prohibition of atomic weapons, Vyshinsky was clearly responding to what he called the "mighty popular movement in all countries for peace."[72] When the Americans campaigned to outvote the Russians at the United Nations, they were also sending a message to the world press. Although they won the battles in the United Nations, they came to realize that these victories brought the Soviet Union no closer to making concessions. In the 1950s, when real negotiations began again, the United States would avoid asking for General Assembly approval of any proposal to which the Soviet Union objected. It was only when this second effort collapsed in 1957 that the United States would again turn to the General Assembly for a propaganda victory.

As McNaughton saw the situation in 1949, the gap in principle on the international control of atomic energy was not "capable" of being bridged.[73] That being the case, External Affairs believed the West should go slow on any proposal which would deprive it of the "major strategic asset which so far has held the balance against vastly superior forces in being."[74] In these circumstances, Canada, as a loyal ally, saw its role as helping the United States to achieve its propaganda goals rather than to negotiate an agreement.

It is true that Canadian diplomats sometimes sought to soften American rhetoric to help the United States make a case that relied less on ideological loyalty and more on reason. Certainly they considered it important always to keep open the possibility of negotiations with the USSR – but they were also convinced that more reasonable proposals made for more effective propaganda if they were rejected. It has been suggested that "Canadians tried hard to meet whatever Russian objections seemed reasonable."[75] In fact, External Affairs believed that the American package was weak in two respects: it ought to give up its demand that the veto not apply to sanctions taken by the Security Council; it ought to accept a timetable that would indicate at what point in the process of establishing international control over atomic energy it would be prepared to stop manufacturing nuclear bombs. But Canada made little effort to press for these substantive changes in the American approach.

For one thing External Affairs was only trying to improve the public image of the United States. It lacked the technical expertise to convince American defence planners that these steps would improve American security. Then, too, these disagreements might eventually be picked up by the newspapers. The department knew that its political masters were reluctant to be seen squabbling with the United States. It was Mackenzie King who had forced Canada to vote for the veto sections of the Baruch Plan despite McNaughton's recommendation, and King remained prime minister until November 1948. Nor would the policy about public disagreement with the United States over disarmament change in the St Laurent era. Pearson, as secretary of state for external affairs, was ready to disagree publicly with the United States on its policy towards the People's Republic of China but not on atomic energy issues.

McNaughton himself would resign on 12 July 1950. Although trained as a soldier, he proved to be first-class diplomat. For more than four years he had worked to devise a plan by which atomic weapons would be taken out of the hands of individual nations. In 1946 he had reason to be optimistic, but from 1947 on it became obvious that prospects for an agreement were declining. Perhaps one reason that he kept trying for three more discouraging years lay in his personal experience of two world wars which had left him in no doubt about the destruction a nuclear war would bring. In the end, the Majority Plan in which he believed would founder; each great power would build its own atomic arsenal and the world would find itself in the dangerous condition which McNaughton had sought to prevent.

CHAPTER FIVE

The Erosion of the Majority Plan, 1950–53

The Soviet explosion of September 1949, the Americans' announcement in January 1950 of their intention to build a hydrogen bomb, and the collapse of negotiations in the Atomic Energy Commission stimulated a period of intense reflection among Canadian diplomats over the atomic impasse. The clash between East and West that began in Korea in June 1950 made the prospect of reaching agreement even more unlikely. The Department of External Affairs doubted that the Soviet Union would ever agree that an international agency should own its atomic facilities as provided for by the ownership provisions of the United Nations Majority Plan. Lester Pearson and his colleagues therefore devoted their efforts to exploring how serious the USSR was about accepting effective inspection. A related concern of External Affairs at this time was the growing divergence between the United States and France over the latter's interest in making German rearmament unnecessary by finding a compromise that would persuade the Soviet Union to disarm. Canada attempted to keep its two Western allies together through a programme of immediate concrete disarmament steps on which both could agree.

1950

PURSUING EFFECTIVE INSPECTION

The United States continued to support the Majority Plan. Yet some American officials were beginning to have doubts about its efficacy.

In August 1950 the secretary of state, Dean Acheson, was asking how there could be assurance "that all accumulated stocks [of nuclear fuel] would, in fact, be turned over to international control."[1] If no such guarantee were possible, then the rationale for international ownership was undermined. George Kennan, chief of the policy planning staff in the State Department, maintained that if his government wished to keep its atomic weapons then it should go on supporting the Majority Plan but not press it with "any particular vigor."[2] If, however, it wished to abolish them, the plan needed to be modified. Underpinning the plan was the premise that the early use of nuclear fuel for peaceful purposes was a serious possibility. If this objective were given up – if there could be an agreement to renounce large reactors and no longer produce nuclear fuel – then it would be possible to dispense with the concept of international ownership to which the Soviet Union objected so strenuously.[3]

Kennan's views made little impression on Canada's diplomats. George Ignatieff saw no possibility of the USSR halting its development of atomic power which was necessary for rebuilding its domestic economy. At the same time, he wanted the United States to keep its lead in atomic weapons so as to be able to deter potential Soviet aggression. He believed that the Soviet Union would attack only if it was certain of victory, and the threat of an American atomic reprisal automatically lessened the chances of such an assault. Thus Ignatieff's argument justified the continual increase in American atomic strength.[4]

After President Truman announced the American decision to build the hydrogen bomb, the Advisory Panel on Atomic Energy asked its secretary, James George, how the Majority Plan might be adjusted to encourage fruitful negotiations with the Russians before they build up their stockpile of atomic bombs. The memorandum that George produced in March 1950 began with the proposition that if nothing was done, by 1954 the Russians would possess enough atomic bombs and bombers to inflict great damage on the United States. The Americans would not dare to use their own nuclear might against the Soviet Union for fear of retaliation. This stalemate could be broken by a surprise atomic attack that would destroy the enemy's capacity to strike back. This situation would favour the Soviet Union which alone was unscrupulous enough to deliver such a blow if it thought it could get away with it. Thus, George argued, it would be in the West's interest to have an atomic control agreement in full operation by 1953.

Unfortunately, the Soviet Union would not agree to the Majority Plan because to do so might curtail its atomic development and would certainly lead to Soviet territory being placed under international inspection while leaving the United States in full control of its atomic bombs. What concessions could be made? The easiest one was to delete from the plan the Baruch proposal on the veto. The Soviet refusal to limit its atomic establishment meant that not much could be done about the provision for international ownership although it might be possible to enlarge somewhat the atomic assets which would remain under national jurisdiction. To meet the Soviet objection to the implementation of any agreement by "stages," all atomic bombs might be put in United Nations escrow, preferably "in some continent remote from both the U.S.S.R. and the U.S.A., such as Africa." George concluded by asserting that there should be no easing of Western demands for unhindered access and continual inspection, and that until the agreement was signed, the United States must be left free to use its atomic bombs as it saw fit.[5]

All in all, these suggested revisions were not practicable. The Soviet Union would not concur in any kind of international ownership, nor would it accept the kind of inspection the West thought necessary. The United States would never agree to placing its atomic bombs in United Nations escrow in Africa. General McNaughton had been genuinely enthusiastic about the Majority Plan. George had come to understand that because it was largely unacceptable to the Soviet Union, it was of little diplomatic use. He and his colleagues had become sceptical about the value of insisting on the ownership provisions; Lester Pearson himself was now suggesting to the Americans that it was time to take a "fresh look"[6] at them.

More and more, Pearson would become interested in pursuing a more moderate scheme with inspection as its centrepiece. But in March 1950 it is probable that what bothered him more than the potential of the Majority Plan was that the Russians had walked out of the AEC meetings and appeared totally indifferent to their resumption. Wrong reported that the only subject that interested them was the admission of the People's Republic of China to the United Nations and its assumption of the China seat on the Security Council. The American position was that if the negotiations were to continue, the Russians must return. Truman declared that there would be no separate talks with the Soviet Union on arms control.

Pearson was worried about the "unyielding position adopted by the U.S. Administration in negotiating with the Russians in general."[7] He was determined to get the talks going again. He told Wrong that "a new initiative in the United Nations, if properly prepared might have some effect."[8] His idea was to explore what Andrei Vyshinsky had meant the previous autumn when he called for "strict inspection and effective control as an integral part of an atomic energy agreement." The Soviet spokesman had also added that "periodic inspection means inspection at intervals, but intervals as determined by necessity and by decision of the international control commission."[9] Yet Pearson had been told often enough by experts that the Soviet Union would never agree to foreign inspectors moving about the country freely.[10] Had Vyshinsky's words offered anything more than the Soviet proposals of June 1947 which fell far short of adequate inspection? Pearson contended that if he meant something new and different, then "it is of the greatest importance that we should know."[11] Vyshinsky might merely be trying to score points by appearing to offer concessions to which the West had not responded. "It is difficult to kill this sort of propaganda," Pearson wrote Wrong, "unless we succeed in pinning down the Soviet representatives to a detailed explanation of their position which will expose it for the sham it is. It seems to me that the only practicable way of trying to do this is by resuming negotiations with the Russians."

Since the six-power talks were stalled because of the controversy over the China seat at the United Nations, Pearson suggested that the possibility of an informal meeting of the United Kingdom, the United States, France, the USSR, and Canada should be investigated. The Russians might refuse, arguing that on such an important subject as atomic energy it was unjustifiable to exclude the world's most populous nation. This claim might offset "the propaganda advantages which we might expect to gain either if the negotiations were resumed or by demonstrating publicly that it is the Russians and not we who are dragging our [sic] feet on this issue. On balance, however, we think we have more to gain than to lose."[12] He wished the United Kingdom and the United States to be sounded out on this initiative. If they agreed, then the Canadian government would be prepared to send out the necessary invitations.

As it happened, Pearson met with high-level United States officials in April. He told them that there had never been a serious exploration of the Vyshinsky proposals of the previous autumn. The Americans suggested that one way of getting around the procedural deadlock in the six-power talks without becoming vulnerable to Soviet criticism was to go back to the original Truman-Attlee-King meeting in Washington and have these three powers invite the French and then the Russians to join them for a new round on atomic energy. Pearson found this a useful suggestion. However, the Americans were not very impressed with the Canadian initiative; they thought that Pearson "seemed to feel that from a public relations point of view we should frequently propose or initiate conversations and let the Russians have the onus of turning them down."[13] In the end, the State Department rejected the idea on the grounds that since Acheson had announced time and again that there would be no concessions to the Soviet Union on the Majority Plan, the United States had nothing new to say. Pearson conceded that if the United States thought this way, then there was no point in more meetings. "It was the hope," he wrote Wrong, "however illusory that something in the way of a fresh start might come out of such consultations that led us to believe the suggestion merited more careful consideration."[14]

A month later, in talks with Prime Minister Attlee and Dean Acheson, Pearson again suggested that another effort be made to renew the talks. In his report on the conversation, Acheson noted that Pearson had no substantive idea in mind, but believed it "was important to smoke out ... the Vishinski proposal and demonstrate that there was nothing in it." Pearson had therefore wondered if there was a way of suggesting that the two sides meet informally (without the Nationalist Chinese spokesman) and "put upon the Russians the burden of refusing."[15] However this initiative was finally killed by the outbreak of the Korean War in June.

As the opening of the General Assembly approached, the Canadians had little hope that any positive steps on atomic energy would be taken. There was little prospect of anything other than a propaganda debate. Pearson continued to push his idea of seeing whether Vyshinsky really would accept the right of unimpeded access, continuous inspection, and search by any means, including observation by air, for undeclared atomic energy facilities. He proposed that the West sponsor a resolution to this effect; it might "smoke out the Soviet spokesmen and expose the hollowness of their arguments on disarmament."[16] If the Russians had really had a change of heart, then there could be real discussions on disarmament, but an American observer reported that Pearson "is under no illusions that such a change had really taken place and was stressing the debating value of a suggested parliamentary procedure."[17]

On 23 October Vyshinsky told the Political Committee of the United Nations that the international atomic energy control body ought to be able to send its inspectors any place and that they ought have the full right to inspect atomic facilities without any previous warning. To the Canadian delegation, this statement seemed to indicate "some slight shift of the Soviet attitude towards international control of atomic energy."[18] The cabinet was informed that "Mr Vishinski during recent weeks had made certain statements which implied that the U.S.S.R. was now prepared to go a great deal further than had been anticipated in the matter of international control of atomic energy."[19] This optimistic assessment turned out to be unwarranted. Vyshinsky's speech had been sufficiently ambiguous to leave the impression that the Soviet Union had made concessions, but in fact it had not accepted the key Western demand of continuous unlimited freedom of access for outside inspectors to all parts of the Soviet Union. Meanwhile the United Kingdom, France, and the United States had decided not to accept the Canadian suggestion of asking the Soviet Union for a more precise definition of inspection. Instead they opted for a totally new resolution supporting the Majority Plan which was duly passed by the General Assembly on 17 November.

James Eayrs has described Pearson's approach as "bargaining in bad faith."[20] It is true that Pearson never overlooked the possibility that if a reasonable proposal to the USSR was turned down, there would still be a pay-off in an enhanced reputation for the West as the side which was sincerely striving for peace. And, like a good salesman, he would naturally choose to emphasize to the Americans the advantages of his scheme that would most likely appeal to them. Yet his lament to Wrong about the need for a fresh start and the message to the cabinet show equally his desire to see the West achieve its aims in the negotiations and his anxiety to reduce the danger of nuclear war.

ESTABLISHING
THE DISARMAMENT COMMISSION

During the year the Americans had been pondering the strategic consequences of the Soviet atomic explosion. Now that the USSR had the secret, there might be some advantage to the United States in an agreement on atomic bombs. But in the March 1950 memorandum, NSC-68, Paul Nitze of the State Department's policy planning staff had warned that such a treaty might be accepted by the Soviet Union in order to take advantage of its conventional strength. It followed that the United States would have to insist "on concurrent agreement on the control of non-atomic forces and weapons."[21] The Truman administration was slow to take this advice. In September 1950, the United States was still insisting that atomic and conventional arms be discussed separately, and it had not backed away from the condition that an agreement on atomic energy must be signed before one on conventional arms was contemplated.

Perhaps the tough fighting in Korea shifted American thinking on this problem. The atomic bombs had clearly not made conventional war obsolete. Controlling Soviet conventional strength seemed more important than ever. The United States administration concluded that there needed to be a new start in arms negotiations. On 24 October, in his address to the General Assembly, President Truman offered some new elements for a viable disarmament plan. It must include all kinds of weapons: the United States would no longer insist that there had to be an agreement on controlling atomic energy before one on conventional arms. The plan must have unanimous consent: this would make negotiations easier because the USSR would realize that it might reject a proposal without having to suffer the adverse propaganda consequences of being out-voted in the United Nations.[22] There had to be safeguards to ensure compliance by all nations: the United States was still abiding by the Majority Plan on atomic energy, with its stringent ownership and inspection provisions. Lastly, Truman suggested that the work of the AEC and the CCA be brought together in a new and consolidated disarmament commission. This was the first time since the days of the Baruch Plan that Truman had personally intervened in arms negotiations. The threat of an atomic war was drawing him into taking the first tentative steps towards arms control – "a joint effort to enforce the military peace while simultaneously conducting the political contest."[23]

Pearson was inclined to dismiss the new American proposal. "I don't know whether it really would be a very great improvement just to have one commission instead of two," he observed. "After all, it's not machinery that we need for disarmament, it's a meeting of minds in respect of disarmament."[24] But he was underestimating the importance of the message that the United States was sending. Any agreement would have to take into account that atomic disarmament would leave the Russians with an enormous advantage in conventional arms. As long as the United States made negotiations on conventional disarmament contingent on a prior agreement on atomic weapons, Soviet strategists could conclude that the Americans were playing to the gallery. A proposal that the separate talks be brought together would eventually be read in Moscow as a signal of serious intent. It is true that progress in disarmament remained impossible because of the Korean War. But once that conflict ended, the start of negotiations was only possible because a consolidated disarmament commission was in place.

At first Pearson seemed to be right – the Soviet Union was slow to realize that it had won an important point. In December, the

General Assembly set up a Committee of Twelve, made up of the current members of the Security Council and Canada to report to the next session of the General Assembly on the advisability of merging the AEC and the CCA. This action had been taken despite a Soviet charge that it would only shelve the question of atomic control for another year. Canada remained lukewarm to the idea and took no part in the debate. Nevertheless the establishment of the committee did open up new possibilities, and Canada was soon trying to moderate the American stance so as to make the proposed merger possible.

1951

Although the work of the Committee of Twelve began in February, it was not until late May 1951 that the United States offered a substantive proposal for merging the two commissions. Embedded in this proposition was a declaration that the Majority Plan must serve as the basis of the work of the new commission. The use of this phrase caused the Russians to reject the American offer. Canadian diplomats were upset by the tone of the American memo-randum. "We do not like the U.S. paper because it is couched in rather provocative language which the U.S.S.R. can scarcely accept," grumbled R.A. MacKay, one of the Canadian officials involved in assessing the proposal.[25] External Affairs worried that the American proposal would only receive the support of a slight majority in the Committee of Twelve. It asked the Canadian delegate on the com- mittee, James George, to evaluate the situation. If the United Kingdom, France, and India did not object and there was general support, then Canada ought not to object. But if the United States was attempting to force its proposition on to the committee and could obtain only seven or eight supporting votes, then George should seek to delay any action: "if the Committee of Twelve tends to gag on it," warned External Affairs, "the Assembly vote will probably be still less favourable."[26]

Under pressure from the United Kingdom, France, and Canada, the United States returned in August with a milder draft that "recalled" that the Majority Plan had been approved by the General Assembly but expressed no opinion on its merits. The Soviet Union was not appeased; the Russians declared that they would only vote for the resolution if the reference to the Majority Plan was dropped. External Affairs believed that no great harm would be done if this concession was made, although it doubted that the Americans would agree. It was apprehensive that both India and Yugoslavia, the emerging leaders of the developing world, might abstain. Canadian fears proved well founded. In the final vote, these countries did abstain on the paragraph which mentioned the plan. But the resolution as a whole was carried by eleven to one, with only the Soviet Union in opposition. This rejection was not very serious since the USSR had made it clear that they agreed with the main thrust of the United States proposal – the merger of the two commissions.

Another incident which illustrates Canadian impatience with American rigidity occurred in September when the Committee of Twelve was preparing its final report to the General Assembly. The USSR had proposed a series of brief amendments which simply amplified the record, changes which most countries thought of little importance. But the United States was determined to oppose Soviet suggestions, no matter how innocuous; the only alternative was a skeleton report that merely listed the dates of the meetings, the official proposals, and the votes on them. When the time came to vote, George observed to the committee that in view of the difficulties of time and desiring to avoid further controversy, he would support the short report, but he would much have preferred the more detailed original to which he believed the General Assembly had a right. The response from External Affairs was that he had not gone far enough; they would have advised him to abstain. "This tendency on the part of the United States to force its view, often ill considered and inconsistent, upon a more or less unwilling committee," an External memorandum declared, "is most unfortunate, and the fact that the issue involved is often relatively minor in no sense justified this practice."[27]

Amalgamating the two commissions was only one facet of the disarmament programme which the United States intended to present to the General Assembly in 1951. In 1949 the CCA had adopted a French suggestion for a census of conventional arms. Now the United States proposed that the accounting should include atomic arms as well. This idea had first surfaced in a memo from the Policy Planning Staff in March 1951.[28] It noted that the American people were concerned that while the United States was embarking on a huge rearmament programme there was "no concurrent program looking toward eventual disarmament." Now that the Soviet Union had become an atomic power, the Americans could no longer agree even to the Majority Plan without compromising their security unless conventional arms were also controlled. A disarmament scheme that was fair to both sides had to begin with a census and verification of existing armaments. The memorandum recommended that the Americans suggest that the census should include nuclear weapons as well. The USSR had always said that it would support a count that included atomic arms. Thus, if the United States now put forward the same proposal, the Soviet Union would be confronted with the dilemma of going back on its own words or allowing broad inspection behind the Iron Curtain.[29]

In a radio broadcast on 7 November 1951, President Truman proposed the principles of a new scheme for a count of existing arms. There would be an inventory done by stages, with each stage to be completed before the next was begun. The least vital information would be disclosed first and the most sensitive last. Unfortunately, but not surprisingly, these proposals failed to attract Soviet support. Beginning with the least vital information essentially meant that data on Soviet conventional arms would become available long before the facts on the American nuclear arsenal were revealed. As well, there was much more public information on American arms than on Soviet arms. In consequence, the census would be more useful to American strategists than to Soviet ones. Moreover, all figures were to be verified, which would mean admitting foreign inspectors to Soviet territory. Finally, the Truman proposal had not announced a date on which the prohibition of atomic weapons would begin – only that it would be sometime in the future.

That same day, the United States, supported by the United Kingdom and France, proposed to the Political Committee that the Committee of Twelve's recommendation for a single disarmament commission be accepted. The mandate of the new Disarmament Commission (DC) would be to prepare a draft disarmament treaty on the basis of certain guiding principles including the progressive disclosure and verification, on a continuing basis, of armed forces and armaments including atomic weapons, effective international inspection, and acceptance of the Majority Plan for the control of atomic energy. The day the tripartite resolution was presented, Pearson lunched with the American ambassador at large to the United Nations, Philip Jessup, and discussed what he could usefully contribute to the debate. It was agreed that he would deal with the Soviet charge that the West was bargaining in bad faith, preaching disarmament while continuing to strengthen the North Atlantic Treaty Organization militarily. In his address to the Political Committee two days later, Pearson justified NATO, supported the merging of the two commissions, argued for the armaments census, and emphasized the importance of inspection.

As expected, the Russians refused to support the resolution. They complained that there was no provision for the immediate prohibition of atomic weapons and that the resolution conformed to the old Baruch scheme of giving a central international control organ the powers of ownership of atomic facilities. They disliked disclosure by stages; information on conventional and atomic weapons should be made available simultaneously. They objected to inspection on a continuing basis. The only part of the resolution acceptable to them was the merging of the commissions. They were unable, however, to prevent the majority of the General Assembly passing the tripartite resolution on 11 January 1952.

Significantly, Pearson had not offered support for the Majority Plan in his speech to the Political Committee. Canadian diplomats were becoming less and less certain about its continuing validity. In view of the great Soviet conventional superiority, they believed the West would be "dismayed" if the USSR were to show any real interest in immediately accepting it. If there were a move towards conventional equality, however, then to get an overall agreement on disarmament the Canadian view was that "in certain respects the present atomic control plan might be modified so as to make it more acceptable to the U.S.S.R. without impairing the effectiveness of the international control which it provides."[30]

In any case these reflections were speculative. There was little sign that concessions that would still preserve the safeguards would be enough to bring the USSR to ease its profound objections to the plan. At the same time the Americans were adamant in not budging from their public support for it. In mid-November 1951 the legal adviser to the State Department wrote Jessup a highly critical note about the plan. It had been based on two unrealistic assumptions: that the United States would have a monopoly of atomic weapons for a number of years and that atomic energy might soon be used for peaceful purposes on a large scale. Given that neither assumption had come to be, were ownership and management provisions still needed, if there was a control system with rigorous inspection? And was it necessary to do away with the veto against sanctions? Could it not remain because its exercise would constitute "a virtual act of war in violation of the most solemn treaty obligations?"[31] He suggested that the United States should take the lead in exploring the possibility of new plans. But this was not a serious possibility. John Hickerson, the assistant under secretary of state for United Nations affairs, wrote to Jessup that "any proposal for reexamination of the atomic energy plan will encounter the strongest opposition and must be initiated directly by the President."[32]

Reporting on the current Assembly session in December 1951, James George, who was now one of Canada's spokesmen at the disarmament talks, expressed satisfaction that the West had taken the initiative in the propaganda wars. He was pleased that the breach between the two sides had not widened; both had agreed to continue discussing disarmament issues. He added: "it is clear that atomic weapons and conventional weapons must be considered together in any scheme leading to effective disarmament."[33] His premise was that the American strategic advantage in atomic bombs would be increasingly neutralized by the Soviet stock, even though the latter was currently much smaller. Consequently, an atomic agreement was desirable. Yet it could not be put into effect until there was a rough parity in conventional arms. Curiously, George did not mention the profoundly contentious question which had been at the root of the impasse all the time. The West insisted that a control system be set up before prohibition of the atomic bomb. The USSR demanded the reverse order. As one observer reported, "controversy over this point arose more frequently than over any other."[34] In fact, the main source of dispute between the two sides would gradually shift from the acceptability of the Majority Plan to which should come first: prohibition or control, an issue which would only be resolved in May 1955.

1952

THE DISARMAMENT COMMISSION AT WORK

Apart from the great powers, Canada was the only permanent member of the new Disarmament Commission. There had been some ambiguity about Canada's status since it was not a member of the CCA, but the British had stated publicly that membership of the Disarmament Commission would be the same as that of the AEC and the Soviet Union had not objected. John Holmes suggests that this gesture "illustrates the particular confidence there was in Pearson at that time."[35] But given their claim to voice the aspirations of the free world, it is more likely that the United States and the United Kingdom believed it important to have within the new commission a small power like Canada which could be counted on, as a loyal NATO member, to support the Anglo-American position.

The tripartite proposal having been dealt with, the General Assembly turned its attention to a Soviet Resolution on measures to combat the threat of war. It consisted of a mixture of political demands such as the condemnation of the Atlantic bloc, immediate cessation of fighting in Korea, and a five-power peace pact along with a number of proposals on disarmament. In January 1952, at the behest of the United States, the United Kingdom, and France, the General Assembly rejected the first three items but transmitted the disarmament measures to the new commission. This step showed that the West intended the Disarmament Commission to be a genuine forum to consider all disarmament measures – those from the East as well as their own.

Canada had shown a strong interest in two of the Soviet disarmament propositions. In presenting the resolution, Andrei Vyshinsky had declared that the "prohibition of atomic weapons and the institution of international control shall be put into effect simultaneously" and that "the international control organ shall have the right to conduct inspection on a continuing basis; but it shall not be entitled to interfere in the domestic affairs of states."[36] David Johnson, Canada's new permanent representative at the United Nations, believed the Russian proposals were ambiguous ploys to influence public opinion. But Pearson was interested enough in what Vyshinsky had said to compose External's dispatch to Johnson himself. Conceding that the new overture was effective propaganda, he nevertheless wondered if the proposal might not represent "a significant change." Did the Soviet Union now believe that an effective international control organ must accompany the prohibition of atomic weapons? Greater clarification was needed. If the Soviet words were only rhetoric, then this fact should be exposed as quickly as possible. "If there is any genuine concession," he concluded, "we have no choice (and I think this is true both for propaganda reasons and from our own direct interest in the matter of content) but to welcome the fact and let the disarmament commission study the question of implementation."[37]

In the Assembly debates Johnson therefore made a valiant attempt to pin Vyshinsky down by a series of direct questions, but the wily Soviet spokesman would not go further in explaining the relationship between the prohibition of atomic weapons and the institution of an effective control system. He left Johnson with the impression that the "Soviet Union was not prepared to make any real concessions on this point."[38] Pearson, always on the lookout for breakthrough, must have been disappointed. The Soviet Union, interested in propaganda victories, was ready to propose inspection on a continuing basis, but, for reasons of prudence, it had added the condition that such inspection should not interfere in the domestic affairs of states. Pearson would continue to insist that unhampered inspection was crucial to any agreement, but the Soviet Union would never lower its barriers.

The main feature of the thirty meetings of the Disarmament Commission in 1952 was the continuing deadlock between the two sides. Most of the Canadian activity in the commission took place in private meetings with the Western big three. In contrast to its prominent role in the AEC, Canada played only a minor role in public sessions of the Disarmament Commission. One reason may have been that it was now much less interested in propaganda and more in genuine negotiation. As the first meetings of the commission approached, External Affairs, unhappy that the commission would meet in public session, wrote Johnson that "nothing will be gained by maintaining the new Commission as a propaganda forum ... any useful work which might be done in the Commission can only be expected to occur in closed sessions."[39] It feared that the intention of both the United States and the USSR was to use the Disarmament Commission to speak to the world press, showing they had no interest in seeking meaningful compromises.

Canadian anxiety increased when at the first business meeting of the commission, the Soviet delegate, Jacob Malik, charged that the United States was using germ warfare in Korea and China. Clearly, the Soviet Union intended to use the commission to score political points rather than to negotiate seriously. There was a danger that the talks would become bogged down in a propaganda issue that had little to do with disarmament. Alarmed, External Affairs instructed Johnson to make every effort "to get the DC into secret sessions as soon as possible."[40] Fortunately, the commission soon ruled that the Soviet charges were out of order. But that left the serious problem of the sessions still being public. In April Canada moved that the work of the commission normally be carried on in closed sessions. The Soviet Union objected that this was merely a Western trick to prevent the world from learning about its stand on disarmament, while the American press, informed through leaks, printed the United States point of view. Perhaps it was this charge that compelled the United States and other countries to abstain, and the Canadian motion was lost. This was the only public initiative that Canada would take in the commission. What it had proposed was necessary if there were going to be a genuine grappling with disarmament, but its motion failed because it was impossible to force the superpowers to enter into serious talks when for the time being their only interest was propaganda.

At the end of March, the Disarmament Commission had two plans of work before it. That of the Americans sought to achieve some means of controlling Soviet armaments and emphasized the gathering of military information, while that of the USSR concentrated on the prohibition of atomic weapons. In the end the commission, by a vote of eleven to one (USSR), adopted a compromise

French plan of work. Two committees were created. Committee 1 would study the regulation of arms and armed forces and the prohibition of atomic weapons; Committee 2 would deal with the disclosure and verification of all armed forces and all armaments including atomic ones. These committees met concurrently during April and May of 1952.

In Committee 2 the Americans presented their five-stage plan for the disclosure of information on armed forces and the locations and facilities concerning armaments of all types including atomic weapons. Gathering such data, they argued, was a necessary prelude to drafting a fair disarmament treaty. The information at one stage would need to be verified before inquiries could begin at the next stage. The aim was to build confidence by going from the least secret to the most sensitive material. But the proposal was immediately denounced by Malik because the United States would be receiving military intelligence during the first four stages without guaranteeing that there would be a fifth stage at which it would reveal its atomic secrets. Earlier, Johnson had written his superiors in Ottawa that "if we could get the Soviet Union to agree to almost any kind of exchange of classified military information with us, we (ie. the West) could hardly be the losers, as their military security is much more strict and comprehensive than ours."[41] Here the "we" speaks volumes; there was no doubt in Johnson's mind that Canada was part of the Western team. And if he could see that the proposal offered an advantage to his side, so could the Soviet negotiators. A major stumbling block to reaching agreement was that each side was concerned not with common security but only with its own. After five meetings, Committee 2 adjourned in late May without any agreed conclusions.

The work in Committee 1 proved equally sterile. At its first meeting, Jules Moch, the French representative, asked whether the Soviet formula for the simultaneous prohibition of atomic weapons and the establishment of an international system of control meant that prohibition would come into force when the control agreement was signed or when the controlling organ was in position and able to work. Malik's response was that when the international control organ was set up and ready to go, "then the prohibition of atomic weapons and the establishment of strict international control over the observance of such prohibition are to go into effect simultaneously."[42] But this proposition did not suit the West. They wished information about Soviet atomic facilities to be gathered and verified before the prohibition of atomic bombs came into effect. At the same time the Americans, for domestic political reasons, were reluctant to commit themselves to a timetable on when, in return for an effective system of international control, they would agree to prohibit atomic weapons. Malik complained that "until there is a decision to prohibit and reduce, there is nothing to control."[43]

But the French had also asked what the Soviet Union meant by continuous control and how was it to be limited so as not to interfere in the domestic policies of states. Johnson also tried to elicit more concrete detail on this point by posing the same questions which Canada had put to Vyshinsky in January. But Malik evaded an answer, except to say that interference in internal affairs meant "not having General Eisenhower and their headquarters staff in their national capitals."[44] This was a fatuous response. Malik could give no useful detail because his government was still fearful about opening its territory to outside inspection. The West was left with no guarantee that international inspectors would have unimpeded access to Soviet atomic facilities.

The debate in the concluding meetings of the committee was merely an elaboration by both sides of what each regarded as the main issue. The essence of their disagreement was this: the USSR called for the immediate prohibition of atomic weapons but refused to offer satisfactory safeguards. The United States was ready to propose the Majority Plan to achieve this goal but would not promise to prohibit atomic weapons at a definite point in time. With such fundamental differences, it was little wonder that the work of Committee 1 was also futile.

Although nothing useful had come from the deliberations of the two committees, the three Western powers were now ready to take a positive step. The USSR had always charged that the West had no real interest in disarmament. To the Western response that disarmament could only take place in an atmosphere of mutual trust, it had maintained that the reduction of armaments would create a sense of international security. In 1946 the Soviet Union had called for the prohibition of atomic weapons. In 1948 it had proposed the reduction by one-third of the conventional military strength of the five permanent members of the Security Council. In view of the Soviet superiority in conventional arms, an across-the-board percentage decrease would have still left it with the advantage. Obviously such a proposal was not very attractive to the West. Yet in the propaganda war to win the important peace constituency, the Soviet Union always appeared to be pressing for real cuts in arms.

To cease being vulnerable on this flank, the three Western powers proposed – at a late May meeting of the commission – an agreement that would provide for a personnel ceiling of between a million and a million and a half for the respective armed forces of the United States, the Soviet Union, and China. For the United Kingdom and France, the level would be between 700,000 and 800,000. Because the offer was not coupled with the prohibition of atomic arms, there was little chance that the USSR would accept it. But it was a measure that would be easily understood by the public. Calling for a reduction of more than one-half in the armed forces of the United States and the USSR would swamp the Soviet proposal for a one-third cut. It would direct public attention away from the American atomic bomb towards the Soviet army. The West argued that the growth in confidence resulting from such an accord would make it easier to abolish nuclear arms, that their proposal was merely one element of a comprehensive disarmament programme which could be put into effect independently of a programme for eliminating atomic bombs. At the end of August, at the last business meeting of the Disarmament Commission, the Soviet Union rejected the plan because the Western proposals merely limited the personnel of the armed forces. What was needed, it insisted, was a substantial reduction of all land, air, and naval forces, the liquidation of military bases maintained on foreign territory, and, above all, the prohibition of atomic weapons.

Yet the tripartite proposal for the limitation of armed forces remained on the bargaining table. If accepted by the Soviet Union, the West would have to live with their offer. If the Russians were serious about atomic disarmament, they would have to agree to some sort of conventional parity. Because the proposal set out a concrete number, it would prove a useful benchmark in the future. In time, the Soviet planners might see that it gave them a definite advantage. Unlike the USSR, the United States had global commitments. If held to a ceiling of a million and a half personnel, it would lack sufficient forces to shore up the Western defence in central Europe until the hoped for West German units began to materialize.

External Affairs was happy about the Western initiative. It contained a provision that the armed forces of other states would be restricted to less than one per cent of the population. Canadian forces would thus remain at their current level, but this presented no problem for the Canadian chiefs of staff. On Pearson's recommendation, the Cabinet Defence Committee gave its support to the proposal. The question then arose about the position Canada ought to take in the Disarmament Commission. James George produced a tough draft, painting the Russians as unreasonable and intransigent. But External Affairs advised him to adopt a milder tone and omit the stronger attacks on the Soviet stand.[45] The statement, read on 1 October by Johnson at the last open meeting of the Disarmament Commission in 1952, was much softer in its approach. Pearson was putting the possibility of substantive progress ahead of propaganda.

DIVERGENCE BETWEEN FRANCE AND
THE UNITED STATES

Perhaps the most notable development in the Disarmament Commission negotiations of 1952 was the split that began to appear between France and the United States. In the late forties the two countries had worked closely together in the AEC, but now they were involved in a fierce conflict over whether to go ahead with the European Defence Community. Although France signed the treaty to set up the community in May 1952, so great was the French popular feeling against rearming West Germany that the French parliament would never ratify the pact. During 1952, therefore, the French government had found itself under pressure from the Americans to propose the ratification of a pact which great numbers of its own people opposed. The Disarmament Commission talks of that spring appeared to offer a way out of its dilemma. If an agreement to disarm could be reached with the Russians, it might no longer be necessary to rearm the Germans.

There was still another reason for French politicians to pay close attention to the Disarmament Commission in 1952. Their government was trying to decide if France should develop atomic weapons. A debate in the assembly in July showed that the French were not ready to take a decisive step to becoming a nuclear power but neither were they prepared to close the door on this option. Even the socialists, who were against nuclear bombs, agreed that France could not do without them if the other great powers continued to have them: a condition for France giving up its programme would be the elimination of all nuclear bombs. Thus the fate of the French atomic programme hung on the success of the talks in the commission.

At the commission, France's policy was admirably expressed by its spokesman, Jules Moch, a naval reserve officer and a former minister of defence. Despite all the changes in government over the rest of the decade, Moch, although a member of the Socialist party, kept his post as his country's negotiator on disarmament. No one could doubt his knowledge of the subject, his intellectual capacity, or his fierce determination to see nuclear weapons eliminated. "I remain an optimist by reason and by faith," he declared.[46] Believing

that the new European Defence Community would result in a re-
surgence of German military might, he had wished the decision to
create it to be put off until the Disarmament Commission's negotiations were complete. Even after the EDC treaty was signed in May,
he still hoped that the commission might work out some solution
that might make this fateful step unnecessary. He calculated that
under the threat of a revived German military presence the Soviet
Union might be more ready to co-operate on disarmament measures that would make the proposed army unnecessary. As Moch
saw it, France and the Soviet Union shared a common objective of
preventing the new army from coming into being. The Americans,
however, were determined to rearm West Germany. From their
point of view any serious disarmament negotiations could only
arrest the progress towards the ratification by France of the EDC
treaty. Moch's views were thus bound to put him on a collision
course with American diplomats.

Canada was a strong supporter of the rearming of West Germany. Nevertheless, its diplomats sympathized a good deal with
Moch's approach to disarmament. They shared his apprehension
that time was running out and that the steady build-up of fissionable materials would soon make effective control of atomic energy
impossible. Like him, they were troubled by the ownership provisions of the Majority Plan which they suspected were out of date,
and they agreed that efficient and continuous international inspection would provide effective control. Moch would certainly have endorsed Pearson's argument that "no general plan of disarmament is
likely to have any prospect of success unless it not only deals at the
same time with both conventional and atomic armaments but also
incorporates all three segments of the problem: the 'decision' to
prohibit atomic weapons and reduce armed forces and armaments
(regarded as essential by the U.S.S.R.); the 'safeguards' of disclosure
and verification of information on such weapons, armed forces and
armaments (regarded as essential by the Western powers); and the
'system of international control' which is essential to enforce the
plan."[47]

The United States had been proposing an elaborate system for
divulging and verifying military information as the first step to
disarmament; the Soviet Union had insisted that it must begin with
an agreement to ban atomic weapons. In June, Moch suggested a
compromise in the form of a three-stage plan in which the counting
of arms would be integrated with actual steps towards disarmament.
After a permanent control organ was established, a timetable would
be implemented with each disclosure of information to be followed

by measures of disarmament. Once the control organ had verified that the disarmament steps had been carried out at one stage, the process would move automatically to the next stage. At the first stage, the divulging of military data, verified by the control organ, would be followed by (1) the prohibition of bacteriological weapons and (2) the limitation of armed forces and all military budgets at the level verified during the first stage. The revelation of additional information at the next stage would bring about (1) a halt in the manufacture of atomic weapons and fissionable materials in dangerous quantities and (2) the prohibition of both qualitative and quantitative increases in conventional armaments. The third disclosure of information would be followed by the establishment of the permanent control of atomic facilities, the prohibition of all use of atomic weapons, the destruction of existing weapons within three months, and, within one year, a first reduction in numbers of conventional armaments and armed forces. Although he set out a way forward, Moch did not specify the amount of information to be disclosed at any one stage.

Johnson was intrigued by the proposal. "Moch's statement," he wrote to External Affairs, "marks a definite shift in the French position in the direction of the Soviet position. In some respects he has gone further than I think the United States would be willing to go in the foreseeable future. On the other hand he has set out concretely and in detail what the rest of us have recognized would sooner or later have to be done – namely he has married up the major components of any comprehensive disarmament scheme (disclosure, verification, control, prohibition, and reduction) and analysed them in relation to the timetable according to which they would be put into operation ... it is an impressive intellectual construction." Johnson's main concern was about the tactical value of making such an offer at that time: "I think it is at least questionable timing to present a major compromise proposal – even in a tentative form – before Malik has shown the least willingness to negotiate a settlement."[48]

The United States found it difficult to accept Moch's design because it violated the principle that disclosure and verification of military information must precede disarmament. Then, too, he had failed to specify that the body to control nuclear energy would have the same ownership powers over atomic facilities which would have been granted by the Majority Plan. Two French scientists visited Washington in September to sell an alternative plan by which all atomic facilities would be nationally owned but subject to continuous international inspection. But they were unable to persuade the

United States authorities that their proposal would guarantee that national governments would not divert fissionable materials in dangerous quantities for their own malign purposes.

Johnson explained the difference this way. Both sides were worried by the existence of an ever increasing number of un-counted atomic bombs. The American answer was to insist on an even tighter control plan. The French argued that the existence of large stockpiles of fissionable materials and weapons made a perfect plan impossible. Certainly "ownership" would no longer solve the problem. Instead, it was necessary to rely on the most extensive powers of inspection to uncover secret atomic facilities and hidden stocks of bombs. They also counted on a comprehensive disarma-ment programme to prevent any aggressor drawing full benefits from a sudden atomic attack.[49]

It is doubtful that either government thought that their scheme would eliminate atomic bombs. But each now had different political agendas. The French, who were at the beginning of their atomic programme, wished for complete freedom from outside restraints. It is true that their disarmament plan called for the type of rigorous inspection which the USSR was not likely to accept. Nevertheless, removing the ownership provisions which the Soviet Union detested might make possible some kind of limited deal that would slow the drive for a rearmed Germany. But for the United States to agree to alter the Majority Plan in a way that seemed to make concessions to the USSR just before a presidential election campaign when the Republicans were promising to end the Democratic policy of being soft on communists was politically impossible. Moreover, as the American negotiators asked themselves, what was there to gain by a more positive approach to the Soviet Union when the latter showed absolutely no interest in compromise?

The rift between the United States and the French was making life difficult for External Affairs. It feared that the Soviet Union was trying, with some success, to weaken French support for the American position. "If the existing divergence of view were to widen, it would clearly place all members of the Western alliance including ourselves in an awkward position," External Affairs warned Johnson. It was ready to propose a moderate course that would command the support of all Western delegations and "enable positive proposals to be put forward which would test the sincerity of the U.S.S.R."[50]

In August, External Affairs produced an internal memorandum which sought to deal with the chief tactical dilemma facing Western planners. American atomic weapons were needed to protect the security of their countries. Yet there was widespread public sentiment in the West in favour of giving them up. As well, specific measures were needed to mollify the French who were not satisfied that enough reasonable concessions were being made to test Soviet sincerity. Current Western proposals tried to tackle, in turn, each element of a comprehensive disarmament programme from its beginning through to its final stage. External Affairs proposed to begin with a manageable "slice" of disarmament that would include enough of each element of a comprehensive programme to allow a substantial beginning in the overall process of disarmament without threatening security. This package would be made up of the balanced reduction of armed forces and conventional armaments, initial steps towards instituting the international control of energy so as to ensure the prohibition of atomic weapons (which External Affairs believed would entail modifying the ownership provisions of the Majority Plan), the disclosure and verification of military information including that on atomic weapons, and, finally, the establishment of an international control organ to ensure the implementation of this "first slice." External Affairs believed that its specific proposals, taken together, would offer a meaningful step towards disarmament without an American commitment to a definite date to eliminate its atomic bombs. Yet the Canadian proposal would test Soviet sincerity and boost Western prestige in the propaganda wars.[51]

Unfortunately the Western allies, when approached, were far from enthusiastic about the Canadian proposal. The French damned it with faint praise: they thought it a small step in the right direction. Both the United States and the United Kingdom doubted that the Canadian package would meet the Soviet complaints that Western disarmament proposals amounted to no more than a means of securing intelligence and postponing the prohibition of atomic arms. Then, too, in the Canadian scheme the first slice of the component of disclosure and verification, following the principle of the exchange of information on the least sensitive areas, would ask the Soviet Union to accept aerial surveys in exchange for their right to examine American atomic facilities from the outside. Finally, both the United States and the United Kingdom remained extremely reluctant to revise the Majority Plan. The chief American disarmament negotiator explained that to attract the USSR, the Canadian proposals would have to go much farther than the United States was prepared to accept; the Americans believed that any concession that the Soviet Union would find significant would weaken the capacity of the United States to defend itself.[52]

Canadian diplomats would have been pleased if there had been agreement to present the package to the USSR and if the latter had shown any interest. Nevertheless their purpose was not to mediate between East and West; this was clearly the case because they argued that one of the advantages of their scheme was that it would test Soviet motives. Any real effort to bring the United States and the USSR together would have assumed that such good will already existed on both sides. In fact the Canadians were pursuing one of their major roles in the disarmament negotiations – protecting Western solidarity. Political strains between France and the United States would cause continual concern in Ottawa, and Canadian diplomats would expend a good deal of energy in trying to smooth over the differences. Unlike France, Canada had no specific security concerns that were not shared by the United States. They believed, however, that many of the French criticisms of the American disarmament proposals were valid. Their self-appointed task would be to find the compromises that would bring the two Western allies back together.

Having finished its work for the present, the Disarmament Commission drew up a report which merely summarized its meetings and offered neither conclusions nor recommendations. The Western powers also included a resolution which approved their own initiatives and instructed the Disarmament Commission to continue its work. This package was passed in the commission on 9 October with only the Soviet Union in opposition. Still, Canada was not anxious for a clash with the Soviet Union on the disarmament issue in the coming session of the General Assembly. The West, dependent on atomic bombs, was unable to offer any concrete proposals for their reduction or control. Yet it was anxious to win the propaganda contest. Canada advised its representatives that "it is most desirable that this dilemma should be concealed from the Assembly."[53] They were to avoid disarmament issues unless the Soviet Union took them up; in that case they were to attack the USSR for intransigence while demonstrating that the West was ready to consider any reasonable proposal. At bottom, what External Affairs feared was that the longer the Soviet Union remained stubborn, the more the United Kingdom and the United States would retreat from their original position on prohibiting the bomb. "This tendency," it warned, "[seems] to be both unreasonable and dangerous."[54] It was crucial that the West continued to stand by its pledge to eliminate atomic weapons. This would not be the last time that External Affairs would worry about the commitment of its allies comprehensive disarmament.

1953

THE BEGINNING OF THE THAW

In the autumn of 1952 the General Assembly had decided to post-pone discussion of the resolution on the work of the Disarmament Commission until the spring of 1953. By that time Dwight D. Eisenhower had become the president of the United States and Georgi Malenkov had succeeded Joseph Stalin, who had died early in March, as premier of the USSR. These leadership changes were soon reflected in the commission's negotiations. On 18 March the Political Committee of the United Nations was considering both a Soviet and a Western resolution. The latter, sponsored by fourteen powers including Canada, was innocuously worded, asking that the Disarmament Commission carry on its work but also commending the commission for its efforts and reaffirming support for the Majority Plan. Countering this was the Soviet resolution blaming the United States, the United Kingdom, and France for proposing mea-sures for illegally obtaining intelligence reports on armaments. In the debate, David Johnson, on behalf of Canada, weighed in on the side of the West, complaining that the Soviet conception of inspec-tion would prevent United Nations inspectors going wherever they thought necessary. In the end the Political Committee endorsed the Western resolution by a wide margin.

The whole dialogue seemed headed for its usual deadlock. But on 15 March, totally unexpectedly, the Soviet premier issued a much publicized statement that there was no issue between the United States and the USSR which could not be settled by peaceful means. On 16 April Eisenhower responded in a conciliatory tone, deploring the arms race and calling on the USSR to co-operate on serious disarmament proposals which would be put into effect under United Nations control and inspection. The signs that, for the first time since the Cold War began, the leaders of the super-powers were beginning to seek ways of easing tensions greatly improved the political climate in which the resolution just passed by the Political Committee was discussed in the General Assembly. Instead of offering his own resolution, the Soviet spokesman sub-mitted two reasonable amendments to the one under discussion. The first of these called for the deletion from the committee's report of the commendation for the Disarmament Commission's attempt to carry out the Assembly's instructions and the implied criticism of the Soviet Union for not co-operating. This was agreed to unanimously by the Assembly. Andrei Vyshinsky also asked for the omission of the phrase denoting Assembly approval of the Majority Plan. But the West refused to budge on this point because they feared weakening political support for it. Vyshinsky's second amendment was defeated, and the resolution as a whole was adopted over Soviet opposition by a substantial majority on 8 April.

Canada supported the resolution but did not take part in the General Assembly debate. Johnson remained sceptical about the Soviet change of heart. Although Vyshinsky had softened his rhetoric and eased his tactics, there was no indication that the USSR had actually altered its stance on disarmament; the press, publicizing the milder Soviet tone, overlooked the fact that the USSR had taken no concrete steps towards meeting the Western position on disarmament.

Although the General Assembly's resolution had called upon the Disarmament Commission to continue its work, there was no point in meeting until an armistice in Korea was declared. On 27 July the two sides agreed to stop the fighting, and eventually this would permit much more realistic disarmament talks. Meanwhile neither side appeared ready with new proposals. On 20 August, the Disarmament Commission, meeting only for one day, approved unanimously a statement which expressed hope that recent international events had created a more propitious atmosphere for disarmament talks and promised to report to the eighth session of the General Assembly in the autumn of 1953.

United Nations anxiety over disarmament became more intense in August with the USSR's test explosion of a hydrogen bomb. Yet at first it seemed that there would be no change in the ritual stands of the superpowers as they approached yet another clash over disarmament at the United Nations. The debate in the Political Committee over the Disarmament Commission report of August began early in November. The Soviet resolution demanded the unconditional prohibition of atomic weapons and the reduction of the armed forces of the five permanent powers of the Security Council by one-third. For its part, the West produced another fourteen-power resolution that implied continued support for the Majority Plan and asked the Disarmament Commission to carry on with its work. In his speech on behalf of Canada, Johnson called on the Soviet Union to recognize that it was unreasonable for it to wish the Assembly to endorse the prohibition of atomic weapons when it was not prepared to discuss a practical system of safeguards through international inspection and control.

The superpowers were still at odds: the Soviet Union demanded the prohibition of the atomic bomb without clarifying what controls it would accept; the Americans insisted that an inspection and control system must be in place before there could be a serious reduction in armed forces and the elimination of the atomic bomb. Yet they avoided committing themselves to any timetable on when this might take place. Into this breach stepped Jules Moch with a speech in which he evoked the spirit of compromise and repeated the proposals which he had put forward in the Disarmament Commission in June 1952. Moch had no reason to expect any support from the West. But undoubtedly he hoped for more understanding from the Soviet Union. Instead Vyshinsky attacked his attempt at compromise as "indistinguishable"[55] from American proposals. We can only imagine what Moch must have thought when dismissed by both sides. Yet he was on the right road. The final report of the Canadian delegation on the eighth session of the General Assembly accurately summed up the situation by noting that neither the United States nor the Soviet Union had shown any intention of changing their respective positions on disarmament but that "the French have indicated the general lines on which a compromise solution might perhaps be sought in private at the appropriate time."[56]

But this was for the future. Meanwhile the prospect of a war fought with hydrogen bombs was driving the prime minister of India, Jawaharlal Nehru, to build a bloc of neutral nations to mediate between the two sides. This message found fertile ground in the General Assembly of 1953 where great numbers of worried delegates showed a fervent desire that the major players seriously tackle the enormously difficult problem of eliminating nuclear weapons. In November, India had attempted to make the fourteen-power resolution more acceptable to the USSR by proposing an amendment that emphasized the danger of atomic weapons but omitted mention of the Majority Plan. To mollify the Indians and appease the growing neutralist sentiment in the General Assembly, the West agreed to this change of language on condition that the resolution acknowledge that any scheme to do away with weapons of mass destruction would need to be under international control. The Indians also proposed that the Disarmament Commission study the possibility of setting up a sub-committee of the United States, the Soviet Union, Great Britain, France, and Canada to hold private talks on disarmament. India had named Canada, its delegate told Pearson, because of Canada's special experience and concern with the atomic side of disarmament. In addition, India saw Canada, its Commonwealth colleague, as an able spokesman for middle powers. The amendment of the fourteen-power resolution to take into account Indian proposals was approved overwhelmingly by the General Assembly. The Soviet Union found itself considering a resolution that suggested a sub-committee but said nothing about the Majority Plan. This allowed it to reverse its United Nations behaviour of the past seven years; instead of voting against the fourteen-power resolution, it abstained. Although there had been no narrowing of the gap between East and West, the establishment of the sub-committee would prove to be an important procedural step that allowed serious negotiations to begin.

EISENHOWER PROPOSES ATOMS FOR PEACE

Another important development for disarmament negotiations was taking place outside the Disarmament Commission. President Eisenhower was beginning to concentrate on the nuclear issue. One writer has suggested that it was his "apparent inconsistency in claiming to work for peace while strengthening America's defense that plagued Eisenhower's efforts to reach a nuclear arms agreement."[57] Nevertheless there is little doubt that he was sincere when he warned the American public in October 1953 that "our former unique physical security has almost totally disappeared before the long-range bomber and the destructive power of a single bomb ... In its wake we see only sudden and mass destruction, erasure of cities, the possible doom of every nation and society."[58]

The president was coming to the conclusion that "as of now the world is racing toward catastrophe" and "something must be done to put a brake on."[59] On 8 December, in a speech to the United Nations, Eisenhower proposed that atomic nations should contribute nuclear materials to be used for peaceful purposes to an international United Nations agency. One advantage of his suggestion was that it would require no on-site inspection. Eisenhower hoped that even a small area in which the two sides could co-operate might lead to bigger things. And there was no danger to American security since the United States, possessing much more fissionable material than the USSR, could afford to reduce its stockpiles by two or three times the amount of a possible Soviet contribution. The Russians responded by pointing out that the Eisenhower proposal would neither check the production of atomic weapons nor limit their use. They were willing to discuss it if at the same time the United States would consider a total ban on nuclear weapons. But after listening to John Foster Dulles, his secretary of state, the president turned this idea down, maintaining that discussions on peaceful uses should be conducted separately from any disarmament talks. Negotiations on the peaceful uses of atomic energy went forward and led to the establishment of the International Atomic Energy Agency in 1957. While this initiative had no direct impact on disarmament negotiations, Eisenhower's powerful rhetoric stimulated the growing consciousness of the American people about the horrors of a nuclear war.

Prime Minister St Laurent hailed the Eisenhower proposal as imaginative and constructive. Canadian diplomats liked it because of its confidence-building aspects. Co-operation in this field of atomic energy, they believed, might lead to progress in disarmament. They were also sensitive to the political benefits of Eisenhower's speech. Because of the great appeal of the Soviet demand that atomic bombs be eliminated, the West was always vulnerable to the charge that they were making no real effort in this direction. Now the United States for once seemed to be taking the initiative. Without giving up their support for the Majority Plan, the Americans had found a brilliant means to demonstrate their sincerity and desire to resolve the atomic problem.

At the end of 1953 prospects for disarmament were therefore marginally better than they had been for three years. Serious disarmament negotiations had been impossible during the Korean War; now at last it was over. Then, too, Stalin had "failed to appreciate," writes an expert on Soviet military doctrine, "that nuclear weapons ... had altered the nature of war." He seems not to have understood that the two superpowers were in "a strategic stalemate reflecting mutual deterrence."[60] Such a premise formed the theoretical foundation for disarmament because it led to the conclusion that neither side could win an arms race. Stalin's death left the way open for Malenkov to proclaim that war in the nuclear age "would mean the end of world civilization."[61]

Still, the obstacles remained formidable. Each side heartily distrusted the other. Eisenhower was integrating the country's atomic weapons with its conventional ones. Then, too, the United States was now without a serious proposal for atomic disarmament. The Majority Plan was simply out of date. Lewis Strauss, the new chairman of the United States Atomic Energy Commission, doubted its effectiveness. Indeed, on 9 September the National Security Council agreed that the plan should not be reaffirmed.[62] The delay in serious negotiations caused by the Korean War meant that each side now had a formidable stock of atomic weapons; there was no longer any foolproof way of ensuring that they had been eliminated. And, finally, the plan was losing its credibility with the allies of the United States, such as France and Canada. The challenge facing the

Americans was to develop a new disarmament strategy that would take these technological and political changes into account.

In this period Canada had continued to develop its role of junior partner to the United States. It had certainly played its part in the propaganda wars by pressing the Soviet spokesmen to be more specific about proposals for inspection and control. Nevertheless it had been dissatisfied with the Majority Plan for some time and wished that the United States would come up with a well-considered comprehensive disarmament scheme on which the USSR could only refuse to negotiate at the risk of losing political prestige. Here, however, Canada was handicapped by an increasing lack of technical expertise. "We are in a dilemma," wrote Pearson to a colleague in October of 1952. "We have to rely exclusively on what the Americans tell us about [the] ... effectiveness [of nuclear weapons] now and later, and there is no way of checking this opinion."[63] Thus Canada was never able to make a useful substantive proposal. The other duty which Canadians had undertaken on behalf of the Western alliance was to attempt to close the rift between the United States and France. This effort placed Canada in something of a predicament. For the sake of Western unity it wished France to abandon its own three-stage plan and adopt Canada's "first slice" proposal. Yet Canadian diplomats could not help but feel that the road that France had indicated might prove useful in finding compromise on disarmament between East and West. The dilemma would be dramatically intensified in 1954.

CHAPTER SIX

Narrowing the Gap between East and West, 1954–55

The main accomplishment of the Disarmament Commission was to give birth to a sub-committee which allowed negotiations between the two sides to be pursued in private. But before that sub-committee could prove useful, each side had to be convinced that the other was serious about reaching an agreement. Up to the end of 1953 the Russians had remained sceptical about the West's seriousness of purpose. They had produced few proposals of their own, being content for the most part to react to those of the West in such a way as to win the propaganda battle. They failed to appreciate that an agreement on disarmament might strengthen their security. But as it became clear that the French shared their apprehension about a rearmed Germany, they began to alter their views. Thus, in November 1953, they had decided not to oppose the resolution setting up the sub-committee. But this new receptivity was still at a low level. As long as the Majority Plan remained part of the formal bargaining position of the West, the USSR would remain suspicious.

Canadian diplomats understood very well that the Majority Plan prevented serious bargaining between East and West. However they lacked the technical expertise to make concrete suggestions for its revision and the political capacity to make the United States pay attention to the need to do so. Yet their diplomatic skills and experience would prove useful to both sides. At a critical juncture the Canadians drafted a United Nations resolution which would allow the negotiations to go forward to an unexpectedly fruitful phase. In return for an Anglo-French offer on behalf of the West to prohibit nuclear arms at a definite point in time, the Soviet Union would agree to reduce its conventional forces and accept an effective system of control.

1956

CANADIAN REFLECTIONS ON THE IMPASSE

The first American H-bomb test on 1 March 1954 revived widespread apprehension, dormant since Hiroshima, about the horrors of atomic war. Some Japanese fisherman, who were unfortunate enough to be subject to the dreadful effects of radioactive fallout, became vivid examples of the harm these terrible weapons could inflict on innocent civilians. Prime Minister Nehru asked rhetorically: "How can we be sure that our children may not gradually go blind or contract some internal disease?" He reminded his listeners that atomic tests always seemed to take place in Asia, and in a formal address to the Indian Parliament on 2 April he called for an immediate "standstill agreement" between the United States and the USSR to prohibit nuclear tests while they worked out a comprehensive arms agreement.[1] This demand would widen the breach between India and the United States and would greatly concern Canadian diplomats in the future.

Meanwhile, at the end of March, Lewis Strauss, the chairman of the United States Atomic Energy Commission happened to observe at a press conference that a hydrogen bomb could wipe out metropolitan New York. This offhand remark touched off an uproar in the United States and Western Europe. As details of the first test became available, it became apparent that Great Britain was vulnerable to complete devastation from a Soviet H-bomb attack. Only with extreme difficulty was the Conservative majority able to defeat a Labour party resolution asking the government to seek a summit meeting with the Soviet Union to arrange for the suspension of tests. The American ambassador to France warned John Foster Dulles that the people of Western Europe were insisting that the tests be halted. NATO governments had no intention of yielding on this score, however. Their foreign ministers agreed with Dulles who, in a meeting of the NATO Council in April, reiterated his conviction that American nuclear weapons were necessary.[2] Nevertheless, something had to be done to ease public anxiety. The British and French began to press for the rapid convening of the Disarmament Commission. "The reason for the [British] initiative," Canada's permanent representative, David Johnson, wrote to External Affairs, "appears to be the very considerable pressure of public opinion that has been aroused in Western Europe and Asia by the US hydrogen bomb test last month. Eden [the British foreign secretary] believes that some gesture must be made even though we are far from having reached substantial agreement on any proposals which might be submitted by Western powers."[3] Norman Robertson, Canada's high commissioner in Great Britain, who would soon be very active in the negotiations, remarked to a colleague that "Dear Old Disarmament is having quite a run after years of sitting on the shelf."[4]

In April the Disarmament Commission met to establish the sub-committee proposed in the Assembly resolution of the previous November. Canada had had no guarantee that it would be a member, for it had not been named in the resolution. The United Kingdom proposed a sub-committee composed of the United States, the United Kingdom, France, the USSR, and Canada. The inclusion of Canada was warmly endorsed by France and the United States, but the Soviet representative was not nearly as enthusiastic. Andrei Vyshinsky asserted: "Clearly, from a military point of view, Canada has not the same importance as the United States. But it is apparently very convenient for the United States to have another vote in the sub-committee, that of Canada, which always and in all circumstances agrees with what is done by the United States State Department."[5] Only the first part of this charge was accurate: Canada had often been unhappy with American policy, but ever since December 1946 it had always voted with the United States. Vyshinsky was not opposed to Canada being a member of the sub-committee but wished to add the People's Republic of China, India, and Czechoslovakia as well. Johnson saw this suggestion as a ploy to fix the blame, if the talks failed, on the West for imposing the composition of the sub-committee.[6] The Disarmament Commission dismissed the Soviet complaint and set up the sub-committee as originally proposed. Vyshinsky's actions showed that the Soviet Union was seeking ways around having to operate in another United Nations committee in which it was always in the minority.

The hydrogen bomb test had impressed Johnson – like so many others – with the critical situation in which mankind found itself. He wrote External Affairs that he was anxious that the sub-committee talks should lead to a genuine effort to find a way out of this dangerous predicament. He conceded that much of the deliberations would be a propaganda exercise, but he added: "it will be that but not only that." He wanted Canada to be fully prepared to pull its weight in "whatever substantive discussions the committee may have."[7] He was particularly insistent that the West should produce fresh proposals: "Something more [is] required than to stand pat on the formulations of 1946–1950. The Western powers should have something new and constructive to offer."[8] Pearson entirely agreed with Johnson. He had earlier warned the Canadian parliament that "in the light of what has happened, we must approach this problem ... with greater urgency,"[9] and he had informed the Standing Committee on External Affairs that his department was making a "complete and exhaustive review" of the past Canadian position on disarmament and attempting to "relate it to the new situation created by the development of the hydrogen bomb, to see if there is anything which can be done to bring the two positions closer together."[10]

Accordingly, an External Affairs interdepartmental working party on disarmament had been asked to review the Canadian position on the Majority Plan. It was also to investigate two new issues. The first of these was the Soviet response to the Eisenhower proposal that states taking part in any agreement on the peaceful uses of atomic energy make an unconditional pledge not to use nuclear weapons. It was possible that the communists might launch an effective propaganda campaign on this theme. Should Canada endorse such an unconditional declaration? Second, the working party was to advise on how to deal with Nehru's proposal for a halt to nuclear bomb tests.[11]

The report of the working party,[12] sent to London for the guidance of the Canadian delegation to the sub-committee, illustrates the difficulty that Canada had in proposing substantive changes to Western proposals. On only one issue was it firm. It argued that the United States, let alone the USSR, would have difficulty surrendering the national sovereignty which the Majority Plan required. It was no longer possible to ensure that, once international control was established, the promised surrender of nuclear materials and destruction of atomic weapons would take place. The report therefore sought to assess whether the French suggestion of an alternative plan based on national ownership of source materials and atomic facilities might be a worthwhile substitute. In any case the report insisted that the Western powers must "concentrate on bringing up to date the international control plan which we ourselves would now genuinely be willing to accept."

On the Indian and Soviet proposals, the report had nothing more to suggest than going along with Canada's Western partners. It agreed that the Soviet call for an unconditional obligation not to use atomic weapons was unacceptable. The working group was comforted by the thought that both the United States and the United Kingdom, which were able "to assess all the strategic and military implications of a Geneva protocol on atomic weapons," were not too concerned with the possible propaganda appeal of the Soviet proposal. Any judgment on Nehru's proposal had to be based on more knowledge about the "present balance of military advantage in this field [of hydrogen bomb explosions]." The only source of such information was the United States. The report concluded with respect to both the Indian and the Soviet propositions that the problem was to preserve Western security while "at the same time taking appropriate counteractions to avoid placing the Western Powers in an embarrassing position from the propaganda point of view."

Lastly, the memorandum maintained that the time had come for the West to amalgamate its various proposals in one comprehensive plan. The French attempt at such an overall design had been interesting enough for Johnson to see it as a possible compromise. But the working party had eventually dismissed the French scheme, explaining that it "would unduly prejudice the position of the West on matters which are dependent on a number of complex political, military and technical problems on which decisions will presumably not be forthcoming during the time which the Sub-committee has at its disposal." This was a reasonable objection. Canadian diplomats might think that, politically, the French proposal was a good one, but they had no first-hand knowledge of the state of Western strategic preparedness and no idea of the military consequences of the French plan.

Canada's lack of strategic knowledge was a serious handicap, as Lester Pearson's opening statement to the sub-committee on 14 May showed. In spite of the hope that he had expressed to the Standing Committee, he was unable to offer any substantive initiative. He raised the possibility of some improvement in the clauses dealing with the international ownership of atomic materials. He tried to meet another Russian objection to the Majority Plan by conceding that it was not necessary for the prohibition of atomic weapons to take place at the last stage of the process. He insisted that a declaration on abolishing the atomic bomb without provision for inspection was meaningless when there was no trust between the would-be signatories. All this may have been true, but it was not new. Canada had failed to find a compromise which might bring the two sides closer together. Robertson, the chief Canadian delegate to this session of the sub-committee, admitted as much when he informed External Affairs that in his speech, Pearson placed "the emphasis more on inspection as the touchstone of Soviet sincerity in these discussions than upon basic principles."[13] Not being able to offer a constructive compromise, Pearson naturally fell back on the other aspect of his policy: trying to embarrass the Soviet Union politically.

THE ANGLO-FRENCH PLAN

The sub-committee met from 14 May to 22 June. On 25 May the Americans presented a working paper on the organization and functions of the proposed control organ. They had entered the sub-committee negotiations ostensibly still standing by the Majority Plan, leading a Canadian observer to complain that "they have therefore I think mistakenly nailed their 1948 colours firmly to the mast."[14] But during the early weeks of the sub-committee meetings they agreed to drop the most contentious features of the plan. Only three weeks previously the French had surrendered the fortress of Dienbienphu to the communist Vietnamese. The Americans believed that there was a serious danger of a collapse of French will, not only to hold on in Indochina but also to participate in the European Defence Community, an issue which was to come up for a vote in the French Assembly in the late summer. No doubt they thought it expedient to make a gesture towards winning French good will in the sub-committee – Robertson was to note "Mr Moch's great delight"[15] when the American representative announced that the United States was not wedded to the Majority Plan. But there were other pressures which made the American administration less enthusiastic about international ownership of nuclear facilities. Major domestic power and chemical corporations were eager to enter a potentially profitable field which under the Majority Plan would be the sole preserve of the international agency.

The new American proposal dropped two features of the Majority Plan to which the USSR had long objected: the concept of international ownership of atomic facilities and the demand that the permanent members of the Security Council give up their veto on sanctions applied to themselves as violators of any agreement. The British spokesman, Selwyn Lloyd, emphasized that what was essential was a system of continuous inspection by a control commission. The West, he said, was leaving aside the question of whether nuclear plants should be owned internationally. Apparently what Lloyd had in mind was a system of national management which would be closely monitored by the international organ. Each government would be left free to develop its own nuclear programme, but the international agency would have its own people in on every national decision so as to ensure that there was no "malign" development.[16] If the West was prepared to give up international ownership, it would continue to insist on a thorough system of continuous inspection and to object strenuously to the Soviet caveat that such inspection should not interfere with the domestic affairs of states.

At first the Russian spokesman, Jacob Malik, refused to discuss the details of the American scheme until the West first accepted the Soviet principle of the prohibition of nuclear arms. But on 1 June he offered a resolution that the states concerned undertake an unconditional obligation not to use atomic or hydrogen bombs. For the first time the USSR was calling for something less than the prohibition of nuclear weapons in advance of agreement on a control system. In view of the uproar over the H-bomb explosions, this proposal was likely to find considerable favour with world opinion. Yet the West believed that demonstrating its willingness to use nuclear weapons was vital to its security. Confronted by this dilemma, the West sought a way out by announcing its readiness to pledge not to use atomic arms except in response to aggression. But Malik rejected this amendment on the grounds that it would legitimize the use of such weapons.

In the middle of June the sub-committee turned to the problem of the phasing of an actual programme of disarmament. How would the prohibition of nuclear arms, the reduction of conventional arms, and the means of control and verification all be fitted together? On 11 June the British and the French jointly proposed a timetable for such a comprehensive programme. At its start, the members of the sub-committee would agree not to use nuclear weapons except in defence against aggression. Then the first phase would begin with the establishment of the control organ. As soon as it was in operation, military manpower and expenditure would be limited to the levels of 31 December 1953. In the second phase, one-half of the agreed reductions in conventional arms would be made and on completion of this cut the manufacture of nuclear weapons would cease. In the third phase, the other half of the reduction in conventional armaments and armed forces would be implemented and after that the prohibition and elimination of nuclear weapons would enter into force. In each phase cuts would be made only when the control organ certified that it would be able to police them effectively.

At a sub-committee meeting on 17 June, Robertson announced Canada's support for the Anglo-French plan. He declared that it differed from the old Baruch scheme in being truly comprehensive, covering both conventional and atomic arms. It met the principal Soviet complaint that the elimination of atomic arms should not be postponed until the last stage by providing for a conditional prohibition at the beginning. And it did not confer on the international control agency the ownership of all atomic enterprises. He pointed out that the West could not agree to the Soviet proposal for unconditional prohibition because it would mean the West giving up its collective right to self-defence against aggression. He noted as well that the USSR had failed to clarify what it meant by "control on a continuing basis without the right to interfere in the domestic affairs of the States."[17] Finally, the Soviet Union would not allow a veto-free decision by the Security Council on any report from an international control agency.

Malik challenged Robertson directly. He claimed that the West was simply unwilling to renounce the use of atomic weapons. Their diplomats spoke about the prohibition of atomic weapons but then said that they needed them to guard against aggression. The Anglo-French plan concentrated on disclosure and verification of conventional arms. It proposed to freeze armed forces and military expenditures; these activities were to be carefully verified by a control organ. "How much time this will require," he complained, "nobody knows." Meanwhile "where is Mr Robertson's prohibition of atomic weapons and reduction of armaments? They are not there, either of them."[18] Only in the remote future did the Anglo-French plan contemplate the total prohibition and elimination of atomic weapons.

The tabling of the Anglo-French plan was nevertheless a significant step in the negotiations. For the first time the Moch concept of a timetable was officially adopted by the West. Nor did the United States object to the document. The first clause was meant to meet the Soviet demand that a decision be taken to prohibit nuclear arms. Yet the memorandum held to the Western position that the control organ be in place before any cuts began and that the elimination of nuclear weapons be postponed until the agreed cuts in conventional arms had been carried out in full. For the present it is true that the Russians rejected it, but they would come to believe that they too could benefit from a timetable, the concept underpinning the Anglo-French design.

What had the sub-committee accomplished? Canada had been most anxious that the talks be conducted in private. This had been done, and it had proved beneficial. There had been some useful exchanges and both sides had emerged with a better understanding of the other's viewpoint. It was later agreed that the record should be made public: the propaganda advantages of such a decision were not lost on the participants!

As to the substance, Robertson reported to External Affairs that the talks had gone as well as could be expected. The West had emerged with a considerable broader and more reasonable position. Nevertheless no possibility of any agreement was in sight and he blamed the Soviet Union for this situation, charging that it did not wish to negotiate. Rather its aim was to launch a propaganda campaign to "neutralize the most powerful weapon of the Western powers." On the bright side, Western unity had been maintained despite the tensions between France and the United States arising from other issues. Canada's role in the negotiations could only be of secondary importance. As Robertson reported: "We tried when possible to keep the temperature of our debates down, to avoid propaganda exchanges, and to take every possible advantage of the privacy of our talks to diminish the areas of real misunderstanding and probe for possible areas of agreement." Here, he was exaggerating the Canadian capacity to mediate between the West and the Soviet Union. He was more accurate when he asserted that "we also endeavoured to pull our weight in the discussions behind the scenes among Western delegations and in drafting Western proposals." Here, no doubt, Canadian diplomatic skills were useful to the Western team.

Robertson was not optimistic about future negotiations, largely no doubt because of his conviction that the USSR was not interested in trying for an agreement. Even if the pressure of world opinion were to force it to modify its position, Robertson thought it was "difficult to see how, without undermining the Soviet system, it could agree to sufficiently broad powers for international control to satisfy the minimum requirements for Western security." Here he was repeating a view common among Canadian diplomats: that the closed nature of Soviet society was in itself an insurmountable barrier to an understanding. In the meantime, with the increase in nuclear stockpiles, the need for disarmament was becoming more and more critical.[19]

The report which the sub-committee submitted to the Disarmament Commission merely transmitted the main proposals on the table: the Anglo-French memorandum, the United States working paper, and a Soviet paper on general disarmament that repeated a number of old proposals such as the unconditional prohibition of atomic weapons and the one-third reduction in the armed forces of the major powers. On 21 July, a day after proceedings began in the Disarmament Commission, Johnson reiterated the Canadian position as enunciated by Robertson. He greeted the new Anglo-French proposals as a major advance and praised Western flexibility on the issue of the ownership of atomic facilities. He asserted that acceptance of the unconditional prohibition of the use of atomic weapons was tantamount to the West renouncing its right to protect itself against aggression. He concluded by sharply criticizing the USSR for not easing its position on inspection.[20] On 29 July the Disarmament

Commission unanimously adopted a report that contained no conclusions or recommendations. It merely sent the documents submitted by the sub-committee on to the General Assembly and the Security Council. Very little progress in reconciling the Western and Soviet positions had been made.

THE CANADIAN PROCEDURAL RESOLUTION

Canada had hoped that the Anglo-French memorandum would be given a prominent place in the 1954 Assembly debate on disarmament. Apart from its intrinsic merit, a Soviet rejection of the proposal would give the West a boost in the propaganda battle. But American support for the proposal was decidedly lukewarm. They were unhappy about the conditional ban on the use of nuclear weapons before proceeding to negotiate a disarmament treaty. They doubted that the suggested measures for control would be as effective in safeguarding their security as those in the Majority Plan. And they were reluctant to hand over any data on their atomic facilities before there had been any reduction in conventional armed forces. External Affairs believed that there was no point in going ahead with this debate, however, unless the West could "present a genuinely united front on the (A/F) which we regard as a major improvement."[21] This did not seem possible, however, and as the Assembly opened on 21 September, External Affairs was frustrated because the West was unable to capitalize on an imaginative and meaningful proposal which, if accepted, would mean a major advance towards disarmament.

Meanwhile, in August the French Assembly had refused to ratify the EDC treaty amid an atmosphere of mutual French and American hostility. The French believed that the United States had let them down in not furnishing the necessary air strikes to defeat the communists in Indochina and that it failed to appreciate their genuine apprehension about German rearmament. The Americans believed the French were evading their responsibilities in Europe and drifting towards neutralism. Alarmed at the French rejection of the EDC, the British with American support had immediately proposed that West Germany have its sovereignty restored and be taken into NATO. This concept was endorsed by a NATO ministerial meeting on 23 October. There would be a separate German army, limited to twelve divisions. West Germany also promised never to produce atomic weapons and to keep its forces under NATO command forever. Late in December the French Assembly ratified this agreement under the American threat to create an exclusive military alliance with West Germany. In the same month the NATO Council decided to equip the alliance's armed forces with tactical nuclear weapons.

Up to this point the major disarmament issue between East and West had been strategic nuclear arms. Now two others, equally divisive, had been added to the agenda. "A German army was crucial to [Eisenhower's] vision of what NATO could become, and NATO was, as always, his first concern"[22] writes one of Eisenhower's chief biographers. It was also clearly the American intention that much of NATO's effectiveness would depend on its possession of tactical nuclear weapons. But these two developments were bound to make disarmament negotiations even more difficult. The USSR could use the disarmament talks to apply diplomatic pressure to prevent the West German army from coming into being. For its part, the United States would reject any proposal that might interfere with the rearming of West Germany.

A minor consequence of the manœuvring of the great powers over German rearmament was to induce the Soviet Union to regard the Anglo-French plan more favourably. Moch's speeches at the Disarmament Commission had demonstrated that the French were anxious to conciliate the USSR. Apparently the Russians had been listening. Early in August, Moch had received a visit from the Soviet ambasssador who asked what could be done to further détente. Moch had advised the Soviet Union to accept the Anglo-French measures. On 22 August, eight days before the fateful vote in the French Assembly on the EDC, Moscow had indicated to Moch that it would take his advice but would postpone the announcement until after the vote to avoid being accused of interfering in France's internal affairs.[23] By the beginning of September, the State Department began to show some anxiety about the possibility of some dramatic Soviet proposal at the General Assembly that would bring its position closer to that of the French.[24] A week later Johnson provided External Affairs with excerpts from *Pravda* that fostered "Mochism to strengthen the hand of these Frenchmen who favour some attempt at rapprochement with the Soviet Union before taking any final decisions on the future of Germany."[25] On 30 September Vyshinsky, on behalf of the USSR, proposed to the General Assembly that the Disarmament Commission be instructed to draft a treaty on disarmament and nuclear weapons "on the basis" of the Anglo-French plan.[26] And on 8 October he presented a resolution to this effect.

In assessing the proposal for External Affairs, Johnson concluded that the Russians had made "substantive concessions." They had dropped their demand for the unconditional ban on the use of atomic weapons as a condition for negotiation. They had abandoned their proposal for a proportional reduction in conventional arms and had instead agreed to bringing them down to "fixed levels." By accepting the heart of the Anglo-French proposals, the principle of a timetable, they had implicitly concurred in the Western concept of stages which had hitherto been anathema to them. However, there were serious weaknesses in their proposals for inspection, despite the reference to the Anglo-French plan. The control organ would be under the Security Council where the veto still applied; it would have the power to receive information but not to conduct on-the-spot inspections to ensure compliance; and it would not be ready to discharge its functions until some time after the declaration of the complete prohibition of atomic weapons. There would thus be a period of time when there would be no means of checking whether the Soviet Union was sincere in its undertaking to prohibit atomic weapons. Still, Johnson believed that with all its short-comings this was a serious proposal that might form "a possible basis for disarmament as an alternative to the prospect of mutual suicide."[27]

Canadian diplomats quite naturally weighed the political consequences of the Soviet initiative. They were concerned with preserving Western unity – the Americans were already pointing out the weaknesses of the Soviet plan while Moch was calling it "the greatest conciliatory step the Soviet government [had] made in any field since the war."[28] The other main Canadian worry was to prevent the Russian offer adversely affecting the talks then going on in London to bring Germany into NATO. The Soviet Union might be sincere about wishing to come to an agreement, but it was also possible that its principal aim was to frustrate German rearmament. It was rumoured that Moch had cabled his premier, Pierre Mendès-France, suggesting that France not ratify the agreement on Germany until the new possibilities for disarmament had been explored.[29] In any case the proposals would give the Soviet Union the initiative in the propaganda war and therefore could not be dismissed out of hand. The way to deal with these dangers, Johnson believed, was to have a resolution passed in the General Assembly as quickly as possible transferring the whole discussion of the Soviet proposals to the sub-committee of the Disarmament Commission. This would allow for serious study of the suggestions and open the way for real negotiations. It would also give the West "some control of the timetable" and prevent interference with "developments concerning defence of Western Europe."[30] All this made good sense to External Affairs which instructed Johnson to proceed along the lines he had suggested.

Paul Martin, the minister of national health and welfare, was the leader of Canada's delegation to the General Assembly in 1954, and he now went to work with gusto to transfer the negotiations with the Russians to the privacy of the sub-committee and was soon discussing a draft resolution to this effect with his Western colleagues. He had hoped that it would be offered by the four Western members of the sub-committee. He was uneasy about having Soviet sponsorship, lest this "give the world a dangerously false impression of unity and imply a much greater agreement than there is yet any evidence for."[31] But Moch warned that four-power sponsorship would weaken any chance of agreement by isolating the USSR. External Affairs, which always believed in smoothing the path of negotiations wherever possible, had some sympathy for what Moch was trying to achieve. Martin's way out of this diplomatic impasse was to suggest the United Kingdom alone offer the resolution. But the British feared that such a gesture might make it appear that Anglo-French solidarity over their memorandum was weakening. Thus, the United Kingdom proposed that Canada alone sponsor the resolution, a suggestion that was enthusiastically supported by both the United States and France. Finally it was agreed that Canada would put forward the resolution and ask the other members of the sub-committee including the Soviet Union to co-sponsor it.[32]

On 12 October Martin asked the Political Committee to endorse a resolution to reconvene the sub-committee of the Disarmament Commission to discuss the Anglo-French memorandum as well as any other proposals. He also proposed that the other members of the sub-committee act as co-sponsors. There was no problem with the Americans, the British, and the French. The USSR, however, hesitated a little. It wanted a serious discussion in the sub-committee, but it seems to have also been interested in deriving as much political advantage out of the situation as possible. Consequently, it moved a series of amendments, the most important of which would have had the Canadian resolution refer to the Anglo-French memorandum and the Soviet resolution of 8 October but not to the American working paper of 25 May on the control organ. Evidently, the Russians wanted to see if an amendment which mentioned their proposals but not those of the Americans might be acceptable. On behalf of the West, Martin responded by suggesting that all three documents be mentioned: the Anglo-French proposal of 11 June, the draft Soviet resolution, and the American working paper. But Vyshinsky rejected any reference to the working paper – to which he objected both in principle and in detail. After consulting his Western colleagues, Martin next proposed a text which made no mention of any individual proposal. Instead, his revised draft resolution requested the Disarmament Commission "to seek an acceptable solution of the disarmament problem taking into account the various proposals referred to in the Preamble of this resolution." As David Johnson, speaking on behalf of Canada, later explained in the General Assembly the preamble referred to the fourth report of the commission with the documents annexed (which included the American working paper of 25 May and the Anglo-French proposal of 11 June) and to the draft Soviet resolution of 8 October.[33] Thus, each party got what it wanted. There was no mention of any specific proposal (including the American working paper) – this suited the Soviet Union. But the working paper would nonetheless be one of the proposals on the table at the coming sub-committee meetings – this was what the United States wanted. Fortunately, the new wording proved acceptable to Moscow, and the Soviet Union agreed to co-sponsor the revised resolution. Adopted by the General Assembly on 4 November, this was the first resolution on disarmament of any importance to be carried unanimously since 1946.

The reactions of Pearson and his colleagues during this period when Canada was attempting to win Soviet sponsorship reveal a strong suspicion of Moscow's motives. Pearson believed that the West should welcome Soviet support and even co-sponsorship of Canada's resolution. Otherwise it would appear that the United States was simply unwilling to consider the Soviet proposals on their merits and was dead set against co-operating with the USSR. The Soviet Union was primarily out to boost its image as a partisan of peace, in Pearson's view, but it was always possible that they were sincere in wishing the sub-committee to do some serious work in the all-important disarmament field. Pearson was a little concerned over Canada's actions because even a procedural resolution had "cold war implications."[34] An accord on procedure might be construed as agreement on the substance of a comprehensive disarmament scheme. In its three major statements in the General Assembly disarmament debate, Canada had therefore emphasized its profound differences with the Soviet Union on the matter of inspection – no member of the United Nations could possibly have mistaken the Canadian stance.

Pearson had also feared that the Soviet Union would find a way to use the negotiations to bring pressure on the French not to ratify the agreement on the rearmament of West Germany. A lot of the difficulty lay with determining whether Jules Moch was acting in good faith; the Americans believed that he often had advance indications of Soviet intentions – information that he did not always share with his colleagues. Moch had confided to Martin, for example, that if Vyshinsky agreed to co-sponsor the resolution, he would "immediately wire Mendès-France urging on him a two months' delay in any steps to debate ratification of France's agreement for German rearmament."[35] The reaction of John Holmes, the assistant under-secretary of state for external affairs, had been that if Moch was hoping to use the five-power sponsorship for this purpose, then it "may be fortuitous that Soviet co-sponsorship is unobtainable."[36] In a telegram to Martin, Pearson expressed a similar thought. The effort to obtain Soviet sponsorship for the Canadian resolution had been necessary to prevent the USSR from complaining that it had been given no opportunity to participate, but he would not be much worried if the Soviet Union refused. Certainly no concession ought to be made that might cause trouble with the United States. "I am strengthened in this view," he continued, "by the information that Moch might counsel delay in Paris on ratification of the London agreement, if the Soviets sponsor our disarmament resolution."[37] These fears about Moch's motives proved groundless. At a lunch with Mendès-France shortly after this, Pearson was told that while Moch was an expert on disarmament he was not very realistic.[38] Clearly, the premier believed that a Soviet agreement to discuss the Anglo-French memorandum in the sub-committee did very little to relieve the American pressure on him to ensure French ratification of West Germany's entry into NATO.

This episode shows that, as Holmes expressed it at the time, Canada's "fundamental purpose [was] to maintain Western unity on disarmament."[39] He might have added that this aim – at its broadest – encompassed bringing West Germany into NATO. If this objective were threatened, then disarmament negotiations with the USSR would have to be sacrificed. Fortunately this proved unnecessary. Canada could have its cake and eat it too. Negotiations in the sub-committee were to continue. The strains in French-American relations had not been exacerbated. Canada had done all this without softening its support for the Western stand. Indeed, according to Martin, it was he who had insisted on including the reference to the American working paper in the resolution which had caused so much difficulty with the USSR.[40]

The Disarmament Commission met briefly on 19 November and decided to reconvene the sub-committee. External Affairs had some concerns lest it meet before the French Assembly endorsed the London and Paris accords on West German membership in NATO.

But there was no need to worry. At the meeting of the sub-committee on 8 December, the Soviet representative made no attempt to torpedo the ratification process. He merely offered a brief statement on the incompatibility of German rearmament with any programme of general disarmament. The meeting ended with a decision to meet again in the latter part of February 1955.

As a consequence of its success in orchestrating the procedural resolution, Canada emerged from the 1954 General Assembly with much prestige. The Swedish delegate praised the "negotiating skill" of the Canadian delegation,[41] and the *Windsor Daily Star*, Martin's home town newspaper, claimed that "Western diplomats here have been heaping praise on Mr Martin for his success as a mediator between the West and Russia."[42] Canada had played a role that hitherto its diplomats had only dreamed about. The positive attitude of both superpowers had allowed them to be nudged into an agreement over a procedural resolution to enable the talks to keep going. As the only small power in the sub-committee, Canada had been in the best position to take the initiative in bringing the two sides together and advancing the cause of disarmament. Yet it was not neutral and, as it made clear, remained deeply committed to the Western position on the need for stringent inspection measures. In fact, unusual circumstances had allowed Canada to play the role of the honest broker *because* it was identified with the West. This episode would be by far the country's most spectacular moment in the disarmament discussions.

1955

On 19 March 1955 President Eisenhower appointed Harold Stassen to be his special assistant on disarmament. Stassen was both bright and ambitious, having previously served as the Republican governor of Minnesota. He was to have cabinet rank, thus reporting directly to the president and bypassing the secretary of state, John Foster Dulles. Stassen was instructed to study American disarmament policy and to present proposals for executive consideration. As a symbol of Eisenhower's deep attachment to peace, the appointment was a brilliant gesture. Yet the most spectacular move in the propaganda war was to emanate from the Soviet Union.

THE SOVIET PROPOSALS OF 10 MAY

In 1955 the confluence of strategic and political interests led to a bold new Soviet initiative in disarmament and arms control. This offer would spring from a self-confidence derived from the strength of Soviet nuclear capacity. Even though its inventory of weapons was much smaller than that of the United States, it was sufficient to deter an American atomic attack. The USSR no longer needed to reject any measures that would have prevented it from catching up with the United States in the field of atomic weapons. Nevertheless, there was always a danger that something might go wrong. Soviet leaders often paid lip service to the idea that only the capitalist world would be fatally wounded in a nuclear war, but they had no illusions about what a catastrophe it would be for their country. Despite their overwhelming conventional strength and considerable atomic capacity, they could not help but be concerned by the entry of West Germany into an alliance that deployed tactical nuclear weapons and by the ring of American military bases which surrounded their country.

The Soviet leaders had also come to see that Stalin's insistence on dividing the world into two camps had only strengthened Western unity. They recognized that there was now a genuine balance of power in Europe; there would be no more significant territorial changes. The tougher the Soviet line and the harsher the rhetoric, the more firmly were Western governments anchored around the United States. What was needed was a relaxation of tensions. Instead of treating the West as a homogeneous bloc, therefore, the Soviet Union would look for diversity in the non-communist world and encourage neutrality. This would help undermine the political forces binding NATO together, weaken the Western determination to increase its military capacity, and sap its resolve to use nuclear weapons. No doubt the Soviet leaders were encouraged in this view because public opinion in Western Europe was losing some of its enthusiasm for NATO and beginning more and more to favour a ban on nuclear weapons.

Nikita Khrushchev and his colleagues continued to believe in the final triumph of world communism. For the present, Western communist parties had little hope, but attractive possibilities were opening up in Asia – India might one day join the socialist camp. What was certain was that the era of peaceful coexistence had arrived; henceforth the forces of world socialism must gain their ends by peaceful means rather than through violent revolutions and bloody wars. Thus there were both political and strategic reasons for easing relations with the capitalist powers. In the spring of 1955 the way was cleared for a fundamental shift in the Soviet posture towards the West; the arch-exponent of the Stalinist foreign policy, Vyacheslav Molotov, was removed from office by a reform group led by Khrushchev who was determined to achieve a détente with the West.

The Russians had already been pressing for a high-level conference with the United States. At first the Americans had put them off on the grounds that this was impossible before West Germany became a member of NATO. But on 5 May West Germany's accession to the North Atlantic Treaty came into effect. In the same month Anthony Eden, the new prime minister of Great Britain, campaigned in a general election on a platform which included a promise to arrange a summit with the USSR. In 1954 Eisenhower had stipulated that there could be no such conference until the Soviet Union – as evidence of good faith – signed a peace treaty with Austria and ended its occupation of that country. In May 1955 the Soviet Union fulfilled this condition – a unilateral concession that entailed real costs – and so conveyed a message to both Eisenhower and the world that Khrushchev and his colleagues genuinely wished for a détente. In June the foreign ministers of France, the United Kingdom, the Soviet Union, and the United States announced that there would be a summit meeting in Geneva in July.

Reasonable proposals on arms control were another way by which the USSR could show its interest in improving relations with the West. Even if rejected by NATO hardliners, such an initiative would be a fine propaganda stroke and might win over Western moderates who wished to see a softer stance towards the USSR. And it was always possible that the West would be sincerely interested in a limited agreement that might improve Soviet security as well as its own.

But would American disarmament thinking change? Late in May Stassen brought down a preliminary report. He concluded that the elimination of nuclear weapons was no longer feasible; instead, they ought to be frozen at current levels. Nuclear testing should be halted. He also proposed the cessation of all nuclear production, the limitation of the manufacture of conventional weapons, and no further expansion of American bases. Surprise attacks were to be made more difficult by stationing foreign inspectors in each superpower and by aerial inspection. Eisenhower found the Stassen proposals too sweeping, however. In theory he favoured reductions in arms but he also believed that the United States would be safe only if its military capacity remained superior to that of the Soviet Union. Eisenhower was never able to reconcile these contradictory feelings. Consequently the appointment of Stassen brought no radical changes in American disarmament policy.

It had been agreed that the sub-committee of the Disarmament Commission would renew its work on 25 February 1955. Canadian diplomats had approached the meeting with ambiguous attitudes. In a memorandum drawn up for the delegation,[43] probably by

David Johnson, it was suggested that there was no real significance to allowing the Soviet Union to use the veto in a Security Council discussion of nuclear issues. As everyone admitted, a serious violation of any disarmament treaty would make the veto academic since it would probably lead to war. Nevertheless, the memorandum added "that the West can derive a propaganda advantage from its position on this matter." Inspection, on which the West could afford no concessions, was fortunately a field in which the Soviet Union was more "vulnerable." At the same time External Affairs refused to limit the purpose of negotiations to propaganda. "We consider," wrote Jules Léger, the newly appointed under-secretary of state for external affairs, "that the present armaments race is in itself a source of tension and, consequently, that the West should explore every possibility of reaching agreement." It was important, he added in his memorandum for Pearson, that any effort to get the Soviet Union to clarify its position should not prompt a negative attitude on its part.[44] External Affairs always hoped that the Soviet Union would eventually accept the kind of international system of inspection that Canada believed would allow the implementation of a serious disarmament programme.

But even efficient inspection was by itself no solution. Johnson calculated that no matter how effective the controls, a government could conceal 20 per cent of its past production of nuclear weapons. Of more importance, American defence strategy depended on the ability to retaliate instantly, which raised the large question of whether the United States would ever agree to give up its nuclear strike force. That there was no guarantee that the USSR would destroy all its atomic bombs even if it signed a disarmament treaty made it all the more impossible to conceive of American nuclear disarmament. Yet the West had maintained again and again that its goal was to eliminate atomic weapons. Johnson believed that it must face up to this difficult dilemma; it "cannot continue to advocate a disarmament programme which it has no intention of carrying out."[45] If it were ever forced to back away from its own proposals just because the Soviet Union accepted them, the latter would be handed a tremendous propaganda victory.

Lester Pearson himself was coming to doubt the value of the sub-committee negotiations in London. Merely to seek to score propaganda victories seemed a little frivolous in view of the gravity of the problem. Was it worthwhile encouraging the public to believe in the possibility of an elaborate disarmament scheme which might demand a degree of inspection which neither the Soviet Union nor any other great power would be likely to accept? Perhaps it would be better to explore a plan that might provide less security than complete disarmament but have a chance of being accepted. On a more practical level, it was absolutely necessary that there be a new examination of the technical aspects of control to see if it was possible to verify the elimination of atomic weapons. If not, he affirmed, "it makes nonsense of the proposals before the sub-committee."[46]

Pearson was so concerned that the sub-committee would fail to meet the challenge of the continuing arms race that he was tempted to go public – "to introduce a little fresh air"[47] into the discussion; but in the end he desisted for fear of undermining the London talks. His commitment to quiet diplomacy and Western unity remained very strong. He did have an opportunity to voice his concerns at the NATO Council meeting in May, but he reported that "the disarmament discussion this morning was disappointingly brief."[48] He had failed to move the council to any action. This episode illustrates Canada's continuing handicap in making substantive disarmament proposals. The problems that Pearson was raising were well known to NATO. Not being a major military power, Canada lacked the technical expertise and experience to suggest new options. At the same time it had insufficient political clout to force NATO to acknowledge these difficulties publicly. It would require the power of the USSR to place new options on the public agenda.

Meanwhile the London negotiations had begun on a discouraging note. At their opening on 25 February, for reasons that are difficult to fathom, the Soviet delegate, Andrei Gromyko, reverted to the traditional Soviet position of demanding the immediate destruction of all nuclear weapons. This action was to be taken independently of the Anglo-French proposals of June 1954. The Soviet Union was asking once again for nuclear disarmament before the creation of inspection machinery and the reduction of conventional forces in which the Soviet Union were clearly superior. He must have known that a proposal that deprived the United States of its main means of defence would be totally unacceptable to the West.

The Soviet action led the four Western powers to wonder if there was any point in continuing the talks. The Americans wanted to quit immediately while it was easy to hold the Soviet Union responsible for their failure. But the British and French delegates maintained that their publics would wish for more proof of Soviet bad faith. External Affairs came down on the side of the latter: "our objective is to try to squeeze some positive result out of the London talks," it insisted, and avoid "a propaganda contest which would only increase the present tension."[49] As always, Canada wished to keep the negotiations going. On 8 March, the Western powers introduced the Anglo-French propositions in the form of a draft resolution. A few days later they publicly declared that they would only continue the negotiations on the basis of these proposals. On 18 March, in response, the Soviet Union softened its stand and in effect accepted the Western conditions; all it had achieved by its initial thrust was a sour atmosphere for the talks.

With the preliminary skirmishing out of the way, a period of serious bargaining ensued. The West was pleased that the Soviet Union had finally accepted the principles underpinning the Anglo-French proposals: that a disarmament plan should include conventional as well as atomic weapons and should be carried out by stages. But the USSR still continued to propose a blanket reduction of one-third of the armaments and armed forces of the five great powers. This would allow the Soviet Union to reduce its numbers but retain its advantage in conventional arms. The West maintained that both sides ought to decrease their forces to equal fixed numerical levels.

The Soviet position on controls also remained unsatisfactory. The Russians were proposing a temporary control organ to supervise the first 50 per cent of the conventional reductions agreed. Yet it would have no right to unlimited access in the territories of those whose forces it was supposed to control, and the West feared that its powers would be limited to checking information submitted by the host government. The apprehension was increased by the refusal of the Soviet delegation to give concrete details of Soviet control proposals. Yet, on the word of this ineffectual body that the first phase of conventional reductions had been completed, the United States would be asked to agree to the prohibition on the use and manufacture of nuclear weapons.

According to the Soviet plan, the prohibition would go into effect simultaneously with the creation of a permanent control organ to supervise the elimination of nuclear weapons. As the West interpreted the Soviet proposal, the control organ would be a complex body composed of hundreds of trained inspectors. It would take a considerable time to build such an organization. The West thus feared that the Soviet proposal of simultaneity meant that prohibition would be put into force before the organ to control it was in place. For its part, the Soviet Union complained that in the Anglo-French proposal the total prohibition and elimination of nuclear weapons would not take place until the second half of the agreed reduction in conventional forces had been completed. Their fear was that once these cuts were made the West might simply refuse to implement the prohibition. This would weaken Soviet security; having surrendered its advantage in conventional arms, it would still be confronted by the superior American atomic forces. The way around this, the Soviet delegate argued, was to accept their compromise suggestion that nuclear weapons be prohibited halfway through the process of conventional arms reduction.

That legitimate concerns existed on both sides provided the elements of a bargain. On 29 March France and Britain proposed that the armed forces of the United States, the USSR, and China be reduced to between 1 and 1.5 million men. France and Britain would accept a ceiling of 650,000. Thus there would be a rough parity between the two sides in conventional armaments and armed forces levels. On 19 April the British and French offered to amend their plan so that the prohibition and elimination of nuclear weapons would begin after 75 per cent of the proposed reductions in conventional arms had taken place. According to British officials, this meant that "no nuclear bomb will be destroyed until three quarters of the total soldiers to be demobilized have actually been discharged and the last nuclear bomb is only destroyed when the last soldier has been demobilized."[50] This concession was contingent on the Soviet Union accepting Western proposals on the reduction of conventional forces and on the institution of an effective control system.

The French supported this offer because they wanted nuclear weapons (of which they had none) eliminated. A Soviet cutback in conventional forces would also lessen the need for a large German army. While the United Kingdom already possessed atomic bombs, its government was under considerable public pressure to move towards nuclear disarmament. The United States, however, had balked at abandoning the principle that all conventional reductions should be completed before the prohibition of nuclear weapons. A strong representation from the United Kingdom would be required before the Americans agreed not to oppose the Anglo-French compromise proposal. The initial American response placed the Canadians in a awkward position. Although External Affairs believed that the Anglo-French statement was sensible and timely, it had no wish to isolate the United States. Nor was it thought appropriate to be on the record (even in the sub-committee) as disagreeing officially with the United States on a matter of security. Consequently, Canada did not co-sponsor the proposal. However, on instructions from External Affairs, its delegate was to say in the sub-committee that he personally could see no reason why the Canadian government would not support the Anglo-French suggestion.[51]

For a while, the intra-allied disagreements seemed rather academic as the Soviet delegate, Jacob Malik, continued to express both criticism and scepticism of the Anglo-French proposition. By the end of the first week in May, Western delegates concluded that this round of negotiations was over. When they met with Malik on 10 May, they therefore suggested a recess in view of the coming Big Four talks at Geneva. But Malik broke in to say that he would be making important proposals in the afternoon. The Soviet government had been re-thinking its position and wanted to propose a comprehensive and radical disarmament plan.

For the first time since 1946 the Soviet Union clearly and unequivocally abandoned its insistence that any disarmament scheme must begin with the elimination of nuclear weapons. They accepted the Anglo-French proposal that nuclear weapons be prohibited only after 75 per cent of the reductions in conventional arms had been completed. They agreed that the USSR, the United States, and China should reduce the number of their conventional forces to between 1 and 1.5 million, and that Great Britain and France should reduce theirs to 650,000 each. They made concessions on the issue of controls as well. There would be two stages. In the first, to prevent surprise attack, they proposed that observation posts be set up in airdromes, on major highways, and at railway junctions; thus, from the beginning of the process the control organ would be able to station some inspectors in the Soviet Union. It would have unimpeded access to the budgetary records of the various states. In the second stage, the control organ would station permanent officials in the atomic states with the right to "inspection on a continuing basis" and "unimpeded access at all times ... to all objects of control." These were far greater powers than the Soviet Union had been willing to concede previously. Perhaps the most important Soviet step was to make a public admission of what all knowledgeable people were painfully aware: "there are possibilities beyond the reach of international control for evading this control and for organizing clandestine manufacture of atomic and hydrogen weapons." In other words, there were so many nuclear weapons in existence that there was no way of guaranteeing that a government that promised to eliminate atomic weapons would do so.

The Soviet Union had made important concessions to the West, but they also put forward a few demands of their own. They proposed a ban on the testing of atomic and hydrogen bombs. Also integral to their disarmament scheme was the elimination of military bases on foreign soil and the withdrawal of occupation troops from Germany. As well, they demanded a freeze of all armaments as of 31 December 1954, without the exceptions of specified nations which the West had proposed; this would work to prevent the rearming of West Germany.[52]

The USSR had made a constructive effort to narrow the gap between the two sides. It would be idle to speculate on its motives. But this much can be said. The Russians had taken a major initiative and certainly would gain in the everlasting propaganda wars. The Soviet offer was later described by Philip Noel-Baker as "the moment of hope,"[53] but this is inaccurate because it was not constructed on the principle of common security. Instead, it strengthened Soviet military capacity at the expense of American. It proposed a ban on nuclear tests which would prevent the further development of atomic weapons. The Soviet leaders also wished to make the use of atomic weapons against aggression subject to their veto in the Security Council. Both measures would work to undermine the threat of American massive atomic retaliation to deter aggression. And even though the Soviet Union had agreed to cut back its conventional forces to 1.5 million (matching those of the United States in number[54]), it would continue to enjoy the advantage of having forces close to central Europe while most of the American ones were stationed across the Atlantic.

The Soviet Union had not met all the Western demands, of course. It was far from clear what they meant that under their proposal inspectors would have "unimpeded access at all times to all objects of control" since they did not define "objects." Nor was it certain that the control organ would be in place before reductions in conventional arms and the elimination of nuclear weapons began. Another source of dissatisfaction was the Soviet contention that nuclear weapons might be used in self-defence only with the approval of the Security Council on which, of course, it had a veto. The Americans were particularly unhappy about the Soviet proposals on control. The American spokesman at the sub-committee complained: "It is not clear that the control organ's inspectors can go everywhere and see everything necessary to make sure that forbidden munitions are not being manufactured or that nuclear weapons are not being secreted."[55] Yet when it came down to real controls, the USSR would not be the only superpower to worry about its sovereignty. None other than President Eisenhower was apprehensive about the effect of controls on the United States. "Are we ready," he wondered, "to open up every one of our factories, every place where something might be going on that could be inimical to the interests of somebody else?"[56]

Perhaps the most troubling issue that the Soviet Union raised was that with so many nuclear weapons in existence there was no scientific way of ensuring that all of them would be detected. Yet the Russians were continuing to propose their total elimination, knowing full well that this procedure could not be verified. Meanwhile the United States had reached the same conclusion. A report from the United States Atomic Energy Commission in November 1954 had stated that the elimination of nuclear weapons was an "unrealistic goal given the large uncertainty associated with verifying past production."[57]

Lester Pearson, too, believed that the Soviet Union had come a long way towards accepting the Anglo-French propositions. There had even been some advance on the matter of inspection – the control organ now proposed by the USSR would have more power than previously. What concerned him, he informed the Standing Committee on External Affairs on 25 May, was the Soviet demand that occupation forces be withdrawn from Germany. If this was an absolute condition for progress in disarmament, then it would be tantamount to saying that there could be "no limitation on armaments and no prohibition of atomic warfare until the American forces were out of Europe and back in the United States"[58] – an impossible condition for the West to accept. Thus, the value of the Soviet concessions might not be as impressive as first appeared. Curiously, in his comments to the Standing Committee, he failed to compliment the Soviet Union for having done what he had wished to see done – open up for public discussion the whole issue of the capacity to check past production of nuclear fuel. Perhaps here he was waiting for a lead from the United States.

The immediate reaction of the four Western delegates to the Soviet proposals of 10 May was positive. The response of Jules Moch was that "the whole thing looks too good to be true." The American delegate said that the United States was "gratified,"[59] and Canada's Johnson proposed to welcome the proposals "because they indicate a real advance in the Soviet position."[60] At the same time the West was not nearly ready to negotiate actively on what was after all a very comprehensive offer and a radical change from previous Soviet positions. On 18 May the sub-committee announced simply that it would take some time to allow the five governments to think about the new situation. And despite Soviet objections, on the first of June it decided not to fix a date for the next meeting. Talks on substance made sense only after considering what the heads of the Big Four governments would decide at Geneva.

Negotiations in the sub-committee had produced some surprises. The initiative on the Western side had been taken by the United Kingdom and France, with the United States holding back to the point where there almost appeared to be three sides at the table.

Canada had played its customary role. Unable to contribute in substance, it had worked to maintain Western unity and had even been prominent in the 1954 session of the United Nations General Assembly in winning Soviet support for procedural resolution that allowed the negotiations to continue. But the big story had been the Soviet Union. Having caught up to the United States in atomic might, it could afford to make concessions in conventional forces. Then, too, it wished to ease tensions for political reasons. With its 10 May proposals it moved from a negative passivity to active pursuit of a disarmament agreement. For the first time there was a public acknowledgment by a superpower that the conditions underpinning a comprehensive disarmament agreement were impossible to achieve. Nevertheless, the Soviet Union kept to its proposal to eliminate nuclear weapons. And, as we shall see, the United Kingdom and France also continued to press for this option. But the Soviet programme pointed to another possibility. The USSR had proposed the reduction of conventional forces, control measures against a surprise attack, and a test ban treaty; each of these could be negotiated outside a complete disarmament package. Together, these partial measures might add up to a programme of arms control, and it was along this path that the superpowers would actually proceed.

CHAPTER SEVEN

Working to Maintain Franco-American Harmony, 1955–56

Perhaps the most important consequence of the Soviet proposals of 10 May was their effect on American rhetoric. It is difficult to believe that either President Truman or President Eisenhower had ever given serious consideration to giving up nuclear weapons; yet ever since Bernard Baruch's opening statement to the United Nations in July 1946 successive American administrations had always maintained that this was the long-term goal of disarmament discussions. Once the USSR had publicly conceded that there was no reliable means of verifying the total elimination of atomic arms, however, the United States stopped declaring that its final aim was to rid the world of the nuclear threat; in short, the United States abandoned the ideal of comprehensive disarmament.

United States policy in the field of atomic weapons was moving from disarmament to arms control. This major shift would change the negotiations in the sub-committee of the Disarmament Commission from an exercise in propaganda to a serious attempt to reach what both sides regarded as achievable goals. Total disarmament would only have been a practical undertaking in an atmosphere of total trust – an obvious impossibility under Cold War conditions. Hitherto both the Soviet and the American disarmament proposals had been designed to embarrass the other side and score propaganda points. Arms control was a different matter – it amounted to a political agreement between the United States and the Soviet Union to regulate military competition and lay down guidelines for its conduct. While accepting the necessity of nuclear weapons, proponents of arms control claimed that the dangers inherent in their existence could be reduced by creating an atmosphere of predictability and therefore of stability. Even American officials like Paul Nitze, who profoundly distrusted Soviet intentions, could see the advantage of an arms control regime for their side.[1] Unlike talks on disarmament, negotiations on arms control might be successful because each side could see that they offered possibilities for strengthening its own security.

The shift to negotiations on arms control would create great difficulties for Jules Moch. France's delegate was convinced that a nuclear war with all its horrendous consequences could only be avoided by the complete abolition of nuclear weapons. Moch did not want to see France acquire a nuclear military capacity. Yet there was a powerful current of French opinion which insisted that if France was to continue to be a great power, it would need these weapons. Since 1952 France's atomic facilities had been working to produce plutonium. In December 1954, the French cabinet had had a thorough discussion on whether a nuclear programme for military purposes was desirable. Premier Mendès-France had adopted an ambiguous position. In secret he launched a study on how long it would take to manufacture an atomic bomb, but in public he stated that France would renounce them if other powers did so. The views of his successors, Edgar Faure and Guy Mollet, would also fluctuate on this issue. Moch nevertheless continued to believe that the move to nuclear arms in France could be resisted – but only if the United Kingdom, the United States, and the USSR gave up theirs. Even he would never agree that France should be the only great power without them.

Harold Stassen and Jules Moch were bound to collide. Stassen had soon seen that the security of the United States demanded the abandonment of the impossible goal of total nuclear disarmament, but the ability of the French government to keep their country from developing nuclear weapons systems depended on the agreement of the other powers to continue to seek the complete elimination of atomic weapons. The Department of External Affairs, which remained convinced that total Western unity was necessary to confront the Soviet threat in Europe, feared that a breach was developing between the United States and France over the issue of nuclear disarmament. Consequently, Canadian diplomats would devote a good deal of energy in the coming months to preventing such a rift.

1955

GENEVA

Canada's secretary of state for external affairs watched the approach of the four-power summit, to be held in Geneva in July, with considerable apprehension. Pearson was worried that the excessive optimism amongst the public generated by this widely advertised event might lead to complacency about Western security. The North Atlantic Council had heard a report from the Big Three foreign ministers about what they expected from the summit. Reporting to the press on the deliberations of the council, Pearson had emphasized the importance of preserving NATO and stressed that there could be no real security until Germany was finally unified. He had also pointed out that foolproof inspection of atomic stockpiles was impossible and that it was doubtful that either side could accept the kind of inspection that would now be necessary to ensure nuclear disarmament.[2]

At the Geneva conference, disarmament issues took second place to what should be done about Germany. The Russians proposed that both the North Atlantic Treaty and the Warsaw Treaty should be replaced by an all-European security agreement within which Germany would be united but neutral. In line with the long-time policy of the American administration, the West insisted that NATO must remain intact and that Germany must be united on the basis of free elections and then allowed to join the North Atlantic alliance if it wished to do so. Arms negotiations were second to this objective. The Soviet Union, however, would begin disarming only if a united Germany were neutral. With this bitter and difficult dispute unresolved, the meeting of heads of government was not likely to give much coherent leadership on disarmament. Nevertheless many American defence experts believed that the Soviet threat was increasing and that the United States should now allow the summit to pass without some disarmament proposal or other – if only to test Soviet intentions. Thus, on 21 July, Eisenhower put forward a suggestion which was soon dubbed "Open Skies." The United States and the USSR would exchange blueprints of their military installations and allow aerial reconnaissance of their countries.

The genesis of Open Skies lay in the American concern about the possibility of a surprise Soviet nuclear attack on the bombers of the Strategic Air Command which would cripple the American capacity to retaliate. A panel of defence experts had estimated that 200 nuclear bombs could defeat the United States.[3] The Americans believed that if the Soviet leaders contemplated attacking the United States, it must be by such a knockout blow; otherwise, their own country would be vulnerable to nuclear reprisal. But to be successful such a nuclear strike at the retaliatory capability of the United States would require surprise. If the Americans had warning of any Soviet preparations to launch a conventional or even a nuclear attack, they could take measures to preserve their ability to strike back. Aerial surveys would provide the necessary information. At the same time Soviet aerial surveillance of the United States would obviate any Soviet concern about an American surprise attack. Hence, arms negotiations should aim to achieve a reliable alarm system against an impending strike instead of trying for the impossible goal of nuclear disarmament. This proposal was not surprising in a country whose strategists had painful memories of the Japanese sneak attack on Pearl Harbor.

But the Soviet leaders were cool to Eisenhower's proposal. There was no political pressure on them to accept. The closed nature of their country meant that they had more to lose from American surveillance of their territory than they would gain from being able to gather aerial intelligence about the comparatively open society of their rivals. Khrushchev's first reaction was that the American proposal was simply another ploy to spy on the USSR's armed forces. (Paradoxically, the stability of the nuclear stalemate later came to depend on the ability of the satellites of each side to observe the territory of the other for signs of hostile action.) To make matters worse, Eisenhower had said nothing about the Soviet Union being able to monitor American bases in Europe and the Middle East from which surprise atomic strikes on the Soviet Union might originate.

Open Skies was a simple idea, easily understood and seemingly fair to both sides, and thus good propaganda. The public reaction was overwhelmingly favourable and Eisenhower emerged from the conference with the gratifying image of a man of peace. For the first time arms control became an integral part of American foreign policy. If Geneva failed to halt the arms race, it had allowed each side to appraise the other more realistically. In fact, each side had convinced the other that it had no intention of beginning a major war which both agreed would only be a common disaster.

THE AMERICANS ABANDON
COMPREHENSIVE DISARMAMENT

At Geneva the Big Four had decided that the sub-committee of the Disarmament Commission should reconvene on 29 August. To ensure that the United States position had been thoroughly thought out, Stassen announced in August the formation of eight task forces to study all aspects of inspection. The American shift away from comprehensive disarmament also occupied the attention of Canadian diplomats. Even before Geneva, Stassen had told the Canadian ambassador in Washington that the United States had decided that even if a workable system of inspection could be devised, there was simply no way of detecting nuclear fuel or weapons which had already been produced. In effect the United States was finally abandoning the Majority Plan of 1948 which assumed that international ownership could prevent nuclear cheating. Instead, the United States would continue to rely for its security on massive nuclear retaliation and would try to obtain Soviet agreement to a warning system against surprise attack.

Before the sub-committee met, Stassen told Paul Martin, who was to be the Canadian representative to that body, that the United States would reserve all its previous positions including its support for the Anglo-French plan for complete nuclear disarmament which it had endorsed barely six months ago. Martin found Stassen's message "disconcerting,"[4] and no wonder. External Affairs had already underlined the importance of the Western powers remaining united when facing the Soviet Union in the sub-committee and had assumed that this could only be done if the United States gave wholehearted support to the Anglo-French proposals. Now there was no hope that this would happen. As might have been expected, Moch also viewed Stassen's intentions with apprehension. But so did Anthony Nutting, the British representative, who explained to Martin that his government had been able to undercut the Ban the Bomb campaign only by making the prohibition of nuclear weapons an essential part of its disarmament policy. Without this promise, British public opinion would have been much more insistent on more direct action on nuclear disarmament. His government would stand by the plan which it had sponsored with the French. But Nutting now had another concern. Moch was determined to table the Anglo-French proposals at the sub-committee, and Nutting was worried about a possible split between Moch and Stassen on the whole issue of comprehensive disarmament.

When the sub-committee began its work on 29 August, Martin found himself dealing with the Soviet offer of 10 May. He was concerned lest a wide-ranging discussion of the Soviet plan, including its observation about the impossibility of checking on previous nuclear production, would bring this troubling issue to public attention. Consequently, he and Nutting and Moch decided to limit their criticisms of the Soviet project to its least credible aspect – inspection and controls. In his opening remarks to the sub-committee, therefore, Martin was quick to ask whether the Soviet proposal really offered progress on the "all-important question of controls."[5] The next day, 31 August, he complained that from his reading of the Soviet text it was not certain that the control organ would be in place before each stage of disarmament began: it was there to provide warning against a surprise attack but not to supervise the first stage of the reduction of arms; it would be empowered to receive information but would not have the right to verify on the spot that the reduction in weapons and forces had actually taken place; it would lack the power to take even interim action against violators of the agreement while waiting for instructions from the Security Council.[6] In this exercise in fault-finding Martin had the hearty support of Nutting and Moch. In response, Arkady Sobolev, the Soviet representative, constantly evaded providing details on the Soviet control proposals and attempted to turn the tables by asking delegates for their reactions to the Soviet plan as a whole which included the measures on nuclear disarmament which they had first suggested.

The sub-committee also spent a lot of time on Eisenhower's Open Skies plan. Stassen began by reading into the record the Soviet statement of 10 May that it was impossible to verify the prohibition of atomic weapons. He went on to remark that it was this consideration that had led President Eisenhower to offer his plan. Martin was painfully aware that the American position gave the Soviet Union a significant tactical advantage. Once the United States was on record as giving up on nuclear disarmament, the Soviet Union could make life miserable for the other members of the alliance – the latter would either have to distance themselves from the Americans on this issue or give up their own longstanding commitment to this goal. It was no surprise, then, that on 1 September Sobolev asked members of the sub-committee whether they still agreed with the Anglo-French proposal that would prohibit nuclear weapons after 75 per cent of the agreed reduction in conventional armed forces had been made and ban them completely after the remaining 25-per-cent reduction had been completed.

In a very strong dispatch to External Affairs,[7] Martin argued that Canada ought to keep to the goal of prohibiting nuclear weapons. The United Kingdom and France had reaffirmed their proposal to abolish atomic weapons on the assumption that there would be effective controls. If the Russians criticized the United States, it would be unfortunate if they were able to attack Canada as well. "It will be much easier to carry other countries in the [General Assembly] with us," he concluded, "if we say that we maintain our objective of disarmament and prohibition of nuclear weapons, provided adequate control arrangements are both feasible and accepted by the USSR." External Affairs agreed, and Martin was eventually able to tell Sobolev that Canada continued to support the total prohibition of nuclear arms.

But the Americans had already delivered a most emphatic answer to the Soviet question on 6 September when their secretary of the air force announced that the United States had no intention of destroying its atomic bombs; it would continue to rest its security on its capacity to retaliate to any attack with overwhelming nuclear power. This uncompromising line was echoed the same day in a meeting of Western delegations to the sub-committee when Stassen announced that he intended to state in the sub-committee that the United States regarded all pre-Geneva positions as having an "inactive and reserve status." Reporting to Ottawa,[8] Martin stated his belief that this decision put the Russians in the happy position of being able to accuse the United States of abandoning the goal of nuclear disarmament and thus score a great propaganda coup in the United Nations. Moch predicted that the Russians would charge that as soon as it had attempted to meet Western demands (in the 10 May proposals), the United States, fearing an agreement, had hurried to disavow its former positions. He believed that European opinion would be deeply offended by the American action. But Stassen remained adamant: prohibition could not be scientifically substantiated and so it was necessary to go with the Eisenhower plan which might lead to a measure of disarmament. This was as far as he went, however; he was careful to avoid any hint that the United States believed that the implementation of Open Skies would eventually lead to prohibition of atomic weapons. Later that day, Stassen made his statement in the sub-committee.

To push his position even further, Stassen proposed to table a resolution calling for the sub-committee to endorse the Eisenhower plan. If the Soviet Union was opposed, he was prepared to see it passed by a margin of four to one. This was to be a first step to winning the approval of the Disarmament Commission. The United States would then be in a better position, he believed, to win the support of the General Assembly and thus put pressure on the Russians to accept the Open Skies plan. But his three Western colleagues thought this a dangerous tactic. Martin was certain that any American attempt to ram the resolution through in the face of Soviet opposition would make it impossible ever to win Russian support for aerial inspection. Nutting believed that the General Assembly would regard the resolution as a Cold War propaganda exercise. Moch asserted that the Russians would argue that the Eisenhower plan was simply a system of espionage designed to defer the banning of atomic weapons.

Amidst this fierce disagreement within the Western camp, Stassen remained stubborn, and Martin despaired of making any impression on him. To the intense annoyance of his colleagues, and without their knowledge, much less consent, Stassen showed the proposed resolution to Sobolev. (Stassen was not one to learn from his mistakes – a similar gesture in May 1957 would ruin his career as an American arms negotiator.) A Canadian delegate to the United Nations, Robert A. MacKay, described the discussions among the Western delegations as "almost brutally frank."[9] Both Moch and Nutting indicated that they would be compelled to offer amendments to Stassen's resolution. Indeed, the British foreign secretary sent a telegram to the State Department supporting Nutting's stand in the sub-committee. Finally, Washington was persuaded that if the resolution could not win the approval of its closest allies, it would do badly if it ever reached the General Assembly. Stassen, much to the relief of his colleagues, finally announced that the United States would not offer the resolution in the sub-committee.

It should not be thought that Canada did not consider Open Skies a good idea. The chairman of the Canadian chiefs of staff, General Charles Foulkes, had already enthusiastically endorsed the scheme, observing that the advantages for Canada far outweighed any inconveniences.[10] Martin's concern was the relationship of the plan to comprehensive disarmament, but he reported that the most Stassen would concede was that it was a "gateway to disarmament"; he would never go so far as to suggest that it might be a "gateway" to the prohibition of nuclear weapons.[11] The Russians soon made it clear that they would only consider the American proposal if it were an integral part of a comprehensive plan. This was the main point of a letter of 19 September from Nikolai Bulganin, chairman of the Soviet Council of Ministers, to Eisenhower. Martin reported to Pearson that he came away from a dinner given by the Soviet foreign minister with the impression that the "Soviet Union is not enamoured with the Eisenhower plan unless it can be made part of a program involving the basic ideas contained in their resolution of May 10th."[12]

The sub-committee terminated its work on 8 October, with the delegates agreeing to suggest no resolution to the Disarmament Commission or the General Assembly. Instead the sub-committee would transmit to the Disarmament Commission a record of its meetings and the documents which had been submitted. The substantive differences between the Soviet Union and the United States were too great to be papered over. Delegates also believed that a meeting of Big Four foreign ministers, scheduled for the end of October, was a much more suitable body to take real decisions. But an even more important reason was that the eight task forces which Stassen had set up to study the question of inspection and control had not yet reported. There could be little progress as long as the Americans were reviewing their policy. In addition, the Western side was at odds with itself. Under these conditions no firm Western programme was possible.

The Americans seemed to have lost ground in these sub-committee deliberations. They had failed to win endorsement for the Eisenhower plan. The Soviet representative had succeeded in bringing the differences on the Western side over the prohibition of atomic weapons out in the open. It is true that in so doing the USSR was, to put it mildly, being inconsistent. The previous May it had explained that, with the best will in the world, it was impossible to check on the earlier production of nuclear weapons and materials. But this declaration had not inhibited the Soviet Union from scoring propaganda points by going after the United States for acknowledging what it itself had so recently maintained. Unfortunately, this course of action must have bolstered American scepticism about the Soviet desire for an arms control agreement.

In one meeting of the Western representatives, Nutting had suggested that the United States need not reject the principle of disarmament. The Anglo-French proposal was based on effective controls and since these were not possible, the United States could be certain that there would be no banning of nuclear weapons. Looking back, some writers[13] have taken up this point, arguing that it was possible both to propose an Open Skies programme and to continue to adhere to the principle of comprehensive disarmament. By being truthful, the United States had become vulnerable to charges of insincerity and inconsistency. Yet there is something to be said for the American approach. If Stassen and his colleagues had come to believe that comprehensive disarmament was impossible, it made sense to educate the American public on this point so as to clear the way for winning their support for a programme of arms control measures including Open Skies.

The meeting of foreign ministers in late October and early November followed the same pattern as the conference of the heads of state at Geneva the previous July. They continued to wrangle over Germany and comprehensive disarmament. Neither the British nor the French pressed for their plan of phased-in nuclear disarmament. In the end the ministers agreed to transmit the record of these discussions to their representatives on the sub-committee with instructions to continue to try to work out an agreement.

On 22 November, the day before the Disarmament Commission was to reconvene, the four Western members of the sub-committee held a strategy meeting. The Americans proposed an attempt to win the commission's endorsement for the Eisenhower plan. Nutting and Moch hoped for a procedural resolution to transmit the records of the sub-committee meetings to the Assembly, fearing that a broader resolution would leave them open to embarrassing Soviet amendments which quoted directly from their own proposals. "We accuse the Russians," Nutting observed, "of advocating disarmament without inspection. The Eisenhower plan on the other hand is inspection without disarmament." Martin could sympathize with what the Americans were trying to do, but he did not believe that the Disarmament Commission was the appropriate body for such a resolution. Thus the meeting broke up without any decision being taken.[14]

When it met, the Disarmament Commission decided to hear only from members of the sub-committee. The highlight was a speech by Moch in which he suggested that the time had come to "synthesize" all the disarmament plans on the table on the basis of three principles: (1) no control without disarmament; (2) no disarmament without control; (3) but, progressively, all disarmament that could be controlled. His proposition excited no great enthusiasm, however, perhaps because the first principle challenged the American position and the second that of the Soviet Union. To satisfy the Soviet Union, Moch proposed to prohibit the use of nuclear weapons as well as test explosions for military purposes. But the Russians were unhappy because under the French plan there would be a stage during which control and inspection were being established without disarmament taking place. To attract the Americans Moch asserted that for the present there ought to be no attempt to destroy atomic stocks because of the impossibility of verification. Instead he suggested periodic conferences to find a scientific method of control, with the aim of destroying nuclear stocks once such a method was discovered. This prospect did not altogether please the United States because a method of detecting nuclear stocks, if found, could lead eventually to the unconditional prohibition of nuclear weapons on which its entire war-fighting strategy was based. Martin, after paying tribute to Moch, affirmed his conviction that it was still possible for the sub-committee to come to an agreement to regulate the arms race. After these interventions, it was decided on 25 November to transmit the report of the sub-committee and the record of the commission's proceedings, without comment, to the General Assembly.

Meanwhile the Western delegates had been trying to agree on a draft resolution for the General Assembly. Once again, the Americans sought an explicit endorsement of the Eisenhower plan. But the United Kingdom was worried about the lack of an agreed Western disarmament policy and continued to fear that any resolution of substance might provoke Soviet amendments that would draw attention to Western withdrawals from previous positions. Moch wanted a call for comprehensive disarmament but realized that neither the United States nor the United Kingdom would support such a resolution. Consequently, both Nutting and Moch preferred to stick to a simple procedural resolution. Canada suggested a resolution that supported the Eisenhower plan for Open Skies and the Bulganin proposals for observation posts on the ground as the first stage of a comprehensive disarmament programme. It also endorsed Moch's dictum calling for the widest possible programme of disarmament that could be effectively controlled. In the end, the four delegations agreed to table a resolution that borrowed much from the Canadian proposal. It called for the Disarmament Commission to reconvene the sub-committee to seek agreement on a comprehensive disarmament plan without specifying whether this included a nuclear component. It also proposed that priority be given to the Eisenhower and Bulganin plans and such measures "of an adequately safeguarded disarmament plan as are now feasible."[15]

The Soviet Union was soon ready with a series of amendments. One would have eliminated references to the difficulties in the way of adequate control of the prohibition of nuclear weapons. Another would have instructed the sub-committee to give priority to both the Soviet 10 May and the Eisenhower plans. But, as a Canadian reporter explained, the former amounted to a general disarmament programme including the prohibition of atomic weapons and was "essentially in contradiction to the thinking behind the present Western draft."[16] Consequently it was unacceptable to the West. India had more luck with some of its amendments. The Indian draft introduced language in the preamble that included a detailed reference to the General Assembly resolution of 4 November 1954, thereby forcing the Western powers to concede that the prohibition of nuclear weapons was still one of the ultimate aims of the United Nations. The West also agreed to another Indian amendment calling for negotiations to suspend the experimental explosions of thermonuclear weapons. To rally many of the smaller nations of the Assembly behind its resolution, the West needed Indian approval and consequently agreed to these concessions.

Speaking in the First Committee on 7 December, Martin attempted to defend the overall Western position without revealing its internal contradictions. He began by asserting that the West continued to support the elimination of nuclear weapons on the understanding that there would be an effective control organ to guarantee implementation. He failed to mention the American reservation of their previous positions, however, and implied that the difficulty was the Soviet lack of response on control. "It might well be," he suggested, "that effective inspection and control would involve difficulties for the Soviet system. Perhaps a completely effective disarmament plan would be possible only if the Soviet leaders relaxed the monopoly over the minds of the people they control." This contradicted the point Martin had made earlier in quoting Eisenhower: "We have not as yet been able to discover any scientific ... method which would make certain the elimination of nuclear weapons."[17] Martin concluded by summarizing the Western programme of action. Since the elimination of nuclear weapons could not be checked, such a programme could not be immediately implemented; governments should therefore proceed in the field of conventional armaments with a kind of disarmament that could be effectively controlled. The early warning system envisaged by the United States should be accepted. Martin made this proposal knowing that the Soviet Union would not agree to the Eisenhower plan without a measure of disarmament. His speech was a clever combination of a propaganda tilt at the USSR along with a practical proposal to enhance Western security. If sufficiently attractive to the public at large, the USSR would either have to accept it, thus strengthening Western security, or lose points in the propaganda battle at the United Nations.

On 16 December, the General Assembly adopted the Western resolution by a count of fifty-six to seven (the Soviet bloc). Technically, the West had achieved its aim to have the sub-committee study the means of establishing the early warning system that the Americans wanted. But politically the resolution was no great triumph. The hope engendered by the Geneva summit was now gone. Few in the General Assembly were optimistic about the future of arms negotiations. The Swedish representative first urged the Soviet Union to give up its "intentional reticence" on controls and then turned on the United States, saying that by "placing reservations on every previously taken position the United States has caused, if not a certain deterioration, at least a deplorable uncertainty in negotiations." The Norwegians observed that the statements of the major powers "seemed to be marked more by anxiety to fix responsibility than concern to find solutions."[18] India was especially critical of the way in which the Disarmament Commission seemed to have been reduced to a rubber stamp for the sub-committee and the disarmament discussions had become the private preserve of the sub-committee's five members, with only occasional interventions by other interested countries. India voted for the Western resolution not because it was satisfactory but partly because its sponsors had accepted some improvements and, as the External Affairs report noted, "partly because to vote against the resolution would be to proclaim to the world that we all abandon hope."[19]

1956

THE REVISED ANGLO-FRENCH PLAN

Once the General Assembly had agreed that the sub-committee was to continue its work, External Affairs turned to planning for the new meetings. The department had no great hopes for a breakthrough: owing to the secrecy of Soviet society, it believed that the USSR would always reject inspection measures such as the Open Skies plan. External Affairs believed that the coming sub-committee talks would be little more than a propaganda duel. If that were the case, a unified Western position would be essential. To develop a unified approach, however, Western members must have enough time to consider any new American proposals. Unfortunately, the Americans had still not completed their studies on disarmament. American decision-making machinery was so complex and slow moving that American officials usually only received their instructions at the last minute. This might leave a little time for Canadians (and other Western delegates) to be briefed but not enough for them to practice quiet diplomacy and shift American policy. Again and again throughout this period the documents reveal Canadian frustration that American administrative procrastination had left insufficient time for the Western four to hammer out a unified position.

On 23 January the Disarmament Commission met and decided that the sub-committee should reconvene at a time convenient to all sides. Norman Robertson, the Canadian high commissioner in the United Kingdom who would shortly be intimately involved in the disarmament talks, believed that the sub-committee should be used as "a forum for negotiations between East and West on the problem of disarmament as one sector of the front which divides them." This being the case, he suggested that it ought not to reconvene until the "US position is settled and a united Western line is agreed."[20] The French also wished for three weeks or so to work out a unified Western position; they were far from happy with what they anticipated would be the American position. External Affairs did not want the sub-committee to meet until at least four weeks after the American proposals were released; otherwise they feared it would begin without the Western delegates having reconciled their positions. But this was not to be. The United States proposed a timetable that would allow only two weeks for allied consultations before the sub-committee began its work on 19 March even though the final American proposals were still not ready and the probability of a gap in policy between them and the French plan was very real.

Meanwhile Moch's position had been greatly strengthened by the January elections in France which had brought to power a minority government headed by his fellow socialist, Guy Mollet. Hitherto France had supported the Western stand that German reunification was a necessary precondition to general disarmament. Mollet reversed this thesis – he asserted that German reunification would result from general and controlled disarmament. Because this was the view put forward by the Soviet Union, it seemed likely that France might be more open to Soviet blandishments. This shift in French views worried the Americans who were unalterably opposed to making disarmament a precondition for German reunification. It was expected that the new Mollet government would press for a more active disarmament policy. Moch would be assured of much firmer cabinet support and encouraged to work even harder to persuade the other Western powers to agree to offer his "synthesis" plan to the Russians at the sub-committee meetings.

The main principle underpinning the Moch synthesis would be comprehensiveness. There would be a timetable which integrated conventional and nuclear disarmament. But the discovery that there was no scientific means of verifying total nuclear disarmament put in question the practicability of any comprehensive plan. For this reason the United Kingdom had begun to think of proposing a reduction in conventional arms alone; the system of verification for that reduction would include the exchange of military blueprints and aerial inspection as well as inspection teams at the main ground control points. Moch was opposed to any scheme for partial disarmament, however, because it failed to provide for the control of nuclear weapons. With or without the British, he was determined to introduce a comprehensive plan. The United Kingdom was also concerned about a possible French drift towards the Soviet camp. Yet they knew that the credibility of Moch on disarmament issues was so great that his endorsement of a Western proposal would help win European public opinion and take the initiative on disarmament away from the Soviet Union. If the British were co-sponsors of the plan, it would be difficult for the French to amend it unilaterally. Consequently, the United Kingdom decided to accept the principle of comprehensive disarmament in return for important French concessions on other points. The first was the deletion of specific numbers to which conventional forces would be reduced – this would please the Americans who, as we shall see, were no longer prepared to reduce their armed forces to 1.5 million. The second was French agreement that "the necessary conditions of confidence" must exist before embarking on succeeding stages of the plan.[21] This would allow governments to take into account their political situation before agreeing to additional measures of disarmament; any one of the signatories could halt the whole process if it believed that a further step would endanger its security.

What emerged was a revised Anglo-French plan. In the first stage, a control organ with the right to use aerial surveys and inspection teams at land control points would be established to forestall a surprise attack. There would also be an agreement on reductions in conventional arms and armed forces. Stage two would see the completion of the first half of the agreed reduction of conventional forces as well as a limitation on nuclear test explosions. Stage three would bring about a prohibition, under control, of nuclear tests as well as the cessation of the manufacture of nuclear arms. After 75 per cent of the agreed reductions in conventional forces had been carried out, there would be a complete prohibition of the *use* of nuclear arms. But there was no provision for the elimination of existing nuclear weapons, just a proposal for a scientific conference to study the possibility of such action.

The initial reaction of External Affairs to the revised plan was critical. The prohibition on the use of atomic weapons would impose a major strategic handicap on the West. There were practical difficulties which made a halt in the manufacture of nuclear weapons very unlikely. External Affairs also ruled out the banning of nuclear tests because it believed them to be crucial to "improving our nuclear defence potential."[22] (The use of the word "our," given Canada's lack of nuclear weapons, illustrates the intense feeling of solidarity which its diplomats felt for the American-led alliance.)

Moreover, it doubted that there was a foolproof way of detecting that an atomic explosion had actually taken place. The department did, however, agree with the insertion of "political" requirements before the next stage of the programme was undertaken. It went further and suggested that these be spelled out and that one condition ought to be the reunification of Germany. While the Canadian suggestion was a fair inference from the Anglo-French proposal of a political veto, it went against the whole Mollet line that disarmament must come before and would eventually lead to the reunification of Germany.

Robertson – at the centre of the negotiations – thought External Affairs' response very shortsighted. In his view, it had greatly exaggerated the security risk. Both Britain and France believed that the implementation of the agreement would take many years. The prohibition on the use of nuclear weapons would not come into effect until the third stage which would not be reached until there had been a vast improvement in political conditions. The Moch synthesis with its promise of comprehensive disarmament would have a very wide appeal not only to the other members of the Disarmament Commission but also to great numbers of people who wished to see the end of the arms race. Because it responded to the aspirations of "all peace-loving countries," the synthesis, Robertson insisted, "can be readily understood and is easily adaptable for publicity purposes."[23] He proposed therefore that Canada give enthusiastic support to the Anglo-French plan but not co-sponsor it for fear of isolating the United States. He wished that Moch would accept the American proposal for aerial inspection and some reduction in conventional arms as stage one of his plan. For its part the United States should raise no objection to the United Kingdom and France discussing the synthesis as a whole with the USSR as these talks would only concern a set of vague propositions for the future. The hard bargaining with the Soviet Union would aim to hammer out an agreement for the first stage.

Robertson's argument won over External Affairs. After all, it was expected that the main American objection to the Anglo-French plan would be that it constituted a comprehensive programme for nuclear disarmament. Canada could support such a scheme because there was no danger that it would be acted on immediately. In fact, the Americans were proposing virtually the same first steps but would oppose an organic link with nuclear disarmament. Canada believed the comprehensive approach was preferable. External Affairs therefore approved the Robertson tactic of working for a Western agreement to present concrete measures for stage one to the Soviet Union. These would be described as part of a comprehensive programme whose implementation would only take place when the necessary political and technical conditions were present. This seemed a reasonable way to close the gap between the French and the United States. But the clash between the two was over a fundamental strategic issue. Having no atomic weapons, the French wished for a nuclear-free defence because this would enable them to participate as an equal in the Western alliance. The Pentagon was so totally dependent on the nuclear deterrent, however, that it could not imagine a security strategy without one. Robertson faced an almost impossible task in trying to reconcile these two approaches to security.

At a 14 March meeting of the Western delegates to the subcommittee, he nevertheless attempted to bring the two together. He observed that Canada supported the comprehensive approach which clearly was not accepted by the United States. He wondered whether the Western powers could achieve "yet another synthesis which would reconcile the United States position with that of France and the UK." On the one hand, the Anglo-French plan would "not come into force until the international situation was more auspicious." On the other hand, the United States was seeking a "limited but immediate"[24] agreement without requiring such an improvement. Robertson proposed to insert elements of the United States position into stage one of the revised Anglo-French plan. Harold Stassen eagerly seized on this idea. He asserted that American objections to the second and third stages of the Anglo-French plan, which involved limiting nuclear capacity, were so fundamental that he would be obliged to oppose publicly certain specific measures, were they to be offered. He suggested that the American proposals (which had been explained to its allies the preceding week) might be incorporated into stage one of the plan without requiring agreement on the ultimate objectives of its second and third stages. But Moch insisted that stage one was only a part of the whole and that concentration on it would destroy the balance of the whole design. Only by putting forward a comprehensive plan, he affirmed, could the West prevent the Soviet Union continuing to appear as the champion of peace because of its 10 May proposals.

Two days later, Robertson reported the American explanation of why they were so opposed to the nuclear sections of the Anglo-French plan. First, they believed that a ban on the use of nuclear weapons could now be no more than a moral prescription and could not actually be enforced. Yet its existence would psychologically inhibit their use of their principle weapon and might convey an impression of declining American strength and will. Second, they were unwilling to halt tests which were so essential to nuclear weapons development; in fact the Atomic Energy Commission was planning a series of hydrogen bomb tests in the Pacific in April. Lastly, they were apprehensive lest the United Kingdom and France contemplate a ceiling on American conventional forces of 1.5 million; if the United States were forced to reduce its forces to that figure it could not carry out its NATO mission and would probably have to withdraw from vital commitments in other areas of the world. When Moch asked Stassen directly why the United States could not accept the revised plan which now included the proviso about political conditions, the latter replied that any plan which led to a substantial weakening of the United States would invite aggression, if not from the USSR then from its satellites or other subversive elements. Even discussions of disarmament would have an adverse effect on American allies, particularly those in Asia.[25] The United States was simply not willing to negotiate seriously about a comprehensive scheme that would weaken its military capacity. Its interest was in a system for early warning against surprise attack which, of course, involved no disarmament at all.

The sub-committee officially reconvened on 19 March. Moch presented his synthesis and the Soviet spokesman asked for some time to consider it. Canadian diplomats were in an unhappy position. They supported Britain and France but were worried about the United States going its own way. They feared that the split between the United States and France would be even more embarrassing when the sub-committee reported to the Disarmament Commission in July. But in fact they had little to worry about. The Soviet Union soon showed that the Anglo-French scheme was a non-starter. Andrei Gromyko maintained that it legalized the use of nuclear weapons and contained no provision for their elimination., There were no definite numbers proposed for the levels to which conventional forces should be reduced. The plan lacked a guarantee that the programme would go from one stage to the next. The Soviet Union would have to agree to aerial inspection as part of the pact. These were all valid objections, but the underlying reason for the Soviet rejection was probably their decision – soon to be revealed – to seek an agreement on conventional arms that was independent of any understanding on nuclear weapons.

Despite the negative Soviet reaction, Lester Pearson was reluctant to give up the comprehensive principle embodied in the Anglo-French plan. He conceded that an approach that sought for accord on immediate concrete measures was crucial; yet he wanted the United States to accept some commitment to ultimate disarmament goals. He believed this was essential not only for propaganda purposes but also to convince the USSR that the West was serious about disarmament. He wondered whether the United States might not accept a more flexible Anglo-French plan that omitted a timetable or a definite sequence for the implementation of its features. Might it be sufficient for an agreement to cover only measures common to all the plans already put forward, with the understanding that "as soon as possible arrangements should be worked out to cover the whole field progressively."[26]

Following instructions, Robertson sounded out the Americans along these lines but with little success. They maintained that they were already committed to continuing the search for a comprehensive disarmament scheme. Nor did they have any difficulty with a stage-by-stage development. What caused them to reject the Anglo-French plan was its specific proposals for the banning of nuclear tests, the prohibition of the use of nuclear weapons, and the reduction of American force levels to 1.5 million. Pearson's tactic might have been successful, had the United States been willing to subscribe to all or even to any of these measures and thus lend credibility to a Western claim that the measures of stage one were but the first steps towards disarmament. But the United States believed that acceptance of *any* of these proposals would threaten its security. What it offered instead, as we shall see, was a limited agreement on a few measures which would strengthen its own safety.

Thus Pearson was to be disappointed. Without any support from the major players, the United States and the USSR, the Anglo-French plan had little relevance to future negotiations. It no longer held the centre of the stage; attention could now shift to the new American and Soviet proposals. This development was not altogether unwelcome to External Affairs. Although it had come to believe that the Anglo-French plan was no longer useful in furthering discussions, it had avoided saying so for fear of offending the French. Now it need no longer pronounce any public judgment on it. More importantly, since the plan was not on the bargaining table, a rift between the United States and France was no longer likely. The Western team could now unite to deal with a new Soviet proposal.

THE ARMS CONTROL SCHEMES
OF THE SUPERPOWERS

The surprising feature of the plan which Andrei Gromyko presented on 27 March 1956 was that the Soviet Union had dropped its ten-year-old demand for the prohibition of nuclear arms. The new focus was the reduction of conventional armaments and armed forces. Section one of the Soviet plan called for a three-year freeze on conventional forces and military budgets at the levels of 31 December 1955 as well as a move to reduce personnel to the levels proposed in the Anglo-French memorandum of 29 March 1955 and the Soviet proposal of 10 May: namely, individual ceilings for the United States, the USSR, and China of 1 to 1.5 million men; 650,000 men for each of the United Kingdom and France; armed forces of no more than 200,000 for other states. To meet a persistent Western demand, section two called for the establishment of the control organ before the reductions in conventional forces began. The Soviet scheme also met much of previous Western criticism by being much more explicit about the aims of control and the methods proposed to attain them. To deal with surprise attack, it suggested ground posts at airports, railway junctions, ports, and highways. It also hinted at the possibility of aerial photography once the requisite confidence had been established. The third section of the Soviet plan offered a zone of limitation and inspection of armaments in central Europe which would include territory of both parts of Germany and adjacent states to them. (Here the Soviet Union was following up a suggestion that had been made by Anthony Eden at the Geneva summit.) Ceilings would be imposed on the number of troops from the USSR, the United States, the United Kingdom, and France to be stationed in the territory of other states in the zone. No nuclear arms would be permitted within this zone. The final section called for the cessation of hydrogen bomb tests and for measures to ensure there were no atomic weapons among the arms of troops on German territory within three months after the treaty was signed.

Once it became a nuclear power, the USSR had much less need for a mass army. Lowering force levels would lessen its military costs and transfer much needed manpower to the home front. But the Soviet plan was also designed to undermine the American position in West Germany. Acceptance of the zone of limitation with its implicit recognition of East Germany would torpedo any serious proposal for German reunification. Yet without some hope of its achievement Chancellor Adenauer would be very handicapped in trying to raise a West German army. With its world-wide commitments, the United States could not reduce its forces to 1.5 million and still keep five divisions in West Germany – the number deemed essential to furnish the necessary political support to the German chancellor in his efforts to build his own army. Moreover, the Soviet proposal to limit the armies of other states to 200,000 would place an intolerable cap on West German strength. The banning of atomic weapons within Germany would also seriously undermine Western defences. The *New York Times* was right to observe that the Soviet plan "would emasculate the German Federal Republic and reduce NATO to the military innocuousness of a debating society."[27] In return for all these concessions the Soviet Union would not be paying much of a price. The United States desired protection against surprise attack through a system of aerial photography and an exchange of military blueprints. The Soviet Union only offered to think about accepting aerial photography in the future, if it were satisfied with the way negotiations were going.

The measures outlined in the Soviet plan would all be beneficial for the Soviet Union. Yet the plan contained enough apparent concessions to make it a realistic offer. To refuse it would furnish grist for the Soviet propaganda mill. Currently, the Soviet Union had some 4 million men under arms compared with 2.8 million for the United States. Bringing the numbers down to 1.5 million would force the USSR to disband 37.5 per cent of its forces compared with a cut of only 14 per cent for the United States. Then, too, in principle the Soviet plan had met the greater part of Western complaints on controls. Most importantly, it had, for the time being, abandoned grandiose schemes for the elimination of nuclear weapons in which no one had really believed. It was not even calling for any ban on the use of atomic bombs. The duel over nuclear disarmament had been a grave obstacle to an agreement because each side was convinced (rightly) that the other would never surrender its nuclear arms. Now that it was admitted that it was technically impossible to verify their elimination, proposals for their prohibition were out of the question. The Americans had acknowledged this in September 1955 when Stassen had reserved all previous American proposals. Now the USSR was saying, in effect, that they agreed with the United States that the only path to a treaty lay through limited, concrete measures which could be implemented immediately and which did not depend on a prior political consensus. For the moment the Soviet Union had abandoned nuclear disarmament and appeared to be interested in an agreement on conventional arms. While there were reasons to reject the Soviet offer, it contained enough concessions to make it difficult to do so. Pearson thought the new proposals "a substantial advance" over previous positions.[28]

The Soviet Union might have solved its immediate tactical negotiating problem, but it still confronted the danger of the spread of nuclear weapons. Gromyko had argued that it might be possible to reach an agreement on conventional arms if it were not tied to a pact on nuclear weapons. But the negative consequences of this position were soon illustrated by the rather vehement reaction of Jules Moch. He conceded that the Soviet proposal might lead to sizable reductions in conventional weapons but warned that it would also result in an accelerated nuclear arms race. Without any controls on atomic weapons the world would be at the mercy of the three nuclear powers. Because countries like France could not accept the prospect of such domination, they would inevitably begin to produce atomic weapons of their own. Moch wanted the Soviet Union to agree to halt the production of fissionable materials for military purposes. Yet he was more than a little inconsistent in his arguments. In their own plan, the French had emphasized the importance of a cut-off in the manufacture of nuclear weapons. Indeed, Moch had warned that without such agreement France reserved the right to make and test its own nuclear weapons. France seemed determined to gain some sort of equality in the nuclear field. Yet there was a flaw in the drive for parity. Even if there was a halt to the manufacture of nuclear arms, the United States, the Soviet Union, and even the United Kingdom already possessed such weapons. Since there was no measure for destroying atomic stockpiles in the Moch synthesis, France would be left with no nuclear weapons even if his plan were carried through.

Nevertheless Moch's attack brought pressure on Gromyko to agree to halt the production of more atomic bombs. Embarrassed to be cast in the role of one who thought nuclear disarmament of little importance, Gromyko later read into the record a statement that the USSR had no objection to considering the prohibition of nuclear weapons and the reduction of conventional forces simultaneously, provided only that an agreement on the latter was not made conditional on achieving one on the former.

Whatever else it had done, Gromyko's plan had pushed Moch's synthesis to the sidelines. The attention of Western delegates now turned to the American plan for "the first phase of a comprehensive programme for disarmament" which Stassen presented to the sub-committee on 3 April. It proposed to begin with some confidence-building steps between Washington and Moscow that would include small demonstration tests of aerial reconnaissance and ground inspection in limited "non-sensitive" areas of both the United States and the USSR. These would be followed by an agreement to set maximum manpower levels at 2.5 million for each of the United States and the USSR and at 750,000 each for Britain and France. After that would come acceptance of a control and inspection plan that would incorporate the Open Skies proposals of Eisenhower and the ground control checkpoints suggested by Bulganin. The next three steps would take place concurrently: (1) an exchange of blueprints of the military establishments of each state; (2) a freeze on defence budgets as of 31 December 1955; and (3) the installation and completion of the inspection and control system. At this point there would be established an Armaments Regulation Organization, with an Armaments Regulation Council composed of all signatories to the treaty, an executive committee of permanent and non-permanent elected members, and a director-general. When the latter reported that the system was ready to verify the reductions in levels of conventional armaments and prepared to provide against surprise attack, the first phase of conventional forces reductions would begin. When the director-general reported that the inspection and control system was prepared to account for the future production of fissionable materials, their manufacture for military purposes would come to a halt. Finally, the testing of nuclear weapons would be limited and monitored in an agreed manner under the control of the Armaments Regulation Council.

The plan of the Soviet strategists had been designed to improve the security of their own country; not surprisingly the aim of the American proposal was to ameliorate the safety of the United States. President Eisenhower and Secretary of State Dulles believed that the Soviet Union was a perpetual enemy whose ultimate intention was to dominate the world. In the Far East the United States seemed to be in a state of continual conflict with communist China; the quarrel over the offshore islands of Quemoy and Matsu made war in Asia a constant possibility. While there appeared to be no immediate threat of Soviet aggression in central Europe, it was necessary to be prepared. Thus the American proposals contained nothing that would weaken their nuclear deterrent, and they made only a slight gesture towards conventional disarmament. The main concern of the United States was the danger of a surprise nuclear strike against the aircraft of the Strategic Air Command. They wanted the Soviet Union to agree to aerial reconnaissance and to exchange blueprints of military establishments. Their plan meant a modest reduction in conventional arms would only take place after the Soviet Union had accepted a system of early warning against surprise attack.

In their plan, however, the Americans did propose a cut-off in the production of nuclear fuel for military purposes. This would have led eventually to an end to the manufacture of new nuclear weapons. Despite opposition from the Atomic Energy Commission and the joint chiefs of staff, Eisenhower had insisted on making this offer to keep the arms control process moving forward.[29] If accepted, each side would be left with its current stockpile of nuclear weapons and the Americans would be in the happy position of having a perpetual superiority. But to verify Soviet compliance with the cessation of the production of nuclear fuels would require a formidable control team roaming around the USSR. As Khrushchev later explained: "we couldn't allow the U.S. and its allies to send their inspectors criss-crossing around the Soviet Union. They would have discovered that we were in a relatively weak position, and that realization might have encouraged them to attack us."[30] Nevertheless, an end to the manufacture of new nuclear weapons was bound to appeal to public opinion. Gromyko did not know how to respond and simply evaded the issue. But the American plan had other features that made it attractive: it would lead to some reduction in conventional arms; it would require no complicated political conditions for its implementation. And because it would certainly help American security the Soviet Union would have to regard it as a serious offer.

Pearson thought that, on the whole, the American plan was a good one. Naturally he would have liked a stronger emphasis on the connection between it and ultimate Western objectives in disarmament. But his greater concern was that halting the production of atomic fuels for military purposes would not stop the proliferation of nuclear weapons. Unless the nuclear bomb was eliminated or an enforceable agreement on the prohibition of its use instituted, non-nuclear countries (perhaps he was thinking of France) would continue to want atomic arms for their own protection; otherwise they might be in the uncomfortable position in which Canada now found itself – forever completely dependent on others for defence against nuclear attack. Moreover, the current atomic powers might transfer nuclear weapons to governments that might be less responsible in their use. Unless past production could be accounted for, it might not even be possible to control such exports. The danger of the use of atomic weapons in local wars would continue.[31]

While Pearson had doubts about this section of the American design, there was not much he could do about it. He had no practical alternative to offer in its place. His options were either to go public with his disagreements or to accept the one dubious proposal for the sake of Western solidarity and the other parts of the package. Because he believed Western unity was crucial in dealing with the Soviet Union, Pearson would have departed from quiet diplomacy only in the event of a disagreement over a strategic issue of enormous consequence. Canadian diplomats were therefore to be found supporting this worrisome cut-off proposal just as strongly as the other parts of the American plan in which they genuinely believed.

A CANADIAN ARMS CONTROL PROPOSAL

Meanwhile, as the sub-committee discussions got under way, Norman Robertson had begun to wonder whether the time had not come for Canada to propose a first-stage programme of its own. He felt a special urgency because of the prospect that the intercontinental missile armed with a nuclear warhead would soon replace the bomber. Time was running out, and the world would soon face the "prospect of push-button nuclear weapons, which might be susceptible of no control whatever and no effective warning system."[32] He was encouraged by the Soviet plan which "set forth a carefully-considered negotiating position." What struck him was that both the United States and the USSR were "seeking an agreement which could be implemented in the near future without any marked change in the international situation."[33] Here was a key point. To make progress in disarmament contingent on improvements in relations between the two sides meant postponing practical measures endlessly. Robertson therefore looked for a scheme which both sides would find acceptable despite the current climate of mutual hostility. The best that could be hoped for was a very few modest steps. At the same time he realized that Canada must be careful in presenting such a programme to avoid upsetting France and even the United Kingdom. It would be necessary to wait long enough for them to understand that a comprehensive programme was not practicable. By the first week in April, he concluded that the "Anglo-French plan as a negotiating document would seem to be virtually a dead letter" and that the "Canadian emphasis in the current talks should be on determining what steps can and should be taken immediately."[34]

Finally, on 20 April, Robertson sounded out Stassen on a modest first-stage accord with the Russians. It was necessary, he told the American representative, to "move from years of discussions to limited practical measures of stabilization." Stassen concurred, although he warned that any proposed pact should not create the impression that the solution of disarmament problems was at hand. Robertson, however, was enthusiastic about the prospects. He wrote External Affairs that "in view of our special position" in the sub-committee it would be useful for Canada to propose a limited agreement which, "however meagre, would in itself be a political development of major importance and could in its turn contribute to an improved atmosphere for tackling the outstanding political questions and for subsequent and more comprehensive measures of controlled disarmament."[35] No doubt Robertson was right in his belief that any kind of arms control agreement would help to ease tensions between the two sides. Nevertheless, his use of the phrase "in view of our special position" is curious. Canada had never concealed its loyalty to the Western side or attempted the role of the honest broker in the sub-committee's deliberations. Why would Robertson have thought that the Soviet Union would see a Canadian initiative as anything but an offer designed to help the West?

A few days later, on 23 April, Robertson presented the sub-committee with Canada's views on how to break the deadlock. A limited agreement, he asserted, should not weaken one side at the expense of the other. He proposed to limit hydrogen bomb tests and stop the manufacture of nuclear fuel for military purposes; in the conventional field, force levels would be reduced to 2.5 million for the United States, the USSR, and China. There was to be an early warning system against surprise attack underpinned by aerial inspection. He emphasized the importance of the American proposals for small demonstration tests in both the United States and the USSR as a means of gaining practical experience in control and inspection. Finally, he stressed that merely because it was proposing a limited first step did not mean that Canada was abandoning its long-range objectives in disarmament.[36] Most of Robertson's proposals were in line with American aims. The single exception was the limitation of nuclear tests. Here, as we shall see, was the beginning of an attempt to develop a somewhat independent Canadian position on the issue of nuclear testing.

Gromyko was not impressed with the Canadian presentation. He would accept neither the figure of 2.5 million for force levels nor aerial surveillance. The Soviet leaders, Bulganin and Khrushchev, happened to be holding talks with the British government in London on the very same day. Stassen met with Khrushchev who expressed his fierce opposition to aerial inspection. These events virtually brought the proceedings of the sub-committee to a close. Stassen and Gromyko held three days of private meetings without results. On 3 May, the day before the sub-committee adjourned, Western delegates submitted a list of six principles which justified the Western position and by implication condemned Soviet intransigence. The text, known as the declaration of 4 May, approved United States proposals for force levels, aerial reconnaissance, and the halting of the production of nuclear materials. It also insisted that the West would not be willing to advance beyond the first stage of disarmament until confidence had been created through the settlement of major political issues (such as German reunification).

Why was it impossible for the sub-committee to produce even a limited agreement? The Soviet leaders desired substantial reductions in their armed forces to lessen the financial burden and help their economy. Because of the tensions in Germany and the Far East, the United States rejected a level of 1.5 million for their forces; to comply, the Americans would have been compelled to dismantle bases and weaken alliances. And it would not have been able to fight brushfire wars if necessary. Open Skies apart, there was in Washington a "robust internal resistance to substantial arms control in general." Some feared that any agreement would diminish public support for defence spending.[37] Consequently, the Soviet leaders saw no advantage in conceding the principal American demand, aerial inspection, which they tended to view as legalized espionage on a grand scale.

Although there was a lack of unity on the Western side – both the Anglo-French plan and that of the United States remained on the table – Pearson was satisfied that there was substantial agreement between these two Western approaches on the requirements for a first-stage negotiation. He observed, quite rightly, that the Canadian delegation "had sought to focus the attention of the Sub-Committee on initial steps."[38] He continued to believe that reconciliation of the opposing Western and Soviet views was possible, and he hoped that further sessions of the Disarmament Commission and its sub-committee would allow this to happen.

WESTERN DISCORD

Although the meetings of the sub-committee had ended in impasse, the Soviet Union soon showed that it was serious about reducing its armed forces. On 14 May it announced plans to discharge 1.2 million men in the course of the next year. Such a move brought economic benefits. It was also a fine propaganda coup. Nevertheless, it was a positive step and showed that unilateral cuts could be made without waiting interminably for a negotiated agreement which was almost impossible to attain because of the mutual competitive drive for advantage. Unfortunately, the value of the Soviet gesture was reduced because of their unwillingness to allow for verification. The West could not be certain that the diminution in forces reduced Soviet military capacity since it could not monitor what was being done with the newly freed up resources of money and manpower. Then, on 7 June, Bulganin wrote the heads of government of

Britain, France, and the United States, calling on them to cut their forces in Germany. He also sent Prime Minister Louis St Laurent a letter complaining that the United Nations discussions had not produced positive results, announcing the cut in Soviet forces, and asking Canada to take steps to solve the problem of disarmament without specifying what these should be. This suggests that the note to St Laurent was more a matter of courtesy to a member of the sub-committee than anything else.

In preparing its response, Canada consulted with its NATO allies to be sure there was no contradiction in principle. The Canadian reply was polite and mild-tempered. It claimed that even after the recent reductions, the Soviet Union would have five times the number of divisions which the West had at its disposal in Europe. It suggested that if reductions were to contribute to international confidence then it must be possible to check them. The letter went on to underline the importance of the sub-committee and to suggest that there was reason for some optimism: Canada never lost faith in the value of negotiations and never lost an opportunity to say so. Finally, the letter made the valid point that a comprehensive agreement would only be possible if there was greater mutual confidence flowing from the solution of dangerous political issues.[39] There was, of course, a danger that the West might decide that the reunification of Germany was such an urgent problem which would have been a mistake: Europe had after all been living peacefully with a divided Germany for four decades. In any case, both the Soviet and Canadian letters were part of the propaganda battle – presumably the next round of real bargaining would take place at the meeting of the Disarmament Commission in July.

Meanwhile the French attitude towards the USSR was hardening. Early in May a delegation led by Premier Mollet had gone to Moscow to solicit support for a general plan to combine German reunification with general disarmament. But Khrushchev was adamant in his opposition to a united Germany. "You keep your Germans," he told the French, and "we shall keep ours."[40] Because of the lack of verification procedures, Mollet was not nearly as impressed with the Soviet cuts in armed forces as their leaders thought he should be. The consequent cooling of relations made it easier for the French to come around publicly to accepting the German-American view that there could be no disarmament before German reunification. Another factor in the stiffening French attitude was the continuing revolt in Algeria. It meant that Moch now placed much less emphasis on the necessity of early restrictions on conventional arms. He was also less wedded to his former assertion that a disarmament agreement was necessary to improve relations with the USSR. Then, too, French government opinion on nuclear arms was changing. Early in 1956, Mollet had shown public support for a multilateral European organization, Euratom, which would build atomic reactors for peaceful purposes. It would own all the nuclear fuel and its member-states would renounce all military use of the atom. But by July Mollet was maintaining that participation in Euratom should not preclude France's right to nuclear arms or interfere with their production if it chose to build them. Even Moch had revised his views and had come to agree with the American position that the limitation and prohibition of test explosions should only come into force as part of a general disarmament agreement. Moch now wished to avoid any embarrassing clause in a comprehensive agreement that might inhibit French military nuclear development. Perhaps the new French attitude was also linked to the announcement in June 1956 that the British intended to test a hydrogen bomb in 1957.

External Affairs had three aims at the forthcoming meeting of the Disarmament Commission. The first was to meet the Soviet challenge on the propaganda front: to criticize the inadequacy of their unilateral disarmament as a means of promoting mutual security by emphasizing the weakness of their control proposals and their refusal to establish an early warning system. The second was to persuade the commission to continue the negotiations in the sub-committee – Canada still hoped that the Soviet Union would eventually embrace the programme suggested by Robertson on 23 April. The third was to bring the views of the French and the United States closer together. Luckily, the Soviet rejection of the revised Anglo-French proposals at the sub-committee meetings had allowed the West to avoid revealing the extent of divergence between Moch and Stassen. Since the debate in the Disarmament Commission was likely to be brief, there was some chance of preventing the differences between the two from becoming more apparent. Thus, a memorandum for the guidance of the Canadian representatives at the Disarmament Commission observed that "it would seem desirable for the Canadian representatives to play much the same role in the private consultations which they played in London i.e. to try to draw the other powers together and to prevent the isolation of any one of them." As well, Canada was to develop a strong public position "in favour of the common elements in the Western proposals advanced in the London discussions."[41]

The Disarmament Commission meetings began on 3 July with two rival resolutions on the table. That of the four Western powers urged that the sub-committee be empowered to continue the search for agreement on the basis of the principles enunciated in the declaration of 4 May. The Soviet Union, dropping its initiative on the reduction of conventional arms for the moment, went back to a purely propaganda motion, calling on all nuclear powers to promise to refrain from using atomic or hydrogen weapons. Two days later, Paul Martin presented a lengthy exposition of the Canadian position. He warned that soon effective control of disarmament would no longer be feasible. The elimination of nuclear weapons was not practicable because of the lack of the means for instituting effective controls. But a programme of "controllable" disarmament was possible and he went on to reiterate the suggestions that Norman Robertson had made in the sub-committee on 23 April. He also praised both the Anglo-French and American proposals. He returned again and again to the importance of aerial photography to guard against surprise attack. Martin also implicitly criticized the Russians for abandoning the urgent task of doing away with nuclear arms. Indeed, he was eloquent on the need to control them before public apathy set in and hydrogen bombs became accepted as ordinary weapons. He demanded that a start be made in their control, but offered no firm proposal, only suggesting here and there that it would be a good idea to halt the manufacture of nuclear fuel. (No doubt he was well aware of Pearson's reservations about this idea.) Overall, Martin's speech could only please the Americans except perhaps for a solitary hint that the limitation of atomic tests might be feasible.[42] But there was little in his speech to attract the Russians. Yet they might have been willing to make concessions on aerial photography in return for significant reductions in the conventional forces of the Western powers.

As things stood, it was evident that the West's resolution would win the approval of the ten members of the Disarmament Commission other than the Soviet Union. Then, on 12 July, Andrei Gromyko not only called for the prohibition of atomic weapons and the ending of nuclear tests but also offered to accept, as a first step to reductions in conventional forces, force levels proposed by the United States (2.5 million for the United States, the Soviet Union, and China; 750,000 for France and the United Kingdom). However, no more than 150,000–200,000 would be allowed other countries (which would of course include West Germany). The offer on conventional forces was not contingent on the Western acceptance of nuclear prohibition. This clever proposal enabled the Soviet Union to appear reasonable and to regain its moral leadership on nuclear disarmament. And, if it were accepted, to prevent the

expansion of the West German army to the size proposed for it by
NATO.

The Soviet proposal also provoked dissension among the four
Western powers. Martin, Moch, and Nutting wished to drop the
earlier resolution in favour of one which simply referred all
proposals before the Disarmament Commission to the sub-committee for study. They expended considerable effort to move the
United States to agree but without success. The Americans insisted
on a resolution which specifically accepted the principles of the 4
May declaration. When the final version of the Western resolution
was presented by Peru, Gromyko, not surprisingly, was not prepared to approve Western principles. Meanwhile Moch had been
talking informally with one of the Russian delegates about the
advisability of a recess to see whether a procedural text acceptable
to all could not be drafted. Unfortunately, he did not bother to
inform his Western partners of what he had done. Thus when a
motion for a recess was tabled, Moch, who favoured the motion,
found himself on the losing side – opposed among others by
Canada, the United States, and Great Britain. Disappointed at the
loss of an opportunity, Moch publicly expressed his regret. Before
the final vote on the Peruvian resolution was taken, Martin attempted to persuade the other members of the commission that it
was in fact only a procedural resolution and so all members could
accept it. On the vote, however, it was adopted with the Soviet
Union in opposition and Yugoslavia abstaining. "Thus the Commission ended on a sour note," commented a member of the Canadian
delegation: "The United States attained its cold war victory but at
the expense of irritating the Soviet delegation, alienating the
Yugoslavs and causing Moch to cry out in indignation."[43]

CONCLUSION

The main Soviet objective in the bargaining discussions on disarmament in 1956 was to reduce American force levels and thereby to
frustrate the Western strategy to depend on West German land
forces; for their part, the Americans wanted an early warning
system against surprise attack. The negotiations foundered because
each thought the asking price of the other side to be too high. An
astute contemporary observer suggested that the real reason for the
American refusal to compromise was that a partial disarmament
agreement would only boost the Soviet campaign to "ease tensions"
and so "tend further to melt the glue of our alliances and bases."[44]
The one change was that both superpowers had implicitly agreed to

abandon total nuclear disarmament as a serious goal. Once President Eisenhower announced this position in Geneva, the United States never budged on this issue. At first the Soviet Union reacted by accusing the United States of backtracking on a long-held commitment, but in the spring of 1956, desiring a substantial conventional disarmament, the Soviet Union dropped its demand for the prohibition of nuclear arms – only to find itself attacked by the West for giving up on the international control of atomic energy. Soviet negotiators never made this tactical mistake again. Their future proposals always had two prongs – one sought the political advantages of advocating nuclear disarmament while the other would propose partial concrete measures that might be negotiated and implemented immediately. Thus, in the July 1956 session of the Disarmament Commission, the Soviet Union came back to its old programme of the prohibition of nuclear arms and the banning of tests while continuing to press for a reduction in force levels. This was a satisfactory political posture – the campaign for nuclear prohibition would perhaps weaken the American will to use atomic weapons while conventional disarmament (if implemented) would help the economic situation at home and certainly undermine NATO.

But abandoning the abolition of nuclear weapons as a feasible goal created a serious problem for those French politicians who were reluctant to see their country acquire atomic arms. Comprehensive disarmament, not merely arms control, was what Jules Moch sought. While he understood that there was no prospect of getting rid of nuclear arms immediately, he pressed the United States fiercely to continue to accept nuclear disarmament as an ultimate Western goal. The rift which developed between France and the United States caused great concern in Canada, where it continued to be an article of faith that unity was necessary if the West was to deal firmly with the Soviet Union. Consequently, Canada was constantly chiding the United States for not providing enough time for consultation among the Western allies to work out an acceptable and agreed position from which to confront the Soviet Union. (The plea for consultation was also an attempt to get the Americans to accept some input on their strategic decisions from lesser NATO powers like Canada.) In the sub-committee, in the Disarmament Commission, at the United Nations, Canada constantly tried to bring the Americans and French together. Of its efforts, the official Canadian report on the July session of the commission comments: "Behind the scenes the Canadian Delegation worked strenuously to maintain solidarity in the Western ranks. This was a continuation of the role which the Canadian representatives had played during the sub-committee session in London. The aim was to reconcile as far as possible the differences in approach among the Western three. At the Commission Session ... Mr Martin was mainly concerned with bridging the gap between M. Moch and Mr Lodge" [the American representative].[45]

In the 1956 discussions in the sub-committee Canada had put forward its own suggestion for a first-stage programme. The plan's main virtue was that it contained measures for immediate action, thus putting to one side the difficult question of whether a first-stage programme should be linked either to the banning of hydrogen bomb tests or to the prohibition of the use of nuclear weapons. It was thought that a programme of immediate measures which were not conditional on any kind of political agreement might well be of interest to both the Soviet Union and Canada's Western partners.

This phase of the negotiations, however, was coming to an end in the summer of 1956. The French were beginning to think more seriously about acquiring nuclear arms, a step which would be very much stimulated by the Suez crisis and the feeling of the French that they had been left in the lurch by the United States. The conviction that in the end they could only rely on themselves would boost the influence of those who had been arguing that France should produce its own nuclear arms. By moving away from nuclear disarmament as a serious policy aim, the French position became more akin to that of the Americans and tensions between Washington and Paris over nuclear issues eased. The French commitment to the international control of atomic energy could now be satisfied by a ritual call for a halt in the production of fuel for military purposes. The issue that would next capture attention was nuclear testing. Oddly enough, it would be Canada that would move a small step away from its powerful partners by proposing their limitation.

CHAPTER EIGHT

Final Negotiations, 1956–57: The Nuclear Test Ban and Aerial Inspection

The impasse which developed at the July 1956 session of the Disarmament Commission had done little to promote harmony between the Soviet Union and the West. These tensions were to be greatly exacerbated by the twin crises of early November stemming from the Anglo-French invasion of Egypt over the Suez Canal and the Soviet army's intervention in Hungary. Yet, curiously enough, it was at this time that both sides began to display more serious interest in reaching an arms agreement. It is probable that the increased tension precipitated by these crises reminded both Khrushchev and Eisenhower how dangerous an uncontrolled arms race might be. There was, as well, considerable public support in the West – and probably in the Soviet Union – for some sort of agreement. And the elements of a practical bargain that might interest the strategic thinkers on both sides had emerged. The United States wanted to install a system for mutual aerial photography; the Soviet Union desired a ban on test explosions designed to improve nuclear weapons. At the sub-committee sessions that ran from March to September 1957, the possibilities for a "trade" were to be explored with a vigour hitherto absent from the discussions.

Canadian diplomats were much more interested in the test ban issue than in aerial photography which would not affect Canada directly. Pearson and his colleagues sincerely supported the need for nuclear testing by the West. However, they were concerned about justifying this position to the Canadian public. Pearson also had a small agenda of his own on the test ban issue. He was convinced that it was important to win the support of the Third World bloc within the United Nations, led by India, for the Western position on arms control. And India had made it clear over the past two years that something should be done to halt these tests. These were among the concerns that led Canada's diplomats to undertake to modify the West's policy on nuclear tests.

INDIA AND THE PRESSURE FOR A TEST BAN

Canada's diplomats had considerable respect for India's leaders and position in the world. As John Holmes was to write some years later: "The eminence of Mr Nehru, the ghost of Mahatma Gandhi, and the cantankerous brilliance of Mr Krishna Menon combined to make India in the 1950s a middle power of such influence that in all things except military and economic strength and a permanent seat in the Security Council it was a great power."[1] In the years following India's independence, a diplomatic entente had developed between India and Canada. Originally based, no doubt, on the Commonwealth link and the assistance programme developed under the Colombo Plan, it blossomed into a much closer collaboration during the crises of the early 1950s.[2] Pearson had co-operated closely with the Indians in pressing for a ceasefire in Korea. Canada had agreed to serve on the International Commissions for Supervision and Control in Indochina only after it was clear that they would be headed by India. And at the time of Suez, both were to agree in rejecting the use of force by France and Britain. Prime Minister St Laurent and Prime Minister Nehru had developed an amiable relationship, and St Laurent believed that Canada had a special responsibility to explain American policy to India and to interpret New Delhi's actions for Washington. For there were profound disagreements between the United States and India.

In the Cold War setting of the 1950s, India described itself as a non-aligned power, a neutralist state which owed loyalty to neither power bloc and hence might play a role in alleviating global tensions. India was stoutly anti-communist. Nehru sometimes criticized Soviet actions, helped suppress Marxist insurrections in Asian neighbours, and often clapped India's own communists in jail. But he did not accept the American contention that the greatest problem in world affairs was the expansionist nature of international communism.[3] The Indian government did not feel threatened by the Soviet Union, which adopted an active campaign of wooing India once Bulganin and Khrushchev came to power. India believed that a more important and more urgent issue was the removal of all traces of colonialism and foreign domination from the countries of Asia and Africa and was less than happy about the intervention of the United States and its allies (often the European colonial powers) in Asian affairs. Most important of all, Nehru believed that the communist regime in China was firmly in control while the United States continued to support the Nationalist leader in his Formosan redoubt. The disparate views of India and the United States on nuclear issues grew out of these differing views of the nature of the threat the two communist giants posed both in Asia and globally.

In March 1954 the crew of a Japanese fishing boat had developed serious radiation sickness because of exposure to the fallout from the first American hydrogen bomb test. The following month Nehru had called for a "standstill" agreement between the United States and the Soviet Union to prohibit such experiments while the Disarmament Commission worked out a disarmament treaty. David Johnson, Canada's permanent representative at the United Nations, had believed that the West might gain a propaganda boost if it agreed to this proposal; he had also thought it would be of military advantage to the Americans because they were well ahead in thermonuclear technology. But the United States Joint Chiefs of Staff were adamantly opposed to an action that would retard continuing nuclear development. Some American officials also feared that halting the tests would advance the Soviet campaign to prohibit nuclear weapons. In June 1954 President Eisenhower had therefore decided against any ban for even a limited period. A few weeks later the United Kingdom had announced its support for the American stand. Canada, too, had fallen into line; after all, it lacked the expertise to judge how a halt in the tests might affect the strategic balance. Essentially Canada took its stand on faith, because of its solidarity with the United States. But in explaining the Canadian position to an anxious correspondent, Pearson had blamed the Soviet Union. "The Western powers," he maintained, "cannot afford to deprive themselves of nuclear weapons or even to stop future tests unless the Soviet Union also agrees to do the same. In order to be effective any such agreement must of course be based on adequate safeguards which the Soviet Union has so far refused to accept."[4]

The Western stance on nuclear explosions did not sit well with India. In the General Assembly's debate on disarmament in the autumn of 1954, its delegate, Krishna Menon, had condemned the refusal of the United States to halt the tests and wondered whether it was right that regions of the world such as his should be left out of the disarmament negotiations – a broad hint that the membership of the sub-committee needed revision. External Affairs had faced an awkward dilemma. India was the last country in the world it wished to see on the sub-committee, because the strength and intensity of the Western argument would be "diluted" by its participation. India's views on disarmament were said to be "rather anti-Western and neutralist in a field in which neutralism can be a very dangerous thing."[5] Yet, given the desire to keep Nehru's goodwill, it would have been foolish for Canada to oppose publicly an Indian candidature for the sub-committee. Fortunately for the department's peace of mind, India had chosen not to press for a change in the composition of the sub-committee at this time although they would do so in 1956.

Menon had decided on another tactic. During the debate in the Political Committee on Canada's procedural resolution to refer all proposals on disarmament back to the sub-committee of the Disarmament Commission, he had offered a draft resolution whose effect would have been to freeze current levels of armed forces and armaments pending an agreement on a disarmament convention. Canada believed this proposal was impracticable because there was no effective mechanism to verify its implementation by the Soviet Union. Moreover such an armaments truce would make the key Western objective of rearming Western Germany impossible. Yet to oppose the Indian amendments would not only shake the Indian-Canadian entente but also result in a bruising debate which might torpedo the procedural resolution which had been constructed with such effort. One way out was to suggest that the Indian resolution be transmitted to the Disarmament Commission without a vote. It happened that the Soviet Union did not want anything to prevent passage of the procedural resolution of which it was now a co-sponsor. The leaders of the Soviet and Canadian delegations had managed to persuade Menon to accept this suggestion. For his part, Menon had declared that he wished only that the Disarmament Commission take the Indian propositions into account. Thus the five sub-committee members had sponsored not only their famous procedural resolution but also one that referred the Indian draft resolution to the sub-committee for consideration. But the sub-committee never got around to discussing the Indian amendments during its 1955 meetings. Apparently the two sides had implicitly agreed that to consider them would only divert time from their own arms control agendas.

Nevertheless it was clear by this time that a test ban had become an increasingly important issue in the disarmament negotiations. The Bandung Conference of twenty-nine Third World countries in

April 1955 had endorsed India's call for a halt to the production of nuclear weapons and an end to nuclear testing. The Soviet Union had proposed such a ban in its paper of 10 May and for good measure had repeated their offer at the Geneva summit in July. Then in August the Russians had begun a series of tests in which they dropped a hydrogen bomb from an aircraft instead of a tower, thus showing that they were ahead of the United States in some areas of arms technology. That September in the sub-committee, the Soviet Union had officially asked the Western countries whether they were prepared to discontinue tests of atomic and hydrogen bombs. The response of the Canadian delegate, Paul Martin, had been that a ban should be instituted only as part of an overall programme to prohibit nuclear weapons. Because there was as yet no practical means of verifying prohibition, Canada was in effect continuing to oppose a ban. In November the Soviet Union, having finished its series of tests, had suggested a reciprocal suspension of tests. But with the adversary seemingly enjoying an advantage, Eisenhower was even more reluctant to agree to a ban. The White House had therefore responded that it had not yet found a formula for a moratorium which would be both dependable and in the interests of the United States. Britain's prime minister had frankly told the House of Commons that he opposed an end to the tests because of the apparent Soviet lead.

In December 1955, at the tenth session of the General Assembly, India had attempted once more to influence events. To receive approval for their own resolution, the West had been compelled to agree to an Indian amendment that called for immediate negotiations between the United Kingdom, the United States, and the USSR for a test ban. The main resolution had also stated that future talks were to take into account India's proposals for an armaments truce and a suspension of nuclear tests. In the preceding debate Menon had complained bitterly that the Indian amendments referred to the sub-committee the previous year had not even been considered.

1956

CANADA'S AGENDA:
LIMITATION OF TESTS 1

The acceptance of the Indian amendment in the General Assembly of 1955 was no doubt due to the rising and insistent global demand that something be done. "The pressure for the banning of tests of nuclear weapons has become considerably greater in the last six months," warned John Holmes in January 1956. "The Minister has been questioned in the House of Commons and further questions ... may be expected."[6] The leader of the Co-operative Commonwealth Federation, M.J. Coldwell, had begun to plead for United Nations action to stop the tests until scientists could determine whether radioactivity from the explosions would endanger future generations. Four prominent Canadian newspapers were urging that the West agree to a ban. To add to External Affairs' concern, Khrushchev and Bulganin had ended their trip to India towards the end of December by joining with Nehru in calling for the unconditional prohibition of the production and use of and experimentation with nuclear weapons. Holmes believed that the "Soviet offer made in India to agree to such a ban has put the West on the defensive. The Minister ... [has pointed] out that it is not good enough merely to argue that such a step must await an over-all disarmament agreement. In the public mind it seems possible to detach this issue because of the possibility of detecting violations."[7] Pearson asked his officials to evaluate a test ban. After a thorough examination, External Affairs advised no change in Canadian policy. There was doubt whether secret Soviet tests could be detected and no proof that radioactive fallout endangered human life. Above all, tests were valuable for "improving [the West's] nuclear defence potential."[8]

There was one possibility for compromise on the testing issue. It was to be found in the revised Anglo-French plan which proposed a limitation of tests with appropriate controls as part of stage two. In the American plan the regulation of tests would come only after agreement that the manufacture of fissionable materials for military purposes had ceased. In discussions with the department over a possible Canadian first-stage proposal, Robertson had suggested that it include a measure for the limitation of tests under controls. This might meet the pressures both "international and domestic."[9] Pearson had liked the idea and asked him to sound out the Americans. Robertson had reported that such a limitation would raise serious difficulties both for the United States and for the United Kingdom. This response suggested that to win its point Canada would have to proceed cautiously. External Affairs nevertheless continued to believe that the limitation of tests would produce "the most beneficial effects in view of the genuine concern of public opinion and *Asian* countries on the subject."[10] Pearson told Robertson that, as part of a partial disarmament programme, such a limitation should begin at an "early stage in view of the widespread interest ... of Western countries and *elsewhere*."[11] Accordingly, when presenting his 23 April proposal to the sub-committee, Robertson had asserted that the ever growing demand for some form of limitation on test explosions was an "important political fact" which the sub-committee should not disregard. He had, however, acknowledged that such "limitation of tests would have to take place in the context of other measures for disarmament under effective control."[12]

Whether the Canadian initiative would satisfy Nehru would soon become apparent, for India had been invited to speak at the Disarmament Commission when it met in July. In his 5 July speech, Paul Martin only noted in passing the need to limit tests. Apparently under pressure from both parliament and public opinion, the British representative unexpectedly proposed some form of limitation. A week later, on 12 July, Krishna Menon devoted most of his eloquent and well-documented statement to a plea for the cessation of tests. He was opposed to mere limitation. There might be disputes over the kind of controls that were necessary. Even limited testing would increase the radioactivity in the atmosphere. The Anglo-French proposal provided for limitation only several years into the future when their programme reached the second stage. To agree to limited explosions was to "go against the basic concept that it is both morally and politically wrong to permit atomic war and the use of atomic weapons."[13] In a response to Menon's statement, Martin argued that there was no scientific basis for the alarm about radioactivity and reiterated Canada's support for the limitation of nuclear tests with the necessary safeguards within the framework of a disarmament programme. Menon could not persuade the Disarmament Commission to agree to ban nuclear tests, but neither, it seemed, was Canada able to convince India that its proposal for limiting nuclear tests was sufficient to deal with the widespread anxiety over the effects of atomic radiation.

Nevertheless External Affairs was firmly convinced that Canada ought to press forward with its proposal on limitation. A ban on nuclear explosions was vigorously opposed not only by its own chiefs of staff but, more importantly, by Great Britain and the United States. The limitation of tests was more acceptable to the chiefs of staff, and the British and the Americans had already agreed to it in principle under certain conditions. Despite Menon's reaction, Canada also hoped that the West might appease the Third World demand for the banning of tests by limiting them.

External Affairs believed that some testing was necessary to ensure Western security. It also doubted that the radiation from tests represented any significant risk. However, the widespread alarm among the public over radioactive fallout was real enough.

External Affairs thus maintained that an agreement to limit the size and number of test explosions "would hardly fail to have a great psychological effect despite the absence of any real practical purpose." It was worried that Western powers were on the "propaganda defensive" over this issue. "The attack," it warned, "has been pressed with increasing vigour by the Asian and African groups in the United Nations as well as by the Communist members."[14] Indeed, India was hardening its stand as the months passed: instead of calling for the suspension of tests it had adopted the Soviet stance of outright prohibition. Holmes was apprehensive that a proposal for the complete cessation of tests might be submitted to the 1956 session of the General Assembly. In his view, it was by no means certain that if the Afro-Asian bloc, combined with the communist countries, tabled such a resolution that it "would fail to carry a majority."[15] To head off such a danger, the West should take the lead to bring tests under control by proposing a scheme for their limitation.

A minor Canadian worry over pursuing a limitation on tests was the effect on its own military capacity. In the absence of a comprehensive agreement, the Canadian chiefs of staff believed it imprudent to "foreclose the possibility of Canada developing and producing nuclear weapons." If, as India proposed, there was a standstill agreement to halt the production of nuclear weapons without any guaranteed protection against a surprise strike, Canada would be completely dependent on the United States or the United Kingdom for the nuclear means of defence against such an air attack. Thus it was not "inconceivable that Canada [might] wish to experiment with small-scale nuclear weapons for interception."[16]

External Affairs' chief concern, however, was the possible adverse reaction of the United States and the United Kingdom. Only these governments knew whether limitation would handicap weapons development. Late in July, Prime Minister Eden announced that Britain was ready not only to limit testing but also to discuss the issue outside an overall disarmament convention. Previously, Canada had always placed its limitation proposal in the context of a partial disarmament plan, but now Pearson was quick to support the idea that "limitation of tests could begin independent of the achievement of any ... broader agreement."[17] Pearson sought some absolute ceiling on the force of each explosion whereas the British envisaged a programme of limitation that would not interfere with their ability to test a hydrogen bomb. Nevertheless the British statement gave the Canadian campaign a boost. As long as limitation remained undefined, both countries could co-operate in pressing for it. As late as January of the following year the British were still thinking of sponsoring a resolution recommending that the sub-committee consider an agreement to limit tests.

In the United States, 1956 was an election year and the test ban issue became entangled with the campaign. The Democratic candidate, Adlai Stevenson, had made a ban a major issue in his campaign, and he seemed to be attracting some support until the Soviet premier, Bulganin, disclosed a letter which he had written to President Eisenhower calling for such a ban and which had noted Stevenson's stand with approval. Seen as a blatant attempt to interfere in American domestic politics, this action helped Eisenhower to win re-election. He had campaigned against a test ban and his easy win seemed to indicate that he had public opinion behind him on this issue. Pearson thought this contretemps most unfortunate.

On 17 November, in a letter to the president of the General Assembly, the Soviet Union again proposed a test ban, and Pearson observed that it was a "pity, especially in light of the Soviet proposals that Western powers cannot quickly agree to ban or at least limit tests." It seemed that the United Kingdom and France were prepared to accept limitation. He added: "it seems fairly well established that the USA govt had planned to announce some such proposal until Stevenson outbid them in the presidential campaign but it may be possible for them to go back to it before [being] placed on defensive by India, Japan ... and Afro-Asians generally, who will demand abolition of all tests and cite Strontium 90 worries as India has done already." Pearson was exasperated. "I realize of course that Canada cannot take the lead in this matter," he continued, "but I also feel that it would be irresponsible of us to remain passive much longer to avoid embarrassing the USA."[18]

Apparently Pearson did decide that the matter was so important that Canada must take the lead. At the beginning of December Canada raised the issue in the General Assembly. The Canadian spokesman, Roch Pinard, maintained that a complete test ban was neither realistic nor necessary. The United Nations must be guided by two considerations: the requirements of the objective scientific situation and its members' defence needs in a world that was dangerously divided. The solution was for the superpowers to set "as a self-denying ordinance, some annual or other periodic limit on the volume of radiation to be generated by test explosions. There would have to be some agreed method of allocating quantities between the powers concerned ... and some arrangements for notification of the proposed tests and for their verification." Pinard added that "this need not in my view give rise to insuperable difficulties."[19] So anxious was External Affairs for this scheme to go through that for the first time it was minimizing the problem of control.

Unfortunately, after a tough election campaign in the United States in which President Eisenhower had stoutly opposed banning tests, the United States was in no mood to make concessions on this issue. Stassen told the Canadian ambassador to the United Nations that the limitation of tests could not be treated separately from a halt in the production of fissionable materials. In response, External Affairs insisted that it was important to respond to the legitimate demands of the "new nations of Asia and Africa" which were being exposed to radiation hazards not through their own doing but because of tests by major powers. They had no recourse except through the United Nations. They might see the limitation scheme as "a prophylactic measure" which would provide protection against the dangers to health. It might also "serve to gain international sanction for the continuance of tests on a scale satisfactory to the military." If this happened, it might also dispose of "one issue on which the Asian-African group are being abetted by the Soviet Union and at least superficially are pursuing a common policy."[20] For Canadian diplomats the limitation of tests was not a military issue since they had no independent means of evaluating nuclear tests. They did believe, however, that the West would lose support for testing unless it responded to the public's concerns about the tests. As well they wished to keep the goodwill of the Third World nations and to undermine the Soviet Union's influence with them. Limiting tests seemed an appropriate measure.

ARMS CONTROL AT THE GENERAL ASSEMBLY

At the conclusion of the Disarmament Commission's meetings in July 1956, the Western countries were somewhat in disarray over arms control. Only the United States, as the great nuclear power, could repair the damage by proposing a programme on which all its Western partners could agree. Unfortunately, the Americans were still not able to offer the results of the study over which their task forces had been labouring since the previous summer. Nor were the prospects encouraging in the late summer and autumn of 1956. Stassen himself had been on a leave of absence in an unsuccessful attempt to prevent Richard Nixon being selected as the Republican vice-presidential candidate. On his return in September, Stassen began to put his arms control programme together – but his proposals were often opposed by both the State Department and the Department of Defense. It would require President Eisenhower to make a ruling. But he was involved in his re-election campaign and, after the Anglo-French invasion of Egypt in early November, with the Suez crisis. It was not until the middle of December that Stassen was able to get Eisenhower's approval for an arms control package.

Pearson found these few months of American inaction highly frustrating. The Americans must be persuaded to move, but Canada lacked any real power and could only exhort. In the middle of August, the United Kingdom suggested that the four Western powers on the sub-committee should meet. Pearson understood that meeting in the midst of the American election campaign would cause difficulties, but bravely asserted that Canada was "unwilling to be guided by the assumption that in a question of this importance U.S. policy is likely to be governed by nothing more objective than party expediency."[21] Unfortunately Arnold Heeney, Canada's ambassador in Washington, was unable to pin the Americans down to a definite schedule. Soon there was another proposal – again from the United Kingdom. The Western four would consult in London in October and the sub-committee would meet in New York late in November. Pearson reiterated the desirability of establishing a common position among the four Western members of the sub-committee as soon as possible: "It does not appear to follow that because the Sub-Committee will not meet until the latter part of November the consultations can also be delayed."[22]

The Americans eventually decided on bilateral talks with each of their Western partners. External Affairs remained worried about the absence of any firm arrangement for four-power talks. If the only talks were bilateral ones, the Americans would be in full control since the others would be unable to join together to put pressure on the United States to change any proposal that they disliked. A four-power meeting would ensure "a common assessment of the nature of the next move and would not leave that question to be judged solely by the U.S."[23] Pearson and his colleagues always saw Canada as a partner – albeit a junior one – in the Western alliance, and this implied some participation in the making of joint Western policies.[24]

After the Soviet Union offered its new disarmament plan on 17 November 1956, there appeared to be an even greater need for a meeting of the Western four. In December, Canada was still urging four-power consultation with no result. Even the Soviet request for a meeting of the Disarmament Commission made no difference. There was no consultation prior to that December meeting – perhaps because the only business transacted was to agree to transmit the third report of the sub-committee (4 May) to the General Assembly and the Security Council. Nevertheless there was some progress. Stassen was anxious to retain the goodwill of his partners; he encouraged bilateral exchanges and made certain his staff was available for briefings. Before the next sub-committee meetings, Canada would have a much more detailed knowledge of the American position than had been the case in the spring of 1956. Heeney would describe this as "at lease some limited progress in the right direction."[25] But there was still no common consultation, and none of the common decision-making for which Pearson yearned.

In preparing for the General Assembly's discussion of disarmament that was to begin in January, External Affairs wished that the United Nations would give "sufficient satisfaction to the group responsive to the leadership of India and Krishna Menon to dissuade them from the submission of unrealistic, unhelpful and even irresponsible substantive resolutions."[26] It was clear from its past record and interest that India would concentrate on nuclear tests. If there was to be a reasonable and smooth transition from the Assembly to the sub-committee, "irresponsible" proposals which might hamper future negotiations should be avoided. Yet there seemed to be a "vacuum of leadership" which might invite "mischievous initiatives." External Affairs believed that Canada ought to step in since it was "on the whole better situated to provide suitable leadership in the direction of moderation than the other Western members of the Sub-Committee."[27] The appropriate question for "positive treatment" is that of nuclear tests.

External Affairs also wanted to help avoid an acrimonious debate between East and West in the Assembly. Yet the American team led by Stassen was considering a resolution designed to win United Nations support for an arms control plan which they would offer. External Affairs feared that any specific, substantive American proposal could only lead to a serious clash. It would be best if the Assembly debate was as brief and non-controversial as possible. Instead of a resolution dealing with concrete proposals, Canada believed a simple call for the sub-committee to carry on its work would be more useful.

1957

On 14 January of the new year, Henry Cabot Lodge, the American ambassador to the United Nations, presented an arms control package to the First Committee. All future production of fissionable materials would be used solely for peaceful purposes. To prevent cheating, this "cut-off," as it came to be known, would be supervised by an international agency. Once this arrangement was in place, it would be possible to limit and ultimately eliminate nuclear tests. The United States also proposed a first-step reduction in conventional force levels to 2.5 million for the United States and the USSR and 750,000 for France and the United Kingdom. Lodge maintained that deeper cuts were not possible until some of the divisive political issues had been resolved. An effective inspection system would be established concurrently with the reduction. Such a verification organization would use appropriate aerial inspection as well as ground units. Lodge especially underlined the importance the American administration placed on aerial inspection as a protection against a surprise atomic attack. Lastly, as a harbinger of the new era that was rapidly appearing, the Americans suggested the international inspection of tests on intercontinental missiles, satellites, and other such developments in outer space.

Broadly speaking, the American programme broke into two parts. The first, the reduction of conventional forces and the use of aerial inspection to guard against surprise attack had to do, as we shall see, with the problem of Germany and European security. The second was the nuclear component: the cut-off and the possibility of an end to tests. External Affairs had been informed of the content of these proposals before they were presented. In general it found the American proposals acceptable, although it doubted that the Soviet Union would agree to a scheme that left the American superiority in nuclear arms intact. The department strongly objected, however, to making the limitation of tests dependent on agreement to the cut-off in the production of fissionable material for military use. It did not believe that the Americans had advanced a convincing argument for not considering the limitation of tests separately; the department believed that it was up to them to show that such a step would lead to a reduction in security for the West.[28]

Although the Americans were dead set against the limitation of tests, they were apparently more open to their registration. The Norwegians had been considering a registration proposal and had sounded out Canada to see if it would agree to act as co-sponsor. At first External Affairs was lukewarm; the resolution seemed complicated and time was needed to study it. However, on the same day as the United States tabled its plan, the Soviet Union proposed a ban on tests. The Soviet draft resolution impelled the West to move to offset the support in the United Nations for such a ban. External Affairs was galvanized into action. The Japanese let it be known that they would be interested in helping to sponsor the Norwegian resolution. Pearson was especially pleased with this possibility. If the Japanese were a co-sponsor, "they were in a strong moral position to lead Asian opinion on this subject." Apparently, Lodge also recognized that a sensible Norwegian/Canadian/Japanese resolution "might prove [a] useful alternative if wilder proposals were inevitable."[29] Thus Canada, along with Norway and Japan, agreed to table a resolution that called for the registration of tests with the United Nations authorities. But neither the USSR nor India was very impressed. The former maintained that registration did nothing to reduce the dangerous consequences of the explosions while Krishna Menon attacked it for condoning the legitimacy of tests. Yet there was an intense desire among the members of the United Nations to take at least some preliminary steps to control the nuclear threat. The Norwegian/Canadian/Japanese resolution thus had considerable support.

But by this time the great powers were in a mood to compromise since each saw an opportunity for benefits. Each believed that there was a chance for real bargaining at the coming meetings of the sub-committee. The Soviet Union hinted that it would support a simple procedural resolution at the General Assembly. Canada, France, and Britain urged Stassen to give up his idea of a substantive resolution. Eager to try his hand at genuine negotiations, Stassen was for once easily persuaded. In this atmosphere of give and take, India also agreed to co-sponsor the procedural resolution. The United States and the Soviet Union still put forward their conflicting proposals in the General Assembly, but the prospect of agreement mitigated the temper with which each side presented its case. It was agreed that neither the resolution on the registration of tests nor that calling for a ban on tests would be pushed to a vote. Pearson maintained that the procedural resolution did not impose any unwanted programmes on governments, nor did it discriminate against one proposal in favour of the other; it simply cleared the way for the renewal of negotiations in the sub-committee. On 25 January the resolution passed with a unanimous vote. A Soviet delegate observed to Pearson that this resolution would get the "sub-committee talks off on the right basis."[30] There was room for modest hope as attention turned to these talks which were to resume in London in March.

CANADA'S AGENDA:
LIMITATION OF TESTS 2

One of Pearson's prime aims was to win the sub-committee's agreement to the limitation of tests. At the General Assembly in December Canada had proposed that the superpowers undertake to limit the volume of radiation generated by the tests and that there be some method of allocating the yields allowed to each side. Now David Johnson, who was the Canadian representative at these sub-committee meetings, was instructed by Pearson to "press hard"[31] on this subject in the discussions. He was to take a moderate position: while East-West political tensions meant nuclear powers had valid reasons for testing to ensure that their weapons were as effective as possible and there was no immediate genetic danger from radiation, it would be prudent not to increase its presence. The Canadian view was to be that "neither the extreme of ... complete cessation of tests nor the retention of full discretion by the testing powers is satisfactory since one neglects defence needs and the other the warnings of competent scientific opinion."[32] Ideally, limits on testing should be one element of a partial plan for disarmament, but if this were not possible, then a separate agreement to limit the radiation from tests ought to be reached.

The Americans, however, remained opposed. They continued to insist that no limitation proposal could be considered unless it was part of a comprehensive disarmament agreement that included effective controls. To this original objection to such a proposal, they now offered a second. The Canadian assumption was that no test which might give one side enough information to provide a military advantage could escape detection. But the Americans denied that this was true; their technical experts advised them that large explosions could be concealed and that even when they were detected, there was no accurate means of measuring the amount of radiation released. Moreover, if the United States were to announce the volume of radiation to be expected from a blast, it would indirectly furnish information on how its bomb was built and what new controls had been developed. Such revelations would seriously erode the West's security.

The United States also pointed to potentially serious political difficulties arising from a separate agreement on test limitations. Without an international authority recognized by both sides, there might be constant disputes about whether explosions had occurred and the amount of radioactivity released. Then, too, the volume of radiation acceptable to Third World nations would probably be too low to allow the United States to proceed with a useful test programme. The real point was that Indian sensibilities were of little importance to the United States when set against the desires of the Pentagon for constant improvements in nuclear weapons. The Americans were unwilling to make concessions to offset some vague political discontent among lesser powers. They were in a mood to bargain, but for anything they offered, they expected something concrete in return. The Soviet Union had not shown the slightest interest in the concept of limiting radiation and, in consequence, Stassen was unwilling to put the issue on the table.

The continuing objections of the United States had led to second thoughts in the British government about the support it had given to a separate agreement on test limitation the previous August. The British need for American nuclear technology forced a reassessment of their position. At their meeting in Bermuda on 26 March 1957, Harold Macmillan, who had replaced Eden as prime minister after Suez, joined Eisenhower in rejecting a limitation agreement because it "could not today be effectively enforced for technical reasons; nor could breaches of it be surely detected."[33]

But even before the Bermuda communiqué, External Affairs had sensed that its proposal was in trouble. The day after he suggested an agreement on the limitation of tests in the sub-committee Johnson reported that Britain would join the United States in its opposition to any separate agreement on test limitation. If Canada persisted, it would meet substantial resistance from its own allies. The loss of British support was a severe blow. Pearson reluctantly concluded that there was no point in continuing to press for the Canadian proposal to be presented to the sub-committee. Perhaps he thought that to insist would work against what Canada deemed its main role to be: to help create and maintain Western unity. Raising such an issue might give comfort to the Soviet Union without changing the mind of the United States.[34]

Pearson had been very enthusiastic about an agreement to limit tests but had failed to persuade the nuclear powers, and in particular the United States, to support it. Canada was a marginal military power. In making an argument on military strategy, it was constantly handicapped by the lack of independent information; for the most part it was forced to rely on Great Britain and the United States for the relevant technical data. Nor did Canada have any significant political power to bring to bear on its partners. Perhaps because they were great powers, they appeared to be much less sensitive to the need to woo Third World support. This episode showed the very severe difficulties Canada confronted in taking any clear-cut initiative on the substance of disarmament issues. It shows why most of the effort of Canada's diplomats was devoted to clarifying and refining the proposals of the other Western allies. It illuminates the limited role that a small player like Canada could play in negotiations over issues of vital concern to the major powers.

Canada was stuck with a policy which its partners would not support. How was it to extricate itself from this awkward position?

Despite the rejection of an agreement on test limitation at Bermuda, Macmillan and Eisenhower had pledged to conduct nuclear tests in a manner that would keep world radiation from rising to more than a small fraction of hazardous levels. They had called on the USSR to exercise the same restraint. This provided External Affairs with a convenient means of escaping its difficulty. In retreating from its support for a limitation treaty, it would not be necessary to "embrace the USA-UK argument about technical difficulties in order to effect a transition from our idea of an agreed 'self-denying ordinance' to the idea of unilateral restraint advocated in the USA and UK Bermuda communiqué." Instead the Soviet Union, because it was unwilling even to consider such an agreement, could be blamed for the need to turn towards unilateral declarations. External Affairs suggested that Johnson ought to be instructed to make such a move "with a minimum of emphasis on whatever temporary retreat from principle may be involved."[35] The new Canadian line would be to appeal to the Soviet Union to make a declaration similar to that of the United States and the United Kingdom in the Bermuda communiqué. In fact the need to employ this tactic would be overtaken by intense negotiations over a test ban. Officially, the limitation of tests remained Canadian policy but it was a dormant one.

CANADA'S AGENDA: REGISTRATION OF TESTS

At first sight the proposal to register tests had better prospects. The Norwegian/Canadian/Japanese resolution had received considerable support in the General Assembly debate including that of the Americans. But a difference soon developed between Canada and the United States over the amount of information which registration should provide. The purpose of the original resolution had been to keep the total actual and expected radiation in the world under constant observation. Canada took this to mean that any country which registered a test would provide "advance notification of the estimated yield in fission product which would be of international concern."[36] This concept was at the heart of a Canadian draft paper on registration of nuclear tests. External Affairs was determined that registration should provide some significant information.

But the Americans were opposed to publication of these estimates, on the grounds that such information might reveal too much about the weapons they were testing. Moreover, they now raised the point that there was no way of verifying Soviet claims about the amount of fission product their tests would produce. External

Affairs was not much impressed by the first argument, and they were dismayed by the talk of verification. The whole point of registration was to try to cope with the problem of radiation without introducing the problems related to control. It was disturbing, as an External Affairs memorandum maintained, "to perceive the tendency to consider registration primarily from the point of view of its potential value as an intelligence instrument." If negotiations were no more than a "formalization of the present system of press releases," it would suggest to the USSR a lack of serious intent to deal with nuclear tests and it would not be likely to "diminish the pressure for concrete action on tests which is a real political factor – and ought not in our view to be dismissed as an Asian-African conspiracy."[37]

The sub-committee was scheduled to discuss nuclear testing early in May. Canada needed to decide whether to hold fast to a position on registration with which the Americans did not agree. The Norwegian/Canadian/Japanese resolution had certainly implied that there would be information furnished on radiation; the countries which had supported it in the General Assembly would not be impressed with an American proposal which suggested publishing little more than the date and location of each test. Yet the United States insisted that announcing a test's estimated yield in fission products would aid Soviet intelligence. Was the issue important enough to expose Canada's differences with the United States? External Affairs' solution was to sidestep the issue by proclaiming that the drive for registration had gone as far as it could go because of the refusal of the Soviet Union to consider it. "The main merit of the somewhat unheroic ideas we are submitting," concluded an External Affairs memorandum for Pearson, "is that they would enable us to avoid undesirable and unfruitful public conflict with the USA and UK without overt retreat from the principles and positions we have been advocating"[38] – that is, without Canada giving up its support for the release of concrete information on the radiation produced by nuclear tests.

This time, however, Pearson decided to hold firm. Canada would continue to support the Norwegian/Canadian/Japanese resolution which had called for some estimate of fission product. As a matter of honour Canada could not just leave its co-sponsors in a lurch. Pearson continued to believe that the resolution's original purpose of appeasing the anxiety of the Indian-led bloc was valid. Now, too, there was the additional advantage of keeping Japanese public opinion friendly towards the West. And on this issue Canada would have the support of France in the sub-committee. Johnson also suggested that because the sub-committee was considering a Soviet paper on partial disarmament it was not a good time to blame the USSR for lack of progress in organizing an acceptable registration scheme. Arguments "alluding to Soviet intransigence" should be held in reserve to be used, if necessary, at "a more appropriate time."[39] On 6 May the British representative tabled a memorandum calling for advance registration of tests as proposed by Canada, Japan, and Norway. Shortly thereafter, Johnson, in supporting the British initiative, went further by calling for "the advanced registration of data concerning the fission products of any proposed explosion."[40]

The Canadian decision to hold firm to the intent of the General Assembly resolution on registration might have led to a serious breach with the United States. That it did not was due largely to the Soviet refusal to take registration of tests seriously: in their view, it would do nothing to lessen the radiation hazard and would simply legalize testing. As Johnson reported to External Affairs, no great difficulties had been created between Canada and its allies because of "the uncompromising attitude taken by Zorin [the Soviet representative] towards the whole scheme."[41] As a result of the earlier discussions in the sub-committee, Canada might still hope for a wider agreement on nuclear testing that would make the registration of tests irrelevant. If this proved impossible, Johnson believed that, despite American opposition, Canada should continue to propose the advance notification of radiation expected. In fact Canada did eventually force a modest change. The United States finally agreed to register in advance the dates of a series of tests; the range of total energy to be released in the series; and to limit the amount of radioactive material to be released into the atmosphere by each test.[42] These proposals were incorporated in the working paper submitted by the West to the sub-committee on 29 August 1957.

Wherever possible and without sacrificing the Western capacity to test its weapons, Pearson sought the means of expressing sympathy with the Asian concerns over the radiation which Western explosions imposed on them. Since a scheme for registration was never implemented, there is no way of knowing whether it would have had the effect of bringing the Asian nations closer to the West. Although registration was marginal to the main arms control issues, it was the kind of helpful proposal which Pearson believed Canada should advance to help the Western cause.

OTHER CANADIAN-AMERICAN ISSUES

Apart from the discussions over the limitation and registration of tests, there were two other matters on which External Affairs wished to iron out any differences with the Americans before the sub-committee talks. The first of these related to the American legislation which prevented the transfer of nuclear weapons to other countries. This had always been a worry for the Department of National Defence because it believed that nuclear weapons were essential for the defence of northern Canada. External Affairs feared that an agreement between the Soviet Union and the United States might make these weapons even more inaccessible.[43] Pearson appears to have been more sanguine and apparently decided to ask for no changes. After all, there were encouraging signs that the Americans would eventually loosen the restrictions against their nuclear arms going to their allies. Stassen, obviously interested in removing Canadian anxiety when he could, soon passed the word that the United States would continue to look after mutual defence needs. Eighteen months later, the United States would offer to supply Canada with Bomarc guided missiles armed with nuclear warheads.

Another and much more important problem was the decision of the Americans to place less stress on verification in any agreement with the Soviet Union. The core of Canadian disarmament and arms control philosophy was the importance of verification. Hardly any Canadian speech on disarmament in the past decade had failed to underline the importance of controls. External Affairs had always believed the Russians vulnerable on this flank and at all sessions of the General Assembly Canadian spokesmen had lambasted them for their secrecy. Now Arnold Heeney reported from Washington that while the United States proposed to inspect future production of fissionable material, it had no intention of demanding a new version of the Baruch Plan. Controls would now be moderate and only sufficient to give reasonable assurance that new Soviet fissionable material was being transferred to non-weapons uses. The Soviet Union would not have to publish an estimate of the amount of fissionable material it had already accumulated. External Affairs was shocked; it made no sense for the United States to insist on elaborate controls to ensure compliance with the limitation of nuclear tests while ignoring the vast nuclear stocks which the USSR now possessed. What value was there to the other measures against surprise attack proposed by the United States, if there were no check on this formidable nuclear arsenal? "We do not see," External Affairs complained in response, "how a contention that the greatest danger is a surprise attack with nuclear weapons leads to a conclusion that the stocks of nuclear weapons should be the only weapons outside the control system even though complete effectiveness cannot be guaranteed."[44]

As External Affairs conceded in this last phrase, there was no way of accurately accounting for past fissile production. It was this fact which had shaped American policy as Stassen would explain to Johnson. An accurate and complete inspection of past production was impossible. The American military, believing their weapons to be technically superior to those of their rivals, would fiercely oppose any inspection by the Soviet Union. External Affairs understood that a completely accurate check of existing nuclear stocks was impossible. Nevertheless its commitment to verification made it uncomfortable with a treaty that would "insist on the inspection of button and glass factories while refusing to include the principle weapon of surprise attack in the operation of the system."[45] Johnson was certain, however, that the Americans had made up their minds; there was no point in pursuing the matter. Reluctantly, External Affairs took his advice; there was no realistic option.

THE FINAL NUCLEAR NEGOTIATIONS

The limitation and registration of nuclear tests were of particular interest to External Affairs because these issues offered some scope for independent Canadian action. But the department knew that the major nuclear questions to be discussed in the sub-committee meetings of 1957 would be a test ban and nuclear restraint. For the first time, there was likely to be serious bargaining on these issues because world public opinion was demanding real progress. Yet all the nuclear powers were nevertheless demonstrating a fierce determination to strengthen their individual nuclear capabilities. Both the United States and the USSR conducted extensive tests that spring, and in the middle of May Great Britain would explode its first hydrogen bomb.

One consequence of the Suez affair of late 1956 was that both France and Britain concluded that they could not rely on the United States in an emergency; they needed their own nuclear deterrents. As well, Suez had shown the British the enormous cost of modern conventional warfare. To deal with both problems, their defence white paper of April 1957 announced that national service would be ended in 1960 and that this loss in conventional strength would be made up by nuclear weapons. France, too, made a radical turn in its defence policy. In the summer of 1956 the French government had still been equivocal about whether it would produce nuclear arms, but the Suez experience convinced Premier Mollet that if it was to remain a great power France would need its own bomb. Any limited Soviet-American agreement might relax tensions and lead to the withdrawal of American and British forces from central Europe. The French would be left to face the Soviet army whose strength might still be intact. Only nuclear weapons could offset such a threat. But an agreement based on the 14 January proposals would destroy forever France's ability to develop its own nuclear weapons because new fissionable materials could only be used for peaceful purposes and nuclear tests would be ended. By itself, an agreement on nuclear issues would do nothing to protect France from a conventional Soviet attack. Once more French politicians realized how vulnerable the security of their country was to shifts in American nuclear policy. It was little wonder, then, that in May 1957 the minister of defence announced that France would create its own nuclear force. It was against this ominous background of increased activity in the development of nuclear weapons that negotiations in the sub-committee took place.

Two substantive issues dominated the sub-committee talks when they opened in London on 18 March: European security and nuclear control. The United States was more concerned with the first item, but the USSR was deeply concerned with a nuclear arms race in which the Americans, by virtue of their technology, seemed to be steadily pulling ahead. Perhaps the Soviet leaders believed that they had sufficient warheads and that they should concentrate on developing intercontinental missiles to carry them. No doubt they wished to prevent nuclear military development in other countries especially the former enemy nations of Germany and Japan. Thus, on the day the sub-committee opened, they submitted a document whose nuclear component completely ignored the view which all had accepted that there was no reliable means of checking on past or illicit manufacture of atomic bombs and demanded their complete prohibition. As well, they called for the cessation of nuclear tests and pledges by states already possessing nuclear arms never to use them. The latter proposal, if accepted, would have constituted a serious moral and political inhibition against the whole United States strategy of massive retaliation.

Two days later, Harold Stassen was ready with the American response. Prohibition was unacceptable because it was impossible to guarantee that all existing nuclear arms had been eliminated. Yet there was cause for alarm over the growing stockpiles of more, and more effective, nuclear weapons. The way to halt this acceleration was to agree that all future stocks of fissionable materials would be used only for peaceful purposes. Fortunately, in contrast to past production, that of the future could be verified. And even if inspection was not one hundred per cent effective, the few extra weapons that might be built could always be countered by the nuclear arsenal of the other side which would continue to exist. The United States would undertake never to use nuclear weapons except in defence against aggression in accordance with the decisions taken by the Security Council. If the United States proposal had stopped there, it probably would have found favour with the USSR since it had a veto in the Council. But Stassen went on to say that the Americans also claimed the right to use nuclear weapons in self-defence as spelled out in article 51 of the United Nations Charter. He also made it clear that the United States would end its nuclear tests only after the cut-off of fuel production for military purposes was in place.

Their Western colleagues in the sub-committee fully supported the American programme. At Bermuda Macmillan had already agreed that nuclear testing must continue. The United Kingdom would not accept the ending of tests apart from other disarmament arrangements. The French, too, linked the cessation of tests to a halt in production of fissionable materials for war purposes. A test ban would have frozen the nuclear superiority of Britain, the United States, and the USSR. Moch also added the condition that there must be substantial conventional disarmament as well. Johnson, on behalf of Canada, enthusiastically approved the American proposals for "bringing the nuclear threat under international control."[46]

The Soviet Union was the first to try to break the deadlock. In a memorandum submitted on 30 April dealing largely with European security, it included some changes in its nuclear stance. The demand that the nuclear states undertake never to use these weapons remained, but the proposal for their immediate elimination was shelved. Instead, the powers were to make every effort to conclude such an agreement in the future. This removed a formidable obstacle to an accord. The United States would never have concurred in the elimination of nuclear arms without any guarantee that the Soviet Union would comply – but there was no reason not to agree that it was desirable to work towards such a goal. Lastly, the Soviet Union proposed to "single out" the discontinuance of nuclear tests from the general disarmament negotiations. Its leaders were apparently determined to make the cessation of nuclear explosions a major test of American goodwill. They insisted that the minimum requirements for a partial disarmament package were the cessation of tests and an unconditional obligation not to use nuclear weapons. On these points they would continue to stand firm.

A wide gap remained between the two sides. In an unusual gaffe, Johnson at the sub-committee meetings continued to criticize the

Soviet stand on prohibition although it was no longer on the immediate agenda. He also discussed the differences between the two sides over the use and testing of nuclear weapons. He had no real alternative – Canada was not of course able to offer nuclear concessions. Any initiative would have to come from the United States. Towards the end of May, Stassen returned to Washington and persuaded Eisenhower that the Russians were serious about negotiating an agreement. The president was anxious to see some progress; he told his advisers that "tangible concessions"[47] would have to be offered. On his return to London, in a written memorandum dated 31 May, Stassen informed the Soviet Union that in return for its agreement to a cut-off on production of fissile materials, the United States would accept a ten-month suspension of verifiable tests. This was an important concession. In January, the United States had maintained that it would halt its experimental explosions only after the production of nuclear fuel for military purposes had been ended. Now, if the USSR would undertake to begin such a cut-off two years later, the United States was proposing to suspend its tests immediately.

Stassen also wished to conciliate the USSR on the matter of using nuclear weapons. Given the Soviet preponderance in conventional forces, the United States would never declare that it would not use nuclear weapons. The Americans claimed the right under article 51 of the United Nations Charter to use nuclear weapons if need be in defence against aggression. But the Russians argued that under this formula any atomic power could legally employ nuclear weapons by labelling its opponent an aggressor even if the conflict was only a minor one. To respond to this flaw, Stassen proposed that a state be entitled to avail itself of nuclear weapons under article 51 if the attack on it either involved their use or was of such a magnitude that it could not be repelled without them. The United States was prepared to promise that while it would keep nuclear weapons as a deterrent, it would not use them in minor wars. This formula pleased none of the other parties. Britain and France believed that limiting the conditions under which it would be employed would weaken the value of the nuclear deterrent on which the West's defence rested. The Soviet Union reiterated that the United States' stand simply legalized the use of atomic arms. The Soviet Union knew that the United States believed it could not meet the Soviet demand without seriously endangering its security. In that sense the Soviet proposal of 30 April was only another round in the propaganda war. It may be that the USSR would have dropped this proposal in return for an unconditional halt to nuclear tests. But, as we shall see, the United States would not go that far; consequently, the USSR saw no advantage in giving up its stand on the high moral ground that nuclear weapons should never be used.

At the moment the Soviet Union was concentrating on achieving a test ban independent of other disarmament measures. At the 14 June meeting of the sub-committee, it tabled a memorandum calling for the immediate cessation of tests for two or three years. To sweeten the offer, it also agreed to a long-standing Western demand that any such ban be verified through reciprocal inspection posts on the territories of the United States, the USSR, and the United Kingdom and in the Pacific. This was a significant concession: for the first time, the Soviet Union had accepted the need for realistic oversight controls with respect to the halting of the tests; the four Western countries were now convinced that the Soviet Union was serious in its initiative.

Moch responded to the Soviet proposal by declaring that France would only agree to a halt in tests if it was accompanied by an end to the production of fissionable materials for military purposes (the American cut-off proposal). This would remain the Western position. In Canada there was no immediate change in policy following the defeat of the governing Liberals on 11 June. A week later Johnson was instructed to follow the American lead in this matter. But the Soviet Union believed that the cut-off entailed a rigid system of international inspection which they found intolerable. There would be no accord on suspending the tests as long as the West insisted that it be conditional on Soviet acceptance of the cut-off. In view of the Soviet position, Eisenhower had been thinking about offering an independent verifiable ban, but in the end he allowed himself to be persuaded by hawkish scientific advisers such as Edward Teller that it would be unwise. He decided to maintain the linkage between the test ban and the cut-off, knowing that this would make an agreement impossible. On 3 July Stassen made a formal offer of a ten-month suspension if the Soviet Union accepted the cut-off, and on 21 August Eisenhower increased the American offer to a two-year suspension of tests. But these proposals elicited no change of position in the Soviet Union.

The position of the United States had the reluctant support of Great Britain and France. Both were unhappy with the cut-off proposal which would leave them with insufficient fissionable material to construct their own nuclear weapons. Macmillan complained that the British might be compelled to abandon their nuclear ambitions. Certainly Britain would be left far behind the two superpowers. France's official position was that it would not accept any nuclear restrictions that did not apply to the present nuclear powers. It would not be bound be a treaty confined only to the test ban. Even after a cut-off was instituted, it would preserve the legal right to acquire nuclear weapons as long as the other powers retained theirs. But in practice a treaty that ended the production of fissionable materials for military purposes and suspended tests would prevent it from entering the military nuclear field. Thus neither Britain nor France had any reason to favour the cut-off. Yet public support in both countries for a test ban compelled their governments to accept the American proposals. Because Canada had no intention of building nuclear weapons, it had nothing to lose by approving the cut-off. Moreover, at a time when a new Conservative government was just taking office, new policy directions were most unlikely; the most sensible thing was to fall in line with the Americans. The Canadian view, explained Johnson to the sub-committee, was that the Soviet proposal of 14 June to suspend tests, though welcome, did not go far enough because it indicated no link "between the suspension of tests and other elements of a partial disarmament agreement."[48]

Meanwhile India, supported by the Soviet Union, had been pressing for an opportunity to appear before the sub-committee. Despite the department's concern to accommodate, where possible, the views of those for whom India spoke, External Affairs feared that once an exception was made, a precedent might be set. Other countries might seek to present their views and so eventually weaken what Canada regarded as one of the sub-committee's main virtues – its small size. A policy guidance document of the previous December maintained that the "Sub-Committee ... represents a shield against the intervention of governments which might choose to adopt the position that because disarmament is of universal concern, all governments should have an equal opportunity of making their views known."[49] No doubt its author had also speculated that preserving the present composition of the sub-committee would allow Canada to continue its unique role as a small player in the big-power disarmament negotiations. But Canada was also worried about what India would actually say.[50] External Affairs judged that there was some possibility of a first-stage disarmament agreement. By May of 1957 it believed that the keys to an accord lay in Soviet willingness to make concessions on conventional force reductions, guarantees that fissionable materials would not be used to manufacture weapons, and safeguards against surprise attack. These were all American concerns, and External Affairs reasoned that some progress here would create "a more favourable framework for considering successive moves for limiting and later ceasing tests." External Affairs was concerned that the emphasis on stopping tests which India was sure to bring to bear in any statement in the sub-committee might exacerbate differences and make agreement more difficult. The Soviet Union, encouraged by India, might sacrifice the possibility of real gains "to score propaganda successes."[51]

It was one thing to wish that India would not insist on appearing before the sub-committee; it was quite another to oppose such an invitation openly. After all, the sub-committee was supposed to be the creature of the Disarmament Commission of which India was a distinguished member. To refuse India would merely invite continued attack on the exclusiveness of the sub-committee. As a small non-nuclear power, Canada was hardly in position to offer a public defence of the sub-committee's present composition, and it wished to avoid needlessly offending a Commonwealth partner and a potential ally against the danger of Soviet expansionism. Accordingly, External Affairs instructed its representative in New Delhi to inform the Indian government that Canada would neither oppose nor support its demand to appear before the sub-committee. He was also to remind New Delhi of the Canadian concern to limit the production of radiation and its strong suggestions for both the limitation and the registration of tests.

The Canadian appeal failed to persuade India. In mid-June the Western representatives to the sub-committee were still wondering whether to allow India to appear. In July and August negotiations in the sub-committee took a turn for the worse and finally broke down. India never did get a chance to present its case. An arrangement whereby a small country like Canada had a voice in crucial disarmament negotiations which was denied to great Asian powers like Japan and India could not last. It was no wonder that the sub-committee had no real support in the United Nations and thus would simply vanish after the Soviet Union announced in the autumn of 1957 that it would no longer participate in negotiations in either the Disarmament Commission or its sub-committee.

SUB-COMMITTEE DISCUSSIONS
ON EUROPEAN SECURITY

The other dominant issue in the discussions of the sub-committee in 1957 – and the matter which was of greater immediate concern to the United States – related to conventional forces reduction and aerial inspection to guard against surprise attack. These matters were part of the intricate problem of European security which remained complicated because of its link with the political question of the reunification of Germany. Through its membership in NATO West Germany had entered into a military alliance with the West and the Adenauer government became vulnerable to a charge from the Social Democrats, their main political opponents, that it had thereby made reunification impossible. Public opinion polls showed that the people of the Federal Republic were much more anxious to see a unified Germany than one which belonged to NATO. Adenauer's political future as well as the fate of the alliance with the United States thus depended on his being seen as a powerful champion of reunification. In 1955 he had told the Bundestag that no European security system (that is, no scheme for disarmament) would be acceptable if it "entailed the continued division of Germany," an assertion with which the Social Democrats agreed.[52]

Nevertheless the introduction into disarmament negotiations of proposals to reduce conventional forces made it more difficult for him to pursue this political strategy, even though there was always a faint hope that in return for an agreement to restrain West German rearmament the USSR might agree to reunification. Nor did the American pursuit of aerial inspection make things easier, once that proposal had been refined and the idea of a surveillance zone in central Europe which might be divided by a demarcation line running between West Germany and East Germany was put forward. Should states require permission of the government of the state over which these aircraft would fly, the Soviet Union would make a great pretence of asking East Germany for such authorization, thus conferring on it the aura of sovereignty. Such an action would undermine the West German argument that East Germany was really a Soviet satellite eager to join the Federal Republic if only the USSR would relax its grip. Clearly, moves towards conventional reductions and aerial inspection threatened reunification. To counter this threat, Adenauer continued to insist that reunification must come before disarmament.

The Americans believed that their security rested on, among other things, NATO's capacity to slow down any massive Soviet ground invasion of Western Europe. If this strategy was to succeed, West German military strength was absolutely necessary to NATO. With the alliance with West Germany forming such a crucial part of the whole American strategy of containing the Soviet Union, the Americans had little difficulty in accepting the German thesis on reunification. On 28 May 1957 Eisenhower would publicly reiterate that the United States would take no disarmament action which would "prejudice the reunification of Germany,"[53] a pledge repeated by the foreign ministers of the United States, the United Kingdom, and France at the end of July.

The Soviet Union also placed the issue of reunification ahead of disarmament – if for different reasons. Presumably the Russians might have won important concessions had they been willing to allow East Germany to join the Federal Republic. But a united German state armed with tactical nuclear weapons was exactly what they feared. Khrushchev had maintained in the summer of 1956 that a "reunited Germany would certainly embark on a new course of agitation and aggression."[54] He absolutely rejected the American-German view that unification must precede any substantive arms control agreement.

While some believed that arms control concessions by the West were out of the question until the Soviet Union agreed to reunification, Canada's diplomats were more flexible. They wished to see Germany united under Western tutelage, and they certainly believed that such a political accord must be a condition for any comprehensive agreement. But a partial understanding on some disarmament issues was another matter – they did not rule out a first-stage reduction in advance of settling the German question.

The disarmament proposals offered by the Soviet Union on 17 November 1956 in the General Assembly had repeated former propositions such as the complete prohibition of atomic weapons, the cessation of all nuclear tests, and the elimination of all foreign military bases from the territory of other states within two years. Its one new and interesting feature was a readiness to consider employing aerial photography in central Europe to a depth of 800 kilometres east and west of a demarcation line between the armed forces of NATO and the Warsaw pact.

Pearson, always ready to give new proposals serious consideration, had adopted a positive attitude towards these Soviet proposals – perhaps to counteract the considerable deterioration in the West's relations with the USSR over events in Hungary and Suez. In January External Affairs suggested a special effort was needed to improve "communications with the Soviet Union on some question of importance."[55] "We trust," it declared some weeks later, "that our partners also will be motivated by such a concern and will be ready to look on the propaganda aspect as secondary."[56] Pearson still believed that the Soviet call for a withdrawal of foreign troops from Germany and Eastern Europe indicated that they were actively seeking the neutralization of Germany, but he considered their acceptance of limited aerial inspection a substantial advance – one of the most important steps ever taken by the Soviet Union towards an effective system of control. To be sure, the proposal was a long way from the Eisenhower concept of open skies over the whole of each other's territory and it would maintain the dividing line between the two Germanies. Nevertheless, the Russians had opened up a new and major area of arms control for discussion and bargaining. On this matter, as on nuclear issues, Pearson wanted the West to move from criticizing Soviet shortcomings to offering positive proposals of its own – an inquiring and constructive approach was in order.

In November the Soviet Union had also proposed that their armed forces as well as those of the West in Germany be reduced by one-third. The West Germans feared that such a serious diminution in troop strength by the West would weaken the pressure on the USSR to trade a comprehensive agreement for reunification. (Indeed Bonn had immediately rejected the Soviet initiative because it made no mention of reunification.) To accommodate the United States, Britain and France decided that they would avoid discussing European security in the sub-committee by maintaining that the topic was outside its terms of reference. Here again, however, External Affairs believed that in the interest of fruitful negotiations it was important to listen to what the USSR had to say about troop reductions in Germany. Of course its aim might simply be mischievous: the disruption of NATO and the freezing of the division of Germany. But the Soviet Union might be genuinely frightened of attack. As External Affairs observed, "if Soviet planners tend to equate U.S. capabilities with U.S. intentions to the same extent that U.S. planners appear to equate Soviet intentions with Soviet capabilities, there must be considerable alarm in Moscow."[57] A refusal to discuss troop levels in Europe might reinforce these fears and make negotiations that much more difficult. Canadian diplomats were not transfixed by German reunification. While acknowledging its importance, they were always ready to explore the possibility of some progress in disarmament with the expectation that, if necessary, some way could be found around German sensibilities about the continuing division of their country.

The desire of the Soviet Union to concentrate on getting the United States to agree to reductions in the overall force levels of both sides had led them to accept a reduction to the figure of 2.5 million which was the lowest the United States would offer. The Soviet concession had come during the meetings of the Disarmament Commission in July 1956. However, the Soviet condition was that this was only to be a first step; there would then have to be a further cut to between 1 and 1.5 million men for the two superpowers.

They had repeated this offer in November 1956 and would do so again in a memorandum for the sub-committee on 30 April 1957.

Canadian diplomats were not impressed by the long-time Soviet argument that only a direct threat to one's own territory justified the maintenance of substantial armed forces on Soviet borders. An indirect threat had caused Canada to participate in World War II and the Korean War, and External Affairs would probably have argued that adhering to collective security meant, by definition, a readiness to cope with indirect threats. Canada certainly believed that in postwar Europe the possibility of Soviet aggression required it to take the unprecedented step of stationing troops in West Germany, far away from North America. It hoped that the United States would not withdraw its troops from Europe before the "removal of the threat which is inherent in Soviet policies and their hegemony in Eastern Europe."[58] This meant no diminution in allied troop numbers until the Soviet Union voluntarily rolled back from Eastern Europe – this might take a long time. Canada therefore continued to support the earlier Western proposal for a first-stage reduction to 2.5 million men for the Soviet Union and the United Stages and 750,000 for France and Britain, conditional upon an amelioration of political conditions. It opposed the Soviet proposal that this step be dependent on agreement to future cuts to 1 to 1.5 million and 650,000, respectively.

Stassen's desire to negotiate an agreement on a test ban during the sub-committee meetings led him to decide to make some concessions on conventional forces. In the 31 May memorandum he handed to Valerian Zorin, he therefore offered a second-stage cut to 2.1 million and a third-stage drop to 1.7 million. But these would not take place automatically; they would be linked to "progress towards the solution of major political issues."[59] Each reduction would require a separate set of negotiations. His proposals received the support of Britain, France, and Canada but did not sit well with the USSR. On 19 July the Russian delegate rejected the offer because further reductions were contingent on the settlement of political problems, that is, German reunification. Stassen could make no concessions on that point. He knew that Eisenhower was committed to keeping United States conventional forces in Germany at the level Adenauer thought necessary. Reductions would only take place when West Germany decided they could and this undoubtedly meant when the USSR agreed to reunification. After 19 July there was no more discussion of this matter in the sub-committee.

Parallel to the lively bargaining between East and West on a test ban was another dialogue on aerial inspection. In its November proposals the Soviet Union had shown some interest in aerial inspection in an area in which the NATO and Warsaw pact forces were stationed, to a depth of 800 kilometres east and west of a demarcation line running between the two sides. This proposal was unacceptable to the West German government because it would be likely to confer international recognition on East Germany. Nevertheless, Stassen was encouraged because the USSR, for the first time, had not dismissed the concept of aerial photography – a concession which the United States had deemed essential to the realization of any partial disarmament scheme.

In March, at the start of the sub-committee sessions, Stassen described to Canada's Johnson an American two-zone alternative to the Soviet proposal. The first, in central Europe, would extend from the North Pole to a 45° north and from 5° east to 30° west. The effect would be to move the proposed Soviet zone farther east to include territory in the western part of the Soviet Union proper. It would cover only a relatively small part of NATO territory but a large portion of that of the Warsaw Treaty countries. A second proposed zone would extend from the Pole to 45° north and from 120° west to 150° east. This zone would cover the Kamchatka Peninsula which the Americans believed would be a major staging area in any attack on the United States. The North American sector would take in Alaska but also the Yukon, the Northwest Territories, and British Columbia. Stassen would need Canadian permission to make this offer to the USSR. In situations like this Pearson was always ready to co-operate. Accordingly, he asked the cabinet to approve the part of Stassen's plan which related to North America. In his supporting memorandum, he noted that Canadian military advisers believed that aerial inspection would allow the West to gain more intelligence than the Soviet Union would because the latter was a closed society. This convinced the Canadian government that Stassen's plan was a good one and worthy of warm support.[60]

Stassen's proposal had also been informally discussed with Zorin and it was now up to Moscow to respond. In its memorandum of 30 April the Soviet Union proposed a European sector bounded on the west by the zero meridian, on the east by 25° east, to the north by 54° north, and to the south by 39°38' north. This would mean that a line bisecting the sector would run near that which currently demarcated the division of the two Germanies. As to the north, it suggested extending the area proposed by the Americans to include the territory of the Soviet Union to the east of 108° east and that of the United States to the west of 90° west. The Soviet Union noted that the two areas were almost equal in extent. But they could hardly have believed that the Americans would accept a scheme whereby a sector in Siberia would be offset by the whole of the United States west of the Great Lakes. As Johnson remarked to the sub-committee, the proposal was "unduly one-sided"[61] in that a vast area of the USSR between its western border regions and longitude 108° east, by far the most developed part of the country, would escape aerial scrutiny.

For the moment, however, the main difficulty which the Soviet memorandum presented to the United States lay in its proposal for a European zone. John Foster Dulles and his colleagues knew how strongly Adenauer opposed this idea. The chancellor was convinced that if East Germany became a party to such an agreement, West German public opinion would believe that the international community approved of the division of Germany, thus weakening his claim that he would unify Germany. So strong was the West German government's opposition to a European zone that its ambassador to the NATO Council took the trouble to read into the record that a German-American understanding precluded the establishment of such an area for aerial surveillance. The issue was especially difficult for Adenauer because of the West German federal elections which were due in September. He could not afford to ignore the growing fear in Germany about nuclear war lest he provide the opposition Social Democrats with valuable electoral ammunition. For the sake of reunification Adenauer would have to prevent a European zone; yet he must not be seen by the electorate as opposing what appeared to be a constructive step towards disarmament.[62]

Adenauer's best tactic therefore lay in stalling the adoption of a European zone until after the election while attempting to escape the responsibility for doing so. Here his friend and ardent supporter, John Foster Dulles, would be extremely useful. The secretary of state announced that as far as the United States was concerned no European zone could be instituted without the agreement of the West European countries; thus West Germany would have a veto. In private he went further. Stassen had returned to Washington for instructions on how to deal with the Soviet memorandum of 30 April. When the matter of aerial inspection came up, Dulles insisted that any proposal for a European zone must be made by the Europeans themselves. The Americans should only suggest that the United States and Canada be opened up in exchange for permission to fly over the USSR. Failing this, a limited Arctic zone should be offered. Stassen objected that the Soviet Union would not accept an American-Russian inspection zone without one in central Europe. In the ensuing dispute Eisenhower came down on the side of Dulles – a European zone would not be part of the American response.

In his subsequent discussions with Zorin, however, Stassen went beyond his instructions. Without authority he handed over a *written* document containing the United States proposals before they had been cleared with its NATO allies. This raised a fierce outcry from the British and West Germans who believed they were being coerced into accepting American positions because it would be difficult to make changes in positions already presented to the Soviet Union. Then, too, Stassen failed to tell Zorin that these proposals were an inseparable package: the Soviet Union would have to accept all the measures. If it agreed to any inspection zones, it would also have to live with the ending of the production of fissionable materials for military purposes. Finally, Stassen had been told to offer a European zone only after NATO agreement. Instead, in his memorandum to Zorin, he stated that the United States was willing to consider aerial inspection in central Europe as well as in a Soviet-American zone. Stassen would later claim that he had given Zorin a written document to prevent a breakdown in the talks. It is more likely that, eager for the personal prestige that would have accompanied success, he made the fatal mistake of ignoring the West European allies. He also weakened his own standing with Eisenhower who confided to Dulles that his confidence in his special assistant for disarmament had been shaken. To fire Stassen would have caused too much confusion, but increasingly Dulles himself took charge of the disarmament negotiations.[63]

During June American policy on a European zone was, to understate it, not very clear. Stassen had offered Zorin a European zone, yet from Bonn, Canada's ambassador, Charles Ritchie, reported that the American ambassador there maintained that the Germans had received an explicit assurance that no aerial inspection zone in Europe would be included in the initial phase of disarmament. This information made Canadian diplomats anxious. They believed that a northern inspection zone would benefit the West more than the USSR. The only kind of aerial inspection which might interest the Soviet Union – as a quid pro quo – was a European zone because it was there that the main NATO forces were deployed. They discussed whether Canada ought not to attempt to persuade the United States to commit itself to a European zone so as to make its northern offer more acceptable to the USSR.[64] In a memorandum for cabinet, External Affairs noted that its military experts advised that Stassen's proposals would benefit the West much more than the

Soviet Union. Consequently, it did not believe the USSR would accept them: "it would not be easy to defend them as equitable to the Soviet Union in terms of relative strategic importance." They were doubtful that Canada's representative should join in presenting such a scheme "since by that act we might expose ourselves to the charge of sponsoring proposals which do not represent a serious effort to meet the Soviet position." The memorandum recommended that Canada take part in a comprehensive North American-Soviet scheme only on condition that "the areas of Soviet Union territory would be of no less relative military importance than the areas of North America."[65]

Canada differed sharply from its allies on the value of a European zone. But then the Europeans differed among themselves as to its worth. Adenauer was hostile to the concept because he believed it would jeopardize his aim of uniting Germany. France and Great Britain, which were more worried about the possibility of a Soviet land attack, though it a splendid idea; they wanted the zone to be extended to include the Soviet Union up to the Urals. Canada, protected by the United States, was less anxious about West European security and more concerned with getting a first-stage arms control agreement with the Soviet Union. External Affairs doubted "that the best way to achieve a system of aerial inspection which would ultimately embrace the entire Soviet Union [was] to present 'tough' proposals at this juncture. We cannot be certain how strong the influences are in Moscow which oppose any negotiation but we think careful consideration should be given to any move which might provide arguments for reversing the present apparent readiness to negotiate seriously."[66] The dispatch went on to hint strongly that the American bases around the Mediterranean, an important source of Soviet anxiety, should also be included in the inspection zone. Canada was now truly out of step with its allies. It was eager for fruitful negotiations but the latter were becoming much less interested in serious bargaining and much more worried about emerging from this impasse with a propaganda victory by being able to blame the failure to reach agreement on their Soviet adversary.

On 29 June, during the election campaign in West Germany, Adenauer responded to an attack that he was obstructing arms negotiations by stating that he had no objection to a European zone which did not work against reunification. A few days later Dulles affirmed that such a zone was acceptable, but he was in no hurry to put forward a clear proposal lest it undermine Adenauer. As he put it, "it will take much longer to work out a European zone than a northern zone which is free of such complications."[67] On 25 July he instructed Stassen to offer a US-USSR zone first in the sub-committee. But the United Kingdom and France objected to this tactic. At this point Dulles decided to take over the negotiations in the sub-committee himself. He found his two important allies absolutely convinced that a European zone must be included in any proposal, and he had the ticklish task of reconciling their position with that of West Germany. In the end, he was able to develop a compromise that satisfied all three. The West would offer air surveillance of the United States, Canada, and the USSR; if that proved unacceptable, Dulles was ready to propose an Arctic zone. If the Soviet Union agreed to either of these, there would be a further offer of a European zone bounded on the south by 40° north, in the west by 10° west and in the east by 60° east. If the Soviet Union refused this proposal, the West was open to a still smaller zone on the understanding that it would cover a significant part of the Soviet Union; this last proviso was a concession to the fears of Britain and France.

Dulles was certain that the Russians would reject these proposals. A straight US-USSR exchange would give the Americans an intelligence advantage. A zone confined to the Arctic would involve a good deal of Canada but very little of the United States – an arrangement which Khrushchev called "quite comical."[68] The proposed European zone would contain much more Soviet territory than the one Stassen had suggested in the spring. Dulles wrote Adenauer that public relations was his main reason for proposing the US-USSR zone. He was certain that the Soviet Union would reject it, and he seriously doubted that the Soviet leaders would accept any European zone that covered an extensive portion of their territory. He was right. The Soviet Union would turn down the Western proposal all along the line: the head of Zorin's staff later told an American colleague that the Dulles proposal for aerial inspection zones was the turning point in the negotiations.[69]

On 2 August the four Western powers made their formal offer on inspection zones. Even if some of its diplomats felt uneasy about Washington's "tough" tactics, it was unlikely that a new Canadian government which still lacked a full-time secretary of state for external affairs would pick a quarrel with its major allies or seek to pursue new and bold arms control policies. On 29 August Canada also supported the Western working paper on partial disarmament measures submitted to the sub-committee that had already been approved by the NATO Council. This was a summary of all current Western proposals: limitation of armed forces to 2.1 million and then 1.7 million given political settlements, fissionable materials not to be used for military purposes, a two-year halt to nuclear testing, and the proposed air inspection zones. The provisions were inseparable; the Soviet Union would have to accept or reject the entire package.

Only two days previously, Zorin had bitterly denounced the entire Western disarmament programme in a prepared statement. He condemned the West for its failure to agree to treat the immediate halting of nuclear weapons testing as a separate issue and to reduce armed forces to 1 to 1.5 million. He declared that the purpose of the Western inspection zones was to gather information on the Soviet Union's most important industrial and communications centres. He pointed out that the Dulles plan omitted aerial reconnaissance over a number of countries in which there were United States bases. He charged that the "ruling circles" of the other countries represented on the sub-committee were not interested in disarmament, that the sub-committee accepted direction from a military alliance that included the Adenauer government (NATO) yet refused to hear the views of countries outside the "military blocs" such as India. Because of its composition the sub-committee was incapable of finding a successful path to disarmament; it would need to be enlarged to include those governments who opposed the arms race. "If a larger number of States representing the various continents and social systems were drawn into the discussion of disarmament questions in United Nations organs," Zorin maintained, "the discussion would be given a more objective character and an opportunity would be provided for the voices of other Governments and peoples to be heard; which, unfortunately, is not possible in the Sub-Committee with its present narrow and one sided-membership." He concluded by insisting that the United States and the other Western powers were using the sub-committee to mislead public opinion and deceive the peoples who wished to end the arms race.[70] Clearly, the USSR intended to break off negotiations.

When the sub-committee recessed on 6 September, the Soviet Union refused to agree to a date to resume discussions – in effect walking out. Later, in November, it formally announced that it would no longer take part in any negotiations conducted in the Disarmament Commission or its sub-committee. So ended the era in which arms control negotiations would be under the aegis of the United Nations and would be largely the province of only five of its member-states.

CONCLUSION

The meetings of the sub-committee of the Disarmament Commission which took place in London in the spring and summer of 1957 were the scene of substantive high-level arms control negotiations.

Unfortunately they ended in failure. External Affairs took them seriously and sent extensive and detailed instructions to Canada's representative, David Johnson, about the line to take on the test ban and aerial inspection. Like Britain and France, Canada approved of a European zone of aerial inspection. It also suggested an approach that paid some attention to Soviet anxieties about security. But Washington was obsessed with the need to keep its alliance with West Germany intact, and the United States government was in no mood to consider a softer stand. In the end, Canada went along with the aerial inspection proposals that Dulles offered the Soviet Union on 2 August.

The test ban issue had presented Pearson with a difficult political dilemma. He believed that the West needed to test to improve its nuclear capability. Yet he recognized that the explosions profoundly offended India and the Third World bloc and inclined them towards neutrality in the great political struggle against the Soviet challenge. He understood that that conflict was global and that Asian and African support was indispensable if the West were to prevail. He attempted to mitigate the harsh effects of the American refusal to give up testing by suggesting both the limitation and the registration of such tests. But Canada was gravely handicapped in trying to persuade the United States to adopt these measures. "It is somewhat difficult," observed Johnson, "for a country which does not have large armed forces and has no nuclear weapons at all and, therefore, carries out no nuclear tests, to take a public position on these issues strongly at variance with the views of a major ally ... we would necessarily be in the rather unsatisfactory position of making proposals which affect other peoples' weapons and forces and have only very slight direct impact on Canadian forces and weapons."[71]

Of course the problem would have been resolved for Pearson if the superpowers had agreed on a test ban. Unfortunately the Americans insisted on linking a ban to the cut-off on the use of fissionable material for military purposes. To make matters worse, both the test ban and the cut-off were only part of an overall Western disarmament plan which included items relating to European security which were unacceptable to the Soviet Union. The whole package was deemed inseparable – no one part could be implemented on its own. This fact in itself would guarantee failure in the negotiations. But the Soviet Union would have rejected the cut-off even if the United States had agreed to treat it and the test ban as separate items. Zorin once explained to Moch that the controls necessary for a cut-off were unacceptable because they "would involve looking into their entire economy."[72] Why did the Americans insist on a cut-off? Dulles asserted that without calling a halt to using fissionable materials to build weapons there would be an uncontrollable spread of such arms throughout the world. Yet less than a year later, in April 1958, President Eisenhower would agree to separate the attempt to achieve a test ban from all other arms control issues.

The political problem facing the American administration was that great numbers of their people found testing repugnant. Leading scientific and moral personalities passionately condemned it. By the spring of 1957, 69 per cent of American citizens favoured a multilateral agreement to halt the tests. But the American military wished them to continue in order to develop different types of tactical atomic weapons on which NATO would depend and to discover a clean bomb that would be free of radioactivity. If the tests were suspended, the scientific organization behind them might dissipate, public interest in them might wane and congressional funds become more scarce, and, finally, psychologically they would be difficult to start up again. The cut-off became a propaganda device to blame the Soviet Union and allow the United States to escape the political penalty of pursuing its testing programme.

It is possible that if the USSR had been willing to make concessions on issues of European security, the United States might have been persuaded to accept a test ban. But this they refused to do. Robert Divine is right when he observes that these negotiations for a test ban failed because at this time "Cold War tensions ... proved too strong to be overcome so easily."[73]

CHAPTER NINE

Conclusion

THE FAILURE OF NEGOTIATIONS

"How did it happen," wondered Andrei Gromyko in 1956, "that after discussing a problem of vital importance to all mankind for a total of ten years, those taking part in these negotiations were, not nearer to, but possibly even farther away from, its practical solution than at the outset of their work."[1] This is no easy question to answer, but at bottom, certainly, was the harsh fact that the negotiations involved two powerful independent sovereign states which were deeply suspicious of each other. Nikita Khrushchev described the political relationship between them as one of peaceful coexistence. This implied that the battle for political mastery of the globe should never be allowed to erupt into world war. But the undisguised hostility between the two countries engendered an active mistrust and suspicion of each other's motives which undermined all efforts to agree on a means to control the arms race.

The sad fact was that the improvement in their respective military capabilities during World War II meant that each was able to destroy the other. By the late 1940s the American air force, armed with atomic bombs, could pulverize Soviet cities and kill millions. By the early 1950s the Soviet Union was capable of an atomic air strike at North America; as well, its army could roll over Western Europe at any time. With such resources of wealth and manpower under its control, it might challenge American power in North America itself. That politicians on either side had no such wild ambitions was beside the point. What concerned strategic planners was not the intentions of the politicians of the other side but the capacity of the armed forces of their potential adversary to inflict horrific damage on their own society and on their own peoples, and so put in question the continued existence of their country. The ugly military reality was that the other side could if it wished, even for the most irrational or mistaken reasons, suddenly launch an entirely unprovoked but nevertheless annihilating attack. The clashes in values and spiralling political hostilities of the ideological Cold War only reinforced this mutual distrust and anxiety. As the military saw it, the only defence was to arm oneself to the point that the other side would be deterred from attacking for fear of retaliation. The heads of government accepted the advice of their strategic planners and made an increase in military capacity their priority. Neither the United States nor the USSR acted on the premise that in the end, no side would be better off if, by increasing its military power, it caused the other to feel so insecure that it was compelled to follow suit.

Yet, in the rush to arm, neither could ignore the current of world opinion which wished instead to see the process reversed and steady progress towards disarmament. This view was an important political element in the ideological conflict between East and West which so often boiled down to which side's view of the world and way of life was morally superior. In the eyes of millions, there was no better proof of the winner in that contest than to be the champion of peace. But how were governments to reconcile their arms control proposals with measures to make themselves stronger militarily? This turned out to be less difficult than it appeared. The purpose of the arms negotiations was transformed; they were directed towards increasing each side's security, not to the reduction of armaments. The measures each side proposed were so framed as to weaken the other. In effect, each would attempt to gain by diplomacy an advantage which was unattainable by military means. These proposals constituted a programme of what the military thought the government should achieve so as to increase its security at the expense of its opponent. As Brigadier-General Thomas Phillips of the United States asserted, American military men regarded the disarmament negotiations as a new form of the struggle for military supremacy.[2]

Because they could be oversimplified and even incorporated into slogans, disarmament measures lent themselves to the illusion that their consequences could be easily understood; thus, they could be made to appear reasonable and attractive and they made for great theatre. Yet, on closer examination, they might constitute a serious threat to the security of the other side. The Baruch Plan seemed a simple and desirable way of establishing international control of atomic energy. Yet, if implemented, it would have allowed the United States to continue as a potential atomic power while preventing the USSR from developing such a capability. The Soviet Union, for its part, constantly proclaimed the need to abolish atomic weapons, a cry sure to touch the humane instincts of people. Had the Americans agreed to destroy their atomic weapons, however, the Soviet army would have been left as the dominant military force in Europe. It was easy for each superpower to shape its disarmament proposals both to appeal to peace sentiment and to place pressure on the other side to accept measures that would weaken its security. If the latter failed to accept proposals because its planners believed them to be harmful to its security, it came under a barrage of abuse from the former. The State Department–Joint Chiefs of Staff working group put it nicely in 1951: "The purpose of this study is the establishment of a foundation upon which positions may be built which would, if accepted by the Soviet Union, be acceptable to the U.S. or, if rejected by the Soviet Union, be advantageous to the U.S. and Western Powers for their propaganda value."[3] Thus, real progress was difficult; the whole process seemed self-defeating. Any measure to strengthen the security of one side would automatically weaken that of the other; no agreement seemed possible.

Fortunately, there were possibilities in the situation that might lead to some restraint in the arms race. To exploit them, two conditions needed to be present at the same time. First of all, the overall international political situation would have to be conducive to meaningful negotiations. Not only would both sides have a need to gain prestige from being seen to be moving towards disarmament; but there would also have to be a sufficient relaxation of tensions between the two antagonists so that each could believe that its adversary was serious about working towards an agreement. The second condition concerned the state of the art of weapons technology itself. It would need to have developed to a point where some compromise would genuinely enhance the security of each side.

Neither of these conditions existed when the Atomic Energy Commission took up the Baruch Plan in June 1946. Baruch delivered his proposals only a few months after Stalin and Churchill had signalled that the Cold War had begun. The plan would have weakened Soviet security. It would have halted their atomic military research; and it would have left the Americans the right to decide when they would destroy their stock of atomic bombs. If there had been a real desire for an accord, surely the United States would have demanded guarantees against a Soviet Army takeover of Western Europe if it agreed to destroy its atomic bombs. But this issue was never mentioned. There was no genuine bargaining; the sessions were public affairs where the protagonists made speeches at each other.

An important change in the strategic balance took place once the Soviet Union exploded its own atomic device in September 1949. With the possibility of atomic parity in sight, it might have been worthwhile discussing restraints on atomic military development. Indeed, the General Advisory Committee of the United States Atomic Energy Commission, which was composed of top nuclear scientists and chaired by Robert Oppenheimer, urged that some approach be made to the Russians. But this suggestion came at the height of the Cold War: a ferocious mutual hostility and fear dominated relations between the two sides. To negotiate some mutual nuclear controls was politically impossible. Then President Truman made the fateful decision to move the world into the hydrogen bomb age. It is likely that neither Truman nor Stalin was particularly anxious to cope with a world in which the dominant weapon was the hydrogen bomb. But neither could be sure that if he abstained, his rival would not go ahead.

A more promising period began with the election of Eisenhower to the presidency, the death of Stalin, and the end of the Korean War. The new Soviet regime claimed it was committed to peaceful coexistence, that it had no intention of winning its goals by violence, and that it understood the catastrophic harm that a nuclear war would inflict on the USSR. As well, the American hydrogen bomb test of 1954 aroused a storm of protest in the West, not least in the United States where an end to testing became an issue in the presidential campaign in the autumn of 1956. President Eisenhower had long warned of the devastating consequences of atomic conflict. Now the pressure of the test ban movement combined with his personal convictions to make him more open to real negotiations. He sent a message to Moscow to this effect by appointing Harold Stassen as his special assistant for disarmament reporting directly to him. The general political thaw worked to make the protestations of sincerity about disarmament by the other side more plausible.

Technical developments in weapons were also creating more favourable conditions for an understanding. By the mid-1950s there were too many nuclear arms in existence to be inventoried and no way of guaranteeing that the elimination of nuclear weapons had taken place. The era of negotiation for complete disarmament could be abandoned in favour of some form of arms control. One positive consequence would be that the Americans might not press for an extensive system of verification – a serious obstacle to the Soviet acceptance of any form of arms restraint. Allowing foreign inspectors to roam the USSR would undermine the long-standing policy of Soviet leaders to keep their society closed and foreign influences out. Then, too, they believed that the less their adversary knew about their military capacity, the better off they would be.[4] In fact, we now know that being able to observe the other side's military activity is an important confidence-building measure. There was another advantage to abandoning total disarmament: on some level it had always seemed impossible – a naive utopian dream unconnected to reality. Arms control seemed much more practical; it made sense to trade a small measure the other side wanted to improve one's own security. Many like Paul Nitze saw such arms control measures as an "auxiliary to national security policy."[5]

The Americans, frightened by the danger of a surprise Soviet attack, wished to take aerial photographs of Soviet territory. For its part the Soviet Union wanted a test ban to stop further American development of nuclear weapons. Here, then, was the possibility of a trade. (Indeed, the chief of Valentin Zorin's staff later told an American diplomat that an agreement on surprise attack zones in Europe and a test moratorium could have been negotiated.[6]) And in April 1957 there began a two-month period of intense private dealing with both sides displaying some flexibility. This effort was the high point of postwar arms negotiations. In the end, however, things went wrong and both sides stepped back from concluding a treaty. Both military and political factors had worked against an agreement.

The American interest in aerial inspection diminished because by 1956 they had developed the U-2 aircraft which could fly at great heights and was equipped with a high-precision camera. Soviet military installations could now be photographed and the extent and nature of the Soviet aerial threat evaluated. The administration was also under heavy pressure from the military not to agree to stop testing. American strategists relied absolutely on the nuclear threat to deter Soviet aggression; continued improvement of the United States' nuclear capability was a priority. They therefore strongly opposed any ban that would constrain their freedom to develop "clean" thermonuclear bombs and low-yield tactical atomic weapons. "In the main," remarked Dulles, "the military people do not have great confidence in the efficacy of any attainable control or inspection system."[7] There was also intense political pressure from both Britain and France not to make a concession on the test ban issue. The former wished to continue to improve its own nuclear military capability and the latter was developing a bomb of its own. From the American point of view, the benefits of an accord became less and less appealing as negotiations proceeded. All they could be certain of was a disgruntled military and an unhappy set of allies.

In the same way, military and political factors combined to make the Russians more intransigent. Washington was unwilling to agree to a test ban but wished to evade the responsibility for torpedoing the negotiations. Consequently, it offered a two-year suspension of tests surrounded by a package of conditions which would make the whole totally unacceptable. If the Russians wanted a test ban, they would have to put up with inspectors swarming over their atomic facilities to make sure none of their fissionable material was being used for military purposes as well as with aerial photography of their most important military facilities. What they would gain in security through a test ban would hardly make up for what they would lose through the military intelligence the United States would obtain. Moreover, the Soviet Union had some reason to feel rather more confident than before about their security because of their enormous progress in missile development. On 26 August 1957, they launched their first rocket. The era in which the bomber was supreme was coming to an end: even North America might not be immune from missile attack.

At the same time Soviet interest in reaching an agreement on arms control took second place to their eagerness to see Adenauer, their great enemy, defeated in the September 1957 elections in West Germany. The chancellor had been pointing to the sub-committee talks as proof that his stand on reunification was not harming disarmament negotiations. The Soviet Union decided to attack Adenauer politically by demonstrating that the negotiations had reached an impasse and that there was little harmony between East and West. Having apparently learned nothing from the failure of its intervention in the American presidential election the previous November, they were trying to frighten West Germany into disowning Adenauer. Zorin made an abusive statement in the sub-committee in which he blamed the West for the obvious failure of the talks. The Soviet tactic failed to prevent Adenauer being returned in September with a great majority.

The possibility of political gain had persuaded the Soviet Union to destroy the sub-committee. It had proved no use to them in the negotiations during the spring and summer of 1957. Perhaps they were tired of always being in the minority. Certainly the sub-committee had become more cumbersome as a negotiating mechanism because in practice all Western initiatives were cleared with the NATO Council. By attacking it as a tool of the West, by complaining that it had no representation from Asia, Africa, or South America, they hoped to win the support of great numbers of middle powers which resented their exclusion from the disarmament process, especially the Afro-Asian neutral bloc headed by India. As advocates of an immediate test ban, the Soviet Union might expect to increase its support in the United Nations. And it was moderately successful: although on 15 November the General Assembly approved the Western resolution by a vote of 57–9 (the Soviet bloc), there were 15 abstentions.

John Holmes has suggested that the talks failed because participating governments "could never come to grips with any proposals which were remotely applicable to the world situation as it existed then."[8] But this judgment is not accurate: a test ban, as was proposed by Eisenhower in 1958, was feasible. Unfortunately, the favourable conditions for an agreement lasted a very short time. Neither superpower would gain much security from compromising. A test ban without conditions was good for Soviet security but bad for the United States. A test ban under American conditions weakened Soviet security. Had Dulles persisted, he would have antagonized his European allies whose support he needed for the basic American strategy of containing the Soviet threat. The Soviet Union, for its part, sought the political advantages of walking out and claiming to be the champion of the Third World's peace aspirations. The conjuncture of security and political factors was no longer favourable to arms control and a major opportunity for a test ban was lost in 1957.

The signing of the Limited Test Ban Treaty in 1963 by the United States and the Soviet Union proved that a test ban was possible. The failure to achieve it in the period under study is symbolic of the decade's futile effort at disarmament and arms control. While great masses of people wished for a compromise, the meaningful decisions were taken by only four men – Truman, Stalin, Eisenhower, and Khrushchev – on the basis of the immediate military and political advantages which might be gained. Moreover, none would suffer any serious political pain because they did not achieve an agreement. None was compelled to concentrate on the serious consequences of failure, as Stalin or Eisenhower had been during the war. Obsessed with the current state of their country's security, they believed that increasing their nuclear might was a necessary evil – even a means of preventing a new world war. None appears to have worried about whether the arms race itself was a source of tension between the two sides. Unfortunately, future generations would have to bear the costs. Billions of dollars were spent to make engines of mass destruction that everyone fervently hopes will never be used. With the end of the Cold War the former antagonists face an additional drain in money and energy to dismantle thousands of nuclear warheads. There is, as well, danger that some of these weapons will find their way into the hands of other governments. There has been a rapid spread in the knowledge and resources necessary to manufacture nuclear weapons. More than half a dozen states have nuclear bombs or are on the threshold of possessing them. Clearly, there has been little benefit and much harm in this arms race.

We can only regret that the two sides did not work harder to find a solution. It is difficult to believe that the leaders of either side seriously considered pursuing genuine disarmament or even the possibility of finding the means to slow down the rate of their arms build-up. Many of their advisers would have warned them that to do so would be construed as a weakening of their determination to confront the adversary. Stalin and Truman never even met to consider this possibility. And at Geneva in July 1955 both Eisenhower and Khrushchev treated arms control as a peripheral issue; the focus was on what should be done about Germany. Granted the latter was a crucial issue but so was the former. After all, there was something totally wrong when, at the end of the Eisenhower regime, the Americans found themselves with thousands more nuclear warheads than they could possibly use in an all-out war. "The search for a preponderance of power," writes John Lewis Gaddis, "led to an obsession with overkill: credibility became an end in itself, without regard to the burdens of maintaining it."[9] Perhaps, given the climate of profound mutual distrust, there was no obvious arms control proposal that would not have given one side or another an advantage. Nevertheless, what is so striking about the documentation that I have seen is that there was hardly any sense of urgency about finding a way of escaping this nuclear impasse.

A VERY JUNIOR PARTNER
IN THE WESTERN FIRM

Canada's approach to the nuclear arms negotiations of the 1940s and 1950s was dictated by global politics. When the discussions first began in 1946, the Cold War had not yet entered its most intense phase and Canadian diplomats had been somewhat optimistic, believing that it might be possible to achieve a world order in which states would surrender some of their sovereignty to the United Nations and its agencies. Hence their initial enthusiasm for the Baruch Plan. But as time went on the divide between the Soviet Union and the West deepened. The Soviet Union seemed to be more aggressive and more dangerous. Canadian diplomats came to believe that an agreement on disarmament was less and less likely, and their consequent assessment of future prospects became much more pessimistic. They came to be convinced that the main task of the West was to unite politically and build its military strength so as to protect its security. In this grand strategy, arms negotiations were seen as a means by which the United States and its allies might strengthen themselves in a peaceful fashion at the expense of the Soviet Union. The latter, of course, wished to use the talks to improve its own strategic position.

Canada's unique status in the United Nations Atomic Energy Commission and the sub-committee of the Disarmament Commission was the result of fortuitous circumstance – its possession of uranium deposits and its location next to the United States. Because it was under the latter's security umbrella, Canada had no specific security goals of its own, unlike the chief Western powers which were all great powers. Its main contribution to the arms talks, External Affairs believed, was to keep the Western powers together: if the West was to make any impression on the Soviet Union, all members would need to present a harmonious front to the world. In a sentence which summed up the whole thrust of Canada's policy in the negotiations, one of its diplomats, probably Norman Robertson, wrote: "Since the essentially Canadian interest in the subject is so closely integrated with the interest of the major Western powers, but principally the United States, there is little scope for an independent Canadian contribution to the work of the Sub-Committee. The Canadian role has largely been to give support to agreed Western positions in the Sub-Committee and to work for the widest possible agreement among the Western Powers in the informal consultations of Western delegations."[10]

Canada had no means of applying pressure, much less the instruments for bullying its allies. It had to rely on sweet reasonableness, that is, skilful diplomacy – the method of a small power. Hence its belief that most of its effective work in eliminating misunderstanding would be done in conversations with other Western delegates. "So far as my own experience goes," Robertson observed, "our only opportunity of putting anything in the pot has been in the private, off-the-record discussions between the Western delegations."[11] But Canada did more than work the corridors. Alarmed by the developing split between France and the United States, it attempted to bridge the gap by suggesting concrete measures. In August 1952, it proposed a "first slice" of disarmament whose first stage would include all the elements of a comprehensive plan which could be supported by both the United States and France. Later, in March 1956, Robertson proposed a first concrete step that would please the Americans but also be part of a larger comprehensive plan to abolish nuclear weapons and thus satisfy the French. Preserving harmony within the Western family was always Canada's major concern.

Apart from facilitating Western agreement on a set of proposals, External Affairs believed that Canada could also help simply by clarifying the texts of the various proposals, so as to make them more acceptable to the world community. In 1956 John Holmes wrote: "Because we do not possess atomic weapons, because our conventional weapons are limited in scope and because we are not fully aware of all the strategic and technical factors involved, our role must of necessity be one of formulating proposals related to a fundamental design laid down by our major allies." And he added: "the best we can hope to do would be to turn our minds to some neat package formula which might have sales value in another propaganda struggle."[12]

It was in the disarmament discussions in the General Assembly that Canada truly came into its own and performed three useful functions on behalf of the West. The first was to offer an effective defence of the Western programme, whether it was the Majority Plan or aerial inspection. At the same time, in almost every speech in the Assembly's disarmament debates, Canada criticized the Soviet Union for not agreeing to the inspection measures which the West believed necessary to any agreement. A second service performed by Canada, either itself or in collaboration with others, was to propose resolutions at the Assembly which would help the Western cause. Thus, Canada offered a useful amendment to the United Nations resolution on the prohibition of atomic arms in December 1946 that was unanimously accepted. In 1948 it was General McNaughton who presented the successful resolution asking for United Nations endorsement of the Majority Plan. In the autumn of 1954, Paul Martin put together the important procedural resolution which won the support of both the United States and the Soviet Union, thus permitting negotiations to continue in the sub-committee. Finally, Canada joined with Norway and Japan in 1957 to suggest a resolution calling for the registration of nuclear tests with United Nations authorities.

Lastly, Canada undertook to rally Third World support for the Western side within the United Nations. In September 1956, Holmes was very concerned that the Afro-Asian countries might combine with the communist bloc and succeed in passing a resolution that called for the cessation of nuclear testing. This possibility presented a rather delicate problem. It was easy enough for the West to attack the communist nations but dealing with the Afro-Asians was a different matter. "Our concern to keep our links with our Commonwealth associates and to hold the affection of Asians and Africans in the United Nations is not just a sentimental frill," wrote Holmes. "It is a thoroughly hard-boiled effort to prevent the Russians from turning our flanks and exposing NATO as a Maginot line."[13] External Affairs believed that among the allies in the sub-committee, Canada was uniquely equipped to line up Asian and African support for the Western programme. A policy guidance document for Canadian delegates to the General Assembly session of 1957 boasted that "the problem may be briefly described as the avoidance of a vacuum of leadership which might constitute an invitation to mischievous initiatives. It would appear that Canada is on the whole better situated to provide suitable leadership in the direction of moderation than the other Western members of the Sub-Committee."[14] Canada had developed a reputation for "objectivity and independence, if not neutrality."[15] No doubt Canada played on its reputation as a middle power to rally support for the Western cause. But during the period under review the West never failed to win a vote on disarmament issues. It would be fair to say that Canada contributed something to this record.

External Affairs was nonetheless keenly aware of Canadian limitations. As a small power, Canada was in no position to offer substantive schemes. When I began this study I was convinced that there was some proposal that would have led to mutual disarmament. Reading the documents I have not been able to find any. I now believe that if the military experts of the West and the Soviet Union were unable to come up with a magic solution, Canada even if it had had the expertise would not have been able to do so. An External Affairs official, Robert A. MacKay, observed that a disarmament agreement would only be reached after hard bargaining between countries which had something of value to trade. Because Canada had nothing to offer, it could hardly influence either side. "Any contribution we can make," he concluded, "will only be in helping to define and support the agreed Western position."[16] Once it became obvious in early 1947 that the Soviet Union would never accept the principles underpinning the Baruch Plan, Canadian diplomats gave up on achieving disarmament. Their main goals became the strengthening of Western unity and the winning of the propaganda war. In this they did what it was possible for them to do. The documents fail to show any means by which they could have been more successful in accomplishing their self-designated task.

The relationship that determined the way Canada operated in the negotiations was the one with the United States. It was probably Norman Robertson who put it this way: "The Canadian representative has from time to time been described as a 'member of the Western team', an 'honest broker', a 'neutral' and a 'representative of the small and middle Powers.' The first of these descriptions is the nearest to being appropriate but only in the sense that Canada is a very junior partner in the Western firm."[17] The "junior" implied that, above all, Canada would be loyal to its friendship with the United States. There was not the slightest doubt that in the case of war with the Soviet Union, the Canadian government intended to be at the side of the United States. Canada openly and enthusiastically acknowledged American leadership. Only the United States had the wealth, the technical expertise, and the political will to take the responsibility for the principal strategic and military decisions essential to maintain the security of the West.

Canada was in no position to challenge any of the basic tenets underpinning American strategy, but it also had no desire to do so. This was no surprise; after all, as a North American country, it was bound to see Soviet military challenges in much the same light. Grant Davy has suggested that because of "her special relationship with the United States Canada found it prudent to follow the American lead on most of the issues."[18] But this is unfair. Keeping in step with the Americans presented no real difficulty for External Affairs because it agreed with the Baruch Plan, with force levels of 2.5 million, with aerial inspection, and with resisting the ending of nuclear tests. Another critic has complained that Canada was neither neutral nor non-aligned but a "small, trusted satellite of the United States."[19] But this is not accurate. Canada had a will and a policy of its own. It rejected neutralism and sincerely believed it was doing the right thing in defending American positions and acting as a spokesman for the West.

The word "partner" implies, however, not only that Canada should take some direction but also that it should have some say – not in American strategic decisions but in how they should be promoted. And on this matter there were sound political factors that gave Canadian diplomats some leverage. Negotiations were being held under the aegis of the United Nations. During the three years of the AEC, the American aim was to discredit totally the Soviet stance on the Majority Plan in the General Assembly. Even after the United States abandoned this sterile method of negotiating the early 1950s, it was accepted by all that crucial decisions would have to be endorsed by the United Nations as a whole. In this kind of situation, Canadian co-operation was important. Canada's steadfast support for the United States helped confer legitimacy on its claim to be the leader of the free world. And in the actual votes the Americans often took the advice of Canadian diplomats who were popular at the United Nations and who had a good sense of what would be acceptable. This being the case, Washington could not afford to treat Canadian diplomats in too cavalier a manner.

External Affairs took its responsibility as a partner seriously. The Americans seemed often to be in the process of formulating policy without ever being able to nail down exactly what they would propose. At these times External Affairs dispatched great numbers of directives to Canadian delegates to the United Nations commissions as well as to Canadian ambassadors in Washington, discussing tentative American proposals in great detail and offering criticisms and suggestions. The Americans listened with what seems like a good deal of patience and always responded to Canadian requests for more information or additional briefing. Over disagreements on tactics, Canada sometimes would give up pushing but occasionally it would persist; nor was there anything in the relationship which inhibited it from so doing. Despite American disapproval, Canada continued to advocate the registration of nuclear tests in 1957. The Americans at no time gave the slightest hint of any intention to bully or coerce. The great number of Canadian commentaries on American disarmament and arms control proposals demonstrated the hope of External Affairs that it was possible to influence the making of American policy. Holmes has testified that Washington was always willing to discuss its plans. Nevertheless, it was difficult to have an effective discussion because United States policy was hardly ever finalized. Internal battles in the administration usually prevented agreed American proposals from being presented to Canada until the eve of the negotiating sessions which left "hardly any time for comment much less major revision."[20] Still, sometimes there were successes. For example, in the autumn of 1955, along with France and Great Britain, Canada succeeded in persuading the United States not to propose a resolution endorsing Eisenhower's Open Skies programme to the sub-committee and the subsequent General Assembly meeting in December.

From December 1946 on, Canada's dialogue with the Americans was carried on without any publicity. Critics of quiet diplomacy have often argued that only by going public can the Canadian government hope to modify American policy. There is certainly a case to be made for this point of view, especially when it comes to major strategic decisions. What can be said about Canada's work behind the scenes in this period is that Canada did help to re-shape minor American tactical initiatives through diplomatic criticism.

In the actual negotiating sessions, Canadian diplomats understood that their main task was to reinforce the attempts of their Western allies to persuade the Soviet Union to accept the Western programme. But this role did not jibe very well with the image of Canada as a peacemaker. There was a perception at the United Nations that Canada was a representative of the smaller powers. Countries like India assumed that Canada would be playing an independent role within the negotiations. More importantly, some of the Canadian public assumed that this was the case. The implication was that the Canadian role was that of an honest broker.[21] On a visit to Moscow in the autumn of 1955, Pearson told the Soviet foreign minister that Canada was anxious to play the part of a peacemaker.[22] Later, in answer to a question in the House of Commons in March 1956, he maintained that "Canada will do its utmost to widen the area of agreement between the east and the west ... to bring about some measure, at least, of effective disarmament."[23] This image has some validity in that Pearson and his colleagues were deadly serious in their desire that the issues between the Soviet Union and the West be settled peacefully. John Holmes wrote that the consciousness of the necessity of a negotiated settlement was what continued throughout the Cold War to distinguish the Canadian approach from that of the United States.[24] This is certainly true of the arms talks. One reason for this attitude was that anti-communism was not so fierce and powerful a political element in Canada as it was in the United States. Another was that, protected by the American umbrella, Canadian officials were not nearly as obsessed with security as were those of the United States. Nor were they prey to the deep nationalist emotions which confrontation with the Soviet Union naturally evoked in the hearts of many American diplomats.

This emphasis on continuing to talk prompted several Canadian initiatives when a breakdown seemed likely. In the autumn of 1947, when it was obvious that the negotiations over the Baruch Plan had reached an impasse, Pearson insisted that they must continue. Nothing should be done to give the Soviet Union an excuse to leave the United Nations. In a world which was fast becoming sharply divided politically and ideologically, it remained the only institution which offered some promise for international reconciliation. Its break-up, Pearson believed, would be an unmitigated catastrophe. And there was always the hope that the USSR would come to its senses and co-operate with the West in controlling atomic energy. After the Soviet Union walked out of the AEC in January 1950, Pearson set to work immediately to find a way of maintaining the talks despite the continuing quarrel over the China seat. He was also anxious to explore whether the Soviet Union was ready to make any concessions on inspection and thus remove a formidable barrier to agreement. Then, in March 1955, when Gromyko showed bad faith in bargaining, External Affairs opposed an American move to break off the talks. Again, it adopted a much more positive attitude to the Soviet proposals of 16 November 1956 than did West Germany. In January 1957 it pressed Washington to give up any idea of a substantive resolution that was bound to be opposed by the Soviet Union and to settle for one that dealt only with procedure so as to enable the sub-committee talks to continue. It suggested that Canadian delegates to the United Nations "assist in making the prospect of negotiations attractive to the Soviet Union by doing what is possible to improve the atmosphere."[25] To prevent a souring of the negotiations in the spring of 1957, Canada was ready to accommodate the Soviet wish to discuss their proposals on troop reductions in Germany within the sub-committee. As well, Canada was uneasy with "tough" Western proposals on aerial inspection because they might weaken a promising Soviet resolve to negotiate seriously.

There were, however, remarkably few serious Canadian attempts to play the role of honest broker and find a compromise between the two sides. In 1946, McNaughton had pressed the Americans to stop insisting that the Soviet Union drop its right to veto any retribution if it should violate the atomic treaty. Nevertheless, in so doing, he made it clear that he continued to believe in the main elements of the Baruch Plan. External Affairs also made tentative attempts to persuade the Americans to clarify the conditions under which they would give up the atomic bomb. And, in April 1950, reacting to the Soviet atomic explosion of the previous September, Pearson sought to persuade senior American officials of the advantages of prohibiting the use of atomic bombs but without success. In April 1956, Robertson sought to bridge the gap between East and West with a set of proposals which were simply an endorsement of American positions, save for the calls for the limitation of atomic tests which were of no interest to the Soviet Union.

Looking back, John Holmes noted that there was a profound scepticism in External Affairs about the prospects for disarmament and suggested that "if there had been desperate conviction in Ottawa that a compromise proposal would have saved the discussions, then the attitude might have been different."[26] Given the great strategic advantages that flowed from the failure to reach an atomic agreement and remembering that the Canadian peace and disarmament movement of the early 1950s was particularly ineffective, it is difficult to believe that the government was greatly concerned about the lack of progress in the arms negotiations, or that it was very upset about that failure. Even if it had wished to, it would have been unable to reconcile the Soviet Union and the United States.

Canada's work in these negotiations was not altogether altruistic. It believed that its own security was very much at stake. Moreover the AEC and the Disarmament Commission, especially its sub-committee, were very prestigious bodies. Canada was the only small player to sit in consistently on a high level East-West diplomatic game in which Western security was the stake. In 1946 and 1947 there was always some chance that the Baruch Plan would be adopted; Canada would then have been on an international committee with enormous power over the vast field of atomic energy. The negotiations often required Canada to take the centre stage at the United Nations, presenting the impression of an energetic middle power using its diplomatic skills to achieve progress on disarmament or arms control. Such an image was no doubt gratifying to the government which was aware of how popular the picture of Canada as peacemaker was with Canadians. Then, too, the negotiations allowed Canada to co-operate with its Western allies enthusiastically on important diplomatic initiatives. No doubt it also helped build good will for Canada in the United States at a time when economic relations between the two countries were developing at an ever quickening pace.

PEARSON AND THE ARMS NEGOTIATIONS

In a column written for the *Toronto Star* in September 1957, when he was out of office, Pearson wrote that "no nation, however pacific its own policy may be, is willing to discard or reduce its weapons if it feels that this would deepen [its] fear and increase [its] insecurity." That anxiety, he went on to explain, could be removed or at least reduced, "by the solution of some of the major political problems that divide the two worlds."[27] Unfortunately this was not to be. During the decade under review, Pearson was confronted by a dilemma about global politics which he once expressed this way:

"I am not sure whether we can constructively cooperate with any communist society to the benefit of the people in this planet ... [but] if we believe that living together on some terms with these people is impossible then we believe in the inevitability of war."[28] He consistently maintained that the Soviet Union with its gigantic army could be constrained only by an enormously expanded Western defence. It is true that, in this view, Pearson echoed the American line, but he sincerely believed in what he was saying. Given his ideological bent and the nature of the Soviet regime, it is easy to see why he thought so. Under these conditions, it is difficult to believe that he thought massive disarmament a realistic possibility.

Yet Pearson's deepest impulse, both as a diplomat and as a liberal, was to search for some way of dealing peacefully with the USSR. "That assumption," wrote Holmes in retrospect, "that what was required was 'a negotiated settlement' was perhaps what continued throughout the Cold War to distinguish the Canadian approach from that of the United States, where the idea of negotiating with the devil rather than making him behave was unpopular."[29] In one of his last interviews as secretary of state for external affairs, Pearson advised the United States "to take advantage of every possible and practicable opportunity to negotiate differences with the Russians."[30] He had maintained this faith in conciliation despite the bellicose rhetoric of Dean Acheson and John Foster Dulles, not to speak of the McCarthyite mood that enveloped American politics for most of the years covered in this study. In retrospect, even if there was no settlement, this was Pearson's most positive contribution to the arms diplomacy of that era. Negotiation was in itself a confidence-building measure. It eased tensions in that it gave each side reason to hope that the other might be prepared to bargain seriously. That each side would have to justify its proposal before world opinion also worked to moderate its programme.

Pearson worried about the growth of nuclear arms and understood the vital importance of the negotiations, but he doubted that Canada could make a difference. The only original Canadian proposals were those on the limitation and registration of nuclear tests, and these were meant to appease India rather than to bring the United States and the Soviet Union together. It is true that from time to time he made some desultory moves. Thus, in 1954, he ordered a review of the Canadian disarmament positions in the light of the development of the hydrogen bomb but the results were meagre. That same year, along with Prime Minister St Laurent, he called for a report on the implications of nuclear weapons and missiles for Canadian defence with the idea of having it tabled in the House of Commons and available to the public. Unfortunately the chairman of the chiefs of staff did not comply on grounds that it would imperil his relationship with the Pentagon.[31] Apparently, Pearson did not insist. A year later he spoke of letting some fresh air into the subject of disarmament but was frustrated when he raised the matter in the NATO Council. Pearson was, after all, the spokesman for a minor power. Henry Kissinger has suggested that the mark of a great statesman is his ability to impose his will on the progress of history.[32] But to be effective, he needs the backing of a world power. Whatever his abilities, Pearson simply lacked the power to make his mark in any significant way on the actual nuclear negotiations. He therefore believed that his attention and energy should be devoted to other issues, ones on which Canada might have a real influence.

Although it is certainly true that within the actual negotiations there was little scope for Canadian initiative, there were some ways in which Pearson might have done something to improve – at least marginally – the political atmosphere in which the arms talks took place. In his memoirs, he wrote that "I was not so naïve as to think we could decisively, or even importantly, influence the policies of the Great Powers, but I hoped that we could influence the environment in which they were pursued."[33] Looking back, it is unfortunate that he did not make a greater effort to do this on three important issues.

First, Pearson's genuine fear of the will and capability of the Soviet Union for aggression prevented him from appreciating its security concerns. In his memoirs, Pearson claimed that Canada "recognized that the USSR had legitimate fears for its security."[34] It is true that at the peak of the Korean War and no doubt on the basis of Pearson's report, the cabinet concluded that the "Soviet Union and communist China were probably quite sincere in their fear of U.S. aggression since they had no contact with sober opinion in Washington."[35] But this was an exception, perhaps prompted by the possibility that the United States would use the atomic bomb in Korea. Otherwise, Pearson showed little public appreciation for Soviet apprehension about its security during the Cold War years. He sincerely believed that the Russians had nothing to worry about since he sensed – rightly – that both the Truman and Eisenhower administrations were firmly opposed to launching a pre-emptive strike. He seems not to have understood that the view from Moscow, where suspicion of Western intentions reigned supreme, differed sharply from that of Ottawa. Only in January 1955 did Pearson concede that "the Soviet people, and even certain Soviet leaders, may at times consider – sincerely consider – that they are threatened by the west."[36] This impression was very much strengthened after his personal conversations with Soviet leaders in the autumn of 1955. But, unfortunately, he acknowledged Soviet concerns only a few times after his return from Moscow. It may be that this potential empathy for Soviet worries over their security was swept away by his anger at their threats over Suez and their occupation of Hungary. Thus, Pearson took little action to educate the Western public that Soviet defence policy was driven by security concerns as genuine and as well founded as those of the West.

Second, Pearson's ideological and political positions make his support for German reunification understandable, but it is possible, with hindsight, to regret that he was ready to forgo calls for an agreement on reducing arms to pursue what was in the circumstances of superpower rivalry at that time an impossible goal. In December 1956 he reported to the cabinet about the possibility of a belt of neutral nations across the centre of Europe including a unified Germany. "The price for this would be the withdrawal of troops both by Russia and N.A.T.O." This arrangement would not be possible, however, without a settlement with the USSR.[37] In fact, three years earlier Dulles had approached Eisenhower with the possibility of making "a spectacular effort to relax world tensions and execute such mutual withdrawals of Red Army forces and U.S. forces abroad" as would permit the stabilization of NATO and of West German forces, "at a level compatible with budgetary relief," and the creation of a "strategic reserve" in the United States. The result would be a "broad zone of restricted armament in Europe, with Soviets withdrawn from satellites and the U.S. from Europe."[38] In 1957, in a series of BBC broadcasts, George Kennan caused a considerable stir by proposing that the United States and the Soviet Union withdraw their armies and nuclear weapons from central Europe and that Germany should be neutralized, largely disarmed, and unified. Was there any real possibility of an arrangement which would have sharply reduced the military presence in central Europe? After all, Khrushchev had offered to withdraw troops from Germany if the Americans would do the same. But by then neither the United States nor West Germany was at all interested in exploring this possibility – but neither was Pearson.[39]

Third, after the outbreak of the Korean War the Americans began a conventional and nuclear arms build-up to deter any potential Soviet attack. Since the United States wished to demonstrate to the USSR its determination to prevail in any conflict, there was no point at which its strategic planners were ever satisfied that their country had enough arms. The only constraint was financial. Pearson agreed with this stance. So great was his desire to ensure American nuclear supremacy over the Soviet Union that he agreed to policies about which he wrote: "Your security becomes their insecurity. So they in turn seek safety in increased arms. A vicious circle commences which in the past has caused untold misery and destruction and might now, if we cannot cut through it, cause mankind's extinction."[40] It is a pity that Pearson did not take more seriously his own memorandum of November 1945 in which he warned of the tragic consequences of atomic rivalry. Perhaps because there was no articulate peace movement of significant proportions, Pearson's efforts to raise the level of public concern about disarmament and arms control were not as extensive as they might have been. They did not come close to those of Howard Green, the secretary of state for external affairs in the Diefenbaker government. Yet up to 1957 the only force which might have caused the superpowers to come to some sort of agreement would have been an aroused public opinion in all countries including Canada.

In later years Pearson complained that the revisionists were unfair to criticize statesmen like himself on the basis of retrospective wisdom. He might have added that historians generally find it easier to say where their hero went wrong than to indicate what he should have done in his specific circumstances. Yet events have shown that the Soviet Union had legitimate security concerns, that the failure to reunify Germany was not a terrible catastrophe, and that a continued arms race put the world into ever greater danger of obliteration, should political relations between the two superpowers have suddenly deteriorated (as they did in the Cuban missiles crisis of October 1962). Pearson certainly had some inkling that the Russians were concerned about the possibility of the long-range bombers of the United States delivering a first strike, that there was an alternative to German reunification, and that trying to halt the arms race by increasing the nuclear strength of the West was a futile and counterproductive policy. No doubt he failed to speak up because of his strong loyalty to the Western cause as well as the political trouble he might get into if he crossed the Americans on a substantial political and security issue. He was the secretary of state for external affairs in a government headed by a prime minister who was a resolute opponent of the Soviet Union. As an ambitious politician he would have been reluctant to upset needlessly St Laurent whose support might be useful in the future.

The Pearson era has been called the golden age of Canadian diplomacy. Is this flattering description borne out in Canada's work for disarmament and arms control in the late 1940s and the 1950s? In many ways, yes. The technical competence of External Affairs was very high. It was clear that its goal was to build Western unity, and in these negotiations it worked efficiently towards that end. But in all these activities Canadian diplomats were still working within the familiar framework of the North Atlantic alliance.

The arms negotiations, however, brought Canada into direct contact with its political enemy – the Soviet Union. How well did its diplomacy bear up in the face of a challenge of a different order? Some foreign observers were not very impressed. Jean Klein described the Canadian contribution as timid, and Alva Myrdal wrote that within the AEC "Canada remained inactive on the burning issues."[41] It is difficult to disagree with this judgment. To be fair, since it was not a great power Canada's effect on arms negotiations was bound to be marginal. The most positive feature of its policy was the insistence that the West continue to negotiate. At the same time, its views on substance, like those of the United States, were formulated on the assumption that Western Europe was in imminent danger of a Soviet attack. It followed, Pearson believed, that the United States needed all the military hardware it could acquire. Here he was mistaken. No one can blame Western politicians including Pearson for being prudent and maintaining an adequate defence. But there is no evidence that the USSR ever intended to attack Western Europe. Overemphasizing the Soviet military threat led to a lack of concern about the escalation of the arms race. If Pearson had been a little less hawkish, he might have come to advocate some measures for slowing it down – a ban on the testing of nuclear weapons, for example.

The end of the Cold War, however, has justified some of Pearson's views on the Soviet Union. He always maintained that the totalitarian nature of the Soviet Union and its secrecy created an understandable suspicion and fear on the part of the West. He was right to maintain that only if the Soviet Union became an open society could an era of reconciliation begin.

Pearson's outlook on the Cold War was the conventional one of Western politicians of the 1950s. He seemed to regard the state of relations between East and West as one of war, except that no military battles were being fought and no one was being killed. Thus, he acted on the assumption that the West was fighting what has been called "an imaginary war"[42] against the Soviet Union. His pre-war and postwar experience and ideological outlook convinced him that the only alternative to a Western nuclear build-up was to allow Western Europe to become open to possible Soviet conquest.

The convergence of extreme East-West enmity with ever improving nuclear weapons created a dilemma of the most serious proportions for which there existed no precedent and to which there simply was no satisfactory and logical solution. For Lester Pearson – as for other statesmen – an escape from this agonizing choice would have required an easing of the Cold War. Unfortunately, with the exception of a brief spurt at Geneva in the summer of 1955, there were very few signs of this happening in the 1950s.

Key Actors
and Meetings

SECRETARIES OF STATE
FOR EXTERNAL AFFAIRS

William Lyon Mackenzie King October 1935–September 1946
Louis St Laurent   September 1946–September 1948
Lester B. Pearson   September 1948–June 1957

UNDER-SECRETARIES OF STATE
FOR EXTERNAL AFFAIRS

Norman A. Robertson   June 1941–September 1946
Lester B. Pearson   September 1946–September 1948
Escott M. Reid (acting) September 1948–March 1949
Arnold D.P. Heeney   March 1949–April 1952
L. Dana Wilgress   June 1952–August 1953
H. Hume Wrong   August 1953–January 1954
R.A. MacKay (acting)   January 1954–August 1954
Jules Léger   August 1954–October 1958

PERMANENT REPRESENTATIVES OF CANADA
TO THE UNITED NATIONS

A.G.L. McNaughton   January 1948–February 1950
John W. Holmes (acting) January–June 1950
R.G. Riddell   June 1950–March 1951

David Johnson   October 1951–June 1955
R.A. MacKay   June 1955–January 1958

AMBASSADORS OF CANADA
TO THE UNITED STATES

Lester B. Pearson   January 1945–September 1946
H. Hume Wrong   September 1946–July 1953
Arnold D.P. Heeney   August 1953–May 1957

IMPORTANT MEETINGS OF UNITED NATIONS
BODIES ON ATOMIC ISSUES

Meeting	*Canada's Spokesman*
Atomic Energy Commission	
14 June–31 December 1946	A.G.L. McNaughton
General Assembly	
29 October–14 December 1946	L. St Laurent
Atomic Energy Commission	
10 March–11 September 1947	A.G.L. McNaughton
Atomic Energy Commission	
19 January–7 May 1948	A.G.L. McNaughton
General Assembly	
30 September–4 November 1948	A.G.L. McNaughton
Atomic Energy Commission	
18 February–29 July 1949	A.G.L. McNaughton
Six-Power Consultation	
9 August–29 October 1949	A.G.L. McNaughton
General Assembly	
23 September–23 November 1949	L.B. Pearson
Committee of Twelve	
February to December 1951	J. George
General Assembly	
19 November–19 December 1951	L.B. Pearson
Disarmament Commission	
1952–54	D. Johnson
Disarmament Commission Sub-Committee	
13 May–22 June 1954	N. Robertson
General Assembly	
11–27 October 1954	P. Martin
Disarmament Commission Sub-Committee	
25 February–18 May 1955	D. Johnson

Disarmament Commission Sub-Committee
29 August–7 October 1955 — P. Martin
General Assembly
30 November–12 December 1955 — P. Martin
Disarmament Commission Sub-Committee
19 March–4 May 1956 — N. Robertson
Disarmament Commission
3–16 July 1956 — P. Martin
General Assembly
January 1957 — L.B. Pearson
Disarmament Commission Sub-Committee
18 March–6 September 1957 — D. Johnson

BIOGRAPHICAL NOTES

JAMES GEORGE (1918–). Joined the Department of External Affairs in April 1945. He was appointed deputy permanent representative to the United Nations in June 1951. Returning to Ottawa in March 1955 he took charge of the United Nations European Division. He went on to a distinguished diplomatic career, becoming high commissioner to India and ambassador to Iran and to Kuwait, Oman, Bahrain, the United Arab Emirates, and Qatar. Since his retirement in December 1977, he has been active on environmental and development issues. In 1984 he became president of the Sadat Peace Foundation.

ARNOLD D.P. HEENEY (1902–1970). A successful lawyer in Montreal, he was invited to become principal secretary to Prime Minister King in 1938. In 1940 he was named clerk of the Privy Council and secretary to the Cabinet. From 1949 to 1952 he was under-secretary of state for external affairs. He was Canada's ambassador to the United States from August 1953 to May 1957. Subsequently, he was head of the Canadian sections of the International Joint Commission and the Permanent Joint Board on Defence. His memoirs, *The Things That Are Caesar's*, appeared in 1972.

JOHN W. HOLMES (1910–1988). Joined the Department of External Affairs in 1943. In 1948 he was attached to the Canadian delegation to the United Nations. He returned to Ottawa a year later to head the department's United Nations Division. In 1953 he was appointed assistant under-secretary of state for external affairs responsible for United Nations, Far Eastern, and Commonwealth affairs. He remained in this position until his resignation in 1960.

He became executive director (and subsequently director general and counsellor) of the Canadian Institute of International Affairs in 1960. He wrote a number of books, including two volumes of essays, *The Better Part of Valour* (1970) and *Canada: A Middle-Aged Power* (1976), and the two-volume work, *The Shaping of Peace: Canada and the Search for World Order, 1943–1957* (1979–82).

GEORGE IGNATIEFF (1913–1989). Joined the Department of External Affairs in 1940, and in 1946 was appointed External Affairs adviser to General McNaughton. In 1949 he went to the embassy in Washington as counsellor and was chargé d'affaires for a brief time in 1953. In 1955 he became chief of the Defence Liaison Division in the department, and he accompanied Pearson to the Soviet Union in the autumn of 1955. He was subsequently ambassador to Yugoslavia, to NATO, and at the United Nations. After leaving the department he was provost of Trinity College, Toronto, 1972–79, and chancellor of the University of Toronto, 1980–86. His memoirs, *The Making of a Peacemonger*, appeared in 1985.

DAVID M. JOHNSON (b. 1902). Entered External Affairs in February 1947. He was secretary to the Permanent Joint Board on Defence 1947–48. He became Canada's permanent representative to the United Nations in October 1951, and it was in this capacity that he represented Canada in the Disarmament Commission meetings. He was Canada's ambassador to the USSR, 1956–60. He retired in January 1960 to practise law.

JULES LÉGER (1913–1980). Joined the Department of External Affairs in 1940. He was twice under-secretary of state for external affairs, from 1954 to 1958 and from 1968 to 1972. He was ambassador to France, 1964–68. In 1974 he was installed as governor general of Canada, a post in which he served with great distinction until 1979.

R.A. MACKAY (1894–1979). A professor of government and political science at Dalhousie University (Halifax), 1927–47, he was a wartime assistant in External Affairs, formally joining the department in 1947. In 1952 he became assistant under-secretary of state for external affairs, rising to deputy under-secretary in January 1954, and finally associate under-secretary in August 1954. He was Canada's permanent representative to the United Nations, 1955–58. He retired from the department in March 1962 and taught at Carleton University (Ottawa) until 1972.

A.G.L. (ANDY) MCNAUGHTON (1887–1966). Trained as an engineer, he went overseas with the Canadian Expeditionary Force in 1914 and at the end of the war was commanding the Canadian Corps artillery. In the Second World War he came to command the Canadian army but resigned in December 1943. He served as minister of national defence, 1944–1945. In 1946 he was named the Canadian representative to the United Nations Atomic Energy Commission and in 1948 appointed permanent delegate to the United Nations. He resigned these positions in 1950, becoming chairman of the Canadian sections of the Permanent Joint Board on Defence (1950–59) and the International Joint Commission (1950–62).

PAUL MARTIN (1903–1992). First elected to the House of Commons in 1935, he entered the cabinet in 1945 as secretary of state and in 1946 became minister of national health and welfare. He undertook diplomatic assignments for both the King and St Laurent governments, and it was in this capacity that he participated in the disarmament negotiations at various times. In 1955 he was instrumental in the negotiations which allowed for the expansion of United Nations membership. He subsequently became secretary of state for external affairs (1963–68), government leader in the Senate (1968–74), and high commissioner to the United Kingdom (1975–79). He published several volumes of memoirs.

LESTER B. PEARSON (1897–1972). Joined the Department of External Affairs in 1928 and in 1935 was sent to London as first secretary in the Canadian high commission. Seven years later he went to the legation in Washington as second-in-command and in 1945 was named Canada's ambassador to the United States. In September 1946 he returned to Ottawa to become under-secretary of state for external affairs. He entered politics and as secretary of state for external affairs from September 1948 until June 1957 set Canada's policies on disarmament issues. Elected leader of the Liberal party in January 1957, he was prime minister from 1963 to 1968. The first volume of his memoirs, *Mike*, appeared in 1972; the second and third volumes were compiled from materials on which he had been working at the time of his death.

NORMAN A. ROBERTSON (1904–1968). Joined the Department of External Affairs in 1929. He was under-secretary of state for external affairs from 1941 to 1946 and went on to be high commissioner to the United Kingdom from 1946 to 1949 and again from 1952 to 1957. During this second term in Britain, he represented

Canada at meetings of the Disarmament Commission in 1954 and the sub-committee in 1956. From 1958 to 1964 he was again under-secretary of state for external affairs. He was subsequently a professor at Carleton University (Ottawa).

H. HUME WRONG (1894–1954). In 1928 Wrong joined the Canadian legation in Washington as first secretary. He spent the next eighteen years in various diplomatic positions before being named Canada's ambassador to the United States in 1946. In 1953 he returned to Ottawa to become under-secretary of state for external affairs but became ill before he was able to take up these duties.

Notes

ABBREVIATIONS

DCER *Documents on Canadian External Relations*
 DEA Department of External Affairs
FRUS *Foreign Relations of the United States*
  NA National Archives of Canada

INTRODUCTION

1 Holmes, *The Better Part of Valour*, 5.
2 See, for example: Minifie, *Peacemaker or Powder-Monkey*; K. McNaught, "From Colony to Satellite," in Clarkson, ed., *An Independent Foreign Policy for Canada?*; Granatstein, *Canadian Foreign Policy since 1945*; and Nossal, *The Politics of Canadian Foreign Policy*.
3 Holmes, *The Better Part of Valour*, 216.
4 Interview with Jacques Monet, who is writing a biography of Jules Léger.
5 Granatstein, *The Ottawa Men*; Granatstein, *A Man of Influence: Norman A. Robertson*; Eayrs, *In Defence of Canada*, introduction to vol. 3; English, *Shadow of Heaven: The Life of Lester Pearson*; Heeney, *The Things That Are Caesar's*; Swettenham, *McNaughton*; Ritchie, *Diplomatic Passport*; Reid, *Radical Mandarin*; Ignatieff, *The Making of a Peacemonger*.
6 Martin, *A Very Public Life*, vol. 2.
7 Ritchie, *Storm Signals*, 162.
8 See, for example, Holmes, *The Shaping of Peace*; also English, *The Worldly Years*.

CHAPTER ONE

1 Quoted in Lundestad, "Moralism, Presentism, Exceptionalism," 528.
2 Schlesinger, "Origins of the Cold War," 36.
3 Gaddis, "The Emerging Post-Revisionist Synthesis on the Origins of the Cold War," 171–90.
4 Ibid., 176–81; also see Taubman, *Stalin's American Policy*, 8–9. For a review of early American Cold War literature, see Lundestad, "Moralism, Presentism, Exceptionalism."
5 Quoted in Gaddis, *The United States and the Origins of the Cold War*, 322.
6 *FRUS 1950*, 1:237.
7 Quoted by McGeehan in *The German Rearmament Question*, 230.
8 Shulman, *Stalin's Foreign Policy Reappraised*, 185.
9 Quoted in Ambrose, *Eisenhower*, 2:373.
10 Ibid., 2:91.
11 Quoted in Bechhoefer, *Postwar Negotiations for Arms Control*, 253.
12 Quoted in *Bulletin of the Atomic Scientists*, 10 (Feb. 1954): 106.
13 Quoted in Ambrose, *Rise to Globalism*, 76.
14 Quoted in Thomas, *Armed Truce*, 672.
15 Quoted in Melvyn P. Leffler, "The United States and the Strategic Imperatives of Reconstruction Policy in Europe 1945–1949," unpublished paper, 26.
16 Quoted in Stursberg, *Pearson and the American Dilemma*, 176.
17 It should be noted that the number of personnel in a division of the American army was three to four times greater than in a division in the Soviet army or in the armies of the European allies.
18 Barnet, "Annals of Diplomacy," 100. Looking back, Paul Nitze observed that "it is untrue that we thought the Russians were about to attack ... our prime concern had remained the economic situation in Europe": quoted in Kaldor, *The Imaginary War*, 90.
19 Quoted in McGeehan, *The German Rearmament Question*, 15.
20 Quoted in May, "The American Commitment to Germany," 448.
21 Quoted in LaFeber, "NATO and the Korean War," 465.
22 In contrast to the Plevan Plan, the EDC would allow German divisions rather than small combat teams in the new army: McGeehan, *The German Rearmament Question*, 206.
23 Quoted in Prittie, *Konrad Adenauer*, 168.
24 Acheson, *Present at the Creation*, 650.
25 Huntington, *The Common Defense*, 62.
26 Quoted in Osgood, *NATO*, 104.
27 Graebner, *The National Security*, 287.
28 Mueller, *Retreat from Doomsday*, 110.
29 Rosenberg, "The Origins of Overkill," 23.

30 York, *Making Weapons, Talking Peace*, 194.

31 Quoted in Holloway, *The Soviet Union and the Arms Race*, 20.

32 McGeehan, *The German Rearmament Question*, 110.

33 Quoted in Newhouse, *War and Peace in the Nuclear Age*, 122.

34 Quoted in Donovan, *Tumultuous Years*, 153.

35 Quoted in Bundy, *Danger and Survival*, 198.

36 Quoted in Malcolmson, *Beyond Nuclear Thinking*, 8.

37 Herken, *Counsels of War*, 66.

38 Dulles, "Challenge and Response in United States Policy," 31.

39 The foreign secretary in the postwar Labour government, Ernest Bevin, justified this decision in the following words: "We have got to have this ... I don't mind for myself but I don't want any other Foreign Secretary of this country to be talked at or by a Secretary of State in the United States as I have just had in my discussion with Mr Byrnes. We have got to have this thing over here whatever it costs ... We've got to have the bloody Union Jack flying on top of it." Prime Minister Attlee agreed with him. Quoted in Kaldor, *The Imaginary War*, 100.

40 Bundy, *Danger and Survival*, 229.

41 Quester, *Nuclear Diplomacy*, 7.

42 Anonymous, "The Balance of Military Power," 25. For Acheson as author, see Osgood, *NATO*, 381, and McGeehan, *The German Rearmament Question*, 100.

43 Holloway, *The Soviet Union and the Arms Race*, 36.

44 Quoted in ibid., 27.

45 Kissinger, *Nuclear Weapons and Foreign Policy*, 364–72.

46 Garthoff, "The Death of Stalin," 10.

47 Michael Carver, "Conventional Warfare in the Nuclear Age," in Paret, ed., *Makers of Modern Strategy*, 779.

48 Newhouse, *War and Peace in the Nuclear Age*, 23.

49 Quoted in Bundy, *Danger and Survival*, 256.

50 Appleby, "Eisenhower and Arms Control," 58–9; Gaddis, *Strategies of Containment*, 150.

51 Osgood, *The Nuclear Dilemma in American Strategic Thought*, 12.

52 Bundy, *Danger and Survival*, 565, 252.

53 Quoted in Rearden, *The Evolution of American Strategic Doctrine*, 39.

54 Bundy, *Danger and Survival*, 247.

55 Osgood, *NATO*, 114.

56 May, "The American Commitment to Germany," 432.

57 Osgood, *NATO*, 119, 146.

58 Quoted in Eayrs, *Canada in World Affairs, 1955–1957*, 55.

59 Quoted in Kissinger, *Nuclear Weapons and Foreign Policy*, 385, 378.

60 Quoted in Freedman, *The Evolution of Nuclear Strategy*, 146.

61 Huntington, *The Common Defense*, 119.
62 Holloway, *The Soviet Union and the Arms Race*, 33.
63 Huntington, *The Common Defense*, 120.
64 Gowing, *Independence and Deterrence*, 1:72.
65 Quoted in Herken, *The Winning Weapon*, 328.
66 Quoted in Dinerstein, *War and the Soviet Union*, 117.
67 LaFeber, *America, Russia, and the Cold War*, 197.
68 Bundy, *Danger and Survival*, 199–200.
69 Quoted in Gaddis, *Strategies of Containment*, 81.
70 Appleby, "Eisenhower and Arms Control," 131.
71 Quoted in the *New Yorker*, 17 Feb. 1986, 100.
72 Quoted in Freedman, *The Evolution of Nuclear Strategy*, 51.
73 Frye, "Disarmament Comes Back to the General Assembly," 333.
74 Howard, *The Causes of Wars*, 20.
75 Quoted in Bechhoefer, *Postwar Negotiations for Arms Control*, 253.
76 Quoted in the *Globe and Mail* (Toronto), 29 Sept. 1989.
77 Ambrose, *Eisenhower*, 2: 107.
78 Quoted in Gaddis, *Strategies of Containment*, 173.
79 Quoted in Divine, *Blowing on the Wind*, 11.
80 Appleby, "Eisenhower and Arms Control," 395.
81 Shevchenko, *Breaking with Moscow*, 83.
82 DEA, 50271–C–40, 23 May 1957, no. 1208, 2.
83 Gaddis, *Strategies of Containment*, 193.
84 Hoffmann, "The Perfect In-and-Outer," 14.
85 Newhouse, *War and Peace in the Nuclear Age*, 113.
86 *FRUS 1952–1954*, 5(part 1): 531.

CHAPTER TWO

1 Canada, House of Commons, *Debates*, 31 Aug. 1950, 90. Geoffrey Pearson doubts that his father ever read Marx seriously. See Gellman, "Lester Pearson, Canadian Foreign Policy, and the Quest for a World Order," 93.
2 Quoted in English, *Shadow of Heaven*, 312.
3 Quoted in ibid., 257–8.
4 Quoted in ibid., 264.
5 Granatstein, *The Ottawa Men*, 234.
6 Quoted in English, *Shadow of Heaven*, 383.
7 NA, Pearson to Robertson, RG 25, access no. 83/84/268, box 245, file (4901–40), pt. 3, 13 March 1946.
8 NA, MG 26, J1, vol. 411, 37385–6.
9 *DCER*, 12(1946): 1671.

10 English, *Shadow of Heaven*, 322.

11 Quoted in Eayrs, *In Defence of Canada*, 4: 11.

12 Page and Munton, "Canadian Images of the Cold War," 581, 584, 599.

13 Spencer, *Canada in World Affairs, 1946–1949*, 79.

14 Kent, "Rising in Favour," 30.

15 Pearson, *Words and Occasions*, 70, 72, 75.

16 *Debates*, 14 Jan. 1957, 175.

17 House of Commons, Standing Committee on External Affairs, *Minutes of Proceedings and Evidence*, 22nd Parl, 3rd sess, no. 1, 12 April 1956, 19.

18 Pearson, *Words and Occasions*, 130.

19 DEA, Statement and Speeches 50/16, 29 April 1950, 5, 2.

20 *Debates*, 31 Aug. 1950, 90.

21 *FRUS 1948*, 3:239.

22 *Debates*, 12 May 1952, 2101.

23 Pearson, "The Development of Canadian Foreign Policy," 18.

24 Pearson, *Words and Occasions*, 112.

25 NA, RG 25, vol. 2412, file 102–AZW–40, pt. 2, Address to Iroquois United Church, 25 May 1952, 3.

26 Pearson, *Words and Occasions*, 112.

27 Ibid., 73.

28 *Debates*, 3 March 1950, 430.

29 DEA, Statements and Speeches 51/46, 12 Nov. 1951, 3.

30 DEA, 50271–A–40, no. D–311, "Disarmament Commission," 2 May 1952, found with memo by Department of National Defence, 26 June 1952, 1.

31 DEA, Statements and Speeches 50/48, 15 Nov. 1950, 4, 5.

32 Pearson, *Words and Occasions*, 124.

33 *Debates*, 3 March 1950, 430.

34 DEA, Statements and Speeches 54/47, 8 Nov. 1954, 1, 5.

35 Ignatieff, *The Making of a Peacemonger*, 137.

36 NA, Cabinet Conclusions 1946–1957, 16 Nov. 1955, 12–13.

37 Pearson, *Words and Occasions*, 138, 139.

38 Standing Committee on External Affairs, *Minutes*, 22nd Parl, 3rd sess, no. 1, 12 April 1956, 10.

39 DEA, Statements and Speeches 57/26, 4 April 1957, 7.

40 NA, MG 26, N1, vol. 65, Pearson to N.S.E. Kelley, editor of the Halifax *Chronicle-Herald*, 3 July 1950.

41 English, *Shadow of Heaven*, 264.

42 DEA, Statements and Speeches 52/15, 21 March 1952, 17.

43 Pearson, *Mike*, 1: 91.

44 English, *Shadow of Heaven*, 198.

45 For a thoughtful examination of how committed Pearson was in practice to collective security, see Gellman, "Lester B. Pearson, Collective Security, and the World Order Tradition."

46 Pearson, *Words and Occasions*, 44.

47 Ibid., 42, 55.

48 Quoted in Eayrs, *In Defence of Canada*, 3: 35.

49 Quoted in English, *Shadow of Heaven*, 239.

50 NA, MG 26, N1, vol. 65, Wrong to Pearson, 7 Feb. 1950.

51 Pearson, "The Development of Canadian Foreign Policy," 25.

52 English, *Shadow of Heaven*, 313.

53 DEA, Statements and Speeches 50/24, 18 June 1950, 2.

54 DEA, Statements and Speeches 50/44, 30 Oct. 1950, 3.

55 DEA, Statements and Speeches 55/21, 1 June 1955, 2.

56 *Debates*, 16 Nov. 1949, 1836.

57 Spencer, *Canada in World Affairs, 1946–1949*, 291.

58 *FRUS 1951*, 2: 891–2.

59 Acheson, *Present at the Creation*, 70.

60 DEA, Statements and Speeches 52/26, 30 June 1952, 5.

61 NA, MG 26, J4, vol. 421, File Privy Council Office Cabinet (Jan.-April), doc. 597, 27 Jan. 1948, "Statement for the Guidance of the Canadian Permanent Delegate to the United Nations and Representative on the Security Council," 1–8.

62 Pearson, *Mike*, 2: 160.

63 NA, MG 26, N1, vol. 2, Pearson to Lower, 12 Oct. 1950.

64 Bothwell and Kilbourn, *C.D. Howe*, 236.

65 Pearson, *Words and Occasions*, 105–7.

66 Ibid., 86.

67 DEA, Statements and Speeches 56/28, 15 Nov. 1956, 5.

68 Quoted in Eayrs, *In Defence of Canada*, 4: 250.

69 DEA, Statements and Speeches 53/17, 15 April 1953, 6.

70 Ross, *In the Interests of Peace*, 45.

71 NA, RG 2, vol. 223, file 1–60–1, "Memorandum by Mr Pearson Regarding Talks in London and Paris on NATO Defence Programmes and Strategy," 22 Sept. 1952, 33.

72 Eayrs, *In Defence of Canada*, 4: 252.

73 Osgood, *NATO*, 388.

74 NA, MG 26, N1, vol. 65, Memo of Discussion between Dulles and Pearson, 15 Feb. 1953.

75 Pearson, *Words and Occasions*, 146.

76 North Atlantic Treaty Organization, *Facts and Figures* (Brussels: NATO Information Services 1984), 276.

77 Quoted in Holmes, *The Shaping of Peace*, 2: 247.

78 Pearson, "Where Canada Stands in the World Crisis," 7.

79 See *Time*, 5 March 1984, 27.
80 *Debates*, 21 April 1955, 3065.
81 Stursburg, *Pearson and the American Dilemma*, 93–4.
82 NA, MG 26, N1, vol. 65, 2 May 1951, 1.
83 Pearson, "Straight Talk from Mike Pearson," 9.
84 Pearson, *Mike*, 2: 181.
85 DEA, Statements and Speeches 53/50, Dec. 1953, 3.
86 *Debates*, 29 Jan. 1954, 1590.
87 Holmes, *The Shaping of Peace*, 2: 196.
88 Cited in DEA, Statements and Speeches 55/14, 21 April 1955, 9.
89 Holmes, *Life with Uncle*, 33.
90 For more on Pearson and the integration of West Germany into NATO, see Eayrs, *In Defence of Canada*, 4: 359–63.
91 *DCER*, 12 (1946):1721–5; Smith, *Diplomacy of Fear*, 177.
92 For an extensive discussion of Arctic defence, see Jockel, *No Boundaries Upstairs* and Eayrs, *In Defence of Canada*, 3: chap. 6.
93 DEA, Statements and Speeches 55/21, 1 June 1955, 8.
94 Jockel, *No Boundaries Upstairs*, 118–29.
95 Davy, "Canada's Role in the Disarmament Negotiations," 306.
96 NA, MG 26, J1, vol. 389, "Canadian Memorandum on Atomic Warfare," 8 Nov. 1945, 349940.
97 Pearson, *Words and Occasions*, 67.
98 *Debates*, 20 Jan. 1955, 362.
99 DEA, Statements and Speeches 50/51, 5 Dec. 1950, 4.
100 NA, MG 26, N1, vol. 4, Pearson to Wrong, 24 May 1951.
101 DEA, Statements and Speeches 51/17, 20 April 1951, 2.
102 Pearson, *Democracy in World Politics*, 22–3.
103 *Debates*, 3 March 1950, 429.
104 Ibid., 29 Jan. 1954, 1588.
105 See Freedman, *The Evolution of Nuclear Strategy*, 125.
106 *Debates*, 31 March 1954, 3540.
107 DEA, Statements and Speeches 54/47, 8 Nov. 1954, 4.
108 DEA, 50115-P-40, Pearson's Memorandum for the prime minister, "United States Defence Policy," 2 Feb. 1954. This memorandum is reproduced in Eayrs, *In Defence of Canada*, 4: 379–82.
109 DEA, Statements and Speeches 54/16, 16 March 1954, 6.
110 Eayrs, *In Defence of Canada*, 4: 260.
111 Pearson, *Democracy in World Politics*, 18–19.
112 DEA, Statements and Speeches 54/41, 23 Sept. 1954, 2–3.
113 Kennan, *The Nuclear Delusion*, 6–7.
114 Quoted in Holmes, *The Shaping of Peace*, 2: 33.
115 Thomson, *Louis St Laurent*, 444.
116 Pearson, *Mike*, 2: 238.

117 Quoted in Eayrs, *Canada in World Affairs, 1955–1957*, 8.
118 Ignatieff, *The Making of a Peacemonger*, 126. Ignatieff went on to suggest that the St Laurent-Pearson combination "was every bit as important for Canada's foreign policy as the Macdonald-Cartier partnership was for Confederation."
119 *Debates*, 6 March 1952, 177.
120 Eayrs, *In Defence of Canada*, 4: 273.
121 See, for example DEA, Statements and Speeches 51/17, 20 April 1951, and Socknat, *Witness against War*, 295.
122 *FRUS 1951*, 1: 847, 846.
123 DEA, 50271–A–40, "Memo for UN Division on Banning of Nuclear Tests," 20 Jan. 1956.
124 Holmes, *The Shaping of Peace*, 2: 294.

CHAPTER THREE

1 Gowing, *Independence and Deterrence*, 1: 8.
2 C.J. Mackenzie, president of the National Research Council, believed that if the Commonwealth co-operated, it could build an atomic bomb (NA, 201(s), vol. 1, "Canada's Position in the Development of Atomic Energy," 29 Oct. 1945, 3–4. Politically this was impossible however. Prime Minister King rejected any united Commonwealth defence projects on principle.
3 *New York Times*, 21 July 1949.
4 Ambrose, "Canada Becomes a Potential Nth Country," 150.
5 Probably some $1.5 billion would have been required: ibid., 193.
6 Eayrs, *In Defence of Canada*, 3: 276.
7 Pickersgill and Forster, eds., *The Mackenzie King Record*, 2: 447.
8 Eayrs, *In Defence of Canada*, 3: 276.
9 NA, MG 26, J1, vol. 389, Pearson to Wrong, 2 Oct. 1945.
10 *FRUS 1945*, 2: 48–50.
11 NA, MG 26, J1, vol. 389, "Canadian Memorandum on Atomic Warfare," 8 Nov. 1945.
12 Eayrs, *In Defence of Canada*, 3: 379.
13 Bundy, *Danger and Survival*, 658.
14 Ibid., 138.
15 Ibid., 148.
16 Canada, House of Commons, *Debates*, 15 Nov. 1945, 2133. The complete statement is reproduced in the *Debates*.
17 Herken, *The Winning Weapon*, 64.
18 Holmes, *The Shaping of Peace*, 1: 207.
19 *Debates*, 17 Dec. 1945, 3637.
20 Ibid., 3646.

21 *FRUS 1945*, 2: 78–80.
22 Herken, *The Winning Weapon*, 67.
23 NA, MG 26, J1, vol. 389, WA–6431, 28 Dec. 1945.
24 Bundy, *Danger and Survival*, 150. For a description of McNaughton at the United Nations, see Ignatieff, "General A.G.L. McNaughton."
25 Quoted in Swettenham, *McNaughton*, 1: 266.
26 Holmes, *The Shaping of Peace*, 2: 46.
27 Powaski, *March to Armageddon*, 41. For more on the Acheson-Lilienthal Report, see Hewlett and Anderson, *The New World*, 1: 533–49.
28 See Gowing, *Independence and Deterrence*, 1: 88.
29 Oppenheimer, "The International Control of Atomic Energy," 2, 3.
30 Hewlett and Anderson, *The New World*, 1: 554.
31 NA, MG 26, J1, vol. 411, Pearson to Robertson, 5 April 1946.
32 After a visit there, John Starnes, secretary to the Advisory Panel on Atomic Energy, wrote: "I do not see how controls can possibly succeed unless there is some form of International Authority responsible for the design and construction of the plants and the production of fissionable material ... The concept of being able to effectively control the production of fissionable materials by an international body of inspectors is impossible ... there are many stages where 'cheating' can occur ... even at a small plant like Chalk River ... they would need a minimum of 20 or 30 *trained* inspectors ... working on 24 hour basis." NA, RG 2/18, access no. 83–84/16, box F, file R–100–A, vol. 1, 1946, Starnes to Ignatieff, 6 Nov. 1946.
33 NA, RG 25, A12, vol. 2118, file 433/1, vol. 2, Ignatieff to Holmes, 17 May 1946.
34 *DCER*, 12 (1946): 446.
35 Ibid., 425.
36 Ibid., 443–4.
37 Hewlett and Anderson, *The New World*, 1: 577–9.
38 Quoted in Bundy, *Danger and Survival*, 167.
39 *New York Herald-Tribune*, 20 June 1946, 25.
40 *DCER*, 12 (1946): 451.
41 Holmes, *The Shaping of Peace*, 2: 47.
42 *FRUS 1946*, 1: 984.
43 Bundy, *Danger and Survival*, 165.
44 Acheson, *Present at the Creation*, 155.
45 NA, RG 25, access no. 89–90/029, file 201–B(s), vol. 2, 18 June 1946.
46 NA, RG 2/18, vol. 114, no. 225, 18 June 1946.
47 Ibid., Atom no. 10, 17 June 1946.
48 Ibid., WA–2496, 18 June 1946.
49 NA, MG 27, III, B20, vol. 11, file 23, "McNaughton Statement to the AEC," 19 June 1946.

50 *DCER*, 12 (1946): 451, 452, 453.

51 *Bulletin of the Atomic Scientists*, "Editorial," 1 (1 Aug. 1946): 32.

52 *FRUS 1946*, 1: 862.

53 For a full description of the work of the committees, see Hewlett and Anderson, *The New World*, 1: 583–94.

54 *DCER*, 12 (1946): 459–60.

55 NA, MG 27, III, B20, vol. 11, Atom no. 68, 24 July 1946.

56 NA, RG 2/28, vol. 114, Atom no. 69, 25 July 1946.

57 NA, RG 25, access no 89–90/029, file 201–B(s), Atom no. 74, 29 July 1946.

58 NA, RG 2/18, vol. 114, Atom no. 80, 1 Aug. 1946.

59 NA, MG 27, III, B20, vol. 11, Atom no. 86, 7 Aug. 1946.

60 NA, RG 2/18, vol. 114, Atom no. 85, 5 Aug. 1946.

61 Hewlett and Anderson, *The New World*, 1: 594.

62 *DCER*, 12 (1946): 468.

63 NA, RG 2/18, vol. 114, Atom no. 127, 27 Sept. 1946.

64 *DCER*, 12 (1946): 461–2.

65 *FRUS 1946*, 1: 945.

66 NA, RG 2/18, vol. 114, "McNaughton speech at the AEC," 17 Dec. 1946, 1.

67 Taubman, *Stalin's American Policy*, 163.

68 NA, RG 2/18, vol. 114, Atom no. 146, 11 Oct. 1946.

69 Shils, "The Failure of the UN AEC," 206.

70 *DCER*, 12 (1946): 781.

71 Spencer, *Canada in World Affairs, 1946–1949*, 128.

72 *DCER*, 12 (1946): 800.

73 Cited in ibid., 782.

74 Quoted in *The United Nations 1946: Report on the Second Part of the General Assembly*, 35–6.

75 NA, RG 2/18, vol. 114, Atom no. 197, 14 Dec. 1946.

76 Hewlett and Anderson, *The New World*, 1: 594–618.

77 See, for example, Eayrs, *In Defence of Canada*, 3: 284–95; Swettenham, *McNaughton*, 3: 104–7; Holmes, *The Shaping of Peace*, 2: 45–53.

78 NA, RG 2/18, vol. 114, Atom no. 235, 31 Dec. 1946.

79 Swettenham, *McNaughton*, 3: 124.

80 Spencer, *Canada in World Affairs, 1946–1949*, 133; Davy, "Canada's Role in the Disarmament Negotiations," 148.

81 Holmes, *The Shaping of Peace*, 2: 48–9.

82 *DCER*, 12 (1946): 490.

83 Ibid., 485.

84 *FRUS 1946*, 5: 68.

85 *Debates*, 17 Dec. 1945, 3637.

86 Pickersgill and Forster, eds., *The Mackenzie King Record*, 3: 367.

87 NA, MG 26, J13, T–237, King Diary, 30 Dec. 1946, 1169.
88 Ibid., 1 Jan. 1947, 00002.

CHAPTER FOUR

1 Bundy, *Danger and Survival*, 613.
2 Ibid., 166.
3 NA, RG 2/18, vol. 114, Atom no. 59, 22 Feb. 1947.
4 Canada, House of Commons, *Debates*, 26 March 1947, 1751–3.
5 For details, see Nogee, *Soviet Policy towards International Control of Atomic Energy*, chap. 4.
6 NA, RG 2/18, vol. 114, Atom no. 89, 15 April 1947, 2.
7 Ibid., Atom no. 91, 17 April 1947.
8 Ibid., Atom no. 95, 22 April 1947.
9 Ibid., Atom no. 121, 4 June 1947.
10 McNaughton's statement is in Standing Committee on External Affairs, *Minutes of Proceedings and Evidence*, no. 7, 5 and 6 June 1947, 249.
11 The Soviet proposals are quoted in Nogee, *Soviet Policy towards International Control of Atomic Energy*, 100.
12 NA, RG 2/18, vol. 114, Atom no. 161, 7 Aug. 1947, 4, 5.
13 Nogee, *Soviet Policy towards International Control of Atomic Energy*, 95–6.
14 NA, RG 2/18, vol. 114, Mota [*sic*] no. 47, 10 July 1947.
15 Nogee, *Soviet Policy towards International Control of Atomic Energy*, 96.
16 NA, RG 2/18, vol. 114, Atom no. 147, 19 July 1947, 2.
17 *DCER*, 12 (1946): 462.
18 McNaughton statement to Standing Committee on External Affairs, 5 June 1947, 253.
19 NA, RG 25, access no. 89–90/029, file 201–B(s), Starnes to Ignatieff, 31 July 1947.
20 NA, RG 2/18, vol. 114, Heeney to Pearson, 8 Aug. 1947.
21 DEA, Statements and Speeches 47/10, 17 May 1947. See also Gellman, "Lester B. Pearson, Canadian Foreign Policy, and the Quest for a World Order," 151.
22 NA, MG 27, III, B20, vol. 13, file 29, McNaughton, "The Development and Control of Atomic Energy," 8 May 1947, 7.
23 McNaughton statement to Standing Committee on External Affairs, 6 June 1947, 257.
24 Eayrs, *In Defence of Canada*, 3: 309–16.
25 NA, RG 2/18, vol. 100 (R–100–A/vol. 2), Heeney to Wrong, 11 Sept. 1947.
26 NA, MG 27, III, B20, vol. 12, file 27, "Memorandum to the Advisory Panel on Atomic Energy," 28 Nov. 1947.

27 *FRUS 1947*, 1: 849.

28 NA, RG 2/18, vol. 115, no. 63, 14 June 1948, 6.

29 Ibid., vol. 114, no. 13, 13 March 1948, 2.

30 Ibid., 3.

31 DEA, Statements and Speeches 48/41, 2 Aug. 1948, 3.

32 NA, RG 2/18, vol. 114, Heeney to Wrong, 16 April 1948.

33 Ibid., vol. 115, Cab. doc. 692, 9 June 1948.

34 Ibid., vol. 115, no. 706, 24 June 1948.

35 DEA, Statements and Speeches 48/52, 30 Sept. 1948, 2.

36 *FRUS 1948*, 1: 382, 6 Aug. 1948.

37 NA, RG 2/18, vol. 115, no. 854, 9 Aug. 1948, 3.

38 *FRUS 1948*, 1: 437, 29 Sept. 1948.

39 NA, RG 25, access no. 89–90/029, file 201–B(s), no. 188, 10 Aug. 1948.

40 Ibid., no. 87, 30 Sept. 1948.

41 Cited in Nogee, *Soviet Policy towards International Control of Atomic Energy*, 140.

42 NA, RG 25, access no. 89–90/029, file 201–B(s), no. 162, 11 Oct. 1948.

43 NA, MG 26, N1, vol. 29, "Advisory Panel on Atomic Energy," 23 Dec. 1948, 2.

44 NA, RG 2/18, vol. 115, no. 570, 18 July 1949.

45 Ibid., no. 169, 16 Feb. 1949.

46 NA, RG 2/18, vol. 115, no. 671, 14 June 1948.

47 Ibid., no. 277, 22 March 1949, 3.

48 Ibid.

49 *FRUS 1948*, 1: 437, 29 Sept. 1948.

50 NA, RG 2/18, vol. 115, no. 224, 1 March 1949.

51 Ibid., no. 179, 16 Feb. 1949.

52 Ibid., no. 565, 4 May 1949.

53 Ibid., no. 501, 3 June 1949.

54 NA, RG 25, access no. 89–90/029, file 201–B(s), Statement by McNaughton to Consultations of Six Sponsoring Powers, 6 Oct. 1949, 12.

55 *Bulletin of the Atomic Scientists*, 5 (Dec. 1949): 351.

56 NA, RG 2/18, vol. 100, file R–100–A(VI), WA–2639, 23 Sept. 1949.

57 Ibid., vol. 115, no. 743, 5 Oct. 1949.

58 Ibid., Pearson interview, 31 Oct. 1949, 4.

59 Ibid., no. 101, 26 Nov. 1949, 2.

60 Ibid., Pearson statement, 7 Nov. 1949, 9; also released as DEA, Statements and Speeches 49/41, 7 Nov. 1949.

61 Bechhoefer, *Postwar Negotiations for Arms Control*, 92.

62 McNaughton statement to Standing Committee on External Affairs, 5 June 1947, 241. Later, John Holmes would hardly have been convinced by this argument. "It would be difficult," he observed in 1961, "to deny that the Western positions were also frequently reversed.

And I think we should say 'we' here, because Canada, as you know, is a member of the Five-Power Sub-Committee which worked for a long time on this subject. As one who often drafted statements explaining why, for instance, we were at one time convinced that the linking of nuclear and conventional disarmament was essential and at other times that it was highly immoral, about the only way I can be one up on the Russians is to blush." Holmes, "The Realities of Disarmament," 80.

63 DEA, 211–G–S, no. 297, 4 March 1948, 2.
64 *FRUS 1948*, 1: 411, 3 Sept. 1948.
65 DEA, Statements and Speeches 49/40, 14 Oct. 1949, 2.
66 NA, RG 218, vol. 115, no. 101, 26 Nov. 1949, 4.
67 *Bulletin of the Atomic Scientists*, 4 (May 1948): 129.
68 Herken, *The Winning Weapon*, 264.
69 Holmes, *The Shaping of Peace*, 2: 48.
70 NA, MG 30, E133, vol. 320, file Solandt, McNaughton to Solandt, 22 Sept. 1958, 3.
71 DEA, 211–G–S, "Letter to Chiefs of Staff," 28 March 1949, 1.
72 *Bulletin of the Atomic Scientists*, 5 (Nov. 1949): 321.
73 NA, RG 2/18, vol. 115, no. 224, 1 March 1949.
74 Ibid., no. 126, 14 Oct. 1949, 3.
75 Holmes, *The Shaping of Peace*, 2: 309.

CHAPTER FIVE

1 *FRUS 1950*, 1: 83.
2 Ibid., 35.
3 For a fuller exposition of Kennan's 1950 views on nuclear weapons, see Mayers, *George Kennan*, 307–9.
4 NA, RG 2/18, vol. 185, R–100–A/vol. 2, 11 Jan. 1950. See attached memorandum by Ignatieff.
5 Ibid., R–100–A/vol. 1, 18 March 1950. See attached memorandum, "Working Paper for Advisory Panel on Atomic Energy: The International Control of Atomic Energy," 14.
6 *FRUS 1950*, 1: 60.
7 NA, RG 2/18, vol. 185, R–100–A/vol. 2, no. 517, 27 March 1950, 3.
8 NA, MG 30, E101, vol. 7, file 42, memorandum to Wrong, 16 Feb. 1950.
9 Canada, House of Commons, *Debates*, 3 March 1950, 431–2.
10 NA, MG 25, box 29, file 278–40, 18 March 1950, 3.
11 *Debates*, 3 March 1950, 431.
12 NA, RG 2/18, vol. 185, R–100–A/vol. 2, no. 517, 27 March 1950, 1–2.
13 *FRUS 1950*, 1: 60.

14 NA, MG 30, E101, vol. 7, file 42, Pearson to Wrong, 22 April 1950.
15 *FRUS 1950*, 1: 562.
16 NA, RG 25, Acc. 89–90/029, file 201–B(s), no. 11, 21 Sept. 1950.
17 *FRUS 1950*, 1: 101.
18 NA, RG 25, Acc. 89–90/029, file 201–B(s), no. 234, 26 Oct. 1950.
19 NA, Cabinet Conclusions, 1945–1957, 25 Oct. 1950.
20 Eayrs, *In Defence of Canada*, 4: 273.
21 *FRUS 1950*, 1: 275.
22 Bechhoefer, *Postwar Negotiations for Arms Control*, 153.
23 Mandelbaum and Talbott, *Reagan and Gorbachev*, 108.
24 NA, RG 2/18, vol. 206, U–41–A/vol. 1, "Memo from Lake Success," 4 Nov. 1950, 5.
25 DEA, 50219–B–40, 28 June 1951.
26 Ibid., no. 423, 29 June 1951, 2.
27 Ibid., no. 582, 4 Oct. 1951.
28 *FRUS 1951*, 1: 452, 8 March 1951.
29 Ibid., 1: 464, 15 March 1951.
30 DEA, 50219–B–40, "Regulation and Control of Atomic Energy and Conventional Armaments," 11 Oct. 1951, 3.
31 *FRUS 1951*, 1: 589, 19 Nov. 1951.
32 Ibid., 1: 599, 4 Dec. 1951.
33 DEA, 50219–B–40, "Final Report on Item Nos 1 and 2 of the Political Committee," 21 Dec. 1951, 5.
34 *Bulletin of the Atomic Scientists*, 8 (April 1952): 117.
35 Holmes, *The Shaping of Peace*, 2: 311.
36 DEA, 50271–40, no. 370, 12 Jan. 1952.
37 Ibid., no. 226, 15 Jan. 1952, 1–2.
38 Ibid., no. 299, 5 Feb. 1952, 3.
39 DEA, 50271–A–40, no. 256, 24 Jan. 1952.
40 Ibid., no. 87, 17 March 1952.
41 DEA, 50271–40, no. 286, 2 Feb. 1952, 3.
42 Quoted in Nogee, *Soviet Policy towards International Control of Atomic Energy*, 184.
43 DEA, 50271–A–40, no. 171, 9 April 1952.
44 Quoted in Nogee, *Soviet Policy towards International Control of Atomic Energy*, 185.
45 DEA, 50271–A–40, letters no. 1024, 27 Aug. 1952, and no. 347, 4 Sept. 1952.
46 United Nations, Disarmament Commission, *Verbatim Record*, 24 June 1952, 27.
47 DEA, 50271–A–40, no. D–311, "Disarmament Commission," 9 May 1952, 2. Printed in *DCER*, 18 (1952): 490.
48 Ibid., no. 383, 25 June 1952.

49 Ibid., letter no. 1247, 25 Sept. 1952.

50 Ibid., no. 239, 23 June 1952.

51 Ibid., "Memorandum for the Joint Planning Committee," 27 Aug. 1952.

52 Ibid., letter no. 1202, 19 Sept. 1952, 3. Printed in *DCER*, 18 (1952): 505–10.

53 Ibid., no. 2, 15 Oct. 1952, 2. Printed in *DCER*, 18 (1952): 512.

54 Ibid., 5.

55 DEA, 50189–40, no. 488, 13 Nov. 1953.

56 DEA, 50271–A–40, "Information about the Eighth Session of the United Nations General Assembly," 20 Jan. 1954, 10.

57 Soapes, "A Cold Warrior Seeks Peace," 63.

58 Quoted in Osgood, *NATO*, 112.

59 Quoted in Gaddis, *Strategies of Containment*, 192.

60 Garthoff, "The Death of Stalin," 10.

61 Quoted in ibid., 12.

62 Appleby, "Eisenhower and Arms Control," 24–5.

63 Quoted in Eayrs, *In Defence of Canada*, 4: 262.

CHAPTER SIX

1 Divine, *Blowing on the Wind*, 20.

2 Ibid., 24.

3 DEA, 50271–A–40, no. 279, 1 April 1954.

4 Ibid., Robertson to Saul Rae, 21 April 1954.

5 United Nations, Disarmament Commission, *Official Records*, 19 April 1954, 6.

6 DEA, 50271–A–40, no. 328, 14 April 1954.

7 Ibid., no. 320, 13 April 1954.

8 Ibid., no. 376, 30 April 1954.

9 Canada, House of Commons, *Debates*, 31 March 1954, 3541.

10 Pearson statement, Standing Committee on External Affairs, *Minutes of Proceedings and Evidence*, 22nd Parl, 1st sess, no. 2, 7 April 1954, 42.

11 DEA, 50271–A–40, "Memorandum," 21 April 1954.

12 Ibid., "Memorandum: Meetings of the Sub-Committee of the Disarmament Commission, London, May 13–July 15 1954," 10 May 1954.

13 DEA, 50271–A–40, no. 509, 14 May 1954.

14 Ibid., George to Rae, 24 May 1954.

15 Ibid., no. 989, 26 May 1954, 2.

16 Noel-Baker, *The Arms Race*, 208.

17 United Nations, Disarmament Commission, Sub-Committee of the Disarmament Commission, *Verbatim Record*, Nineteenth Meeting, 17 June 1954, 9.

18 Ibid., 14–15.
19 DEA, 50271–A–40, no. 1179, 22 June 1954, 3–5.
20 DEA, Statements and Speeches 54/35, 21 July 1954.
21 DEA, 50189–40, no. 426, 1 Sept. 1954.
22 Ambrose, *Eisenhower*, 216.
23 Moch, *Destin de la paix*, 66–7.
24 DEA, 50189–40, no. 426, 1 Sept. 1954.
25 Ibid., no. 794, 8 Sept. 1954.
26 The Russian draft is reprinted in Denise Folliot, ed., *Documents on International Affairs 1954* (London: Oxford University Press for Royal Institute of International Affairs, 1957), 294–6.
27 DEA, 50189–40, no. 14, 1 Oct. 1954, 1–3.
28 Ibid., no. 93, 30 Sept. 1954.
29 Ibid., no. 154, 6 Oct. 1954, 2.
30 Ibid., no. 90, 30 Sept. 1954, 2.
31 Ibid., no. 180, 8 Oct. 1954.
32 Ibid., no. 191, 9 Oct. 1954, and no. 201, 11 Oct. 1954.
33 DEA, Statements and Speeches 54/46, 22 Oct. 1954, 6.
34 DEA, 50189–40, no. 139, 14 Oct. 1954, 20.
35 Ibid., no. 583, 20 Oct. 1954.
36 Ibid., no. 165, 20 Oct. 1954.
37 Ibid., no. 846, 21 Oct. 1954.
38 Ibid., no. 856, 23 Oct. 1954.
39 Ibid., no. 165, 20 Oct. 1954, 2.
40 NA, MG 26 N1, vol. 29, no. 313, 21 Oct. 1954, 2.
41 Quoted in Davy, "Canada's Role in the Disarmament Negotiations," 285.
42 *Windsor Daily Star*, 4 Nov. 1954.
43 DEA, 50271–A–40, "Disarmament," 22 Feb. 1955.
44 Ibid., "Memorandum for Minister," 21 Feb. 1955, 2.
45 Ibid., no. 807, 6 May 1955, 8.
46 Ibid., no. 360, 2 March 1955.
47 Quoted in Holmes, *The Shaping of Peace*, 2: 315.
48 DEA, 50271–A–40, no. 605, 11 May 1955.
49 Ibid., no. 384, 5 March 1955.
50 Ibid., copy of British Foreign Office telegram to Washington, 29 April 1955.
51 Ibid., UN Division memorandum to the under-secretary, 18 April 1955, 1; also attached, telegram of 18 April 1955 from secretary of state for external affairs to the high commissioner in the United Kingdom.
52 An English translation of the Soviet statement of 10 May is to be found in United Nations, Disarmament Commission, DC/SC.1/26, 10

May 1955. For summaries, see Bechhoefer, *Postwar Negotiations for Arms Control*, 290–5; DEA, 50271–A–40, no. 697, 11 May 1955.

53 Noel-Baker, *The Arms Race*, 12.

54 Much to their embarrassment, the Americans would be later forced to repudiate this figure because they needed 2.5 million personnel, if they were keep up to their world-wide responsibilities. With fewer troops, they would have to consider withdrawing some American forces from Germany. To do that would multiply the political difficulties in the way of the Adenauer government building a powerful West German army, a goal for which the Americans had been struggling since 1949.

55 Quoted in Patterson, "President Eisenhower and Arms Control," 10.

56 Quoted in Ambrose, *Eisenhower*, 247.

57 Appleby, "Eisenhower and Arms Control," 65.

58 Pearson Statement, Standing Committee on External Affairs, *Minutes of Proceedings and Evidence*, 22nd Parl, 2nd sess, no. 13, 25 May 1955, 562.

59 Quoted in Noel-Baker, *The Arms Race*, 21–2.

60 DEA, 50271–A–40, no. 704, 11 May 1955, 3.

CHAPTER SEVEN

1 Talbott, *The Master of the Game*, 70.

2 *New York Times*, 17 July 1955, 1.

3 Appleby, "Eisenhower and Arms Control," 136.

4 DEA, 50271–A–40, no. 459, 26 Aug. 1955, 1.

5 United Nations, Disarmament Commission, DC/SC.1/PV.52, 30 Aug. 1955, 20.

6 Ibid., DC/SC.1/PV.53, 31 Aug. 1955, 34–5.

7 DEA, 50271–A–40, no. 503, 7 Sept. 1955.

8 Ibid., no. 498, 6 Sept. 1955.

9 Ibid., "Disarmament," United Nations Division, M. Cadieux to J.W. Holmes, 9 Sept. 1955.

10 Legault and Fortmann, *Une diplomatie de l'espoir*, 119.

11 DEA, 50271–A–40, no. 529, 10 Sept. 1955, 2.

12 NA, MG 32, B12, vol. 10, file 100–7, 22 Sept. 1955, Martin to Pearson, 4.

13 Nutting, *Disarmament*, 19; Spanier and Nogee, *The Politics of Disarmament*, 90–1; Bechhoefer, *Postwar Negotiations for Arms Control*, 312.

14 DEA, 50189–40, no. 328, 22 Nov. 1955, 3.

15 Ibid., "Disarmament," 2 Dec. 1955.

16 Ibid., no. 402, 7 Dec. 1955, 2.

17 United Nations, General Assembly, 10th session, First Committee, 805th meeting, 7 Dec. 1955, 250.
18 Davy, "Canada's Role in the Disarmament Negotiations," 343.
19 DEA, 50189–40, "Tenth Session, First Committee, Final Report on Agenda Items No. 17 and 66," no date, 10.
20 DEA, 50271–A–40, no. 124, 2 Feb. 1956, 1–2.
21 Ibid., no. 192, 24 Feb. 1956, 2.
22 Ibid., no. V–348, 2 March 1956, 2.
23 Ibid., no. 266, 9 March 1956, 3.
24 Ibid., no. 295, 14 March 1956, 4–5.
25 Ibid., no. 315, 16 March 1956, 4.
26 Ibid., no. V–520, 3 April 1956, 3.
27 New York Times, 2 April 1956, 10.
28 DEA, 50271–A–40, no. V–520, 3 April 1956, 4.
29 Appleby, "Eisenhower and Arms Control," 126.
30 Quoted in Newhouse, War and Peace in the Nuclear Age, 141–2.
31 DEA, 50271–A–40, no. 569, 10 April 1956, 1–3.
32 Ibid., no. 362, 23 March 1956, 4.
33 Ibid., no. 385, 29 March 1956, 5.
34 Ibid., no. 411, 5 April 1956.
35 Ibid., no. 521, 20 April 1956, 2–4.
36 Ibid., no. 537, 24 April 1956. The Robertson proposals are also to be found in United Nations documents: DC/SC.1/PV.82, 23 April 1956.
37 Appleby, "Eisenhower and Arms Control," 154.
38 DEA, 50271–A–40, DL–471, 15 May 1956, 2.
39 Ibid., United Nations Division, "Reply to Bulganin letter," 5 July 1956.
40 Quoted in Dallin, Soviet Foreign Policy after Stalin, 242.
41 NA, MG 32, B12, vol. 11, "Disarmament," June 1956, 2, 12.
42 United Nations, Disarmament Commission, Official Records, 53rd meeting, 5 July 1956.
43 DEA, 50271–A–40, no. 598, 17 July 1956, 4.
44 Frye, "Disarmament," 266.
45 DEA, 50271–A–40, "Report on the Session July 3–16, 1956 of the Disarmament Commission."

CHAPTER EIGHT

1 Holmes, The Better Part of Valour, 19. Gary R. Hess notes in a recent article ("Accommodation amid Discord") that "by 1954 when India played a prominent role in the Geneva settlement on Indochina 'never had India's – and Nehru's – reputation stood higher in the world.' British Prime Minister Winston Churchill wrote to Nehru that

as 'the light of Asia ... you might be able to do what no other human being can, in giving India the lead, at least in the realm of thought, throughout Asia, with the freedom and dignity of the individual as the ideal rather than the Communist Party drill book.' " Hess is quoting from the biography of Nehru by Sarepelli Gopal.

2 Escott Reid, Canada's high commissioner to India between 1952 and 1957, suggests that "in 1953 and 1954 the special relationship between India and Canada and, indeed, in India's relations with the West reached its high point. A process of erosion then set in. It was caused by the resentment aroused in India by the U.S. military aid agreement with Pakistan concluded early in 1954; the differences in opinion between the West and India over Indo-China and Kashmir; the resentment aroused in the West by the treatment accorded by India to Krushchev and Bulganin on their visit to India in the autumn of 1955; and the attitude of the Indian government to the Hungarian revolution of 1956 and the Soviet-imposed counter-revolution." *Radical Mandarin*, 277.

3 As Hess notes ("Accommodation amid Discord," 7), "John Foster Dulles dismissed non-alignment as 'immoral.' [He] resented the inconsistency of Indian foreign policy, which seemed forever condemnatory of any semblance of Western imperialism while tolerant of arbitrary actions by the Soviet Union and Chinese People's Republic." No doubt many American officials considered the leaders of India to be closet communists.

4 NA, 11456–40, Pearson to Hoskins, 22 Sept. 1954.

5 DEA, 50271–A–40, "Memorandum for the Minister," 14 Oct. 1954, 4.

6 Ibid., "Memo for UN Division on Banning of Nuclear Tests," 20 Jan. 1956.

7 Ibid.

8 Ibid., no. V–348, 2 March 1956, 2.

9 Ibid., no. 363, 23 March 1956, 2.

10 Ibid., "Memorandum for the Minister," 17 April 1956, 2. My italics.

11 Ibid., no. V–626, 19 April 1956, 1. My italics.

12 Ibid., no. 537, 24 April 1956, 4.

13 United Nations, Disarmament Commission, *Official Records*, 58th meeting, 12 July 1956, 13.

14 DEA, 50271–A–40, "Memorandum for the Minister," 18 July 1956, 4.

15 Ibid., no. V–1170, 5 Sept. 1956, 1.

16 Ibid., "Memorandum for the Minister," 18 July 1956, 6.

17 Canada, House of Commons, *Debates*, 1 Aug. 1956, 6792.

18 DEA, 50271–A–40, no. 1360, 21 Nov. 1956.

19 Ibid., no. V–649, 7 Dec. 1956, 3. See also DEA, Statements and Speeches 56/38, 5 Dec. 1956.

20 Ibid., no. vv–43, 27 Dec. 1956, 2–3.
21 Ibid., no. v–364, 25 July 1956, 2.
22 Ibid., no. v–1150, 27 Aug. 1956, 1.
23 Ibid., no. v–1370, 9 Oct. 1956, 1.
24 On the problem of consulting with the United States, John Holmes was later to write: "When Canada was a member of the five-power United Nations' Sub-Committee on Disarmament, its position was peculiarly frustrating. It was unwilling to act irresponsibly on its own in matters involving world security, but it was unable to have effective discussions of policy with the United States. The willingness of Washington to discuss was not in doubt, but the preliminary battle of Washington would inevitably result in an agreed American policy on the eve of the opening of the sessions of the Sub-Committee, leaving no time for comment, certainly not for substantial revision." Holmes, *The Better Part of Valour*, 153–4.
25 DEA, 50271–C–40, no. 530, 6 March 1957, 1.
26 DEA, 50271–A–40, "Disarmament Discussions in the Assembly," 9 Jan. 1957, 2.
27 Ibid., no. v–7, 7 Jan. 1957, 1–2.
28 Ibid., no. vv–5, 12 Dec. 1956, 4–6.
29 Ibid., no. 184, 15 Jan. 1957, 1.
30 Ibid., no. 412, 30 Jan. 1957.
31 DEA, 50271–C–40, no. v–141, 17 March 1957, 1.
32 Ibid., 3.
33 United States, Department of State, *Documents on Disarmament*, 2: 272.
34 DEA, 50271–C–40, no. v–156, 21 March 1957.
35 Ibid., no. v–291, 2 May 1957, 2.
36 Ibid., no. v–187, 29 March 1957, 1.
37 Ibid., no. v–223, 3 April 1957, 3–4.
38 Ibid., no. v–291, 2 May 1957, 5.
39 Ibid., no. 949, 6 May 1957, 1.
40 Ibid., no. 979, 8 May 1957, 2.
41 DEA, 50271–A–40, no. 1092, 18 May 1957, 6.
42 United States, Department of State, *Documents on Disarmament*, 2: 871.
43 DEA, 50271–A–40, no. v–67, 6 Feb. 1957, 3.
44 Ibid., no. v–109, 1 March 1957, 2.
45 DEA, 50271–C–40, no. v–174, 26 March 1957, 2.
46 Ibid., no. 554, 21 March 1957, 4.
47 Quoted in Appleby, "Eisenhower and Arms Control," 201.
48 DEA, 50271–C–40, no. 1640, 2 July 1957, 2.
49 DEA, 50271–A–40, "Regulations, Limitations and Balanced Reductions of all Armed Forces and All Armaments," 28 Dec. 1956, 11.
50 Looking back, John Holmes commented on this feeling of apprehen-

sion among Canadian diplomats: "There had been too great a tendency, particularly in the United Nations, for the Great Powers and Canada ... to feel: 'Keep out the neutrals; it is tough enough now, but what if we have Krishna Menon in here.' This was rather unwise in the long run because it meant that Krishna Menon was being very much more difficult outside of the discussions than in. You cannot deny that all these countries have a tremendous interest in disarmament; if they are kept out, their attitude is much more likely to be irresponsible." Holmes, "The Realities of Disarmament," 85.

51 DEA, 50271–C–40, no. V–366, 31 May 1957, 2–3.
52 *New York Times*, 17 July 1955, 3, col. 5.
53 United States, Department of State, *Documents on Disarmament*, 2: 790.
54 *New York Times*, 4 June 1956.
55 DEA, 50271–A–40, no. V–23, 14 Jan. 1957, 4.
56 DEA, 50271–C–40, no. V–119, 6 March 1957, 2.
57 Ibid., no. V–276, 23 April 1957, 2.
58 Ibid., no. V–302, 9 May 1957, 2.
59 *Documents on Disarmament*, 2: 817.
60 DEA, 50271–C–40, "Memorandum to the Cabinet: Proposal for Zones for Aerial Inspection," 29 March 1957.
61 Ibid., no. 1055, 15 May 1957, 2.
62 Charles Ritchie, Canada's ambassador in Bonn, believed that the Adenauer government had little interest in disarmament but claimed a veto over any negotiations which went further than was "healthy or desirable." DEA, 50271–C–40, no. 293, 13 June 1957, 3.
63 Appleby, "Eisenhower and Arms Control," 202–8.
64 DEA, 50271–C–40, no. V–359, 30 May 1957, 2.
65 See "Memorandum to the Cabinet: Zones of Aerial Inspection," attached to DEA, 50271–C–40, "Memorandum for the Minister: Zones of Aerial Inspection," 11 June 1957, 4, 6.
66 DEA, 50271–C–40, no. V–411, 17 June 1957, 2.
67 *Documents on Disarmament*, 2: 830.
68 Quoted in Bechhoefer, *Postwar Negotiations for Arms Control*, 391.
69 Appleby, "Eisenhower and Arms Control," 216–17.
70 *Documents on Disarmament*, 2: 865.
71 DEA, 50271–C–40, no. 795, 17 April 1957, 8.
72 Ibid., no. 971, 8 May 1957.
73 Divine, *Blowing on the Wind*, 157.

CHAPTER NINE

1 United Nations, Disarmament Commission, *Official Records*, 57th meeting, 12 July 1956, 2.

2 United States, Department of State, *Documents on Disarmament*, 2: 821 (as paraphrased by Zorin).

3 *FRUS 1951*, 1: 479, 6 July 1951.

4 Bundy, *Danger and Survival*, 612.

5 Talbott, *The Master of the Game*, 375.

6 Appleby, "Eisenhower and Arms Control," 217.

7 Quoted in Huntington, *The Common Defense*, 361.

8 Holmes, "The Realities of Disarmament," 80.

9 Gaddis, "How Wise were the 'Wise Men'?" 100–3.

10 DEA, 50271–A–40, General Assessment of the Proceedings in the Disarmament Sub-Committee in London, 19 March to 4 May 1956, 8 May 1956, 12.

11 NA, MG 26, N, vol. 29, "L.B. Pearson Disarmament 1948–1955," quoted in Léger to MacKay, 28 Nov. 1955, 2.

12 DEA, 50271–A–40, no. GX: 114, 21 Jan. 1956, 1.

13 Quoted in Robinson, *Diefenbaker's World*, 28.

14 DEA, 50271–A–40, "Regulation, Limitation and Balanced Reduction of All Armed Forces and All Armaments," 28 Dec. 1956, 12.

15 Holmes, *The Better Part of Valour*, 8.

16 DEA, 50271–A–40, no. 68, 8 Feb. 1956, 3.

17 Ibid., General Assessment of the Proceedings in the Disarmament Sub-Committee in London, 19 March to 4 May 1956, 8 May 1956, 12.

18 Davy, "Canada's Role in the Disarmament Negotiations 1946–1957," iv.

19 Warnock, *Partner to Behemoth*, 149.

20 Holmes, *The Better Part of Valour*, 154.

21 DEA, 50271–A–40, no. 68, 8 Feb. 1967, 20.

22 Ignatieff, *The Making of a Peacemonger*, 137.

23 Canada, House of Commons, *Debates*, 20 March 1956, 2298.

24 Holmes, *The Shaping of Peace*, 2:36.

25 Ibid., no. v–7, 7 Jan. 1957, 1.

26 Holmes, *The Shaping of Peace*, 2: 320.

27 Quoted in Pierson, *The Four Faces of Peace*, 171–2.

28 Pearson statement, Standing Committee on External Affairs, *Minutes of Proceedings and Evidence*, 22 Parl, 3rd sess, no. 1, 12 April 1956, 24.

29 Holmes, *The Shaping of Peace*, 2: 36.

30 Pearson, "Where Canada Stands in the World Crisis," 7.

31 Letter: Ignatieff to the author, 2 May 1986.

32 Beisner, "History and Henry Kissinger," 514.

33 Pearson, *Mike*, 2: 35.

34 Ibid., 25.

35 NA, Cabinet Conclusions, 21 Dec. 1950, 23.

36 Canada, House of Commons, *Debates*, 20 Jan. 1955, 373.

37 NA, RG/16, vol. 5775, Report of Cabinet Meeting, 19 Dec. 1956, 9.
38 Quoted by John Lewis Gaddis in Immerman, ed., *John Foster Dulles*, 67–8.
39 Alexei Filitov, a Soviet specialist on post–World War II Germany writes: "There existed the possibility that the Cold War would have been aborted and that Soviet-American cooperation on the German problem could have been begun on several occasions in the last forty-five years, notably in 1947 and 1948, or from 1953 to 1955 or even ... from 1955 to 1958. Such cooperation would have produced a settlement for the division of Germany similar to what was achieved in 1990, with much less waste of human and material resources." Filitov, "Victory in the Postwar Era," 55.
40 Pearson, "After Geneva: A Greater Task for NATO," 15.
41 Klein, *L'Enterprise du désarmement depuis 1945*, 138; Myrdal, *The Game of Disarmament*, 77.
42 Kaldor, *The Imaginary War*. See also Ronald Steel's citation ("The End and the Beginning," 299): "The purpose of the Cold War was not victory but the maintenance of a controlled contest."

Bibliography

MANUSCRIPT SOURCES

DEPARTMENT OF EXTERNAL AFFAIRS (DEA)

211–G, United Nations Discussions on Disarmament, vols. 1–2

50189–40, United Nations Discussions on Disarmament, vols. 1–6

50189–B–40, United Nations Disarmament Commission, vols. 1–8

50189–C–40, United Nations Disarmament Commission, Sub-Committee, vols. 1–4

50219–B–40, United Nations Atomic Energy Commission

50271–40, Reduction of Armaments at the United Nations General Assembly, 1951–2

50271–A–40, United Nations Disarmament Commission, vols. 1–34

50271–C–40, United Nations Disarmament Commission, Sub-Committee Meetings

NATIONAL ARCHIVES OF CANADA (NAC)

Cabinet Conclusions, 1946–1957

MG 26, J1, W.L. Mackenzie King Papers, vols. 389, 411

MG 26, N1, L.B. Pearson Papers, vols. 29 (Disarmament, 1948–1955) and 65

MG 27, III, B20, C.D. Howe Papers

RG 2/18, Central Registry File of the Privy Council, vols. 100, 114–116, 166–167, 185–186, 205–206

RG 25, Acc. 89–90/029, file 201–B(s), United Nations Atomic Energy Commission

GOVERNMENT PUBLICATIONS

Canada. Department of External Affairs. *Canada and the United Nations.* Volumes for 1946 through 1957
- *Documents on Canadian External Relations.* 12. *1946.* Cited as *DCER.*
- *Documents on Canadian External Relations.* 18. *1952.* Cited as *DCER.*
- Statements and Speeches, 1947 to 1957. Various.
Canada. House of Commons. *Debates.* Various.
- Standing Committee on External Affairs. *Minutes of Proceedings and Evidence.* Various.
United Kingdom. Central Office of Information. *The Disarmament Question 1945–1954.* London: Reference Division, Central Office of Information, 1954.
United States. Department of State. *Disarmament: The Intensified Effort, 1955–1958.* Washington DC: Government Printing Office, 1958.
- *Documents on Disarmament 1945–1959.* 2 vols. Washington DC: Government Printing Office, 1960.
- *Foreign Relations of the United States.* Volumes covering the years 1946–1954. Washington DC: Government Printing Office. Cited as *FRUS.*
- *The Record on Disarmament.* Washington DC: Government Printing Office, 1954.

INTERVIEWS

ARTHUR CAMPBELL. On the secretariat of the Disarmament Commission 1954; on the disarmament desk of the United Nations Division, Department of External Affairs, May 1955 to the end of 1956.
MARSHALL CROWE. First secretary, Canada's Permanent Mission to the United Nations and adviser to Canada's representative to the Disarmament Commission, 1954–7.
GEOFFREY PEARSON
GEOFFREY MURRAY. Senior counsellor, Canada's Permanent Mission to the United Nations, 1955–7.
JOHN STARNES. Secretary to the Advisory Panel on Atomic Energy, 1946.

SECONDARY SOURCES

Acheson, Dean. *Present at the Creation: My Years in the State Department.* New York: Norton, 1969.
Ambrose, Paul B. "Canada Becomes a Potential Nth Country: 1943–1951." Doctoral dissertation, University of Pennsylvania, 1966.
Ambrose, Stephen E. *Eisenhower.* 2: *The President.* New York: Simon & Schuster, 1984.

– *Rise to Globalism: American Foreign Policy since 1938*. New York: Penguin Books, 1973.

Anonymous [Acheson, Dean]. "The Balance of Military Power." *Atlantic* 187 (June 1951): 21–7.

Appleby, Charles Albert. "Eisenhower and Arms Control 1953–1961: A Balance of Risks." Doctoral dissertation, The Johns Hopkins University, 1987.

Barnet, Richard J. "Annals of Diplomacy," *New Yorker*, 10 October 1983: 53–105.

Bechhoefer, G. Bernhard. *Postwar Negotiations for Arms Control*. Washington DC: Brookings Institution, 1961.

Beisner, Robert. "History and Henry Kissinger," *Diplomatic History* 14 (fall 1990): 511–27.

Bothwell, Robert. *Pearson: His Life and Work*. Toronto: McGraw-Hill Ryerson, 1978.

– "Radium and Uranium: Evolution of a Company and a Policy." *Canadian Historical Review* 64 (June 1983): 127–46.

– and William Kilbourn. *C.D. Howe: A Biography*. Toronto: McClelland & Stewart, 1980.

Bottome, Edgar. *The Balance of Terror: Nuclear Weapons and the Illusion of Security 1945–1985*. Boston: Beacon, 1986.

Bundy, McGeorge. *Danger and Survival: Choices about the Bomb in the First Fifty Years*. New York: Random House, 1988.

Clarfield, Gerard H., and William M. Wiecek. *Nuclear America: Military and Civilian Nuclear Power in the United States 1940–1980*. New York: Harper & Row, 1984.

Clarkson, Stephen, ed. *An Independent Foreign Policy for Canada?* Toronto: McClelland & Stewart, 1968.

Dallin, David J. *Soviet Foreign Policy after Stalin*. New York: Lippincott, 1961.

Davy, Grant. "Canada's Role in the Disarmament Negotiations 1946–1957." Doctoral dissertation, Fletcher School of Law and Diplomacy, 1962.

Dinerstein, Herbert S. *War and the Soviet Union: Nuclear Weapons and the Revolution in Soviet Military and Political Thinking*. Second edition. New York: Praeger, 1962.

Divine, Robert A. *Blowing on the Wind: The Nuclear Test Ban Debate, 1954–1960*. New York: Oxford University Press, 1978.

Donovan, Robert J. *Conflict and Crisis: The Presidency of Harry S Truman, 1945–1948*. New York: Norton, 1977.

– *Tumultuous Years: The Presidency of Harry S Truman, 1949–1953*. New York: Norton, 1982.

Dulles, John Foster. "Challenge and Response in U.S. Policy," *Foreign Affairs* 36 (October 1957): 25–43.

Eayrs, James. *Canada in World Affairs: October 1955 to June 1957*. Toronto: Oxford University Press for the Canadian Institute of International Affairs, 1959.

– *In Defence of Canada*. 3: *Peacemaking and Deterrence*. Toronto: University of Toronto Press, 1972.

– *In Defence of Canada*. 4: *Growing Up Allied*. Toronto: University of Toronto Press, 1980.

Eggleston, Wilfrid. *Canada's Nuclear Story*. Toronto: Clarke, Irwin, 1965.

English, John. *Shadow of Heaven: The Life of Lester Pearson*. 1: *1897–1948*. Toronto: Lester & Orpen Dennys, 1989.

– *The Worldy Years: The Life of Lester Pearson*. 2: *1949–1972*. Toronto: Alfred A. Knopf Canada, 1992.

Filitov, Alexei. "Victory in the Postwar Era: Despite the Cold War or Because of It?" *Diplomatic History* 16 (winter 1992), 54–60.

Freedman, Lawrence. *The Evolution of Nuclear Strategy*. New York: St Martin's Press, 1981.

Fry, Michael G., ed. *Freedom and Change: Essays in Honour of Lester B. Pearson*. Toronto: McClelland & Stewart, 1975.

Frye, William R. "Disarmament Comes Back to the General Assembly," *Bulletin of the Atomic Scientists* 13 (November 1957): 333–5.

– "Disarmament: The Bargain Counter," *Bulletin of the Atomic Scientists* 12 (September 1956): 265–7.

Gaddis, John Lewis. "The Emerging Post-Revisionist Synthesis on the Origins of the Cold War." *Diplomatic History* 7 (summer 1983).

– "How Wise Were the 'Wise Men'?" *Atlantic* 269 (February 1992), 100–3.

– *Strategies of Containment: A Critical Appraisal of Postwar American National Security Policy*. New York: Oxford University Press, 1982.

– *The United States and the Origins of the Cold War, 1941–1947*. New York: Columbia University Press, 1972.

Garthoff, Raymond L. "The Death of Stalin and the Birth of Mutual Deterrence," *Survey* 25 (spring 1980): 10–16.

Gellman, Peter Stuart. "Lester B. Pearson, Canadian Foreign Policy, and the Quest for a World Order." Woodrow Wilson Department of Government and Foreign Affairs, University of Virginia, 1987.

– "Lester B. Pearson, Collective Security, and the World Order Tradition." *International Journal* 44 (winter 1988–9): 68–101.

Gowing, Margaret. *Britain and Atomic Energy 1939–1945*. London: Macmillan, 1964.

– *Independence and Deterrence: Britain and Atomic Energy, 1945–1952*. 1: *Policy-Making*; 2: *Policy Execution*. London: Macmillan, 1974.

Graebner, Norman A. *The National Security: Its Theory and Practice 1945–1960*. New York: Oxford University Press, 1986.

Granatstein, J.L. *A Man of Influence: Norman A. Robertson and Canadian Statecraft, 1929–1968*. Ottawa: Deneau, 1981.

- *The Ottawa Men: The Civil Service Mandarins, 1935–1957*. Toronto: Oxford University Press, 1982.
- ed. *Canadian Foreign Policy since 1945: Middle Power or Satellite?* Toronto: Copp Clark, 1970.

Grosser, Alfred. *The Western Alliance: European-American Relations since 1945*. Translated by Michael Shaw. New York: Continuum, 1980.

Harrington, Michael. *Socialism: Past and Future*. New York: Little, Brown, 1989.

Harrison, W.E.C. *Canada in World Affairs: 1949 to 1950*. Toronto: Oxford University Press for the Canadian Institute of International Affairs, 1957.

Heeney, Arnold. *The Things That Are Caesar's: Memoirs of a Canadian Public Servant*. Toronto: University of Toronto Press, 1972.

Herken, Gregg. *Counsels of War*. New York: Knopf, 1985.
- *The Winning Weapon: The Atomic Bomb in the Cold War 1945–1950*. New York: Vintage Books 1981.

Hess, Gary R. "Accommodation amid Discord," *Diplomatic History* 16 (winter 1992): 1–22.

Hewlett, Richard G., and Oscar E. Anderson, Jr. *The New World, 1939–1946*. 1: *A History of the United States Atomic Energy Commission*. University Park: Pennsylvania State University Press, 1962.

Hoffmann, Stanley, "The Perfect In-and-Outer." *New York Review of Books*, 23 November 1989.

Holloway, David. *The Soviet Union and the Arms Race*. New Haven CT: Yale University Press, 1983.

Holmes, John W. *The Better Part of Valour: Essays on Canadian Diplomacy*. Toronto: McClelland & Stewart, 1970.
- *Life with Uncle: The Canadian-American Relationship*. Toronto: University of Toronto Press, 1981.
- *The Shaping of Peace: Canada and the Search for World Order, 1943–1957*, vol. 2. Toronto: University of Toronto Press, 1982.

Holmes, John, et al. "The Realities of Disarmament." In D.L.B. Hamlin, ed., *Diplomacy in Evolution: 30th Couchiching Conference*. Toronto: University of Toronto Press for the Canadian Institute on Public Affairs, 1961.

Howard, Michael. *The Causes of Wars and Other Essays*. Cambridge MA: Harvard University Press, 1984.

Huntington, Samuel P. *The Common Defense: Strategic Programs in National Politics*. New York: Columbia University Press, 1961.

Ignatieff, George. "General A.G.L. McNaughton: A Soldier in Diplomacy." *International Journal* 22 (summer 1967): 402–14.
- *The Making of a Peacemonger: The Memoirs of George Ignatieff*. Toronto: University of Toronto Press, 1985.

Immerman, Richard H., ed. *John Foster Dulles and the Diplomacy of the Cold War*. Princeton NJ: Princeton University Press, 1990.

Jockel, Joseph T. *No Boundaries Upstairs: Canada, the United States, and the Origins of North American Air Defence, 1945–1958*. Vancouver: University of British Columbia Press, 1987.

Kaldor, Mary. *The Imaginary War: Understanding the East-West Conflict*. Cambridge MA: Basil Blackwell, 1990.

Keirstead, B.S. *Canada in World Affairs: September 1951 to October 1953*. Toronto: Oxford University Press for the Canadian Institute of International Affairs, 1956.

Kennan, George F. *The Nuclear Delusion: Soviet-American Relations in the Atomic Age*. New York: Pantheon, 1976.

Kennedy, Paul. *The Rise and Fall of the Great Powers: Economic Change and Military Conflict from 1500 to 2000*. New York: Random House, 1987.

Kent, Tom. "Rising in Favour." *Canadian Forum* 68 (December 1989): 30–1.

Kissinger, Henry. *Nuclear Weapons and Foreign Policy*. New York: Harper & Row, 1957.

Klein, Jean. *L'Entreprise du désarmament depuis 1945*. Paris: Éditions Cujas, n.d.

LaFeber, Walter. *American, Russia, and the Cold War, 1945–1980*. Fourth edition. New York: John Wiley, 1980.

– "NATO and the Korean War: A Context," *Diplomatic History* 13 (fall 1989): 461–77.

Legault, Albert, and Michel Fortmann. *Une diplomatie de l'espoir: le Canada et le désarmament 1945–1988*. Quebec: Les Presses de l'Université Laval/ Centre québécois de relations internationales, 1989. Also published in English as *A Diplomacy of Hope: Canada and Disarmament, 1945–1988*. Montreal & Kingston: McGill-Queen's University Press, 1992.

Lundestad, Geir. "Moralism, Presentism, Exceptionalism, Provincialism and Other Extravagances in American Writings on the Early Cold War Years," *Diplomatic History* 13 (fall 1989): 527–45.

McGeehan, Robert. *The German Rearmament Question: American Diplomacy and European Defense after World War II*. Urbana: University of Illinois Press, 1971.

MacMillan, Margaret O., and David S. Sorenson, eds. *Canada and NATO: Uneasy Past, Uncertain Future*. Waterloo: University of Waterloo Press, 1990.

Malcolmson, Robert W. *Beyond Nuclear Thinking*. Montreal & Kingston: McGill-Queen's University Press, 1990.

Mandelbaum, Michael, and Strobe Talbott. *Reagan and Gorbachev*. New York: Vintage, 1987.

Martin, Paul. *A Very Public Life*. 2: *So Many Worlds*. Toronto: Deneau, 1985.

Masters, Donald C. *Canada in World Affairs: 1953 to 1955*. Toronto: Oxford University Press for the Canadian Institute of International Affairs, 1959.

May, Ernest L. "The American Commitment to Germany 1949–55," *Diplomatic History* 13 (fall 1989): 431–60.

Mayers, David. *George Kennan and the Dilemmas of US Foreign Policy*. New York: Oxford University Press, 1988.

Mendl, Wolf. *Deterrence and Persuasion: French Nuclear Armament in the Context of National Policy 1945–1969*. London: Faber, 1970.

Minifie, James. *Peacemaker or Powder-Monkey: Canada's Role in a Revolutionary World*. Toronto: McClelland & Stewart, 1960.

Moch, Jules. *Destin de la Paix*. Paris: Mercure de France, 1969.

Mueller, John. *Retreat from Doomsday: The Obsolescence of Major War*. New York: Basic Books, 1989.

Myrdal, Alva. *The Game of Disarmament: How the United States and Russia Run the Arms Race*. Manchester: Manchester University Press, 1977.

Newhouse, John. *War and Peace in the Nuclear Age*. New York: Knopf, 1989.

Noel-Baker, Philip. *The Arms Race: A Programme for World Disarmament*. New York: Oceana, 1958.

Nogee, Joseph L. *Soviet Policy towards International Control of Atomic Energy*. Notre Dame IN: University of Notre Dame Press, 1961.

Nossal, Kim Richard. *The Politics of Canadian Foreign Policy*. Second edition. Scarborough, Ont.: Prentice-Hall, 1989.

Nutting, Anthony. *Disarmament: An Outline of the Negotiations*. New York: Oxford University Press, 1959.

Osgood, Robert E. *NATO: The Entangling Alliance*. Chicago IL: University of Chicago Press, 1962.

– *The Nuclear Dilemma in American Strategic Thought*. Boulder CO: Westview, 1988.

Oppenheimer, Robert J. "The International Control of Atomic Energy," *Bulletin of the Atomic Scientists* 1 (1 June 1946).

Page, Don, and Don Munton. "Canadian Images of the Cold War 1946–7." *International Journal* 32 (summer 1977): 577–604.

Paret, Peter, ed. *Makers of Modern Strategy: From Machiavelli to the Nuclear Age*. Princeton NJ: Princeton University Press, 1986.

Patterson, David S. "President Eisenhower and Arms Control," *Peace and Change: A Journal of Peace Research* 11 (no. 3/4, 1986): 3–24.

Pearson, Lester B. "After Geneva: A Greater Task for NATO." *Foreign Affairs* 34 (October 1955): 14–23.

– "The Balance of Power," Address to the World Affairs Council, Philadelphia, Pennsylvania, 4 October 1957.

– *Democracy in World Politics*. Toronto: Saunders, 1955.

– "The Development of Canadian Foreign Policy." *Foreign Affairs* 30 (October 1951): 17–30.

– *Mike: The Memoirs of the Right Honourable Lester B. Pearson. 1: 1897–1948*. Toronto: University of Toronto Press, 1972.

- *Mike: The Memoirs of the Right Honourable Lester B. Pearson*. 2: *1948–1957*. edited by John A. Munro and Alex I. Inglis. Toronto: University of Toronto Press, 1973.
- "Straight Talk from Mike Pearson." *Maclean's* (15 October 1949): 8–9, 62–5.
- "Western European Union: Implications for Canada and NATO." *International Journal* 10 (winter 1954–55): 1–11.
- "Where Canada Stands in the World Crisis." *Maclean's* 70 (6 July 1957): 13–14, 47–52.
- *Words and Occasions: An Anthology of Speeches and Articles Selected from His Papers by the Right Honourable L.B. Pearson*. Toronto: University of Toronto Press, 1970.
Pickersgill, J.W., and D.F. Forster, eds. *The Mackenzie King Record*. 2: *1944–1945*; 3: *1945–1946*. Toronto: University of Toronto Press 1968, 1970.
Pierre, Andrew J. *Nuclear Politics: The British Experience with an Independent Strategic Force 1939–1970*. London: Oxford University Press, 1972.
Pierson, Sherleigh G., ed. *The Four Faces of Peace and the International Outlook*. Toronto: McClelland & Stewart, 1964.
Powaski, Ronald E. *March to Armageddon: The United States and the Nuclear Arms Race, 1939 to the Present*. New York: Oxford University Press, 1987.
Prittie, Terence C. *Konrad Adenauer, 1876–1967*. Chicago: Cowles, 1971.
Quester, George H. *Nuclear Diplomacy: The First Twenty-Five Years*. New York: Dunellen, 1970.
Rearden, Steven L. *The Evolution of American Strategic Doctrine: Paul H. Nitze and the Soviet Challenge*. Boulder CO: Westview, 1984.
Reid, Escott. *Radical Mandarin: The Memoirs of Escott Reid*. Toronto: University of Toronto Press, 1989.
Rhodes, Richard. *The Making of the Atomic Bomb*. New York: Simon & Schuster, 1986.
Ritchie, Charles. *Diplomatic Passport: More Undiplomatic Diaries, 1946–1962*. Toronto: Macmillan, 1981.
- *Storm Signals: More Undiplomatic Diaries, 1962–1971*. Toronto: Macmillan, 1983.
Roberts, Chalmers M. *The Nuclear Years: The Arms Race and Arms Control, 1945–70*. New York: Praeger, 1970.
Robinson, H. Basil. *Diefenbaker's World: A Populist in Foreign Affairs*. Toronto: University of Toronto Press, 1989.
Rosenberg, David Alan. "The Origins of Overkill: Nuclear Weapons and American Strategy, 1945–1960," *International Security* 7 (spring 1983): 3–71.
Ross, Douglas A. *In the Interests of Peace: Canada and Vietnam 1954–1973*. Toronto: University of Toronto Press, 1984.

Schlesinger, Arthur, Jr. "Origins of the Cold War," *Foreign Affairs* 46 (October 1967): 22–52.

Shevchenko, Arkady N. *Breaking with Moscow*. New York: Alfred A. Knopf, 1985.

Shils, Edward A. "The Failure of the UN AEC: an Interpretation," *Bulletin of the Atomic Scientists* 4 (July 1948): 205–10.

Shulman, Marshall D. *Stalin's Foreign Policy Reappraised*. New York: Atheneum, 1963.

Smith, Denis. *Diplomacy of Fear: Canada and the Cold War, 1941–1948*. Toronto: University of Toronto Press, 1988.

Soapes, Thomas F. "A Cold Warrior Seeks Peace: Eisenhower's Strategy for Nuclear Disarmament," *Diplomatic History* 4 (winter 1980): 557–71.

Socknat, Thomas P. *Witness against War: Pacifism in Canada, 1900–1945*. Toronto: University of Toronto Press, 1987.

Spanier, John W., and Joseph L. Nogee. *The Politics of Disarmament: A Study in Soviet-American Gamesmanship*. New York: Praeger, 1962.

Spencer, Robert A. *Canada in World Affairs: From UN to NATO 1946–1949*. Toronto: Oxford University Press for the Canadian Institute of International Affairs, 1959.

Steel, Ronald. "The End and the Beginning," *Diplomatic History* 16 (spring 1992), 294–301.

Stursberg, Peter. *Lester Pearson and the American Dilemma*. Toronto: Doubleday, 1978.

Swettenham, John. *McNaughton*. 1: *1887–1939*; 2: *1940–1943*; 3: *1944–1966*. Toronto: Ryerson, 1968–9.

Talbott, Strobe. *The Master of the Game: Paul Nitze and the Nuclear Peace*. New York: Alfred A. Knopf, 1988.

Taubman, William. *Stalin's American Policy: From Entente to Detente to Cold War*. New York: Norton, 1982.

Thomas, Hugh. *Disarmament – The Way Ahead*. London: Fabian Society, 1957.

– *Armed Truce: The Beginnings of the Cold War 1945–1946*. London: Hamish Hamilton 1986.

Thomson, Dale C. "India and Canada: A Decade of Co-operation 1947–1957." *International Studies* 9 (April 1968): 404–30.

– *Louis St Laurent: Canadian*. Toronto: Macmillan, 1967.

Warnock, John. *Partner to Behemoth: The Military Policy of a Satellite Canada*. Toronto: New Press, 1970.

York, Herbert F. *Making Weapons, Talking Peace: A Physicist's Odyssey from Hiroshima to Geneva*. New York: Basic Books, 1987.

Index

Acheson, Dean, 14, 20, 21, 25, 31, 34, 39, 57, 79, 85–7, 90, 138, 141, 280

Acheson-Lilienthal Report, 85–8, 97

Adenauer, Konrad, 17, 20, 22, 23, 65, 211, 252, 255, 256, 259, 260, 261, 269

Advisory Panel on Atomic Energy (Canada), 85, 98, 104, 113, 114, 138, 301n.32

aerial inspection, 34, 194, 195, 197, 198–200, 202, 204, 213, 214, 218, 253, 255–60, 273, 275, 276

Anglo-French Plan (1954), 172–6, 187, 190, 196

Arctic zone, for aerial inspection, 256–60

atomic bomb, 9, 16, 23, 30, 32, 38, 40, 61, 64, 67, 68, 73, 75, 77, 87, 92, 200, 206–11, 216, 230, 231

atomic energy, control of, 29, 39, 67, 77–81, 84, 86, 100, 103, 111, 121, 127–9, 132, 155; authority to oversee, 88, 91, 108, 113, 117, 133, 149, 151, 155, 158, 173, 177, 186, 188, 189, 197, 211

Atomic Energy Commission (AEC), United Nations, 5, 85, 90, 91, 94, 99, 100, 108, 126, 133, 134, 139, 150, 266, 272, 279, 284; Committee 2, 95–9, 109, 112, 113, 117; established, 84; first report, 102, 108, 109; Scientific and Technical Committee, 94, 97; second report, 108, 114, 115; third report, 116, 118, 119, 125; Working Committee, 109–11, 117, 124; work ends, 124, 131

Atomic Energy Commission (AEC), United States, 26, 41, 164, 167, 190, 209, 214, 267

Attlee, Clement, 28, 61, 78, 80, 81, 141, 295n.39

Australia, 94, 95, 112, 115, 123

Baruch, Bernard, 84, 85, 88, 90, 91, 102, 107, 113, 192, 266

Baruch Plan (1946), 85, 86, 88–93, 95, 97–9, 101–4, 107, 113, 114, 118, 120, 136, 143, 172, 244, 266, 272, 274, 275, 277–9. *See also* Majority Plan

Berlin blockade (1948–49), 18, 24, 31

Bohlen, Charles, 41

Bulganin, Marshal Nikolai, 15, 199, 202, 214, 217, 218, 226, 230, 233, 311n.2

Bulletin of the Atomic Scientists, 92, 134

Bundy, McGeorge, 80, 84

Byrnes, James, 83, 85, 295n.39

Canada: a junior partner, 4, 5, 63, 66, 165, 235, 275; as a marginal power, 185, 240. *See also* External Affairs; Pearson disarmament proposals (in chronological order): resolution supporting Majority Plan (4 Nov. 1948), 123, 124; resolution (with France) calls on every nation to limit its sovereignty to permit the international control of atomic energy (Nov. 1949), 130; George memorandum (March 1950), 138; Pearson formula for successful negotiations (9 May 1952), 155; External Affairs memorandum on manageable "slice" of disarmament (Aug. 1952), 157, 158; External Affairs interdepartmental working party on disarmament (spring 1954), 169, 170; procedural resolution (Oct. 1954), 178, 179; Robertson's attempt to break Soviet-American deadlock (23 April 1956), 217; External Affairs memorandum on aerial surveillance (11 June 1957), 258, 259; Western formal offer on inspection zones (2 Aug. 1957), 249; Western package of all current Western proposals (29 Aug. 1957), 260–1
Canadian Peace Congress, 67, 73
Chalk River, nuclear reactor, 75, 76, 87

China, 48, 63–6, 72, 112, 118, 123, 127, 131, 133, 139, 150, 168, 227
Churchill, Winston, 13, 15, 20, 21, 27, 28, 69, 81, 266, 310n.1
Commission for Conventional Armaments (CCA), 131–4, 143
Committee of Twelve, United Nations, 144–6
Co-operative Commonwealth Federation (CCF), on Canadian foreign policy, 72, 230
Council of (Big Four) Foreign Ministers, 14, 17, 99
Czechoslovakia, 14, 25, 49, 168

Davy, Grant, 3, 275
Dienbienphu, 22, 61, 171
Disarmament Commission (DC), 6, 95, 146, 148, 149, 160, 166, 167, 176, 207, 227, 228, 261, 279
sessions: 1952, 149–59; Aug. 1953, 161; April 1954, 168; July 1954, 174, 175; 19 Nov. 1954, 180; Nov. 1955, 201; Jan. 1956, 204; July 1956, 220–2, 231; Dec. 1956, 235
sub-committee, 162, 166, 168, 177, 192, 272; May-June 1954 meeting, 171–4; Feb.-May 1955 meeting, 185–90; Aug.-Oct. 1955 meeting, 195–9; March-May 1956 meeting 209–17; March-Sept. 1957 meeting, 246–62
Disarmament Conference, Geneva (1932), 44, 54, 84
Dulles, John Foster, 22,

23, 42, 62, 181, 258, 263, 268; on aerial inspection, 259–61; and ban on nuclear tests, 167, 270; on forces in Europe, 282; on negotiations with USSR, 14, 39, 163, 214, 286; nuclear strategy, 27, 33, 68

East Germany (German Democratic Republic), 17, 23, 51, 252–3, 256–60
Eayrs, James, on Canadian policy, 3, 73, 79, 142
Eden, Anthony, 22, 29, 71, 168, 183, 232, 240
Eisenhower, Dwight D., 12, 21, 26, 61, 152, 183, 214, 258, 267, 282; and alliance with West Germany, 19, 23, 38, 174, 252, 255, 271; anxiety to avoid nuclear war, 15, 30; negotiating with the USSR, 16, 41, 42, 160, 163, 181, 235, 248; nuclear strategy, 27, 30, 33, 34, 164, 192, 223; and nuclear tests, 229, 233, 234, 240, 241, 249, 263, 270; Open Skies proposal, 194–203, 213
English, John, on Pearson, 8, 46, 53, 56
Endicott, James, 73
European Defence Community (EDC), 20, 21, 65, 154, 155, 171, 175, 176
European zone, for aerial inspection, 256–60

External Affairs, Department of, 4, 58, 92, 112, 135, 144, 145, 150, 158, 159, 198, 204; on Anglo-French Plan, 176, 178, 185, 187, 206; on Baruch Plan, 91, 101, 107; on India, 228, 230, 236, 250, 251, 274; on limitation of tests, 231, 232, 234, 240, 241; on Majority Plan, 125, 137; on reports from Johnson, 156, 167, 168, 176, 243; on reports from Mc-Naughton, 95, 98, 102, 130, 134; on reports from Martin, 197; on reports from Robertson, 170, 173, 207, 216; on the USSR, 119, 126, 127, 253, 254, 259, 278; on Western unity, 157, 193, 194, 205, 235, 272, 273, 275, 276

Faure, Edgar, 193
Federal Republic of Germany. *See* West Germany
First (Political) Committee, United Nations, work of, 100, 101, 115, 121, 122, 127, 141, 146, 147, 160, 161, 178
fissionable material. *See* nuclear fuel
France: as a nuclear power, 30–1, 154, 224, 245–6. *See also* Moch
disarmament proposals (in chronological order): census of conventional forces of United Nations members (Oct. 1949), 133; resolution (with Can-

ada) calling on every nation to limit its sovereignty to permit international control of atomic energy (Nov. 1949), 130; supports American demand for single disarmament commission (7 Nov. 1951), 146; joins United States and Britain in proposing personnel ceiling (May 1952), 152–3; proposes three-stage timetable for disarmament (June 1952), 155; joins Britain in proposing timetable for disarmament (11 June 1954), 172; joins Britain in proposing comprehensive disarmament plan (29 March 1956), 187; joins Western powers to make a formal offer on inspection zones (2 Aug. 1957), 260; joins Western powers to offer package of current Western proposals (29 Aug. 1957), 260–1

General Assembly, United Nations, meetings: 1946, 99–102; 1947, 115; 1948, 121–4; 1949, 127–30, 133, 135; 1950, 141–4; 1951–52, 146–9; spring 1953, 160–1; autumn 1953, 161–3; autumn 1954, 175–9, 227–8; Dec. 1955, 203–4, 229; Jan. 1957, 236–8
Geneva summit (July 1955), 15, 183, 190, 194–5, 271, 285
George, James, 138–9, 144–5, 147, 153, 289

German Democratic Republic. *See* East Germany
Green, Howard, 283
Gromyko, Andrei, 93, 99, 107, 117, 132, 264; and AEC first report, 103, 106; on atomic weapons, 94, 111, 185; on Baruch Plan, 108–9, 114; at Disarmament Commission (July 1956), 221–2; and Soviet proposals, 91, 110, 210; at sub-committee meeting (March-May 1956), 209–10, 212, 215, 217

Heeney, Arnold, 6, 116, 235–6, 244, 289
Hickerson, John, 57, 147
Holmes, John, 3–4, 6, 63, 73–4, 85, 104, 134, 148, 180, 226, 230, 232, 270, 273–4, 276–8, 280, 289, 304n.62, 312n.24, 312n.50
Hungary, 52, 96, 99, 225, 253, 282
Hydrogen bomb (H-bomb), 15, 26–7, 29, 34, 36, 38, 52, 67, 69, 137, 161, 164, 167, 227, 229, 245, 267, 280

Ignatieff, George, 6, 71, 85, 87, 108, 111, 138, 290
India, 7, 63, 122–3, 130, 144, 167–8, 182, 202, 204, 226–30, 232–3, 236, 238, 250–1, 261, 270, 277, 280, 311n.2
Indochina, 4, 15, 29, 61, 65, 175, 226

Inspection, to verify disarmament measures, 97, 100, 104, 109–11, 117, 130, 137, 140–1, 149, 155, 157, 160, 171, 174, 177, 184, 190, 194, 197, 203, 244, 273. *See also* aerial inspection
International Atomic Energy Agency, 164

Japan, 233, 238, 243, 246, 251, 273
Jessup, Philip, 146–7
Johnson, David, 6, 167–8, 169, 170, 176–7, 227, 262, 290; at the Disarmament Commission (1952), 150–2, 156–7; at the Disarmament Commission (July 1954), 174; at the General Assembly (1951–52), 149; at the General Assembly (spring 1953), 160–1; at the General Assembly (autumn 1954), 179; at the sub-committee (Feb.-May 1955), 184, 190; at the sub-committee (March-Sept. 1957), 239–43, 245, 247, 250, 256–7

Kennan, George, 13, 70, 93, 138, 282
Khrushchev, Nikita: on Geneva (1955), 195, 271, 311n.2; on Germany, 17, 219, 253, 282; and India, 226, 230; negotiating with the West, 16, 215, 217, 260; nuclear war, 30, 41–2; peaceful coexistence, 12, 15, 51, 182–3, 264
King, William Lyon Mackenzie, 46, 54, 70–1,

77–82, 103, 105, 136, 300n.2
Kissinger, Henry, 62, 281
Klein, Jean, on Canada's role, 284
Korea, 5, 14–15, 19–20, 24, 40, 49, 58, 107, 137, 141, 143, 148, 150, 161, 164, 226

Lawrence, George, 85
Léger, Jules, 6, 184, 290
Lilienthal, David, 86
Lippmann, Walter, 15–17, 90
Litvinov, Maxim, 44, 55
Lloyd, Selwyn, 171
Lodge, Henry Cabot, 224, 236–7
London Naval Conference (1930), 54

MacArthur, Douglas, 59, 64
MacKay, R.A., 144, 199, 274, 290
Macmillan, Harold, 240, 241, 247, 249
McNaughton, Andrew G.L., 5, 6, 102, 108, 112, 113, 116, 117, 119, 125, 126, 132, 135, 291; appointment to AEC, 84, 85, 87, 88; on inspection, 109, 110; resignation, 136; on safeguards, 94, 95, 98; supports Baruch principles, 114, 118, 121, 123, 127, 128; and veto, 90, 103, 104
Majority Plan, 124–9, 136–9, 141–8, 152, 155–8, 160, 161, 164–6, 171, 196, 273, 276
Malenkov, Georgi, 15, 36, 160, 164
Malik, Jacob, 128, 150–2, 156, 172, 173, 188

Marshall, George, 17, 115
Marshall Plan, 48, 54, 59, 118, 134
Martin, Paul, 6, 181, 229, 273, 291; at the Disarmament Commission (1955), 201; at the Disarmament Commission (July 1956), 221, 222, 224; at the General Assembly (autumn 1954), 178–80; at the sub-committee (Aug.-Oct. 1955), 196–9
May 4 (1956) Declaration by the West, 217, 221, 222
May 10 (1955) Soviet proposal, 188–92, 196–8, 202, 208, 211, 229
Mendès-France, Pierre, 22, 29, 177, 180, 193
Menon, Krishna, 226–8, 231, 236, 238, 313n.50
Mexico, 94, 102
Mikoyan, Anastas, 36
Moch, Jules, 151, 154, 171, 190, 196, 199, 201, 202, 222, 224; and European Defence Community, 155; and Canadian procedural resolution, 177, 178, 180; Moch's synthesis, 155, 156, 162, 173, 176, 205, 207–9; on nuclear weapons, 193, 198, 213, 219, 220, 223
Mollet, Guy, 29, 193, 205, 219, 220, 245
Molotov, Vyacheslav, 36, 51, 99–102, 182
Myrdal, Alva, on Canada's role, 284

Nehru, Jawaharlal, 7, 162, 167, 169, 170, 226, 227, 228, 230, 310n.1
Nitze, Paul, 13, 42, 142, 268, 294n.18
North Atlantic Council, 19, 21, 22, 60, 62, 69, 72, 176, 185, 194, 257, 270, 281
North Atlantic Treaty Organization (NATO), 18, 20, 35, 42, 51, 52, 60, 61, 62, 65, 68, 72, 146, 167, 175, 180, 182, 183, 194, 222, 252, 263, 282
Norway, 238, 243, 273
nuclear fuel, 24, 27, 29, 33, 86, 89, 97, 111–14, 155, 157, 163, 190, 196, 213, 215, 217, 246, 269; proposed halt in production for military purposes, 214, 215, 236, 237, 247, 249, 250, 262, 263
nuclear tests: Bermuda communiqué on, 240, 241, 247; cessation of, 27, 73, 169, 183, 188, 189, 203, 206, 211, 221, 224, 228–30, 245–50, 262, 268, 270; limitation of, 217, 221, 230, 232–4, 237–9, 270, 280; proposal for registration of, 237, 241–3, 273, 276, 280
Nutting, Anthony, 196, 199–202, 222

Open Skies. See aerial inspection
Oppenheimer, Robert, 27, 86, 267
Osborn, Frederick, 107, 116

Pearson, Lester B., 42, 84, 90, 105, 143, 146,

153, 169, 185, 194, 221, 235, 256, 291, 300n.118; on Anglo-French Plan, 210; on arms negotiations, 279–85; Baruch Plan, 91, 107; on comprehensive disarmament, 209; on India, 123, 162, 225, 226; on inspection, 122, 129, 133, 137, 142, 170, 278; on Majority Plan, 147, 184; on Moch's synthesis, 155; on national sovereignty, 114; on negotiating with USSR, 7, 8, 17, 43–53, 93, 116, 119, 179, 180, 190, 212, 218, 227, 253, 254, 277; on North American defence, 66; on nuclear arms, 67–70, 79–81, 87, 92, 128, 165, 215, 244; on nuclear tests, 230, 232, 233, 237, 240, 242, 243, 262; on policy towards Germany, 65; political strength of, 70–4; on relationship with the United States, 53–65, 136
Pinard, Roch, 233
Progressive Conservative party, views on Canadian policy, 71

Reid, Escott, 46, 311n.2
Ritchie, Charles, 6, 45, 87, 258, 313n.62
Robertson, Norman, 6, 44, 45, 168, 220, 221, 291; Acheson-Lilienthal Report, 87; Anglo-French Plan, 207; limitation of nuclear tests, 230; on negotiations with the USSR, 204, 205, 272,

275; rejects proposal to outlaw atomic bomb, 92; at subcommittee meeting (May-June 1954), 171–4; at subcommitee meeting (March-May 1956), 208, 210, 216, 217, 273, 278
Roosevelt, Franklin D., 81, 105
Rose, Fred, 82
Rotmistrov, General, on surprise attack, 37

safeguards, to ensure disarmament, 81, 84, 98, 99, 100, 120, 122, 123, 143, 147, 161
sanctions, to enforce disarmament proposals, 91, 92, 101
Security Council, work of, 45, 57, 58, 83, 84, 90, 94–6, 100, 102, 108, 119, 120, 123, 125, 129, 130, 132, 133, 173, 189, 197, 247
Smith, Arnold, 61
Sobolev, Arkady, 197–9
Social Credit party, on Canada's policy, 71
Social Democratic party (West Germany), and reunification, 23, 252, 257
stages, in arms reduction proposals, 89, 125, 139, 146, 151, 177
Stalin, Joseph, 12, 46, 102, 129, 160, 270, 271; and atomic bomb, 25, 39, 82, 93; Berlin blockade, 18; consequences of death of, 36, 40, 51, 164, 267; on disarmament, 134; on

Germany, 17, 21; hostility towards the West, 13, 14, 182, 266; on international control of atomic energy, 99, 118; strategic views, 30, 32, 37

Stassen, Harold, 183, 234, 235, 236, 240, 244, 245, 267; appointed, 181; on comprehensive disarmament, 193; at General Assembly (January 1957), 238; at subcommittee meeting (Aug.-Oct. 1955), 196–200; at sub-committee meeting (March-May 1956), 208, 209, 212, 213, 216, 217; at sub-committee meeting (March-Sept. 1957), 246–9, 255–7, 260

Stevenson, Adlai, 233

Stockholm Petition (1950), 40

St Laurent, Louis, 43, 47, 61, 68, 70, 71, 105, 108, 113, 136, 164, 219, 226, 280, 283, 300n.118

Strauss, Lewis, 26, 27, 164, 167

Sub-Committee of the Disarmament Commission. See Disarmament Commission

Suez crisis, 4, 53, 62, 71, 72, 224–6, 235, 240, 245, 253, 282

Teller, Edward, 249

test ban. See nuclear tests

timetables, for implementation of disarmament proposals, 89, 135, 152, 155, 172, 173, 177

Truman Doctrine, 13

Truman, Harry S., 12, 14, 126, 139, 270, 271; approves NSC–68, 13; on arms control negotiations, 15, 143, 146; on atomic bomb, 24, 25, 31, 38, 93, 192; and Baruch Plan, 88, 102, 128, 134; on Germany, 19; on hydrogen bomb, 26, 138, 267; strategic views, 30; and Washington Conference (1945), 77–81

Union of Soviet Socialist Republics (USSR), disarmament proposals (in chronological order): international control of atomic energy (11 June 1946), 110, 111; one-third cut in the Big Five's armaments coupled with prohibition of atomic weapons (Sept. 1948), 133; resolution to ban atomic weapons and to institute international control of atomic energy simultaneously (2 Oct. 1948), 122; resolution that governments undertake unconditionally not to use atomic or hydrogen bombs (1 June 1954), 172; 10 May 1955 comprehensive and radical plan, 188, 189; arms control plan of 27 March 1956, 210, 211; for a test ban and a readiness to consider aerial surveillance (17 Nov. 1956), 233, 253; test ban and zones for aerial surveillance (30

April 1957), 247, 256; test ban for two or three years to be verified through reciprocal inspection posts (14 June 1957), 249

United Kingdom: as a nuclear power, 28, 29, 245 disarmament proposals (in chronological order): supports American demand for a single disarmament commission (7 Nov. 1951), 146; joins United States and France in proposing a personnel ceiling (May 1952), 152, 153; joins with France to propose timetable for disarmament (11 June 1954), 172; joins with France to propose comprehensive disarmament plan (29 March 1956), 187; joins with Western powers to make formal offer on inspection zones (2 Aug. 1957), 260; joins with Western powers to offer package of current Western proposals (29 Aug. 1957), 260–1

United Nations, 39, 40, 45, 50, 53, 61, 63–5, 71, 80. See also Atomic Energy Commission; Disarmament Commission; First Committee; General Assembly

United States: NSC–68 memorandum, 13, 14, 34, 39, 142; views of joint chiefs of staff on arms control, 16, 18, 19, 42, 66, 214, 227, 266. *See also* Acheson, Dulles, Eisenhower, Stassen, Truman

disarmament proposals (in chronological order): Baruch Plan (14 June 1946), 88, 89; Truman plan to consolidate consideration of nuclear and conventional arms (24 Oct. 1950), 143; Truman plan for an arms census (7 Nov. 1951), 146; five-stage plan for disclosure of information on armed forces and armaments (spring 1952), 151; personnel ceiling for the permanent members of Security Council (May 1952), 152, 153; organization and functions of proposed control organ (25 May 1954), 171; first phase of a comprehensive programme (3 April 1956), 213–15; arms control package (14 Jan. 1957), 236, 237;

in return for cut-off, a ten-month suspension of verifiable tests and manpower cuts (31 May 1957), 248, 255; a ten-month suspension of tests if the USSR accepted a cut-off (3 July 1957), 249; formal offer on inspection zones (2 Aug. 1957), 260; formal offer of a two-year suspension of tests if the USSR accepted the cut-off (21 Aug. 1957), 249; final Western offer of a package of all current Western proposals (29 Aug. 1957), 260–1

Veto, 184, 189; and Baruch Plan, 83, 89–92, 95, 101, 102, 105, 108

Vyshinsky, Andrei, 14, 102; at Disarmament Commission (April 1954), 168; at General Assembly (1947), 115; at General Assembly (1948), 122; at General Assembly (1949), 129, 135; at General

Assembly (1951–52), 149; at General Assembly (spring 1953), 160, 161; at General Assembly (autumn 1953), 162; at General Assembly (autumn 1954), 176, 178; on inspection, 139–42

Washington Conference (1945), 81–3, 105

West Germany, 9, 16, 19, 23, 29, 34, 36, 38, 52, 62, 65, 134, 154, 155, 175, 176, 179, 180, 182, 183, 189, 211, 252, 255–60, 262, 269, 278, 282

Wilgress, Dana, 44

World Congress of Partisans of Peace, 135

Wrong, H. Hume, 6, 44, 55, 64, 67, 87, 92, 115, 139–42, 292

Yugoslavia, 18, 49, 144, 222

Zhdanov, Andrei A., 14

Zorin, Valerian, 243, 255, 258, 260–2, 268, 269